ALFRED PORTALE'S 12 SEASONS COOKBOOK

ALSO BY ALFRED PORTALE

Alfred Portale's Gotham Bar and Grill Cookbook

Alfred Portale's
12 Seasons
COOKBOOK

Alfred Portale
with Andrew Friedman

PHOTOGRAPHS BY GOZEN KOSHIDA

BROADWAY BOOKS
NEW YORK

BROADWAY

ALFRED PORTALE'S TWELVE SEASONS COOKBOOK.
Copyright © 2000 by Alfred Portale. All rights reserved. Printed in Japan.
No part of this book may be reproduced or transmitted in any form or by
any means, electronic or mechanical, including photocopying, recording, or
by any information storage and retrieval system, without written permission
from the publisher. For information, address Broadway Books, a division of
Random House, Inc., 1540 Broadway, New York, NY 10036.

Broadway Books titles may be purchased for business or promotional use or
for special sales. For information, please write to: Special Markets Department,
Random House, Inc., 1540 Broadway, New York, NY 10036.

BROADWAY BOOKS and its logo, a letter B bisected on the
diagonal, are trademarks of Broadway Books, a division of Random
House, Inc.

Visit our website at www.broadwaybooks.com

Library of Congress Cataloging-in-Publication Data
Portale, Alfred.
    Alfred Portale's twelve seasons cookbook / Alfred Portale with
Andrew Friedman—1st ed.
        p.   cm.
    Includes index.
    1. Cookery. 2. Menus. 3. Gotham Bar and Grill. I. Title.
    TX714.P68 2000
    641.5   99-087943

FIRST EDITION

Book design by Marysarah Quinn

ISBN 0-7679-0606-3

00 01 02 03 04 10 9 8 7 6 5 4 3 2 1

FOR Helen, Olympia, AND Victoria

Acknowledgments

Every book has two stories to tell: the one between the covers and the one behind the scenes. This is the behind-the-scenes story of the *Twelve Seasons Cookbook* and the people who made it happen. Thanks to all . . .

After a year or two had passed and I had some perspective on the experience of writing the *Gotham Bar and Grill Cookbook,* I decided it was time to start work on a new project. My coauthor, Andrew Friedman, and I sat down to explore some concepts. We developed several, but eventually settled on the one that shapes this book.

Several of the people who contributed to the *Gotham Bar and Grill Cookbook*'s success also participated in this project: David Kratz, my agent and publicist, shared our enthusiasm and offered some useful advice; our editor, Judy Kern at Doubleday, committed to the project; and Marysarah Quinn again lent her keen talent to the design.

My great Gotham chefs, Martin Burge and Jacinto Guadarrama, were invaluable in helping me test the recipes, as was talented chef Lincoln Engstrom. Gotham pastry chef Joseph Murphy shared many of his own dessert recipes. And Mary Goodbody assisted in the final days of recipe editing.

Special thanks also to my wife, Helen Chardack, who contributed several personal recipes to the book. Additionally, she helped me develop some of the new dishes that appear here and made a crucial editorial pass over most of the written recipes when they were in first-draft form.

Gozen Koshida flew to New York from Japan to photograph the book, aided by his assistant and interpreter, Hiromi Hayashi.

A number of friends provided time, services, and properties to make the photo shoots a success. They were David Samuels from Blue Ribbon Seafood; the Gossman family, proprietors of Gossman's Dock in Montauk, Long Island;

Ron from Stokes Farm; Tim Starks from Eckerton Hills Farm; Claws on Wheels in East Hampton, Long Island; Elizabeth Fonseca; Scott from Quail Hill Farm; Joel Patraker, the Director of the Union Square Green Market; Porcelaines Bernardaud, Lalique North America, and Viking Range Corporation for the use of their world-class equipment.

In all of the above, I was supported on a day-to-day basis by Gotham's Saundra Blackman and Lisa Scott.

Michael Greenlee, the Gotham's Wine Director, offered advice for the "What to Drink" sidebars.

Also, thanks to my business partners, Rick and Robert Rathe, Jeff Bliss, and especially my friend Jerome Kretchmer, who has always generously shared his wisdom and encouragement.

To the food writers and community in New York City and around the country: thanks for fifteen years of supporting the Gotham team's effort.

And, of course, to the Gotham staff, past and present, for all of their loyalty, hard work, and dedication to excellence. And, as well, to our loyal customers, who make every season a rewarding one in which to cook.

In addition, Andrew would like to thank his wife, Caitlin, for her devotion and support; Judith Weber, a thoughtful, wise, and trustworthy agent and friend; Pascal Beric and Dominic Cerrone, two excellent culinary teachers; Kit Golden and Tom Mangan (belatedly); and Alfred Portale, for his early belief and a great opportunity.

Contents

ALFRED PORTALE'S 12 SEASONS COOKBOOK

Introduction

It's a Thursday night late in May and I'm sitting in the Gotham Bar and Grill's office, a small room tucked behind the sprawling kitchen downstairs at 12 East 12th Street in New York City. I'm leaving soon for the long Memorial Day weekend, but not before I finish fine-tuning the June menu, which I've been working on over the past few days by making handwritten notes on a photocopy of the May dinner menu. While certain dishes stay on year-round due to their popularity, several offerings change every four weeks or so; each time the calendar turns over to the 1st, we debut creations designed for the new month and occasionally bring back favorites from our repertoire.

Looking over May, I see that I've already slashed a line through the Atlantic Salmon with Morels, Ramps, Sweet Peas, and Chervil because I think it belongs in the expiring month; it's extremely tender and delicate and will feel out of place on the June menu. I've also omitted Veal Chops with Spring Leeks and Soft Polenta because it, too, seems so decidedly springlike to me. Other dishes have been similarly retired for the year, but a few final decisions remain. Chilled Pea Soup with Lobster, Crème Fraîche, and Caviar? It's a keeper; peas are well within their prime for all of June, and lobster is right at home during the first month of summer. Warm Asparagus and Oregon Morels with Fava Beans, Chervil, and Mushroom Jus? I grant it a reprieve. We'll take it off mid-June, after the morels have faded out for the year, then replace it with a Shellfish Risotto, or something along those lines.

Once this holiday weekend has passed, the entire city will be in a summer state of mind, and I want to reflect this. I jot down a short list of candidates that includes grilled dishes and seafood, such as Grilled Lobster with Grilled Corn, Potatoes, and Roast Garlic–Tarragon Butter. Seeking others, I stop for a moment, close my eyes, and think of some of my favorite warm-weather destinations, such as the Mediterranean and Morocco. With them in mind, I begin to work out ideas for dishes such as Seared Mackerel with Orzo Salad and Toasted Cumin Seed Dressing *and* Grilled Marinated Leg of Lamb with Tabbouleh and Minted Aioli. This last one is brand new; I haven't even cooked it yet, but it's been on my mind for weeks, and I resolve to perfect it before the 1st and introduce it to the kitchen staff.

Anything else? Oh, yes—across the top of the menu, in capital letters, I jot the words Ginger-Berry Lemonade. June is the time when we begin selling this adult fruit punch, and I want to be sure we have some ready at the beginning of the month because, now that it's come to mind, I find that I am already looking forward to my first taste of the year.

I close the menu and slip it into my desk drawer. I'll take one final pass at it after the weekend—my first weekend of summer. Who knows what inspiration may strike as my wife, Helen, and I spend the next four days visiting roadside produce stands and cooking for our family and friends? The dish we'll make for dinner Sunday night might turn out to be the next big thing at the restaurant. A beach house, after all, is a much better place to think about summer cooking than a subterranean office, so my hopes of returning with at least one new recipe are actually pretty high.

I go through this enjoyable and challenging exercise every month at the Gotham Bar and Grill, adjusting the menu to reflect the changes around us that influence not only what is available to eat, but what we want to eat as well—the seasonality of ingredients, the weather, and the emotions triggered by the month at hand. Traditionally, chefs alter their menus once each season, but I find that a monthly audit always results in substantial changes. Not only do many ingredients peak well before the full season has ended, but each month of the year is defined by its own distinct set of events or associations that simply cannot be ignored. For example, December and January are both winter months, but they stir such different feelings that I don't think of them as related by anything other than weather and the fact that one immediately precedes the other.

In other words, when it comes to cooking, as far as I'm concerned, there are twelve seasons—each month distinguishing itself from the one that precedes and the one that follows it. The traditional four seasons are always with us, of course, but practically speaking, the twelve-seasons approach proves more useful and better attuned to how we live from day to day.

The transformations that occur throughout the year take place on a daily basis themselves. Think about it—as you're reading this, we are participating in a natural phenomenon as inspiring as it is terrifying. The Earth is rotating on its axis, spinning at an astonishing rate, as it takes its annual trip around the sun, getting farther and farther away before working its way dependably back. This never-ending cycle creates the seasons and everything they bring.

Our lives are so defined by technology that it's easy, and in some ways tempting, to ignore this power of nature. We often consider the weather merely as ambiance, rather than as the product of such profound celestial machinations. But the ceaseless movement of the planet affects us all. It affects the air, temperature, and precipitation. And it plays on our emotions, as when we speak of winter depression and spring fever.

This book, then, is a chef's-eye view of the relationship between human beings and animals, fruits, and vegetables as the Earth revolves around the sun, taking all of us through our intertwined annual cycles. In it, I've tried to look at how climatic shifts are reflected both in the raw ingredients we are presented with and in our cultural traditions and day-to-day appetites.

To be more specific, this book is focused on how these forces act upon that body of land located roughly between 30° and 50° latitude and 70° and 125° longitude known as the United States. Though it would be fascinating to examine this on a global level, it would take an encyclopedia to accomplish such a feat. In fact, even the U.S. approach is imperfect. December is very different in New York, for instance, from what it is in Florida, and there are even vast differences between northern and southern California.

This book looks at the twelve seasons in the United States from the vantage point of New York City and the Northeast. This isn't just a matter of convenience—I happen to live and work in New York—but because this book is focused as much on cultural tradition as it is on the seasonality of individual foods, the Northeast offers the best model available. This region, more than any other, follows the seasonal arc that we hear about in songs, read about in literature, and watch in the movies.

I've also taken a thematic, rather than an ingredient-driven, approach to most of the months, so almost all of the ideas and recipes presented will have universal appeal no matter where you live.

The Twelve Seasons In thinking about the most

practical way to share my feeling about each month of the year, each of the twelve seasons, I've tried to honor all of the considerations I make when cooking both at the Gotham Bar and Grill and at home. To me, there are many factors that must be considered when thinking about cooking during a particular month, and not all of them have to do with the seasonality of ingredients. Don't you find that each month brings certain emotions, memories, challenges, and desires to mind?

I know I do. For example, January to me is a time for reflection and renewal, a time to set new goals and to repent for the culinary sins of the holidays. So, in "January: A Fresh Start," I offer recipes that are relatively light to help make up for December's indulgences.

Similarly, I always find September to be a rather stressful time because the whole world seems to be readjusting to the post–Labor Day focus on work, work, work. Accordingly, "September: Recipes for Busy Times" is devoted to relatively simple and quick dishes for those taxing weeks.

There are, of course, months in which the subject matter wasn't open for discussion. In a few cases, this owes to cultural tradition. November, for example, means just one thing to me—Thanksgiving—so I've devoted the entire chapter to ways of "Giving Thanks" with recipes that use ingredients associated with that holiday, just as December focuses on "Celebrations" with a full range of recipes from canapés and cocktails to more formal meals for Christmas and New Year's Eve.

In a related vein, there are a few months in which the available ingredients dictate the menu. Foremost among these is May, which I've dubbed "The Big Bang of the Culinary Year" because of the astonishing proliferation of vegetables that explode onto the scene this month. On the other side of the calendar, October marks the beginning of our descent into the colder months with the arrival of the ingredients that constitute the autumn palate in the chapter titled "Sweater Weather."

Other months bring nostalgia. As much as I love spring, when March rolls around, I find myself already missing the chill of winter, celebrated here with classic French cuisine in "Last Chance for Winter." In much the same way, at the end of summer, I find that August produces the identical response. Consequently, that chapter—"Seize the Day"—offers recipes intended to facilitate entertaining and being outdoors as much as possible in the last days of your vacation.

Then there are months that are defined by transition as they ease us into a new season. To me, there's a fundamental shift that happens every June as "Summer Settles In," which is why that month's chapter features recipes that reflect the summer lifestyle, with grilled dishes, picnic suggestions, and abundant uses for stone fruits and seafood. The same can be said of April, "Return of the Light," when the last traces of winter are mingled with the anticipation of spring.

Finally, in a few cases I offer a highly personal, you might say idiosyncratic, view of the month at hand. I grew up in the bitter cold of Buffalo, New York, and now live in almost-as-frigid New York City. As a result, I'm constantly seeking ways to combat the winter blues, and one of my favorites is what I call "Culinary Sunshine"—cooking bright, vibrant dishes that are like a tropical vacation on a plate—and these are what I've offered in the month of February.

But the most personal chapter you'll find in the following pages is July, in which I've shared some childhood memories of family holidays spent on Crystal Beach and the recipes those recollections have inspired. I've included them here not only because they sum up, truly, what July means to me, but also to provide a sense of how you might weave influences from your own experiences into your cooking. With home cooks, as with professional chefs, recipes can be a form of autobiography, and I wish you all the best as you cook, or create, dishes to suit the seasons of your life.

ALFRED PORTALE
NEW YORK CITY
MAY 2000

How to Use This Book

Since this book operates on the principle that each month of the year constitutes a season unto itself, each chapter is devoted to one of those "seasons." It's worth noting that since May is the most bountiful month, and reverberates with signs of new life, this book begins in May rather than January.

Each chapter begins with an introduction in which I share my general observations about the month, both an overall point of view and a practical discussion of the ingredients that flourish during its four weeks. For example, the introduction to "August: Seize the Day" will describe, among other things, the abundance of tomatoes and eggplant, as well as a diverse range of recipes for them, while the opening pages of "December: Celebrations" will discuss how to infuse menus with holiday spirit, offering canapés and cocktails, and will preview the upcoming recipes featuring truffles, caviar, and foie gras.

Each chapter introduction will be followed by the recipes that reflect the theme of the month. In many cases, when an ingredient or technique appears several times in a chapter, I've grouped the corresponding recipes together and have preceded them with a short essay that offers some information and advice about that subject. For example, "September: Recipes for Busy Times," features an essay on the technique for making pan sauces that will prove helpful when cooking both Seared Halibut with Haricots Verts, Scallions, and White Wine Sauce (page 181) and Chicken Breasts with Rosemary and Chanterelles (page 183), while "July: Birthdays and Barbecues" includes an essay on berries that will guide you in the preparation of all three desserts in that chapter. These essays are indicated in the recipe list that precedes each chapter.

The recipes are also supported by several features, many of which will be familiar to readers of *Alfred Portale's Gotham Bar and Grill Cookbook* (Doubleday, 1997):

Each recipe is preceded by a headnote, which is essentially an introduction to the dish itself and includes information ranging from the inspiration for the recipe to practical cooking advice that will help you make it successfully the first time.

In most cases, the headnote is followed by a note on "Thinking Ahead" which provides suggestions for steps that might be executed in advance to minimize last-minute preparations. In those rare instances that require special equipment, such as a mandoline or a conical strainer, this is noted immediately after "Thinking Ahead."

Following the recipe itself, two features provide directions for how you can adjust it to accommodate factors ranging from personal taste to seasonality of ingredients:

Variations

Suggestions intended to help (a) free you from recipe dependence by offering ways to vary a dish to suit your taste, or (b) provide alternate ingredients to use in case some are unavailable. "Variations" also offer seasonal substitutes should you wish to make, say, Atlantic Salmon with Morels, Ramps, Sweet Peas, and Chervil (page 33) in November rather than May, by substituting another mushroom (such as chanterelles) for the morels and leeks for ramps, or using the vegetables in the dish to accompany a simple sautéed chicken.

Flavor Building

Ways to augment a dish by adding ingredients that will increase its complexity or render it more sophisticated. (In cases where a recipe from the Gotham Bar and Grill has been simplified, this is where you will learn how to return the omitted ingredients to the dish.) Examples of "Flavor Building" include topping May's Chilled Maine Lobster and Avocado Cocktail (page 16) with Sevruga caviar and supplementing August's Grilled Tomato *Bruschetta* with Lemon Thyme (page 136) with Roquefort cheese or Anchovy Vinaigrette (page 97).

Additionally, the recipes are complemented, and punctuated, by a range of sidebars. These include:

What to Drink

Here you'll find advice ranging from the ideal wine to accompany a particular dish to cocktails that complement the month. For example, in October I provide you with the recipe for a Beaujolais Kir (Beaujolais Nouveau, cassis, and a splash of Grand Marnier) to commemorate the arrival of Beaujolais Nouveau, or suggest a Sauternes or a late-harvest Riesling to accompany Seared Foie Gras with Poached Quince, Tangerine, and Pomegranate Juice (page 200). A dramatically different example is June's Spiked

Lemonade (page 87), which demonstrates some ways of turning a childhood staple into an adult punch.

Preserving
Recipes and techniques that show you how to save time in a bottle, capturing the charms of in-season ingredients for months to come. Examples include Apricot Preserves (page 85) and Plum Jam (page 81) in June, Strawberry Preserves (page 114) in July, and Concord Grape Jam (page 190) in September.

Menus
Menus for special occasions that unite recipes featured in the chapter and elsewhere in the book, and integrate hors d'oeuvres, main meal, dessert, and wines or cocktails to achieve a culinary mood appropriate to the occasion or time of year. Examples include a Father's Day Potluck Dinner (page 89) in June, a Superbowl Party (page 323) in January, and two French Dinners (page 387) in March.

In the back of the book, you'll find a few helpful appendices:

Basics
Recipes that are called for throughout the book. These include white chicken stock, brown chicken stock, double turkey stock, vegetable stock, mayonnaise, and basic vinaigrette.

Mail-Order Sources
A list of some of my favorite purveyors that will be useful in obtaining some of the more hard-to-find ingredients in the book, such as foie gras, caviar, truffles, duck or duck confit, and salt cod.

Citrus Salad with Lemongrass, Toasted Almonds, and Mint

Chilled Maine Lobster and Avocado Cocktail

Chilled Pea Soup with Lobster, Crème Fraîche, and Caviar

Asparagus

Warm Asparagus and Oregon Morels with Fava Beans, Chervil, and Mushroom Jus

Asparagus Soup

Grilled Soft-Shell Crabs with Asparagus, New Potatoes, and a Lemon-Caper Vinaigrette

Fiddleheads, Ramps, and Morels

Atlantic Salmon with Morels, Ramps, Sweet Peas, and Chervil

Veal Chops with Spring Leeks and Soft Polenta

Asparagus, Prosciutto, and Spring Onion *Frittata*

Pancakes with Honey-Almond Butter

Jelly-Filled Doughnuts

Lemon Parfait

Tangerine and Blood Orange Terrine

Mother's Day Brunch

MAY
THE BIG BANG OF THE CULINARY YEAR

If a chef rather than an astronomer had devised the calendar, the year would begin not in January but in May, when the vegetables that appear are a cook's dream come true. May is the time of life beginning anew, of optimism and promise, and this spirit is revealed in the fragile shade of green that infuses the entire landscape—a pale, expectant hue that announces tender young buds and shoots as they sprout into being. Not coincidentally, this color also defines many of the foods of May, such as pea shoots, fava beans, and asparagus—many of which rank among my favorites of any month.

These vegetables share a similarity of spirit, a vulnerability if you will, that is wonderfully appropriate to the time of year. This month is also cherished a bit more than the others because many of its culinary gifts are as fleeting as daffodils. Ramps (sweet, wild leeks) and fiddleheads, for instance, truly flourish only during these few short weeks, a rare instance where nature prevails over the blurring of the seasons brought on by the year-round availability of most produce in supermarkets. Personally, I don't mind the limitation; while it would be tempting to have these divine ingredients all the time, part of their charm is the anticipation created by this strict seasonality.

When cooking in May, try to find some quiet time in your routine to relax and give yourself over to the tenderness of the season. When I think of this month, I envision recipes that use several of these ingredients on the same plate, often juxtaposing them against one dominating element to emphasize their endearing fragility. A good example is Atlantic Salmon with Morels, Ramps, Sweet Peas, and Chervil (page 33), in which the accompaniments are rather poignant compared to the fillet, an effect that is echoed in Veal Chops with Spring Leeks and Soft Polenta (page 37).

May is also the time to avail yourself of vegetables so flavorful they can stand as a course by themselves. A superb illustration of this is Warm Asparagus and Oregon Morels with Fava Beans, Chervil, and Mushroom Jus (page 25), in which plump stalks of asparagus act as a perfect foil to the meaty, woodsy mushrooms—a fully rounded dish that doesn't seem to be lacking a thing despite the fact that there's no fish, poultry, or meat on the plate. Similarly,

I've held off on garnishing the Asparagus Soup (page 27), permitting its sylvan grace to speak for itself.

You might wonder where one would find such idyllic inspiration in the rigid, grid-patterned arena of New York City. For me, and for many other chefs, the answer is the Union Square Green Market—a diverse gathering of farmers who brave the urban jungle several times a week to set up camp on a plaza of sorts between Fourteenth and Seventeenth streets. As soon as the market is up and running each year, my cooks and I drop by every day that it's open, roaming the stands, smelling the herbs, handling the produce, and catching up with the farmers. After months of winter, this is a very effective and enjoyable way for us to reconnect with the earth.

My wife, Helen, and I do our own, cosmopolitan brand of cultivating this month as well. In March, we germinate a variety of heirloom seeds twenty-three stories above the city on the terrace of our apartment. There, in a cold frame I've fashioned out of Plexiglas and wood, young vegetable plants soak up the first rays of spring. In May, we load them into the back of our Jeep and drive them out to our country home, where we carefully transplant them into our garden, which we refer to affectionately as our "edible landscape." Our daughters, Olympia and Victoria, take great pleasure in watching tomatoes, beans, and cucumbers make their annual debut, and we all reap the bounty of this shared endeavor throughout the summer.

For my family, this month is an especially meaningful one, since it brings Helen's birthday and, of course, Mother's Day. We don't offer brunch at the Gotham Bar and Grill, so—in the name of a Mother's Day Brunch (page 49)—I'm delighted to have this opportunity to share some of our personal, favorite breakfast recipes. These include Pancakes with Honey-Almond Butter (page 40) and Citrus Salad with Lemongrass, Toasted Almonds, and Mint (page 15). And, if you've ever wondered how to make doughnuts, here's your chance—this chapter includes a primer as well as my recipe for Jelly-Filled Doughnuts (page 43).

Finally, to help you make something unexpected and special for Memorial Day, you'll find a recipe putting that great American cooking machine, the outdoor grill, to surprisingly sophisticated use. Delight your first guests of the season by making Grilled Soft-Shell Crabs with Asparagus, New Potatoes, and a Lemon-Caper Vinaigrette (page 28) the centerpiece of your holiday feast. It perfectly complements a cold beer under the hot sun, the ideal way to welcome the summer days ahead.

Citrus Salad with Lemongrass, Toasted Almonds, and Mint

MAKES 4 SERVINGS

4   clementines
4   tangerines
4   blood oranges
2   pink grapefruit
1   lime
6   kumquats
     Juice of 1 lemon
$^1/_4$ cup chopped lemongrass (1 stalk)
2   medium Kaffir lime leaves
4   tablespoons sliced almonds
1   tablespoon gently packed fresh mint, cut into chiffonade

Using a sharp, thin-bladed knife, cut off and discard the peel and white pith from the clementines, tangerines, oranges, grapefruit, and lime. Working over a small bowl to catch the juices, cut between the membranes to remove the segments. Put the segments in the bowl and squeeze any juice from the membranes. Discard any seeds. Pour $^3/_4$ cup of the juice into a measuring cup and set it aside.

Thinly slice the kumquats and discard any seeds. Combine the kumquat slices with the citrus fruit segments. Cover and refrigerate.

In a small saucepan, combine the lemon juice, reserved citrus juice, lemongrass, and lime leaves. Bring to a boil over medium-high heat and remove from the heat. Set aside for about 30 minutes to infuse with flavor. Strain through a fine-mesh sieve into another bowl, cover, and refrigerate until chilled.

Preheat the oven to 350°F. Spread the almonds in a single layer on an ungreased baking sheet and bake, stirring occasionally, for about 5 minutes, until lightly and evenly browned and fragrant. Transfer to a plate to cool and halt the cooking.

Divide the fruit sections among 4 rimmed soup bowls. Spoon 2 tablespoons of sauce over each serving, and garnish with the mint leaves and almonds.

VARIATIONS: Don't be discouraged if you don't have lemongrass and Kaffir lime leaves; the salad will still be delicious without them.

If you'd like to make enough for a large group, or to have planned leftovers, the recipe multiplies very well.

Substitute oranges for the tangerines or clementines, if necessary.

When I was a kid, my mother would often purchase glass jars of orange and grapefruit sections from our local supermarket. Swimming in a tart citrus juice, along with maraschino cherries, this "salad" wasn't very good; my mouth still curls when I think of its too-bitter quality and chemical taste. Not only that, but suspended in their cloudy juice, the citrus sections looked to me and my sister like something that belonged on a shelf in our school's science classroom rather than in our refrigerator at home.

Nevertheless, I have fond memories of the times this salad evokes. So, for Mother's Day one year, I thought it would be fun to make my version of this dish part of a buffet brunch for my family. I was surprised at how well it came out. In fact, I now make it in large batches so I have leftovers for days to come—my own version of my mother's tradition.

Chilled Maine Lobster and Avocado Cocktail

MAKES 4 SERVINGS

One of the most important and elusive instincts for a chef to develop is how the proportions, or relative amounts of different ingredients, will register in a dish. In a salad, the challenge is usually to create a suitable dressing and use just enough of it to enhance and unite the flavors and textures without overwhelming any of them.

This recipe was inspired by the decadent, but enormously successful, proportion of lobster to its supporting players in a cool, creamy salad served at Gossman's Point, a harborside shop in Montauk, Long Island, that prepares a variety of memorable dishes from the fish and shellfish caught just offshore. Their lobster salad makes quite an impact because it's loaded with meat, accounting for most of its volume.

A similar ratio is adopted here, rounding out the composition with diced potatoes, slivers of avocado, celery dice, and a touch of tarragon.

(continued)

THINKING AHEAD: The dressing can be made a day in advance. The lobsters can be cooked and shelled the morning you plan to serve this cocktail. (Keep the lobster meat covered in the refrigerator.)

LOBSTER AND AVOCADOS

$1/4$	cup white wine vinegar
2	$1^{1}/4$-pound live lobsters
3 to 4	small new potatoes
1	rib celery, peeled and diced
1	medium yellow or red beet
2	ripe Haas avocados

Using a large stockpot, bring salted water and the vinegar to a boil over high heat. Add the lobsters and cover the pot. Return to the boil and cook for 8 to 10 minutes, or until the shells are bright red. Lift the lobsters from the pot with tongs and set them aside to drain and cool. When cool enough to handle, crack the shells and remove the meat. Discard the shells or reserve them for another use, such as shellfish or fish stock. Transfer the meat to a bowl, cover, and refrigerate.

In a small saucepan, cook the potatoes in boiling salted water over medium-high heat for about 15 minutes, or until tender when pierced with the tip of a small, sharp knife. Drain and, when cool enough to handle, cut the potatoes into $1/2$-inch dice. Put them in a bowl and set aside.

In a small saucepan, cook the celery in boiling salted water for about 2 minutes, until bright green. Using a slotted spoon, remove and rinse them under cold water to set the color. Set aside.

Let the water return to a boil. Add the beet, reduce the heat, and simmer for about 35 minutes, or until tender when pierced with the tip of a small, sharp knife. Drain and, when cool enough to handle, peel, and cut the beet into $1/2$-inch dice. Set it aside.

Cut the avocados in half lengthwise and remove the pits with the heel of the knife. Peel and cut the avocados into quarters. Using a sharp, thin-bladed knife, cut each quarter lengthwise into $1/8$-inch-thick slices, keeping the slices attached at one end. Fan the slices gently and set them aside.

The cooked beets, which are visually brilliant, serve to pace the experience of eating the salad by inviting the diner to slow down and savor their sweetness. A simple but elegant presentation is pictured here, but you might also pack the salad in a container on ice for a picnic. (If you do, omit the beets, which will bleed out into the salad and turn everything red.)

Properly made, this salad should have just a bit of a kick, thanks to the pinch of cayenne pepper. Be careful to use just a bit; as with all the ingredients, it's important to keep this one in proper proportion.

WHAT TO DRINK: Serve this with a Krug Grand Cuvée Champagne to embellish its elegant nature.

ASSEMBLY

1	cup gently packed romaine lettuce, cut into chiffonade
4	tablespoons mayonnaise, preferably homemade (page 420)
	Coarse salt, freshly ground white pepper, and cayenne pepper to taste
$^1/_2$	teaspoon fresh lemon juice, or to taste
1	tablespoon chopped fresh tarragon
1	tablespoon finely minced chives

In a medium bowl, combine the lobster meat, potatoes, celery, and romaine. Add the mayonnaise, a tablespoon at a time, until the salad is nicely dressed. Season with salt, white pepper, cayenne pepper, and lemon juice. Fold in the tarragon and chives.

Divide the salad among 4 martini glasses or salad plates and garnish each with 2 avocado fans and a portion of the diced beets.

VARIATION: Cooked, sweet shrimp make a fine substitute for the lobster. Use 1 pound and reduce the cooking time to 4 minutes.

FLAVOR BUILDING: For an opulent flourish, top each serving with hard-boiled quail eggs and about half an ounce of Osetra caviar.

THINKING AHEAD: The lobster can be prepared one day in advance, chilled, wrapped tightly in plastic, and refrigerated. The soup itself can be made one day ahead as well. Allow it to cool and keep it tightly sealed in the refrigerator.

Chilled Pea Soup with Lobster, Crème Fraîche, and Caviar

MAKES 4 SERVINGS

SOUP

1	tablespoon olive oil
1	onion, chopped
$^{1}/_{2}$	rib celery, chopped
1	quart White Chicken Stock (page 421)
4	cups shelled fresh peas
	Coarse salt and freshly ground white pepper to taste
2	tablespoons unsalted butter
2	tablespoons sugar, or to taste, optional

In a stockpot, heat the oil over medium heat. Add the onion and celery and cook, stirring, for 3 to 4 minutes, or until softened. Add the stock, raise the heat to high, and bring to a boil. Add the peas and return to a boil, reduce the heat, and simmer for about 12 minutes, or until the peas are tender. Remove from the heat and season with salt and pepper.

While the soup simmers, set a strainer over a bowl large enough to hold the stock. Set another bowl in a larger one holding ice cubes and ice water to chill the soup. Also have a blender and ladle on hand.

Strain the soup into the bowl. Transfer the vegetables to the blender and purée, adding only enough of the strained stock to make a fine, thick purée. Add the butter, and pulse or stir until it melts and enriches the purée.

Scrape the contents of the blender into the bowl set in the ice bath. Add the remaining stock, a little at a time, until the soup reaches the desired creamy consistency. Season with sugar, if desired, cover, and refrigerate.

LOBSTER

$^{1}/_{4}$	cup white wine vinegar
1	$1^{1}/_{2}$-pound live lobster

Using a large stockpot, bring 8 quarts of salted water and the vinegar to a boil over high heat. Add the lobster and cover the pot. Return to the boil and cook for 8 to 10 minutes, or until the

Peas embody the qualities of spring in their size, brilliant green color, short peak season (mid-May through late June), and their own delicate nature. Within hours of picking, a pea's natural sugars begin turning into starch, taking with them their sweetness. For this soup to have the best flavor and texture, then, you should use extremely fresh peas.

You'd never know it from looking at the final product, but making this innocent-looking soup requires the cook to be intensely focused during its preparation. Before revving up the stove, do yourself a favor and set up a small production line comprising (a) a fine-mesh strainer (set over a bowl), (b) a blender, and (c) a bowl set into an ice bath. Having this little soup factory ready to go before you begin cooking will make your life easier, at least for the 30 minutes or so it takes to complete the recipe.

(continued)

The rest of the procedure is fairly simple and yields a satiny smooth purée to which just enough stock is added to achieve a soup consistency. Cooked lobster dressed with lemon and crème fraîche is mounded in the center of each bowl, rendering the soup more substantial and complex.

The dish should be served cool, but not frigid. If refrigerated, allow it to come up a few degrees before serving.

shell is bright red. Lift the lobster from the pot with tongs and set it aside to drain and cool. When cool enough to handle, crack the shell and remove the meat. Cut the meat into spoon-sized pieces. Discard the shells or reserve them for another use, such as shellfish or fish stock. Transfer the meat to a bowl.

ASSEMBLY

$^1/_3$ cup crème fraîche
2   teaspoons fresh lemon juice, or to taste
Coarse salt and freshly ground white pepper to taste
1   cup lightly packed fresh pea shoots
1   ounce Sevruga or Osetra caviar

Remove the soup from the refrigerator about 20 minutes before serving so that it is chilled but not ice cold.

In a small bowl, whisk together the crème fraîche, lemon juice, and salt and pepper.

Select 8 of the best-looking pea shoots and set them aside. In a small sauté pan, bring 1 cup of water to a boil over medium-high heat and cook the remaining pea shoots for about 15 seconds, until wilted. Lift them from the pan with a slotted spoon and drain them on a clean kitchen towel.

Arrange a tight mound of wilted pea shoots in the center of each soup bowl. Toss the lobster with a few tablespoons of crème fraîche until nicely dressed. Carefully spoon the lobster on top of the pea shoots. Pour the soup around the lobster, and then garnish the soup with swirls of crème fraîche, the caviar, and the reserved fresh pea shoots.

VARIATIONS: The lobster can be replaced with lump crabmeat or peekytoe crab. In months other than May and June, you can replace the fresh peas with high-quality, frozen *petits pois*; keep in mind that they will cook more quickly than fresh peas.

If you cannot obtain pea shoots, substitute an equal amount of wilted watercress.

As extravagant and satisfying as this soup is, the pea soup by itself (i.e., without the lobster) is also delicious.

Asparagus

Asparagus are one of the quintessential spring vegetables. They first appear in mid–March and their season lasts until the end of June, but they peak in May, the only time when the dramatic, plump Jumbo and Colossal varieties are readily available.

When they're young, asparagus have a purple tip and green stem, which grows thicker as they ripen. Asparagus are generally classified by size. In nonpeak months, Pencil, Large (a bit of a misnomer because these are actually rather thin), and Extra Large are the options. The recipes in this book primarily use these varieties, although there is one that calls for white asparagus, which, because it is imported, is the most expensive.

White asparagus is produced via a blanching process in which sand is piled up around the vegetable as it grows up out of the ground. Though quite lovely, this variety can also sometimes be unpleasantly bitter. Like Belgian endive, it should be checked carefully for freshness—if shopping for white asparagus, be sure that the base of the stalk is not withered.

When purchasing any variety of asparagus, examine the tips for signs of freshness because this is the portion most likely to break or spoil. The tips should be tightly closed and not too dry. Old asparagus are identified by a "wrinkle" in the stem or a breaking down of the tip, so even if an asparagus stem hasn't matured to this point, bear in mind that dryness is a sign that the end is near.

While it's not imperative that asparagus be peeled, doing so is beneficial for a number of reasons, including a superior look, mouth-feel, and taste. Not only is this a simple procedure (except with Pencil asparagus, which should be left unpeeled), but peeling the stem makes more of it edible and allows the vegetable to cook at the same rate from top to bottom. To peel an asparagus, start about an inch below the tip and, peeling away from the top, remove the skin in one swift, deft movement with a vegetable peeler, then rotate the asparagus to peel the next portion. Rest the asparagus on a flat surface to provide leverage and help ensure that you don't snap the stalk as you work.

There are a number of methods for cooking asparagus. The three most common are in boiling salted water, simmering them in a large skillet, or steaming them. Many chefs tie asparagus in bundles when boiling them to facilitate their removal from the hot water. If you do this, do not bind them too tightly or the string will cut into them and mar their delicate surface.

If asparagus are to be served cold, and are being cooked in advance, be sure to shock them in ice-cold water to stop the cooking and keep the color and flavor from dissipating. After cooking, set them on a plate with a clean towel underneath to soak up the moisture so that it doesn't dilute the vinaigrette or sauce with which you'll ultimately be dressing the asparagus.

THINKING AHEAD: The asparagus can be cooked as many as 6 hours in advance, kept covered in the refrigerator, and reheated before serving. Be sure to dip them in ice water for a few seconds after precooking to shock them and preserve their natural color.

1	tablespoon canola oil
1	pound fresh morel mushrooms, ends trimmed, large caps halved
	Coarse salt and freshly ground white pepper to taste
1	shallot, peeled and finely minced
$^1/_2$	clove garlic, peeled and finely minced
$1^2/_3$	cups Vegetable Stock (page 425) or White Chicken Stock (page 421)
$1^1/_2$	pounds fresh fava beans
$2^3/_4$	pounds Jumbo asparagus, peeled, ends trimmed (24 to 36 spears)
2	tablespoons unsalted butter
2	tablespoons finely minced chives
12	sprigs fresh chervil

In a large sauté pan, heat the oil over medium heat. Add the morels, season them with salt and pepper, and cook, stirring occasionally, for 4 to 5 minutes, until softened. Add the shallot and cook, stirring, for about 4 minutes, or until softened. Add the garlic and cook, stirring, for about 3 minutes longer.

Add the stock, raise the heat, and when the stock comes to a boil, reduce the heat and simmer for about 5 minutes. Remove from the heat and set aside, covered, to keep warm.

Bring a saucepan of salted water to a boil over high heat. Add the fava beans and cook for one minute. Drain and rinse under cold water. Remove the thick peel from each bean and set aside.

In a large pot, bring salted water to a boil over medium-high heat and cook the asparagus spears for 4 to 5 minutes, until tender when pierced with the tip of a sharp knife. You may have to cook the asparagus in batches. Drain them on a clean kitchen towel.

Arrange the asparagus in the center of a serving platter or on individual serving plates. Using a slotted spoon, distribute the mushrooms evenly over the asparagus.

Reheat the sauce over high heat until boiling. Taste it for seasoning and, if necessary, cook it a little longer to reduce slightly and intensify the flavors. Remove it from the heat and swirl in the

In recent years, many restaurants have taken a "full disclosure" approach to menu writing, providing exhaustive details about each dish, from the source of the ingredients to the technique used to cook each and every one of them. Often, the result more closely resembles a recipe than a name.

With most of the selections on the Gotham menu, and to some extent in my books, we make a point of leaving one or two essential ingredients out of the title to allow an element of surprise at the table. But this recipe is so simple that it's actually difficult to find something to omit. Maybe that's why we rarely feature it on the Gotham menu, saving it instead as an unexpected gift from the kitchen. You might find that it suits the same purpose at home—try it as a starter or midmeal offering in a multicourse dinner, or make it the centerpiece of a vegetarian meal.

Visually, these quintessential spring vegetables, both at their peak of flavor in May, are a stunning couple—as starkly distinct and complementary to the eye as they will be to the palate.

butter to enrich the sauce. Add the fava beans and the chives and spoon the sauce over and around the asparagus. Garnish with the chervil and serve.

VARIATIONS: White asparagus can be used to make the dish a bit more unusual. Substitute cremini mushrooms for the morels, if necessary.

THINKING AHEAD: This soup can be made a day in advance. Allow it to cool, then cover and refrigerate it. Reheat gently, stirring occasionally, over medium heat.

2	medium leeks, white part only
1	tablespoon canola oil
1	medium onion, chopped
2	cloves garlic, peeled and sliced
3	cups White Chicken Stock (page 421)
1	medium russet potato, peeled and cut into medium dice (about $1^1/4$ cups)
2	bunches asparagus, cut into $1/4$-inch rounds (about $3^1/2$ cups)
	Coarse salt and freshly ground white pepper to taste
1	bunch fresh spinach, stemmed, washed, and coarsely chopped (about 8 ounces)
2	tablespoons unsalted butter

Chop the leeks and rinse well. In a stockpot, heat the oil over medium heat. Add the leeks, onion, and garlic, and cook, stirring, for about 4 minutes, or until softened. Add the stock and potato, raise the heat to high, and boil for about 5 minutes. Add the asparagus and season with salt and pepper. Reduce the heat and simmer for 12 to 14 minutes, or until the asparagus is tender. Stir in the spinach and cook about 2 minutes longer, until it just wilts. Remove from the heat.

Working quickly so that the soup does not cool too much, purée the soup in a blender or food processor, working in batches if necessary. Strain it through a fine-mesh sieve, pressing firmly with the back of a spoon to remove the asparagus fibers and extract as much liquid and flavor as possible. Swirl in the butter to enrich the soup and serve.

VARIATION: This soup is just as good chilled as it is hot—serve it cool, but not frigid. If refrigerated, allow it to come up a few degrees before serving.

Does "Asparagus, Spinach, and Potato Soup" sound appealing to you? Me neither. But spinach and potatoes play crucial roles in allowing this asparagus recipe to live up to expectations.

To make soup from asparagus, the stalks must be cooked until their stringy fibers break down completely. By the time this happens, their pale green color boils away, leaving a less-than-compelling complexion. The concentrated chlorophyll in the spinach compensates for this by supplying a natural "artificial coloring" that provides the soup a familiar, comforting appearance.

The potatoes are included for textural support. When heated, they release a natural starch that is ultimately blended into the stock, providing the appropriate thick consistency.

As good as this soup is hot, I also love serving it chilled, especially outdoors on a sunny, slightly warm May afternoon. (See Variation.)

Grilled Soft-Shell Crabs with Asparagus, New Potatoes, and a Lemon-Caper Vinaigrette

MAKES 4 SERVINGS

Like many of the ingredients in this chapter, blue crabs are at a point of immaturity in May. They are also, quite literally, vulnerable as they molt, or shed their hard outer shell, in order to grow. (Soft-shell crabs are blue crabs caught within 6 hours of shedding.) While soft-shells are available for several months, emotionally they belong to May because their arrival is always much heralded by food lovers, especially on the East Coast, where signs announcing "We have soft-shells!" begin to pop up in fish-store windows, and restaurant chefs scramble to add soft-shell dishes to their menus.

This recipe is for people who love their soft-shell crabs crisp, as I do. It's included here in hopes of correcting the very common, and

POTATOES

1¹/₂	pounds fingerling or small new potatoes
3	large cloves garlic, peeled and crushed
1	leek, split lengthwise
1	tablespoon whole black peppercorns
2	sprigs fresh thyme
1	bay leaf
	Coarse salt to taste
2	tablespoons extra-virgin olive oil

In a large pot, combine the potatoes, garlic, leek, peppercorns, thyme, and bay leaf. Add enough cold water to cover by 2 inches. Season with salt. Bring to a boil over high heat, reduce the heat, and simmer for about 15 minutes, until the potatoes are tender when pierced with the tip of a knife.

Remove the pot from the heat. Add the olive oil and set the potatoes aside in their cooking water. The oil will infuse the cooking water with flavor and permeate the potatoes. Cover and keep warm. To serve, lift the potatoes from the liquid with a slotted spoon.

ASPARAGUS

1¹/₂	pounds Extra Large asparagus, peeled, ends trimmed (about 12 spears)
2	tablespoons extra-virgin olive oil
	Coarse salt and freshly ground white pepper to taste

In a large pot of boiling salted water, cook the asparagus for about 4 minutes, or until just tender. Lift them from the pot with tongs and drain them on kitchen towels.

Transfer the asparagus to a serving platter and drizzle with the olive oil. Roll the asparagus in the oil to coat them. Season with salt and pepper.

LEMON-CAPER VINAIGRETTE

5	tablespoons extra-virgin olive oil
¹/₄	cup fresh lemon juice
1	tablespoon drained capers
1	shallot, peeled and finely minced
	Coarse salt and freshly ground white pepper to taste
2	plum tomatoes, halved, seeded, and cut into ¹/₄-inch dice
2	tablespoons finely minced chives

In a small bowl, stir together the oil, lemon juice, capers, and shallot, and season with salt and pepper. Just before serving, stir in the tomatoes and chives.

SOFT-SHELL CRABS AND ASSEMBLY

12   jumbo soft-shell crabs (3 per serving), cleaned at right, below
3   tablespoons canola or vegetable oil
      Coarse salt and freshly ground white pepper to taste

Build a charcoal fire in a grill, banking the coals on one side, and let them burn until covered with white ash. Lightly oil the grill grate.

Pat the crabs dry with paper towels. Brush them with oil and season with salt and pepper. Grill them near but not over the coals for 6 to 8 minutes, turning once, until the crabs look burnished with a golden brown color and feel firm to the touch. If the legs begin to burn, move the crabs farther from the coals. Serve immediately, while piping hot, drizzled with vinaigrette, with the asparagus and potatoes on the side or arranged on the individual plates next to the crabs. (Note that the vinaigrette is not emulsified and needs to be stirred as you spoon it over the crabs.)

VARIATION: The crabs can be sautéed rather than grilled. To do this, preheat your oven to 450°F. Season the crabs with salt and pepper. Pour 2 tablespoons of canola oil in each of two ovenproof 12-inch sauté pans (4 tablespoons total) and set the pans over high heat until the oil is very hot but not smoking. Add the crabs, shell side down, and cook until crisp, about 4 minutes. Turn the crabs and place the sauté pans in the oven. Roast until the crabs are golden brown and cooked through, about 5 minutes.

(continued)

logical, misconception that crabs must be dredged in flour in order to produce this effect. In reality, all that's needed is extremely high and, most importantly in the case of grilling, indirect heat. By allowing the crab to cook a bit longer than you would over direct heat, the exterior turns very brittle. I especially love to grill soft-shells because the smoky flavor has a great affinity with so many sauces. (See page 70 for grilling tips.)

SOFT-SHELL CRABS: Soft-shell crabs are sold in four sizes: prime, jumbo, hotel, and small. The blue crabs are caught and kept in special "floats," where they are carefully watched so that they can be harvested as soon as they molt.

They are best if bought live and will keep for a few days in the refrigerator covered with wet newspaper. They must be dressed before being cooked; have the crabs cleaned at the fish store (if you plan to cook them soon after purchase) or dress them yourself in the following manner: Cut or pull off the apron that folds under the rear of the crab. With scissors, snip off the "face" just behind the eyes. Clean out the gills located on either side of the crab and rinse under cold water.

FLAVOR BUILDING: For a richer alternative to the Lemon-Caper Vinaigrette, try this butter sauce— a fairly traditional *beurre blanc,* made with whole butter that is emulsified into a reduction comprising white wine, vinegar, and shallots. Heavy cream is added to aid emulsification, as I have done here. Feel free to modify the recipe to suit your own taste by adding lemon juice, lime juice, or a small amount of minced garlic. You might also add a few tablespoons of chopped herbs such as chervil, chives, parsley, tarragon, mint, dill, or basil. Garnish with tomato dice, scallions, and/or capers.

Basic *Beurre Blanc*
MAKES ABOUT 4 SERVINGS; $1/2$ CUP

$1/3$ cup dry white wine
2   tablespoons champagne or white wine vinegar
1   tablespoon finely chopped shallot, from about 1 small shallot
2   tablespoons heavy cream
1   stick unsalted butter, cut into 8 equal pieces
$1/8$ teaspoon cayenne pepper
    Coarse salt and freshly ground white pepper to taste

BUTTER-BASED SAUCES can be kept warm for up to 1 hour by placing the saucepan in a skillet filled with hot tap water. Keep the water hot, but not simmering, over very low heat, or pour the sauce into a large-mouthed vacuum jar (warm the jar first by rinsing it out with hot water) and close tightly.

Combine the white wine, vinegar, and shallot in a small saucepan. Cook over medium heat for 4 to 5 minutes, until reduced to about 2 tablespoons. Add the heavy cream, raise the heat, and bring to a boil. Immediately reduce the heat to low and, whisking constantly, stir in the butter one piece at a time. When all the butter has been added, pour the mixture through a fine mesh strainer. Discard the shallot. Season the sauce with cayenne pepper, salt, and pepper. Keep warm until ready to use.

Fiddleheads, Ramps, and Morels

This triumvirate of vegetables virtually defines May cooking. They are among the most fleetingly available of all the year's ingredients and, happily, get along very well in a variety of contexts. Fiddleheads, ramps, and morels are also very easy and quick to cook, making them attractive last-minute additions. I purchase them throughout the month, using them in as many dishes as possible, both at the Gotham and at home.

Fiddleheads

In the wild, fiddlehead ferns have a papery brown scaling or skin. Rub this layer off under cold running water, and a verdant green is revealed. This color, along with the delicate grassy flavor and fresh crunch of the fiddlehead, reminds me of everything I love about May. So perhaps it's not surprising that the fiddlehead's season runs only four or five weeks, most of which fall in this month.

Fiddleheads are the shoots of ostrich ferns, named for the way they coil up into a tight spiral, like an ostrich burying its head in the sand. They can be steamed or cooked in boiling salted water, very much like green beans, or they can be sautéed raw in a little olive oil or butter. When purchasing them, choose the tight young, baby ones over those that seem to be trying to open, because, as they mature, they become fibrous, bitter, and inedible.

Ramps

Ramps, or wild leeks, also have a very short season of little more than a month. They look like a hybrid of a scallion and a small leek and have a soft, sweet onion flavor. Because their tops are more delicate than those of regular leeks, the entire vegetable is edible. They are foraged in the wild and are usually purchased in bunches, tied with a piece of twine. Ramps must be thoroughly washed to remove all grit, and the root end should be trimmed before cooking. Like fiddleheads, they are good quickly steamed, blanched, or sautéed.

Morel mushrooms To my mind, morels—with their distinct conical cap and honeycombed surface—are the quintessential spring mushrooms. As you might expect from their deep woodsy flavor and aroma, morels are most abundant during a wet spring, although their season runs all the way to September.

Because they're unlike any other mushroom, morels are among the most highly prized of the family and come in many varieties, the most familiar being the practically, if uninventively, named "common." Other varieties include "white" (actually cream or tan in color) and "black." Whatever the variety, a morel's cap is generally 2 to 4 inches long and flows seamlessly into the stem, which is usually pale, brittle, and yellow.

Oregon is a major source of morels, though they are also foraged in northern California, the Midwest, and as far east as Virginia. They are most often found in North American apple orchards, under elm trees, and in low, damp areas.

When purchasing morels, seek out those with an absolutely dry cap and, when you get them home, refrigerate them in a brown paper bag. (Plastic will trap their moisture, which causes them to go bad almost immediately.) Keep in mind that morels must be cooked, because if eaten raw, they have been known to cause stomachaches. To ready them for cooking, trim the very bottom portion of the base.

Throughout the year, keep dried morels in mind as well. To me, they're one of the two most useful dried mushrooms (the other being porcini). There's no better way to impart an intense mushroom flavor to stock or soup. Reconstitute dried morels in warm water, then rinse them in several changes of water to get out all sand. Be sure also to cut the larger ones in half lengthwise to check for stones that may be trapped in the hollow cap.

THINKING AHEAD: The vegetables can be blanched as many as 4 hours in advance. (Be sure to reserve 1 cup of the cooking liquid.)

Atlantic Salmon with Morels, Ramps, Sweet Peas, and Chervil

MAKES 4 SERVINGS

VEGETABLES

1/2	cup fresh peas
12	ramps
5	medium leeks, white parts and about 1 inch of the green
5 to 6	small-to-medium fingerling or creamer potatoes
3	tablespoons unsalted butter
6	ounces fresh morel mushrooms, ends trimmed, large caps halved
	Coarse salt and freshly ground white pepper to taste

In a saucepan, bring about 2 cups of salted water to a boil over high heat. Add the peas and cook for about 4 minutes, or until just tender. Using a slotted spoon, transfer the peas to a bowl filled with ice water.

Cut about 1 inch off the green tops of the ramps. Put the ramps in the boiling water and cook for about 3 minutes, or until just tender. Using a slotted spoon, transfer the ramps to the same bowl of ice water.

Cut the leeks on the bias into 1/2-inch-thick slices. Rinse well and separate the slices into separate rings. Cook the leeks in the boiling water for about 3 minutes or until just tender. Using a slotted spoon, transfer them to the bowl of ice water with the other vegetables. Drain the vegetables and set them aside. Reserve 1 cup of the cooking liquid.

In a saucepan, cook the potatoes in boiling salted water for 12 to 15 minutes, or until tender. Remove from the heat and cover to keep warm in the cooking liquid.

In a medium sauté pan, melt the butter over medium heat. Add the mushrooms, season with salt and pepper, and cook, stirring occasionally, for 6 to 8 minutes, or until softened. Remove from the heat and set aside, covered, to keep warm.

This dish sums up the spirit of May cooking in an impressionist display of colors and textures—pale pink salmon riding above a lightly buttered broth and attended by wispy wild leeks, delicate green peas, and musky morels. The very essence of leeks and ramps—which are among the sweetest varieties of onion—is captured by cooking them in a carefully measured amount of water. The cooking liquid is then used as a base for the sauce, permeating it with gentle, aromatic flavor.

ASSEMBLY

$1/2$ cup heavy cream
$1/4$ cup unsalted butter, cut into pieces
  2 tablespoons fresh lemon juice
     Coarse salt and freshly ground white pepper to taste
  4 7-ounce Atlantic salmon fillets, each about $3/4$ inch thick
  2 tablespoons canola oil
  2 tablespoons finely minced chives
  8 beautiful-looking chervil sprigs

In a saucepan, bring the reserved 1 cup of cooking liquid to a boil over high heat. Add the cream and cook for about 5 minutes to reduce slightly. Lower the heat and add the butter, 1 piece at a time, whisking well after each addition and not adding the next piece until the preceding is incorporated to create a rich, creamy emulsion.

Drain the potatoes and slice them into $1/2$-inch-thick rounds. Add the potatoes, peas, ramps, leeks, mushrooms and their juice to the sauce and heat, stirring gently, until heated through. Stir in the lemon juice, and season with salt and pepper. Cover and keep warm.

Season the salmon with salt and pepper. In a 12-inch sauté pan, heat the oil over medium heat until it is very hot but not smoking. Cook the salmon, skin side down, for 3 to 4 minutes, or until golden brown on the bottom. Turn and cook about 2 minutes longer, until the other side is lightly browned and the salmon is medium-rare.

Using a slotted spoon, mound some of the vegetables in the centers of 4 warmed dinner plates. Top each mound with a salmon fillet and a few more vegetables. Add chives to the sauce and spoon a few tablespoons of sauce over and around each serving. Garnish with the chervil sprigs.

WHAT TO DRINK: Serve this dish with a lush white French Burgundy (such as a Puligny-Montrachet or Chassagne-Montrachet) or a California Chardonnay made in the French style.

VARIATIONS: If unavailable, simply omit the ramps. Also, just about any white-fleshed fish (e.g., halibut or grouper) can be substituted for the salmon.

FLAVOR BUILDING: You can augment the butter sauce with a touch of mint or dill to create a more herbaceous result.

Fiddleheads can be added to expand the spring theme. Cook them in boiling salted water for 3 to 4 minutes, drain them, transfer them to a bowl of ice water to "shock" them, and drain again. Reheat with the other vegetables before serving the dish.

THINKING AHEAD: The polenta can be made in advance and kept warm for up to 2 hours using the following method: Transfer the polenta to a container with a small diameter; a stainless-steel *bain-marie* or a 2-quart sauce pot works well. Smooth the surface with a rubber spatula to further reduce the surface area. Then melt 1 tablespoon of unsalted butter over the surface to keep it from drying out. (When using the polenta later, the butter can be stirred in and will provide additional flavor and richness.) Cover with a sheet of foil or parchment paper that makes contact with the surface of the purée. Cover the pot or *bain-marie* again with foil and place it in an oven set to the lowest possible setting (usually 180°F). If necessary, prop the door slightly ajar with a kitchen towel to keep the heat from building up. The polenta will keep like this for up to 2 hours. (This method also works for potato purées and vegetable purées.)

The vegetables can be cooked as many as 6 hours in advance and reheated before serving.

LEEKS AND PEAS

1   cup fresh peas
4   medium leeks, white parts only

In a saucepan, bring salted water to a boil over high heat. Add the peas and cook for about 4 minutes, or until just tender. Using a slotted spoon, transfer the peas to a bowl filled with ice water to stop the cooking and set the color. Drain and set aside.

Cut the leeks on the bias into ¼-inch–thick slices. Rinse well. Cook the leeks in the boiling water for about 5 minutes, or until just tender. Using a slotted spoon, transfer them to a bowl filled with ice water to stop the cooking. Drain and set aside. Reserve 1 cup of the cooking liquid.

Veal Chops
with Spring Leeks and Soft Polenta

MAKES 4 SERVINGS

This dish, like the one that precedes it, displays a quiet array of seasonal colors—peas, morels, and pearl onions. The vegetable ensemble is a versatile side dish that makes an equally compelling match with roast chicken, roast pork, pork loin, or even a roasted pork chop. The same can be said of the savory, stock-based polenta that rounds out this main course with some welcome heft.

Even if you usually like your meat on the rare side, let the veal cook a bit longer. Like spring lamb, it needs to be at least medium-rare to reach its optimum flavor and texture.

SOFT POLENTA

2$^1/_2$ cups White Chicken Stock (page 421)
2   cups whole milk
    Coarse salt and freshly ground white pepper to taste
1   cup instant polenta

In a medium saucepan, combine the stock and milk. Season with salt and pepper, and bring to a boil over high heat. Stir in the polenta. Reduce the heat and continue stirring with a wooden spoon for about 5 minutes, or until the polenta is smooth and pulls away from the sides of the pan. Cover to keep warm and set aside.

ASSEMBLY

4   rib veal chops, each approximately 14 ounces
    Coarse salt to taste
2   teaspoons cracked white peppercorns
2   tablespoons canola oil
$^1/_4$ cup (4 tablespoons) unsalted butter
    Freshly ground white pepper to taste
3   tablespoons water, red wine, or chicken stock

Preheat the oven to 400°F.
Season the veal chops on both sides with salt and cracked peppercorns, using approximately $^1/_4$ teaspoon of peppercorns per side. In a large, ovenproof sauté pan, heat the oil over high heat and sear the chops for about 3 minutes on each side, until nicely browned. Put the pan in the oven and roast for about 6 minutes, turning the chops once, until medium-rare. Transfer the chops to a serving platter and keep warm.

Meanwhile, bring the reserved cup of cooking liquid from the vegetables to a boil over high heat. Lower the heat to medium and whisk in 2 tablespoons of the butter, about a teaspoon at a time, to make a buttery emulsion. Add the peas and leeks, season with salt and ground white pepper, and cook for about 5 minutes, until heated through. Cover and set aside.

Return the sauté pan used to cook the chops to the burner and add the water, wine, or stock. Deglaze over high heat, scraping up the browned bits on the bottom of the pan, until the liquid is reduced by half. Add any juices that have collected on the platter from the chops. Swirl in the remaining 2 tablespoons of butter to enrich the sauce. Place a chop on each plate and spoon some polenta and vegetables next to it. Spoon the sauce over the chops and serve.

WHAT TO DRINK: Serve this dish with a light-style red Burgundy from Gevrey-Chambertin, or a California Pinot Noir, ideally one produced in the Russian River Valley.

VARIATIONS: For mushroom polenta, add 2 ounces of dried porcini or black trumpet mushrooms to the stock. For a garlic-and-herb-flavored polenta, infuse the stock with 2 crushed garlic cloves and 1 sprig each of rosemary and thyme, and bring to a boil. Remove from the heat, cover, and let stand for 10 minutes. Strain the liquid before proceeding with the recipe.

A pork chop, or the gentle flavor and soft texture of pork loin, are viable alternatives to the veal.

$^1/_2$	pound small red potatoes, unpeeled
4	ounces jumbo asparagus, peeled, ends trimmed
1	cup finely sliced spring onions or scallions
8	whole eggs
3	tablespoons heavy cream
2	tablespoons coarsely chopped chervil
	Coarse salt and freshly ground white pepper
1	tablespoon unsalted butter, cut into several small pieces
3	ounces *prosciutto di Parma,* thinly sliced and cut into strips
4	ounces fresh goat cheese, crumbled into small pieces

Asparagus, Prosciutto, and Spring Onion *Frittata*

MAKES 6 TO 8 SERVINGS

Preheat the oven to 375°F.

In a large pot of boiling salted water, cook the potatoes over high heat until tender when pierced with the tip of a knife, about 15 minutes. Drain and, when cool enough to handle, thickly slice. Set aside.

In a large pot of boiling, salted water, cook the asparagus over high heat until just tender, 3 to 4 minutes. Using tongs or a large skimmer, remove the asparagus from the water. (Do not remove the pot from the heat.) Plunge the asparagus into a bowl of ice water to cool and set the color. Drain, then cut the spears in half crosswise. Set aside.

Add the onions to the boiling water and cook for 4 minutes. Drain and set aside.

In a large mixing bowl, whisk together the eggs and heavy cream until thoroughly incorporated. Stir in the spring onions and chervil. Season with salt and pepper. Set aside.

In a 10-inch nonstick ovenproof sauté pan, arrange the asparagus spears in a spoke pattern. Place the pan over medium heat and distribute the butter between the spears. When they begin to sizzle in the pan, after about 2 minutes, whisk the egg mixture to recombine and pour it into the pan. Evenly distribute the prosciutto, potatoes, and goat cheese pieces around the pan, being sure not to neglect the outer edges. Cook for 2 minutes.

Transfer the pan to the hot oven and bake until fully set, about 12 minutes. It will be a little loose in the center. Pass the pan under the broiler for 1 minute, or until the *frittata* is lightly browned on top. Invert it onto a warm serving plate, slice into wedges, and serve immediately.

VARIATION: This recipe can also be enjoyed at room temperature.

A *frittata* is an Italian version of an omelet, and it is a useful technique to learn because it doesn't require the same finesse as the latter—there's no flipping or folding required to make a perfect one. Eggs and the other desired ingredients are heated briefly on the stove top, then finished in the oven and browned under the broiler. For this occasion, I've selected the classic Italian combination of asparagus and prosciutto, which often turn up together in salads. But the technique described below may be adapted to include countless ingredients and combinations. *Frittatas* may be served hot or warm, and also make wonderful leftovers.

Pancakes
with Honey-Almond Butter

MAKES APPROXIMATELY 12 PANCAKES

This batter could single-handedly eliminate the phrase "flat as a pancake" from the national vocabulary because it produces such thick, fluffy results. I'm presenting it here as a Mother's Day offering (see menu on page 49), but this is actually a recipe I picked up from my father. Don't be surprised or discouraged when the batter doesn't form perfect circles in the pan; its thickness prevents it from flowing out evenly from the center. But what these lack in aesthetics they more than make up for in flavor.

If you're making a large batch, or cook pancakes on a regular basis, invest in a rectangular non-stick griddle that will expand two burners into a restaurant-style cooking surface. These can be purchased at houseware or cooking-equipment stores; ask the merchant to help you select a heavy-duty griddle that distributes the heat evenly.

1 cup all-purpose flour
4 teaspoons baking powder
1 tablespoon sugar
3/4 teaspoon salt
1 cup whole milk
2 large eggs
5 tablespoons unsalted butter, melted
3 tablespoons canola oil, for cooking the pancakes
  Honey-Almond Butter (page 41)

In a bowl, sift together the flour, baking powder, sugar, and salt.

In another bowl, whisk together the milk and eggs. Add the melted butter and blend well. Fold in the dry ingredients, taking care not to overwork the batter.

In a skillet set on medium heat, heat a little canola oil. When hot, spoon about 2 tablespoons of batter into the pan to make one pancake. If the pan is large enough, cook 2 or 3 pancakes at a time. Cook for 3 to 4 minutes, until golden brown on the bottom. Turn and cook for a few more minutes, until golden brown on the other side. Repeat with the remaining batter and oil until all the pancakes are cooked. Serve the pancakes, with Honey-Almond Butter on the side, while still hot enough to melt the butter.

DRESS (YOUR PANCAKES) FOR SUCCESS: Most inexpensive supermarket syrups are made from corn syrup, caramel color, and artificial maple flavoring. If you're going to go to the extra effort of making your own pancakes, splurge on a high-quality syrup.

FLAVOR BUILDING: In the upcoming months, fold fresh blueberries into the batter just before cooking.

Honey-Almond Butter

MAKES 1 1/2 CUPS

Just as a high-quality syrup merits some extra consideration when making pancakes from scratch, butter can be a make-or-break condiment. This recipe could become a family heirloom that you make for every special-occasion breakfast or brunch. Unsalted (sweet) butter is sweetened further with honey and perfumed with orange zest, and toasted almond slices are added to provide flavor and texture. It's equally delicious on waffles and French toast.

THINKING AHEAD: The butter can be made a week in advance and kept tightly wrapped in the refrigerator, or one month in the freezer.

1/4	cup sliced almonds
1	cup unsalted butter, softened
2	tablespoons honey
2	tablespoons golden raisins
1	tablespoon finely chopped orange zest
1/4	teaspoon fine salt

Preheat the oven to 350°F.
Spread the almonds in a single layer in a shallow baking pan and toast for about 6 minutes, until lightly browned and fragrant. Shake the pan or stir the nuts several times during toasting. Transfer the nuts to a plate to cool completely.

In a bowl, combine the butter, honey, raisins, zest, salt, and toasted almonds. Mix with a fork until the ingredients are well distributed in the butter. Serve immediately, or cover and refrigerate for up to 2 days. Leftover butter can be frozen, well wrapped in plastic, for up to a month.

VARIATIONS: Feel free to adapt this recipe to suit your own taste, perhaps adding ground cinnamon or vanilla extract, grated orange zest, or toasted pistachio nuts. You can also replace the chopped orange zest with chopped lemon zest and/or the sliced almonds with the same quantity of toasted pistachio nuts.

THINKING AHEAD: The dough must be made at least 8 hours in advance.

SPECIAL EQUIPMENT: You will need a small, home electric fryer, which is a good investment for other uses, including French fries. You can substitute a heavy-bottomed, stainless-steel or cast-iron pot fitted with a clip-on thermometer.

2	tablespoons plus 1 teaspoon milk
3^1/$_2$	teaspoons active dry yeast
6	tablespoons warm water
1	tablespoon plus 1 teaspoon unsalted butter, melted
1	large egg
2	cups all-purpose flour
^{1}/$_4$	cup sugar
^{3}/$_4$	teaspoon salt
	Canola oil for deep frying
1 to 1^1/$_4$	cups raspberry jam

Pour the milk in a small bowl and sprinkle with the yeast. Whisk until the yeast dissolves.

In a bowl, combine the water and butter. Whisk in the egg and then the milk and yeast mixture.

Put the flour, sugar, and salt in the bowl of an electric mixer. Using the paddle attachment, begin mixing the dry ingredients. Slowly add the milk and egg mixture, and beat at low speed until the batter comes together in a cohesive mass. Cover with plastic wrap and refrigerate for at least 8 hours or overnight. The dough will rise in the bowl during chilling.

Turn the dough out onto a lightly floured surface and punch it down to release the trapped air. Using a lightly floured rolling pin, roll the dough out to a thickness of ^{1}/$_4$ inch. Using a 3-inch-round cookie cutter, cut out 8 to 10 rounds. Set them aside to rest for about 30 minutes.

In an electric deep fryer or a large, deep pot, heat the oil to 350° to 375°F. If using an electric deep fryer, use as much oil as is called for by the manufacturer. If using your own pot, pour in enough oil to reach a depth of 3^1/$_2$ to 4 inches.

When the oil is hot, fry the doughnuts for about 5 minutes, turning them to brown on both sides. Fry only a few doughnuts at a time; do not crowd the pan. Let the oil regain its temperature

Doughnuts are such a singular pleasure that they might seem best left to bakers who specialize in them. But making homemade doughnuts is, in reality, no more difficult than making a cake. And the memory of warm, homemade doughnuts is one that children and grandchildren will cherish forever.

Here, I've provided a recipe for yeast-raised doughnuts that are fried in canola oil. When cooked, they "puff up," allowing you to insert the filling of your choice. (See Variations.)

After the oil cools down, you can strain it and store it for another use. It can be used until it begins to darken, at which point it should be discarded.

between batches. Drain the doughnuts on paper towels and then cool them completely on wire racks.

Fill a pastry bag fitted with a large, plain tip with jam. Insert the tip in the side of a doughnut and squeeze about 2 tablespoons of jam into the hollow interior. Repeat with the remaining doughnuts. Serve.

VARIATIONS: Fill these doughnuts with Strawberry Preserves (page 114), Blueberry Jam (page 116), or Apricot Preserves (page 85).

PRESERVING:
Kumquat-Orange Marmalade

MAKES TWO 4-OUNCE JARS

Traditionally, orange marmalade is made with Seville oranges, which are grown primarily in England and the South of France and impart an essential balance of sweet and bitter flavors. Since it's nearly impossible to obtain these oranges in the United States, I make marmalade with kumquats—small, bitter oranges with an edible peel that happen to be in season during May.

Kumquats approximate the qualities of Seville oranges very well. A dear friend of our family, Dr. Tony Federico, makes a fantastic marmalade down in Florida with an orange variety called calamondin. He has a tree in his front yard that supplies him and his extended family and friends with an entire year's worth of marmalade. The calamondin oranges, with their combination of sweetness and bitterness, are so perfect for marmalade that I don't understand why a whole industry has not grown up around this fruit.

20	kumquats
5	oranges
$1/2$	cup sugar

Slice and pit the kumquats. Peel and segment the oranges.

Put the kumquats, oranges, and sugar in a saucepan and cook over high heat for 20 to 25 minutes, until thick. Let the mixture cool slightly.

Spoon the hot marmalade into hot sterilized canning jars (see note page 81), leaving about $1/4$ inch of headroom. Screw on the lids. Let cool completely and then store in a cool, dry place. The jars should not touch each other during cooling. Refrigerate after opening.

Lemon
Parfait

MAKES 6 PARFAITS

THINKING AHEAD: The parfait and the granité can be made as many as three days in advance and frozen.

1 cup heavy cream
2 eggs, separated
8 tablespoons sugar
Grated zest of 2 lemons

Pour the cream into a large stainless steel mixing bowl and whisk by hand or with a hand-held mixer until it forms soft peaks. Set aside. Combine the egg yolks and 3 tablespoons of the sugar in the bowl of an electric mixer and whip at high speed until they double in volume, approximately 3 minutes. Set aside. Place the egg whites into a second mixing bowl and whip at high speed until they reach the stiff peak stage, approximately 4 minutes, then add remaining sugar and whip for 1 minute more. Using a rubber spatula, fold the zest into the yolks, then carefully fold in the whites, followed by the cream. Fold quickly and gently, keeping the mixture light and airy; do not overmix. Fit a pastry bag with a plain tip and pipe the mixture into 6 individual ring molds measuring 2^1/$_2$" in diameter by 1" high. Smooth the tops with the back of a knife. Arrange molds on a parchment-lined cookie sheet. Cover the entire cookie sheet with plastic wrap and freeze the parfaits for a minimum of 4 hours, preferably overnight.

LEMONGRASS SAUCE
3 stalks lemongrass
Zest of 1 lemon
1 tablespoon fresh lemon juice
1^1/$_2$ cups milk
2^1/$_2$ tablespoons sugar

Using a heavy-bladed chef's knife, finely chop the lemongrass and set it aside. In a medium non-reactive saucepot, combine the zest, lemongrass, lemon juice, milk, and sugar. Cover and bring to a boil over high heat. Remove the cover and let the sauce steep for 30 minutes off the heat. Pass it through a fine-meshed strainer and allow it to cool at room temperature for 20 minutes, then cover and refrigerate until completely cool, approximately 1 hour.

Though frozen parfait and ice cream look somewhat similar, the technique for making a frozen parfait (also known as a frozen soufflé) varies from that used to make ice cream in two significant ways: The egg whites and yolks are whipped separately with sugar, then folded together, flavored, and frozen. Because, unlike an ice cream, the custard here isn't cooked, this produces a light, airy result.

In this recipe, the parfait is flavored with quite a bit of lemon zest, and its tartness is echoed with a Meyer Lemon Granité (page 320), as well as a mango and grapefruit garnish. A dramatic contrast is provided by the unusual and delicious sauce in which milk is infused with lemongrass and sugar.

(continued)

ASSEMBLY

  2   ripe mangoes
  1   red grapefruit
  1   recipe Lemongrass Sauce
  1   recipe Meyer Lemon Granité (page 320)
  6   sprigs mint, for garnish

Peel, halve, and pit the mangoes. Cut the flesh into $1/2$-inch dice. Transfer the flesh to a small bowl and set it aside. Using a sharp thin-bladed slicing knife, cut the ends off the grapefruit, then cut away the peel. Working over a small bowl, segment the grapefruit by cutting between the membranes. Cut the segments into $1/4$-inch dice and set them aside.

Remove the parfaits from the freezer. To unmold, first rub the sides of the molds between your hands to slightly warm them, then push the edges out with your fingers. Place the parfaits in the centers of 6 chilled soup plates. Scatter the diced mangoes and grapefruit around. Next, spoon the lemongrass sauce over the fruit. Top each parfait with a scoop of granité. Garnish with the mint and serve.

VARIATION: Instead of making a granité, use a store-bought mango or raspberry sorbet.

Tangerine and Blood Orange Terrine

MAKES 8 TO 10 SERVINGS

Made with a variety of citrus fruits, this stunning dessert—a glorified Jell-O mold when you get right down to it—displays a beautiful mosaic of color set in a light jelly made from tangerine juice and late-harvest Riesling.

THINKING AHEAD: This recipe must be made at least 8 hours in advance and will keep well overnight.

10	tangerines
7	blood oranges
1	375 ml bottle late-harvest Riesling wine
3	tablespoons sugar
2	tablespoons water
2	tablespoons powdered gelatin
8 to 10	sprigs fresh mint

Peel and segment the tangerines, holding them over a bowl to catch the juices. Measure and set aside 1 tablespoon of tangerine juice. Peel and segment the oranges. Lay the segments on clean, dry kitchen towels to drain.

In a large saucepan, combine the wine, sugar, water, and reserved tangerine juice. Stir to mix and then transfer $2^1/2$ cups of the liquid to a small bowl. Sprinkle the gelatin over the liquid in the bowl. Set aside for at least 5 minutes to give the gelatin time to soften and dissolve.

Heat the liquid in the saucepan over medium-high heat until warm to the touch, but not boiling or even simmering. It should reach about 115°F. Remove from the stove. Add the gelatin mixture and whisk until the gelatin dissolves completely.

In a ceramic terrine mold measuring approximately 10 by $3^3/4$ inches, arrange enough tangerine and orange segments to cover the bottom in a single layer. Spoon enough of the gelatin mixture over them to barely cover. Continue layering tangerine and orange segments and the remaining gelatin mixture until the terrine is full or all the fruit is used. Cover with plastic wrap and refrigerate for at least 8 hours or overnight.

To serve, dip the bottom portion of the terrine in hot tap water for 30 to 40 seconds. Invert the terrine on a baking sheet or flat serving platter. Cut into slices with a sharp knife and serve, garnished with mint sprigs.

VARIATIONS: Blood oranges, Minneolas, or clementines can be substituted for the tangerines.

FLAVOR BUILDING: Add a chiffonade of mint to the jelly.

Mother's Day Brunch

Here are three Mother's Day menus that can be served anytime from late morning until well into the afternoon. They all begin with the same cocktail and canapé. The first menu is intended to be presented as a buffet; the other two as seated meals.

COCKTAIL
POUSSE RAPIER **(page 262)**

CANAPÉ
SALMON RILLETTE **(page 271)**

MENU 1—BUFFET MENU
WARM POTATO AND SMOKED EEL SALAD **(page 274)**

CITRUS SALAD WITH LEMONGRASS, TOASTED ALMONDS, AND MINT **(page 15)**

PANCAKES WITH HONEY-ALMOND BUTTER **(page 40)**

ASPARAGUS, PROSCIUTTO, AND SPRING ONION *FRITTATA* **(page 39)**

JELLY-FILLED DOUGHNUTS **(page 43)**

MENU 2
CHILLED MAINE LOBSTER AND AVOCADO COCKTAIL **(page 16)**

ATLANTIC SALMON WITH MORELS, RAMPS, SWEET PEAS,
AND CHERVIL **(page 33)**

TANGERINE AND BLOOD ORANGE TERRINE **(page 48)**

MENU 3
CITRUS SALAD WITH LEMONGRASS, TOASTED ALMONDS,
AND MINT **(page 15)**

LEMON RISOTTO WITH SPOT PRAWNS **(page 339)**

MILK CHOCOLATE *PETITS POTS* WITH LINZER COOKIES **(page 413)**

Lobster Summer Rolls with Mint, Cucumber, and Lemongrass Dressing

Salad of Local Wax Beans, Shell Beans, and Mint

Soupe de Poisson

Seared Mackerel with Orzo Salad and Toasted Cumin Seed Dressing

Seared Yellowfin Tuna Burger with Lemon Aioli

Shellfish Risotto

Grilling

Grilled Lobster with Grilled Corn, Potatoes, and Roast Garlic–Tarragon Butter

Grilled Marinated Leg of Lamb with Tabbouleh and Minted Aioli

Plums

Black Plum Tart with Vanilla Bean Ice Cream

Cherry Cheesecake

Father's Day Potluck Dinner

JUNE

SUMMER SETTLES IN

In New York City, June ushers in outdoor dining, short summer Fridays, weekends at the beach, and Shakespeare in Central Park. It's the time for T-shirts, shorts, sneakers, and sunglasses. It's the time for movies on weeknights and long, aimless strolls through the evening rays of a late-setting sun. It's when young and old alike seem to hear the cry "School's out!" and adopt a relaxed state of mind.

This change rides, or surfs, in on a wave of water—which becomes an unusually prevalent part of daily life come June. In fact, water is so welcome in June that the sight of a sky gray with afternoon storm clouds doesn't bring disappointment, but rather the anticipation of those moments after the tempest when the air will be damp and the pavement cool beneath our shoes.

The ultimate expression of how water and recreation are united in June is the quintessential image of summer in the city—neighborhood kids romping through the geyser of a fire hydrant.

At the Gotham Bar and Grill, where we try to maintain a relatively informal mood year round, things lighten up even more than usual this month, which is a transitional time for us. Memorial Day in late May marks the unofficial beginning of summer, but it can still feel like spring when June begins. In fact, at the restaurant, our menu changes two or three times during this month as leeks, morels, and other ephemera gradually fade away.

Not only that, but for all the insouciance of May, the food it inspires remains somewhat formal and classic, at least it does for me. It isn't until June that irreverence descends—dishes lighten up with less butter and cream, and the crowd at the Gotham transforms as an influx of out-of-town guests, clearly enjoying the respite of a vacation, fill the dining room. Fewer suits occupy the lunchtime seats, and the dinner crowd, more raucous than even a few weeks back, lingers later into the evening. Yes, they would like an after-dinner drink.

When it comes to cooking in June, the growing heat suggests more exotic locales than the ones that surround me. If I close my eyes, it's easy to imagine that I'm strolling through a market in Thailand instead of the Green Market at Union Square, lunching at a café beside the Mediterranean rather than one on Fifth Avenue, or trekking through the desert to Morocco rather than walking to work at the Gotham. These welcome, heat-induced illusions are reflected in such culinary mirages as Seared Mackerel with Orzo Salad and Toasted Cumin Seed Dressing (page 61) and a *Soupe de Poisson* (page 58) that is based on the classic Mediterranean fisherman's soup.

The backyard grill's three-month tenure as a social center kicks in during this month, so there are a few grilled dishes in this chapter, including Grilled Lobster with Grilled Corn, Potatoes, and Roast Garlic–Tarragon Butter (page 74) and Grilled Marinated Leg of Lamb with Tabbouleh and Minted Aioli (page 77). To help you with these and other recipes, there's a primer on grilling that you should find useful all summer long or—if you live in the South or on the West Coast—all year.

After the vegetables of May, fruits take their turn this month. Plums, which may be the ultimate summer snack, are featured in a Black Plum Tart with Vanilla Bean Ice Cream (page 83). Apricots, too, reach their annual prime, the perfect time to capture them with the art of preserving as on page 85.

June is also a time for picnicking in earnest. My wife and I enjoy spending considerable extra time with our two daughters during this month, and any parents reading this will relate to the fact that, if you have kids, you have to do a lot of planning around food. There are a host of family favorites that we rely on when we head to a state park or the beach. I've shared a few here, including Lobster Summer Rolls with Mint, Cucumber, and Lemongrass Dressing (page 54) and a Salad of Local Wax Beans, Shell Beans, and Mint (page 57).

Here, too, are some of my favorite versions of Spiked Lemonade (page 87) to help you put an adult spin on this childhood favorite. Like all of this chapter's offerings, my hope is that it successfully combines a youthful spirit with sophisticated pleasure.

Lobster Summer Rolls with Mint, Cucumber, and Lemongrass Dressing

MAKES 6 SERVINGS; 12 ROLLS

The classic Vietnamese summer roll features shrimp, basil, lettuce, julienned vegetables, scallions, fresh coriander, and bean-thread noodles, wrapped in rice paper and intended for dipping in a potent sauce. I developed something of a summer-roll addiction several years ago while vacationing on Saint Bart's. A local Vietnamese-French restaurant proved so dependable that I dined there almost every day and always started with a round of summer rolls, which they made to order.

As much as I loved them, however, it occurred to me that there's something less than ideal about summer rolls for American diners: because the contents are unadorned, their success depends on constant dipping. This is especially inappro-priate if the rolls are used for enter-

THINKING AHEAD: The rolls themselves can be made as many as 4 hours in advance, wrapped tightly in plastic wrap, and stored under a damp towel in the refrigerator. If you prefer to make the rolls just before serving, the lobster can be prepared the morning of the day you will be serving them; the dressing as much as 1 day in advance.

NOTE: A Japanese-style mandoline is a good tool to use to julienne the vegetables.

LOBSTER

4	quarts water
$1/4$	cup red or white wine vinegar
	Coarse sea salt to taste
2	$1^{1}/_{4}$-pound live lobsters

Using a large stockpot, bring the water, vinegar, and salt to a boil over high heat. Add the lobsters and cover the pot. Return to the boil and cook for 8 to 10 minutes, or until the shells are bright red. Lift the lobsters from the pot with tongs and set them aside to drain and cool. When cool enough to handle, crack the shells and remove the meat. Discard the shells or reserve them for another use, such as shellfish or fish stock. Cut the meat into $1/2$-inch-thick pieces. Transfer the meat to a bowl, cover, and refrigerate.

ASSEMBLY

1	cup Lemongrass Dressing (page 56)
2	tablespoons chopped fresh cilantro
	Coarse salt and freshly ground white pepper to taste
12	sheets rice paper (6-inch diameter)
1	small carrot, peeled and julienned
1	medium cucumber, peeled and julienned
20	fresh mint leaves, cut into chiffonade
1	avocado, halved lengthwise, pitted, peeled, and thinly sliced
$1/2$	head radicchio, cut into julienne
6	scallions, white parts only, thinly sliced
1	small head Bibb lettuce, cut into chiffonade

Toss the lobster with about 2 tablespoons of the dressing, or more to taste, and the cilantro. Season with salt and pepper.

Have all the ingredients for the rolls prepared and assembled. Fill a bowl with warm water.

Dip a single sheet of rice paper in the warm water and let it soak for 30 seconds, or until pliable. Do not leave the rice paper in the water for too long or it will absorb too much water and tear. Lift the sheet from the water and lay it on a dry work surface.

Across the bottom third of the paper, spoon a little of the lobster, leaving a $1/4$-inch border. Layer a little carrot, cucumber, mint, avocado, and radicchio on top of the meat. Season with salt and pepper, and drizzle with dressing. Scatter with scallions and lettuce.

Working slowly and carefully, roll the rice paper tightly into a cylinder. The roll should be $3/4$ to 1 inch in diameter. Set it aside on a tray, covered with a damp, well-wrung kitchen towel. Repeat with the remaining ingredients to make 12 rolls. Keep the rolls covered with the towel until ready to serve.

VARIATION: For a less time-consuming option, you can substitute shrimp for the lobster; allow two large shrimp per roll, poach them for five minutes, and split them in half lengthwise.

taining, when it's impolite at best, and unsanitary at worst, to dip repeatedly.

When *New York* magazine asked me to contribute a recipe to their annual "Summer Entertaining" issue a few years ago, I saw it as a chance to Americanize the summer roll. I developed an aromatic and boldly seasoned, emulsified dressing of lemongrass oil, ginger, garlic, and lemon juice. This is used to dress the lobster, a more luxurious choice than the traditional shrimp, before it is wrapped in the roll, eliminating the need for dipping altogether.

The rolls produced by this recipe are almost transparent—the dressing dampens the rice paper, affording a sneak peek at the contents inside. The flavors and textures unfold in the mouth—creamy dressing and avocado, matched by herbaceous notes of cilantro and mint and the heat of cayenne pepper.

A brief word about rolling: The proportion of vegetables to the rice paper is all-important, much like the proportion of fish to rice in sushi. Summer rolls must be rolled tightly—to about the diameter of a quarter—for the flavors to mingle appropriately. The rice paper itself should be white (not yellow) and unbroken; discoloring and cracking signify aged paper, which is to be avoided.

Lemongrass Dressing

MAKES ABOUT 1 CUP

1	cup plus 2 tablespoons canola oil
1	stalk lemongrass, finely chopped
1	large egg yolk, at room temperature
2	teaspoons Dijon mustard
1	teaspoon fresh lemon juice
1/4	teaspoon cayenne pepper, or to taste
	Coarse salt and freshly ground white pepper to taste
1/2	clove garlic, peeled, sprinkled with salt, and mashed to a paste

In a small, nonreactive saucepan, heat the oil and lemongrass over medium heat and simmer for about 5 minutes. Remove from the heat and let cool to room temperature. Strain through a fine-mesh sieve into a bowl and discard the lemongrass.

In a medium bowl, whisk the egg yolk, mustard, lemon juice, and cayenne until smooth. Season with salt and pepper. Whisk in the oil, drop by drop, until the dressing begins to thicken. Add the remaining oil a little faster. When all the oil is absorbed, stir in the garlic. Taste and adjust the seasonings. The dressing should have a little heat and a bright, citrusy edge.

VARIATION: Substitute the grated zest of 1 lemon for the lemongrass and double the amount of lemon juice.

Salad of Local Wax Beans, Shell Beans, and Mint

MAKES 6 SERVINGS

A composition of pale yellows and greens, pastoral and summery as a cornfield, this dish belongs at any June picnic or open-air meal. Don't skip the step of shocking the beans; it's essential to preserving their individual colors. The lemon vinaigrette dresses the salad in agreeable warm-weather attire—keeping things light, crisp, and crunchy—and the mint's perfume underscores this effect.

THINKING AHEAD: All of the vegetables can be shocked, drained, covered, and refrigerated as many as 8 hours in advance.

SALAD
$1/2$	cup fresh cranberry beans
$1/2$	pound wax beans, trimmed
$1/2$	cup fresh peas
$1/2$	cup shelled fresh fava or lima beans
$1/2$	pound haricots verts, trimmed
$1/4$	cup minced shallots
	Lemon Vinaigrette (recipe follows)
	Coarse salt and freshly ground white pepper to taste
1	tablespoon fresh mint leaves, cut into chiffonade

In a saucepan, cook the cranberry beans in boiling salted water over high heat for about 20 minutes, until just tender. Using a slotted spoon, transfer the beans to a large bowl filled with ice water to stop the cooking and set their color. Return the water to the boil and cook the wax beans and peas for about 5 minutes, until just cooked; transfer them to the ice-water bath. Repeat with the fava beans, cooking them for about 4 minutes; transfer to the ice-water bath. Return the water to the boil and cook the haricots verts for about 4 minutes, until just tender; transfer to the ice-water bath. Drain the vegetables and pat them dry with paper towels. Rub the thin brown skin from the fava beans.

In a bowl, combine the beans and shallots. Add the vinaigrette and toss to mix. Season with salt and pepper. Just before serving, toss in the mint chiffonade.

LEMON VINAIGRETTE
$1/2$	cup extra-virgin olive oil
3	tablespoons fresh lemon juice
1	teaspoon Dijon mustard
	Coarse salt and freshly ground white pepper to taste

In a small bowl, stir together the oil, lemon juice, and mustard, and season with salt and pepper.

Soupe de *Poisson*

MAKES 8 SERVINGS

In French gastronomy, three fish soups reign above all *others—bouillabaisse,* the world-renowned boiled fish stew served atop a crouton spread with rouille; *bourride,* a Provençal fish soup that is thickened with aioli (my personal favorite); and *soupe de poisson,* which is the French equivalent of Manhattan clam chowder, because it's a universally adored and recognized soup. Recipes for each of them vary from region to region— from Provence to Brittany, for example—owing to the differences in available fish and local cooking styles. So you are sure to see different versions depending on where you are in France.

This is my New York regional version of *soupe de poisson,* featuring whatever catch is on hand. It incorporates some of the primary flavors of Provençal cooking— saffron, fennel, garlic, and orange zest—and a crouton topped with rouille, which, incidentally, is named for its rusty color. In many ways, the final dish suggests a bouillabaisse that has been passed through a food mill.

Soupe de poisson is traditionally

THINKING AHEAD: The entire soup can be prepared a day in advance and reheated over medium heat, stirring occasionally. The rouille can be made a day in advance and kept covered in the refrigerator. You can cut the vegetables and clean and prepare the fish several hours before making the soup.

SPECIAL EQUIPMENT: A food mill and a large conical strainer.

5	pounds fish, such as wolffish, blackfish, rockfish, or scrod, or a mixture, skinned and cleaned by the fishmonger
1	eel, about $1^1/4$ pounds
	Coarse salt and freshly ground white pepper to taste
1	cup extra-virgin olive oil
$1^1/2$	cups dry white wine
2	pounds lobster bodies (see note below)
2	whole heads garlic
1	3-inch piece leek, white part only
1	small head fennel, trimmed
1	small onion
3	tablespoons tomato paste
2	28-ounce cans whole plum tomatoes, drained, juice reserved, and tomatoes crushed
2	quarts White Chicken Stock (page 421)
2	cups bottled clam juice
3	sprigs fresh flat-leaf parsley
2	bay leaves
1	small bunch fresh thyme
	Zest of $1/2$ orange
2	pinches saffron threads
1	teaspoon crushed red pepper flakes
$1/2$	teaspoon white peppercorns
16	$1/2$-inch-thick slices bread, cut from a baguette and toasted to make croutons
$1^1/2$	cups Rouille (page 60)

Preheat the oven to 425°F.
Cut the fish and eel into $3^1/2$-inch-long pieces and season them with salt and pepper. In a large skillet, heat $1/4$ cup of the olive oil over high heat and sauté the fish and eel for 3 to 4 minutes, until golden brown. Cook the fish in batches or in 2 pans, if necessary. Transfer it to a plate and set aside.
Add $1/2$ cup of the wine to the pan and deglaze over medium

heat, scraping the bottom of the pan with a wooden spoon. Set aside.

Cut the lobsters into quarters and put them in a roasting pan oiled with about $1/4$ cup of the remaining oil. Roast in the preheated oven for about 30 minutes, or until the shells turn bright red. Set aside.

Separate the garlic into cloves and crush the cloves. Discard the peels. Heat about $1/4$ cup of the remaining oil in a skillet and sauté the garlic for about 12 minutes. Set aside.

Thinly slice the leek, fennel, and onion. Heat the remaining $1/4$ cup of oil in a large stockpot over medium heat. Cook the vegetables for about 12 minutes, or until soft. Add the garlic, raise the heat to high, and cook the vegetables about 8 minutes longer, stirring them until caramelized. Reduce the heat to medium, add the tomato paste and cook, stirring, for about 2 minutes.

Add the crushed tomatoes and the reserved juice to the pot and simmer for 6 to 8 minutes, stirring occasionally. Add the fish, deglazed liquid, and lobsters. Add the stock and clam juice, parsley, bay leaves, thyme, orange zest, saffron, red pepper flakes, and peppercorns. Raise the heat and bring the soup to a boil. Skim any foam that rises to the surface, reduce the heat, and simmer for about 1 hour.

Pass the soup through a food mill or purée it in a food processor fitted with the metal blade just until all solids are coarsely chopped. You may have to do this in batches. Strain through a mesh sieve, season with salt and pepper if necessary, and serve in large bowls. Pass the croutons and rouille on the side.

VARIATION: To make a rich and complex sauce from leftover broth, strain a cup of soup through a fine-mesh strainer. Cook slowly over medium heat until reduced by half or until the flavor is deeply concentrated. Off the heat, whisk in 3 tablespoons of butter. Finish the sauce with a tablespoon of finely minced chives and, if desired, a splash of Pernod. Spoon it over sautéed halibut, bass, or cod.

WHAT TO DRINK: Accompany this soup with any of the great rosés of Provence or the Languedoc, or the Rhône Valley's highly esteemed Tavel rosé.

made with inexpensive fish such as porgy, rockfish, wolffish, or blackfish. Here, I've added eel for the extra body its backbone provides and for its unique flavor.

Because this recipe calls for proficiency with a food mill and, more importantly, the ability to obtain a freshly killed eel, passionate and experienced home cooks will probably fare better with this recipe than novices, who should feel free to replace the eel with sea bass, black sea bass, or red snapper.

The use of whole fish demands a comparable amount of liquid, so this recipe yields enough soup to accommodate a patio full of guests. If you're feeding a smaller group, freeze the remaining portion in small batches.

NOTE: Lobster bodies, which are the heads and upper portions of the lobsters, can be obtained in two ways: (a) Reserve them, frozen in Ziploc bags, after making another recipe that uses the other parts of the lobster, such as the Chilled Maine Lobster and Avocado Cocktail (page 16) or the Lobster Summer Rolls with Mint, Cucumber, and Lemongrass Dressing (page 54); or purchase them from a fish store that does a brisk lobster business. Often these stores will have lobster bodies for sale.

Rouille

It wasn't until a few years ago that I was confident of the difference between rouille and aioli. While I knew that the use of red pepper was what distinguished rouille, I wasn't sure how the pepper was cooked in the classic recipe. Some research revealed that there are, indeed, many different approaches to rouille. Some people make it with a great deal of cayenne, while others balance the cayenne with roasted red pepper— which appeals to me and is the method used here. It should also be noted that this recipe does not follow the traditional step of using bread as a binding agent, because I don't feel the benefits warrant the inconvenience and mess it entails.

1	red bell pepper
	Coarse salt and freshly ground white pepper to taste
1	large egg yolk, at room temperature
2	tablespoons plus 1 teaspoon fresh lemon juice
¹/₄	teaspoon cayenne pepper
1	cup canola or grape-seed oil
2	tablespoons extra-virgin olive oil
2	tablespoons warm water

Char the pepper over a gas burner turned to medium heat or under a broiler, turning as it blackens on all sides and until it is soft on the inside and takes on a nice smoky flavor. This will take about 15 minutes. Use large tongs or two long-handled forks to handle the pepper. Transfer the pepper to a bowl and cover it tightly with plastic wrap to allow the pepper to steam as it cools. Peel the skin, which should pull right off. Scrape out the seeds and coarsely chop the pepper. In a food processor fitted with a metal blade, purée the pepper until smooth. Season it with salt and pepper, and set aside.

In a medium bowl, whisk the egg yolk, lemon juice, ¹/₂ teaspoon coarse salt, and the cayenne until smooth.

Mix the canola oil with the olive oil. Whisk the oil, drop by drop, into the egg-yolk mixture until the mayonnaise begins to thicken. Add the remaining oil a little faster. When all the oil is absorbed, thin it with a little water if it gets too thick. Stir in the reserved red-pepper purée. Taste the mayonnaise and adjust the salt, cayenne, and lemon juice, if necessary.

Seared Mackerel with Orzo Salad and Toasted Cumin Seed Dressing

MAKES 4 SERVINGS

WARM CHICKPEA SALAD WITH LEMON THYME, GARLIC, AND EXTRA-VIRGIN OLIVE OIL

1	cup dried chickpeas
1	cup White Chicken Stock (page 421)
1	whole head garlic, halved
2	sprigs lemon thyme or English thyme
	Coarse salt and freshly ground white pepper to taste
2	tablespoons extra-virgin olive oil
1	tablespoon fresh lemon juice, or to taste

In a large pot or bowl, soak the chickpeas in cold water to cover by about an inch for 4 hours or overnight. Drain, rinse well, and transfer to a medium saucepan.

Add the chicken stock, garlic, thyme, and enough water to cover by 2 inches. Bring to a boil over high heat. Reduce the heat to low and simmer, uncovered, for about 20 minutes. Taste the liquid and season it with salt and pepper. Cook for 20 to 30 minutes longer, until the chickpeas are very tender but still hold their shape. Remove the pan from the heat. Remove the garlic and thyme. Discard the thyme and all but 2 or 3 cloves of garlic. Mash the reserved garlic cloves and stir them into the chickpeas. Add the olive oil and just enough lemon juice to heighten the flavor. Stir until mixed. Adjust the seasonings, cover, and keep warm.

TOASTED CUMIN SEED DRESSING

2	teaspoons whole cumin seed
1	large egg, at room temperature
4	teaspoons fresh lemon juice
1	tablespoon Dijon mustard
$^3/_4$ to 1	cup canola oil
	Coarse salt and freshly ground white pepper to taste

My fondness for mackerel originated in France, where I learned to cook it *à la nage* in a highly aromatic broth with plenty of cut vegetables. But it was years later that I realized how much I prefer this method. Its high oil content enables mackerel to stand up to high heat very well, allowing you to turn the skin rich and crispy without overcooking it. Here, mackerel is contrasted with the orzo, which is bound in a thick, emulsified cumin seed vinaigrette that's enlivened with fresh lemon juice and also includes diced cucumbers and niçoise olives.

Mackerel is a cousin to the barracuda and feeds almost as voraciously as its more ferocious relative, sometimes devouring entire schools of shrimp, producing a sweet flavor in the fish. Mackerel is also highly perishable, so be sure to buy yours from an especially reputable fishmonger.

In a small sauté pan, toast the cumin seeds over high heat for about 2 minutes, stirring constantly, until lightly browned and fragrant. Transfer them to a spice grinder or mortar and grind to a fine powder. Set aside.

In a medium bowl, whisk the ground cumin seed, egg, lemon juice, and mustard until smooth. Whisk in the oil, drop by drop, until the dressing begins to thicken. Add the remaining oil a little faster. When all the oil is absorbed, taste and season with salt and pepper.

ORZO SALAD

1	quart water
	Coarse salt to taste
1	cup (8 ounces) orzo
1	cup peeled, diced cucumber
1/3	cup pitted, sliced kalamata or niçoise olives
1/3	cup thinly sliced scallions
	Freshly ground white pepper to taste
	Fresh lemon juice to taste

In a medium saucepan, bring the water and a little salt to a boil over high heat. Add the orzo, stir, and boil for 8 to 10 minutes, or until tender. Drain, transfer to a bowl, and set aside to cool.

When cool, stir in the cucumber, olives, and scallions. Add enough cumin seed dressing to moisten and flavor the orzo, and season it with salt and pepper. Taste, and add enough lemon juice to raise the acidity.

SEARED MACKEREL

2	tablespoons canola oil
4	4-ounce mackerel fillets, skin on
	Coarse salt and freshly ground white pepper to taste

In a large sauté pan, heat the oil over high heat. When hot but not smoking, add the fillets, skin side down. Season with salt and pepper. Reduce the heat to medium and cook for 2 minutes. Turn over the fillets and cook for 2 minutes longer, until medium. Remove them from the pan and set aside to keep warm.

SHALLOT VINAIGRETTE AND ASSEMBLY

2	tablespoons fresh lemon juice
1	tablespoon champagne vinegar
1/2	teaspoon Dijon mustard
	Coarse salt to taste
2/3	cup extra-virgin olive oil
	Freshly ground white pepper to taste
4	cups loosely packed salad greens such as *frisée* (curly endive), watercress, and radicchio
2	tablespoons finely minced shallot
2	tablespoons finely minced chives

In a bowl, whisk together the lemon juice, vinegar, and mustard. Season with salt. Whisk in the oil, drop by drop, until the dressing begins to thicken. Add the remaining oil a little faster. When all the oil is absorbed, taste the vinaigrette and season it with salt and pepper. Remove $1/4$ cup of the vinaigrette and set aside the remaining so that you have 2 containers of vinaigrette.

Place a mackerel fillet on each of 4 dinner plates. Spoon orzo salad and chickpea salad around the fillet.

Dress the greens with the reserved $1/4$ cup of vinaigrette and season with salt and pepper. Arrange the greens on the plates.

Stir the shallot and chives into the remaining vinaigrette. Spoon it over the mackerel, letting a little drizzle onto the plates. Serve immediately.

VARIATIONS: The orzo salad is wonderful as a stand-alone pasta salad, and it also has a great affinity with squab.

Seared Yellowfin Tuna Burger with Lemon Aioli

MAKES 4 SERVINGS

In June, when even the most dedicated carnivores might be pushing to trim those last few pounds for summer, keep the tuna burger in mind. Tuna is a wonderful alternative to beef because—unlike turkey—it can be eaten rare, which in this case approximates the qualities of a traditional beef burger. The one concession that must be made is that you cannot grill this tuna burger because no binding element (an egg, for example) is used and it would break up and fall through the grate when heated.

To help the burger hold together, the tuna in this recipe is chopped very fine, but it must not be ground. To achieve the desired effect, first slice the tuna thin, then chop it with a sharp knife. This texture is essential to attaining the proper adhesion effect.

I take rare tuna in an Asian direction, adding cilantro, ginger juice, sesame oil, shallots, and mushroom

THINKING AHEAD: The tuna can be chopped and the other ingredients prepared as many as 6 hours in advance, provided that you keep each one separately wrapped in the refrigerator.

$1^1/_2$	pounds sushi-quality yellowfin or bluefin tuna, chilled
1	heaping tablespoon finely chopped shallots
1	tablespoon chopped fresh cilantro
2	teaspoons extra-virgin olive oil
2	teaspoons mushroom-flavored or regular soy sauce
1	heaping teaspoon finely chopped jalapeño pepper
1	teaspoon Ginger Juice (page 65)
$^1/_2$	teaspoon sesame oil
	Coarse salt and freshly ground white pepper to taste
1	tablespoon canola oil

On an impeccably clean cutting board and using a sharp chef's knife, slice the tuna as thin as possible. Dice and then finely chop the tuna slices. Transfer the tuna to a stainless-steel bowl set in a larger bowl filled with ice to keep the ingredients cold during mixing.

Add the shallot, cilantro, olive oil, soy sauce, jalapeño, ginger juice, and sesame oil, and mix gently. Season with salt and pepper, keeping in mind that soy sauce is salty.

With moistened hands, form the tuna into 4 patties and transfer them to a wax paper–lined tray. Refrigerate for at least 15 minutes.

In a nonstick sauté pan, heat the canola oil over high heat until very hot but not smoking. Cook the burgers for about 2 minutes, until nicely seared and browned. Using a spatula, carefully flip the burgers and cook about 2 minutes longer, until medium-rare.

ASSEMBLY

4	slices country-style bread
$^1/_2$	cup Lemon Aioli (page 65)
1	head Bibb lettuce, washed and separated into leaves
1	ripe beefsteak tomato, thinly sliced

Lightly toast the bread and spread it with aioli. Lay lettuce leaves and tomato slices on the toast and then top with a tuna burger. Serve, passing the remaining aioli on the side.

VARIATION: Go a more traditional burger route and serve the tuna burger on a soft roll.

GINGER JUICE

8   ounces fresh ginger (the fresher the ginger, the more juice)

Using the medium-fine holes of a cheese grater, grate the ginger onto a board or plate. Wrap a few tablespoons of the grated ginger in the corner of a piece of cheesecloth or a clean kitchen towel and squeeze over a bowl to extract as much juice as possible (you should have about a quarter cup). Discard the squeezed ginger and continue with the remaining ginger until it is all squeezed of juice. Use the juice immediately or within a day or two. Store it in a tightly lidded jar in the refrigerator.

Lemon Aioli

MAKES ABOUT 1 CUP

1   large egg yolk, at room temperature
1   tablespoon plus 2 teaspoons fresh lemon juice
1   teaspoon minced lemon zest
1   teaspoon Dijon mustard
1   teaspoon minced garlic
$^{1}/_{4}$ teaspoon freshly ground black pepper
1   cup canola oil
2   tablespoons extra-virgin olive oil
   Coarse salt to taste

In a medium bowl, whisk together the egg yolk, lemon juice, lemon zest, mustard, garlic, and pepper to combine.

Combine the canola oil with the olive oil. Whisk the oil, drop by drop, into the egg-yolk mixture until the aioli begins to thicken. Add the remaining oil a little faster. When all the oil is absorbed, taste the aioli and season it with salt. Adjust the seasoning with pepper and lemon juice.

soy—powerful flavors all, which means that keeping them in balance with one another is especially important.

WORKING WITH RAW TUNA: To keep the tuna from sticking to you when forming the patties, run your hands under cold water just prior to working with the fish.

THINKING AHEAD: A recipe like this requires you to be organized and plan ahead. It's best to do most of the prep work—like cleaning the clams and mussels, readying the onions and garlic, and making the stocks—in the morning. Also, to really plan ahead, save the lobster head and shells that will be left over from the recipes on pages 16 and 54 for use here. To prepare the risotto itself in advance, follow the steps on page 339.

The broth can be made up to a day ahead and refrigerated until ready to use.

In taste, this risotto—populated with lobster and a variety of clams, mussels, squid, and shrimp—resembles something you might be served in a seaside Italian town like Monterosso. But in appearance, the ratio of fish to rice makes it look more like a Spanish paella.

The stock, a defining component of any risotto, is made from the shells of the lobster and shrimp, with garlic, onion, chicken stock, and tomato added to deepen the flavors.

LOBSTER AND SHRIMP

1	quart water
	Coarse salt to taste
2	$1^{1}/_{4}$- to $1^{1}/_{2}$-pound live lobsters
1	pound unshelled jumbo shrimp, with heads if possible

Using a large stockpot, bring salted water to a boil over high heat. Add the lobsters and cover the pot. Return to the boil and boil for about 4 minutes. Add the shrimp, cover, and steam for 2 minutes longer.

Using tongs, lift the lobsters from the pot. Drain the shrimp. Both the lobster and the shrimp will be parcooked at this stage. Set them aside to cool. When cool enough to handle, crack the lobster shells and remove the meat. Cut the meat into $1/_2$-inch-thick pieces, and transfer to a bowl. Save the lobster shells.

Peel the shrimp and cut off the heads, reserving both shells and heads to flavor the broth. Slice the shrimp in half lengthwise and combine them with the lobster meat in the bowl. Cover and refrigerate.

SHELLFISH BROTH

1	tablespoon extra-virgin olive oil
1	large onion, sliced
1	small, whole head garlic, halved
3	sprigs thyme
1	bay leaf
2	quarts White Chicken Stock (page 421)
1	28-ounce can whole plum tomatoes, drained, juice reserved, and tomatoes crushed

1	teaspoon black peppercorns
1/2	teaspoon crushed red pepper flakes
4	fresh flat-leaf parsley sprigs or stems

In a large pot, heat the olive oil over medium heat. Cook the onion and garlic for about 3 minutes, until softened. Add the thyme and bay leaf, and cook for 1 minute longer. Stir in the reserved lobster and shrimp shells and the shrimp heads, and sauté for about 10 minutes, until the lobster shells turn bright red.

Add the chicken stock, tomatoes and their reserved juice, the peppercorns, red pepper flakes, and parsley to the pot. Raise the heat to high and bring to a boil. Reduce the heat to low and simmer for about 40 minutes, until the broth is richly flavored and fragrant. Strain through a colander into a bowl to remove the large shells and vegetables. Set a fine-mesh sieve over the pot and strain the broth again. Cover and keep warm.

CLAMS AND MUSSELS

2	cups dry white wine
1	small onion, sliced
3	cloves garlic, peeled and smashed
3	sprigs fresh thyme
12	littleneck clams, well scrubbed
2	pounds cultivated black mussels, well scrubbed

In a large saucepan, combine the white wine, onion, garlic, and thyme. Cover and bring to a boil over high heat. Reduce the heat and simmer for 6 to 8 minutes, until reduced by about half. Add the clams, cover, raise the heat to high, and steam for about 2 minutes. Add the mussels, cover, and steam about 5 minutes longer, stirring occasionally, until the clams and mussels open. Using a slotted spoon or tongs, lift the clams and mussels from the pan. Discard any that have not opened and spread out the rest to cool. Transfer them to a bowl and cover with a kitchen towel.

Strain the cooking liquid through a fine-mesh sieve into a glass measuring cup. It should measure about 1 1/2 cups. Reserve.

ASSEMBLY

7	tablespoons unsalted butter
3	tablespoons extra-virgin olive oil
2	large shallots, minced
2	pounds arborio rice
1	cup dry white wine
10	ounces raw squid, cut into rings
1	teaspoon chopped fresh thyme
	Coarse salt and freshly ground white pepper to taste
3	tablespoons chopped fresh flat-leaf parsley

In a stockpot, combine the reserved shellfish cooking liquid and shellfish broth. Bring to a boil over high heat. Reduce the heat to low and simmer gently.

In a stockpot, combine 3 tablespoons of the butter and the olive oil, and heat over medium heat until the butter melts. Add the shallots and cook, stirring, for about 1 minute. Add the rice and cook, stirring with a wooden spoon, for 7 to 10 minutes, until it turns milky white and opaque and begins to stick to the bottom of the pan.

Add the wine and stir for about 2 minutes, until nearly absorbed. Ladle about 1 cup of the simmering broth into the rice. Cook for about 2 minutes, stirring often, until the broth is almost completely absorbed. Add more broth, a cup at a time, stirring gently until it is absorbed by the rice before adding the next cup. After about 15 minutes, begin tasting the rice. At this point, add the broth judiciously. The rice should be firm, yet cooked through in 18 to 20 minutes total cooking time.

About 8 minutes before you anticipate the rice will be done, add the squid and thyme, and cook for 2 minutes. Add the lobster and shrimp meat, the clams and mussels, and season with salt and pepper. Cook for 4 to 6 minutes longer, stirring, until the rice is creamy but still firm to the bite.

Stir in the remaining 4 tablespoons of the butter and the parsley. Adjust the seasonings and serve.

VARIATIONS: Vary the mix of shellfish to suit your taste, or concentrate on just one flavor.

Grilling

We've come a long way since the days when grilling was the only way to cook a piece of meat. Today, the convenience of electric and gas ovens has turned outdoor grilling from a daily necessity into a special event.

What a shame. As simple as grilling seems—it's really nothing more than cooking food by ambient heat from a source beneath the grate—the chemistry it triggers is wonderful: As the fats are rendered out of the beef, chicken, or what-have-you, the drippings plummet to the depths of the fire, from which they are returned to the cooking food via the smoke coming off the coals. Essentially, these drippings, which would normally reduce or collect in a pan, reduce directly on the food's surface, creating an intensely flavored exterior that gives way to a tender, juicy inside. In other words, the cavemen had it better than they could possibly have realized.

I personally have loved grilling since well before I knew I wanted to be a chef. When I was growing up, my family had an old-fashioned barbecue in our backyard before upgrading to a more serious, gas-powered model that was anchored in place with a central pole that went right through the grill and into the ground. But that was nothing compared to my wife's family. Helen's father, William, had a setup that allowed him to grill right in the family's living-room fireplace, and later he installed a gas grill in their kitchen.

I had always thought of such a spectacle as a restaurant-only proposition, and in fact, the next time I encountered it was at Michel Guérard's restaurant in France, where Helen and I worked together after graduating from the Culinary Institute of America. At one end of

Guérard's kitchen, there was a wood-burning fireplace where the grilled dishes featured on the menu were prepared. The grill cook would rake the coals forward and replenish them from the fire as they burned down to ash.

Grills are not only part of Helen's and my mutual heritage, but are part of our contemporary cooking life, as well. In our Manhattan apartment, we had a grill on the balcony until we found out that it was against the regulations in our building, and we gave it away.

Eventually, we invested in a very serious grill at our summer house—so serious that it came with a lifetime guarantee. It also came with 100 pounds of hardwood lump charcoal. Having grown up on low-grade, chemically treated briquettes, it was a revelation for me to taste food cooked over real wood. Simply put, there was no going back. My advice to you is to stay far away from briquettes because they can transfer an unpleasant flavor to what's being cooked. Steer clear of starter fluid and pre-soaked charcoal briquettes for the same reason.

Despite my love for cooking over charcoal, it must be said that gas grills are a more convenient and perfectly respectable alternative and eliminate the need for fretting over such details as the timing of the fire. A gas grill doesn't yield the same results as a real fire, but depending on your priorities, it can be a logical choice to make.

By far the most useful grill feature is an adjustable coal bed, which can be raised or lowered to control the intensity of the heat. Obviously, an adjustable grate will serve the same purpose. This is not common to most popular brands, but it's worth seeking out if you do, or plan to do, a lot of grilling.

As far as starting the fire, if an electrical outlet is convenient, an electrical fire-starter is a clean and fast way to go, but other approaches, such as an all-natural fire-starter, also work well. If using charcoal, it's important that the fire be lit long enough in advance to burn down. You'll see the recurring instruction "let the coals burn until covered with white ash" throughout this book. While many people think of grilling as cooking over a flame, the desired heat source is really a flameless fire. This takes about 40 minutes to achieve, depending on the type of fuel you use. (A good test of the heat itself is to hold your hand about 5 inches above the coals. If you can leave it there for five seconds, it's ready; if you cannot leave it there that long, it's still too hot.)

Preparing the Food In addition to using marinades, cooking over hardwood (mesquite, hickory, apple) coals adds flavor to grilled dishes, as do branches of herbs tossed on the fire to smolder and impart their flavor to the food that is being cooked. Helen and I love using rosemary branches, thyme branches, and sage, and we pick and dry them at the end of the season for this very purpose.

Direct versus Indirect Heat Any food that takes more than 15 minutes to cook should be grilled over indirect heat to avoid overcooking or charring. I keep a portion of my grill warm with indirect heat for another, pragmatic reason: As ingredients are cooked, you can simply move them to the indirectly heated area, where they will keep warm as other items are cooked. For this reason, I recommend a large, square or rectangular-shaped grate, rather than a circular one, to get as much usable surface area as possible.

The Ultimate Grilling Experience Open-pit grilling is the purest form of this technique. It requires a lot of time because it involves working with hardwood logs which take about two hours to burn down. My favorite foods to cook over an open pit are steak, shrimp, vegetables, corn, lobster, potatoes, and homemade sausage.

If you live near a beach, you should get out there and do some open-pit cooking at night. And not just for the food. Under the light of the moon, watching the silhouettes of your friends against the flames and listening to the water crash against the shore, you get a sense of what it must've been like to live in ancient times, cooking with fire. This is part of the appeal of grilling for everyone, I think—the attraction to the flame itself, an almost genetic nostalgia for our collective, primal past.

Grilled Lobster with Grilled Corn, Potatoes, and Roast Garlic–Tarragon Butter

MAKES 4 SERVINGS

This practical recipe invites you to do most of the work in advance, dispensing with the messiness of preparing whole lobsters well before mealtime. In fact, the lobster can be blanched in the morning, when I also suggest you split the lobster and crack the claws. This advance work will reduce your actual cooking time to a mere 8 minutes—leaving you an extra half-hour to soak up the last of the day's sunshine before getting down to grilling.

This recipe was inspired by my days working for the great French chef Michel Guérard. One of the dishes prepared in his kitchen's fireplace was Chimney-Smoked Lobster. (See Grilling, pages 70–72, for more on this.) Among its unique charms are an aromatic compound butter that melts into, and is trapped by, the shells during cooking, and a

THINKING AHEAD: The lobster can, and should, be blanched several hours ahead of time and refrigerated. The Roast Garlic–Tarragon Butter can be made 3 days in advance and refrigerated, or up to 1 week in advance, wrapped tightly in plastic wrap, and frozen.

ROAST GARLIC–TARRAGON BUTTER
3	tablespoons Roast Garlic Purée (page 317)
8	tablespoons (1 stick) unsalted butter, softened
2	teaspoons finely chopped fresh flat-leaf parsley
1	teaspoon chopped fresh tarragon
1	teaspoon fresh lemon juice
$1/8$	teaspoon cayenne pepper
$1/2$	teaspoon coarse salt, or to taste
	Freshly ground white pepper to taste

In a small bowl, fold the roast garlic purée into the butter, then fold in the parsley, tarragon, lemon juice, and cayenne. Season with salt and pepper. Use while at room temperature or cover and refrigerate. Allow the butter to come back to room temperature before using it.

GRILLED CORN AND POTATOES
8	ears unhusked fresh sweet corn
$1^1/2$	pounds small new potatoes, about 2 inches in diameter
3	tablespoons extra-virgin olive oil
	Coarse salt and freshly ground white pepper to taste

Pull the husks from the ears of corn, leaving the leaves attached at the base. Remove the silks and then pull the husks back over the corn. Using a strip of the husks, tie the ends closed. Soak the corn in cold water to cover for about 20 minutes.

Build a charcoal fire in a grill and let the coals burn until covered with white ash. Spread them out in the grill, leaving a portion of the grill free of coals for indirect cooking. Lightly oil the grill grate.

In a bowl, toss the potatoes with the oil and season with salt and pepper. Lay the potatoes on the grill grate or arrange them in a single layer in a mesh grill basket. Grill for 20 to 25 minutes over indirect heat, turning frequently, until tender. (If the potatoes are very small—$1^1/2$ inches in diameter or smaller—they will cook in about 15 minutes.)

Lift the corn from the water and grill for 10 to 15 minutes over indirect heat. Remove the potatoes and corn from the grill and set them aside to keep warm.

LOBSTER

1 quart water
  Coarse salt to taste
4 1¼-pound live lobsters

Using a large stockpot, bring the water and salt to a boil over high heat. Add the lobsters and cover the pot. Return to the boil and boil for about 2 minutes. Using tongs, lift the lobsters from the pot. The lobsters are parcooked at this stage. Set them aside to cool. When cool enough to handle, break off the claws and crack them. Turn the lobster bodies upside down on a cutting board and split them in half lengthwise with a sharp knife. Remove the intestines.

Put the claws and lobster bodies, cut sides down, on the grill and cook for 1 to 2 minutes, until slightly browned. Turn the bodies over and spread each with about 2 tablespoons of the herb butter. Cover the grill with its lid and grill the lobsters for about 6 minutes longer, until they are cooked through and the butter melts into the lobster meat. Serve with the potatoes and corn.

VARIATION: Grill and serve the lobster with simple drawn butter and lemon.

FLAVOR BUILDING: To add another dimension of flavor to the lobster, add some wood to your fire in the following manner: Soak chips of cherry, apple, or oak wood in water before wrapping them in heavy-duty aluminum foil. (Larger pieces, if you can get them, do not require soaking.) Poke a few holes in the foil and place the wrapped wood on the edge of the coal bank. Give it a few minutes to start smoldering and smoking.

smoker effect that is achieved by keeping the grill cover sealed.

Just as lobsters are best cooked in gently simmering water, here they should be grilled over moderate heat to avoid toughening the meat.

NOTE: If you use larger potatoes, parcook them for about 10 minutes in boiling salted water. Drain and proceed with the recipe as directed.

Grilled Marinated Leg of Lamb with Tabbouleh and Minted Aioli

MAKES 6 SERVINGS

THINKING AHEAD: Marinate the lamb 12 to 24 hours in advance. The aioli can be prepared in the morning, provided it is kept covered and refrigerated.

LAMB AND MARINADE

$^2/_3$	cup extra-virgin olive oil
$^1/_2$	cup fresh lemon juice
1	medium onion, quartered and thinly sliced
2	tablespoons minced garlic
2	tablespoons dried oregano
1	tablespoon freshly ground black pepper
1	teaspoon ground cinnamon
1	butterflied leg of lamb, cut from a $4^1/_2$-pound leg
	Coarse salt to taste, for grilling

In a large, shallow, nonreactive dish, combine the olive oil, lemon juice, onion, garlic, oregano, pepper, and cinnamon. Stir well. Add the lamb and rub thoroughly with the marinade. Cover with plastic wrap and refrigerate for at least 8 hours or overnight.

MINTED AIOLI

6 to 7	scallions, green parts only, left whole
1	cup loosely packed fresh mint leaves
2	large egg yolks, at room temperature
2	cloves garlic, peeled and mashed to a paste with a pinch of coarse salt
$^1/_2$	teaspoon Dijon mustard
$^1/_8$	teaspoon cayenne pepper
	Coarse salt and freshly ground white pepper to taste
1	cup canola oil
$^1/_2$	cup extra-virgin olive oil
1	teaspoon fresh lemon juice, or to taste

In a medium saucepan, cook the scallions in boiling salted water for about 10 seconds. Add the mint leaves and cook for 10 seconds longer, or until the leaves wilt and turn bright green. Lift the scallions and mint from the water with a slotted spoon or strainer and transfer them to a bowl of ice water to stop the cooking and set the color. Drain and then very gently squeeze out the excess water.

Transfer the scallions and mint leaves to a blender or food processor fitted with a metal blade and process until puréed. Scrape

When assembling a dish, most chefs—myself included—consider the primary ingredient before the accompaniments. But the opposite approach can often be more inspirational. Like featured or supporting actors in a movie or play, "featured" ingredients often have a more intense and memorable role than the main ingredient.

This dish resulted from my desire to assemble a contemporary Mediterranean menu, and the first component I settled on was the tabbouleh; its Middle Eastern mix of bulgur wheat, tomatoes, parsley, and mint seems to me a powerful representative of Mediterranean cooking. As someone who never tires of lamb, I decided to make it the central component here, marinating it in copious amounts of garlic and lemon juice to reinforce the theme. And to make it feel familiar to American diners, a fresh mint purée is incorporated in a unique, pale green sauce.

This recipe is also a great picnic dish that travels very well. The grilled meat, tabbouleh, and herbaceous dressing all feel right at home in the outdoors.

WHAT TO DRINK: Enjoy this dish with a spicy Rioja or a juicy Barbera.

down the sides of the bowl several times during processing. Add the egg yolks, garlic, mustard, and cayenne, and season with salt and pepper. Process for about 20 seconds longer, until well combined.

Mix the canola oil and olive oil in a glass measuring cup, and with the blender or processor running, slowly add the oil in a steady stream. Scrape down the sides of the bowl several times during blending. When the emulsion is thick and fluffy, season with lemon juice, salt, and pepper. Cover and refrigerate until ready to serve. The aioli will keep for up to 2 days; it will retain its bright green color for only about 8 hours.

TABBOULEH

1	cup cracked bulgur wheat
2	cups hot tap water
$1/2$	cup finely chopped fresh flat-leaf parsley
2	tablespoons mint leaves, cut into chiffonade
3	tablespoons fresh lemon juice, or to taste
2	tablespoons extra-virgin olive oil
2	plum tomatoes, peeled, seeded, and cut into $1/4$-inch dice
3	scallions, white parts and about 1 inch of the green parts, thinly sliced
1	clove garlic, peeled and very finely minced
	Pinch of ground cinnamon
	Coarse salt and freshly ground white pepper to taste

In a medium stainless-steel bowl, combine the bulgur and hot water. Let stand uncovered for 35 to 40 minutes, until most of the water is absorbed and the bulgur is soft but still has a bite. Drain off any excess water. Scrape the bulgur onto a clean kitchen towel and gently squeeze to remove any remaining moisture. Return the bulgur to the bowl.

Add the parsley, mint, lemon juice, olive oil, tomatoes, scallions, garlic, and cinnamon. Season with salt and pepper, stir gently to mix, and set aside for about 20 minutes for the flavors to develop. Taste and adjust the seasonings. Add more lemon juice for a citrusy edge, if necessary.

THINKING AHEAD: You could bake this tart ahead of time, but I would strongly encourage you to serve it fresh out of the oven. The ice cream must be made at least 4 hours in advance.

BRÛLÉE SUGAR

1	cup light brown sugar
1/2	cup granulated sugar

Preheat the oven to 250°F.
Combine the sugars, mixing well to integrate them evenly. Spread the mixture on a baking sheet and dry it in the oven for about 1 hour. Transfer to a blender and process to a fine powder. Set aside.

QUICK PUFF PASTRY

4 1/2	cups all-purpose flour
1	tablespoon salt
2 1/2	cups unsalted butter, cut into pieces and chilled
1/2	cup cold water

In a mixing bowl, whisk together the flour and salt. Add the butter and, using your fingertips or 2 forks, work the butter into the flour until the mixture resembles coarse crumbs. Do not overmix. Add the water all at once and stir to just combine. There will be small chunks of butter in the dough.

Turn the dough out onto a lightly floured surface and, using a lightly floured rolling pin, roll it into a large rectangle approximately 1/2 inch thick. Fold one side of the dough into the center and then fold the other side over it, so that the rectangle is folded in thirds, like a letter. Roll the dough into another 1/2-inch-thick rectangle and fold it again in similar fashion and in the same direction. Repeat the rolling and folding process 4 times. To do so will form buttery, flaky layers in the baked crust. Use immediately or wrap in plastic and refrigerate for up to 1 hour.

ASSEMBLY

8	black plums, peeled, pitted, and sliced into 1/4-inch-thick wedges
1/4	cup unsalted butter, cut into small pieces
	Vanilla Bean Ice Cream (page 84)

Black Plum Tart with Vanilla Bean Ice Cream

MAKES 8 SERVINGS

Years ago, I was preparing to go on national television for the first time, to show Regis Philbin and Kathie Lee Gifford how to make this dessert on their show *Live! with Regis and Kathie Lee,* and I was more than a little nervous. Though I've become far more comfortable on camera, the first time was more than a little daunting.

So one weekday morning, there I was, waiting in the wings just off-stage. I had all of the ingredients prepared, lined up in sequential order, and ready to be wheeled out to the set, when word came through that the United States had just bombed Libya and the show would be interrupted by the news department. I breathed a sigh of relief, returned all the ingredients to their individual containers, packed up my gear, and headed down the hallway for the elevator, trying to conceal my relief with feigned disappointment.

But as I was on my way out, a

production assistant caught up with me and told me that the news report had concluded—we were going back on the air! Shocked, I hurriedly unpacked all the ingredients in a matter of moments, whereupon I was all but thrust onto the set to show a few million people how to bake this tart. Miraculously, the demonstration went off without a hitch and the dessert came out just right.

The point of this story is that this dessert is very simple to make. It shows off the qualities of June plums, which are plentiful but not yet supersweet, as they will be just a few weeks later. Their tartness perfectly complements the rich vanilla bean ice cream.

Preheat the oven to 350°F.

Roll the pastry dough to a free-form rectangle about $1/4$ inch thick. Using a $3^3/4$-inch round cutter or a sharp knife, cut out 8 circles. Reroll the dough if necessary to get enough circles. Carefully transfer the circles to an ungreased baking sheet. Prick them all over with a fork.

Fan the plum slices on the pastry rounds. Sprinkle each with a generous layer of brûlée sugar. Bake for about 10 minutes. Remove from the oven but do not turn off the heat. Sprinkle more sugar over the plums and dot each tart with butter. Bake for 10 to 15 minutes longer. Sprinkle with more sugar as soon as they are removed from the oven. Serve hot or warm, with scoops of ice cream.

VARIATION: Ginger Ice Cream (page 218) works very well as an accompaniment to this tart.

Vanilla Bean Ice Cream
MAKES ABOUT 1 1/2 QUARTS

2	cups heavy cream
1	cup milk
10	tablespoons sugar
2	Tahitian vanilla beans, split lengthwise
8	large egg yolks

In a large saucepan, combine the cream, milk, 5 tablespoons of the sugar, and the vanilla beans. Bring to a simmer over low heat, stirring occasionally to help the sugar dissolve.

In a bowl, whisk the egg yolks with the remaining 5 tablespoons of sugar. Add about 1 cup of the hot cream mixture to the beaten egg yolks, whisking to mix. Add this mixture to the saucepan, whisking well to combine. Cook over low heat for 4 to 6 minutes, stirring constantly until the custard is thick enough to lightly coat the back of a wooden spoon. Strain through a sieve into a stainless-steel bowl. Remove the vanilla beans from the sieve

PRESERVING:
Plum Jam

MAKES THREE 8-OUNCE JARS

To keep a natural plum flavor, this jam uses less sugar than you'll encounter in most preserving recipes, resulting in a very soft, spoonable consistency.

4	pounds ripe plums, peeled, pitted, and sliced
1	cup water
$^{1}/_{4}$	cup sugar

In a large saucepan, bring the plums, water, and sugar to a boil over high heat. Reduce the heat to medium-high and cook for about 55 minutes, until thick, using a wooden spoon to mash the fruit during cooking. Reduce the heat to low and simmer for about 10 minutes longer, until very thick.

Transfer to a container to cool. Cover and refrigerate and serve within a week.

For longer storage, spoon the hot jam into hot, sterilized canning jars, leaving about $^{1}/_{4}$ inch of headroom. Screw on the lids. Let cool completely, and then store in a cool, dry place. The jars should not touch each other during cooling. Refrigerate after opening.

NOTE: To sterilize the jars, set them in a large pot and cover with enough water to fill them and cover them by an inch or so. Let the water come to a boil over high heat, remove from the heat, but leave the jars in the hot water until ready to fill. Put the lids in a bowl and pour boiling water over them. Do not let the lids boil. Leave in the water until ready to use.

and, using the tip of a small knife, scrape the tiny, black vanilla seeds into the custard. Discard the beans.

Set the bowl in a larger bowl filled with ice and water and let it stand for about 40 minutes, stirring occasionally, until chilled.

Pour the custard into the container of an ice-cream machine and freeze according to the manufacturer's directions. Transfer to a covered container and freeze for at least 4 hours or overnight, until firm.

PRESERVING:
Apricot Preserves

MAKES THREE 8-OUNCE JARS

I love apricots, so it's an annual disappointment to me that their peak season is as short as it is. (We even have difficulty getting superior specimens at the Gotham for more than a few weeks each year.) Because they're so elusive, I try to capture apricots in a preserve and enjoy their sweetness again and again all summer long.

Apricots should be picked when they're underripe, and home cooks would do well to seek them out at a farm stand offering locally grown fruit.

4 pounds apricots, peeled, pitted, and sliced
3 cups water
$^1/_2$ cup sugar

In a large saucepan, bring the apricots, water, and sugar to a boil over high heat. Reduce the heat to medium-high and cook for about 55 minutes, until thick, using a wooden spoon to mash the fruit during cooking. Reduce the heat to low and simmer for about 10 minutes longer, until very thick.

Transfer to a dish to cool. Cover, refrigerate, and serve within a week.

For longer storage, spoon the hot jam into sterilized glass canning jars (see note, page 81), leaving about $^1/_4$ inch of headroom. Screw on the lids. Let cool completely and then store in a cool, dry place. The jars should not touch each other during cooling. Refrigerate after opening.

Cherry
Cheesecake

I grew up on Italian cheesecakes made with ricotta cheese. Because they are not baked in a water bath, these cheesecakes are more dry and boast a browner crust than the quintessential New York–style cake that's made primarily of cream cheese. (There's also a lighter French version that includes a lot of crème fraîche and less cream cheese, isn't baked, and as a result, requires a small amount of gelatin to get it to set up.)

This recipe is based on the classic New York–style cake. It's rich and creamy, and while the cherry compote is a sweet and satisfying topping that makes great use of fresh fruit this month, the cake can certainly be served without it.

THINKING AHEAD: This dessert must be made at least 8 hours in advance.

CHEESECAKE

1	pound cream cheese, at room temperature
1	cup sugar
1	Tahitian vanilla bean, split
	Grated zest of $^1/_2$ orange
1	tablespoon fresh orange juice
$^1/_4$	teaspoon coarse salt
4	large eggs, at room temperature
3	cups crème fraîche, at room temperature

Preheat the oven to 350°F. Butter a 10-inch cake pan.

In the bowl of an electric mixer set on medium-high speed, cream the cream cheese, sugar, and vanilla bean until smooth. (The bean will not disintegrate but will flavor the batter as it mixes.) Add the orange zest, juice, and salt, and mix briefly. Add the eggs one at a time, mixing after each addition until just incorporated. Do not overmix. Too much air incorporated into the batter can produce air pockets in the baked cake. Add the crème fraîche and beat until just mixed. Remove and discard the vanilla bean.

Scrape the batter into the prepared pan, and put the pan in a larger roasting or baking pan set on the oven rack. Pour enough hot water into the larger pan to come about halfway up the sides of the smaller pan. Bake for $1^1/_2$ to 2 hours, until very lightly browned and firm around the sides. The center should be a little soft; it will firm up during cooling. Cool completely on a wire rack. Cover with plastic wrap or aluminum foil and refrigerate for at least 8 hours or overnight.

LINZER CRUST

$^3/_4$	cup chopped hazelnuts
$^1/_2$	cup plus 2 teaspoons sugar
$^1/_4$	cup plus $^1/_2$ tablespoon almond flour (see Mail-Order Sources, page 426)
$^3/_4$	cup unsalted butter
1	large egg
$1^1/_2$	cups all-purpose flour
$1^1/_2$	tablespoons ground cinnamon
2	teaspoons baking powder
1	tablespoon butter, for cake pan

P reheat the oven to 350°F.
Spread the hazelnuts in a single layer in a shallow baking pan and toast in the oven for about 6 minutes, until lightly browned and fragrant. Shake the pan or stir the nuts several times during toasting. Transfer the nuts to a cutting board. Finely chop them. Transfer to a bowl and set aside.

Increase the oven temperature to 400°F. Lightly spray a 10-inch tart pan with a removable bottom with vegetable oil.

In the bowl of an electric mixer set on medium-high speed, cream the sugar, almond flour, and butter for 3 to 5 minutes, until smooth and light colored. Add the egg and whisk to just combine.

In another bowl, whisk together the flour, cinnamon, chopped hazelnuts, and baking powder. With the electric mixer set on medium-low, gradually add the dry ingredients to the dough. Mix until just incorporated.

Lightly butter the bottom of a 10-inch cake pan and line it with parchment paper. On a lightly floured surface, roll the dough to a circle about 13 inches in diameter and $1/4$ inch thick. Using the bottom of the pan as a guide, trim the dough into a 10-inch circle. Roll the dough around the rolling pin. Place the pin over the cake pan and unroll the pastry over the pan. Ease the dough into the pan, pressing gently against the bottom to fit it securely. Smooth out any cracks. Prick the dough all over with the tines of a fork. Bake for about 10 minutes. Press down any swelling or bubbles in the crust. Return it to the oven for about 5 minutes, or until golden brown. Cool on a wire rack. When completely cool, run a knife around the inside of the pan and pop out the linzer circle.

(continued)

WHAT TO DRINK:
Spiked Lemonade
MAKES 8 SERVINGS; ABOUT 1 QUART

The word *spiked* connotes the covert pouring of alcohol into a fruit punch and conjures up images of a drunken office party scene in a 1960s comedy where a character inevitably concludes, "Somebody must've spiked the punch bowl."

But, so long as your guests know what's in their glasses, a spiked punch can be a great, colorful "house cocktail" for a summertime gathering. With that in mind, here are some of my favorite ways of sprucing up the ultimate thirst quencher—lemonade.

	Juice of 18 lemons
$1/2$	cup sugar
$1/2$	cup water
1	lemon, finely sliced into rings, for garnish
1	sprig fresh mint, leaves picked, for garnish, optional
$1^1/2$	cups (12 ounces) raspberry vodka

I n a large pitcher, stir together the lemon juice and sugar until the sugar dissolves. Add the water, stir, and taste. Add more sugar, if necessary, for sweetness. Keep in mind that when served, the ice in the glasses will dilute the lemonade a little.

Fill another pitcher or individual glasses with ice. Add the lemon slices and mint leaves, if using them.

Mix the lemonade with the vodka and pour it over the ice. Stir and serve.

NOTE: For pink lemonade, add a splash of cassis. The lemonade can be spiked with other flavored vodkas, such as mandarin, lemon, or orange.

FLAVOR BUILDING: Make colorful, flavorful ice cubes by filling a tray with 2 cups of the fruit juice of your choice. To obtain an intense flavor, I like to buy organic, frozen fruit concentrate and make the concentrate with less water than its label suggests. You might also use bottled fruit nectars such as boysenberry, raspberry, blackberry, or strawberry for this purpose.

CHERRY COMPOTE AND ASSEMBLY

- 20   fresh Bing cherries, stemmed and pitted
- 2   cups dried cherries
- 1   cup dry red wine, such as Merlot
- $^1/_4$ cup sugar
- 1   tablespoon fresh orange juice
      Grated zest of $^1/_2$ orange
- $^1/_4$ cup raspberry jam

In a large saucepan, combine the fresh cherries, dried cherries, wine, sugar, orange juice and zest, and bring to a boil over medium-high heat. Cook, stirring, for about 6 minutes, until the flavors meld and the cherries soften. Set aside, covered, to keep warm.

Remove the cheesecake from the refrigerator. Spread the linzer disc with jam. Working carefully, invert the cheesecake onto the linzer layer. Tap on side of cheesecake pan to loosen and slide the pan off. Cut cake into wedges and serve with the warm compote on the side.

VARIATION: Omit the cherry topping and adorn the basic cheesecake with fresh fruit such as strawberries or blueberries.

Father's Day Potluck Dinner

Since many family members often contribute to a Father's Day meal, here are some dishes that will travel very well to your celebration. This menu can also be used as the basis for a complete buffet to be prepared by one household, thanks to a few important efficiencies—it features two cold dishes that can be made in advance; the two hot dishes are both cooked on the grill; and the desserts can be baked ahead of time as well.

LOBSTER SUMMER ROLLS WITH MINT, CUCUMBER,
AND LEMONGRASS DRESSING **(page 54)**

GRILLED CHICKEN MARINATED IN CUMIN, LEMON,
AND GARLIC **(page 112)**

GRILLED MARINATED LEG OF LAMB WITH TABBOULEH
AND MINTED AIOLI **(page 77)**

SALAD OF LOCAL WAX BEANS, SHELL BEANS, AND MINT **(page 57)**

COCOA COOKIES **(page 292)**

CHOCOLATE BISCOTTI **(page 293)**

GINGER-BERRY LEMONADE **(page 124)**

Brandade with Radish, Red Onion, and Olive Salad

Grilled Yellowfin Tuna Salad with Anchovy Vinaigrette

Montauk Chowder with Clams, Wild Striped Bass, Tomatoes, and Yellow Finn Potatoes

Linguine with Grilled Shrimp, Cranberry Beans, and Pesto

Grilled Soft-Shell Crabs with Israeli Couscous and Summer Vegetable Sauté

Angel Hair Pasta with Lobster, Tomatoes, Garlic, and Flat-Leaf Parsley

Grilled Wild Striped Bass with Grilled Fennel, Tomatoes, and Picholine Olives

Grilled Chicken Marinated in Cumin, Lemon, and Garlic

Grilled Marinated Rib-Eye Steak

Berries

White Angel Food Cake with Raspberries and Nectarines

Blueberry Croustade with Sweetened Mascarpone

Ice Cream

Strawberry Ice Cream

Summer Dinner Party

JULY

BIRTHDAYS AND BARBECUES

For me, July is a month of memories. Sandwiched between June—when the current season is just dawning—and August—when cool nights begin to creep back in—July means pure, unadulterated summer.

A lot of New Yorkers find this month's heat unbearable, but I welcome the remembrances it sparks of my fondest summer moments, everything from recent vacations with my family to childhood days long gone.

Among my most vivid summertime recollections are those of my family's annual stay in the 1960s on Crystal Beach, on the Canadian side of Lake Erie. Summertimes at our cottage come back to me in a rush of images—of barbecues and beach parties, the Ferris wheel that rolled over and over in the lakeside amusement park, and the fireworks stands that beckoned to my friends and me.

In Canada, fireworks—illegal in the United States—were as easy to purchase as bubble gum. The one obstacle to pyrotechnic gratification was my father, who for years prohibited us from buying anything but unsatisfying small sparklers and ladyfingers.

But when I turned fifteen, I got a restricted driver's license from New York State and—almost as important—an unrestricted fireworks license from my father. My friends and I spent days preparing an Independence Day extravaganza for the 150 or so people who gathered at the cottages for our annual reunion. We not only purchased hundreds of dollars' worth of fireworks, we

actually made our own aerial shells and successfully engineered an entire show complete with the requisite big finale.

And the best part of it all was that July Fourth happens to be the day on which I celebrate my birthday, adding a personal significance to the extravaganza.

I've rummaged through such memories to find the inspiration for the recipes in this chapter. Here you'll find adaptations of some of my favorite childhood dishes and those my own family has enjoyed over the years.

Among the latter group are Linguine with Grilled Shrimp, Cranberry Beans, and Pesto (page 102), which was conceived on a trip to Italy's Cinque Terre; Montauk Chowder with Clams, Wild Striped Bass, Tomatoes, and Yellow Finn Potatoes (page 99), inspired by our daughters' first clamming expedition; and Angel Hair Pasta with Lobster, Tomatoes, Garlic, and Flat-Leaf Parsley (page 107), which was improvised one Saturday night a few years ago and became an instant classic at our weekend home. The Brandade with Radish, Red Onion, and Olive Salad (page 94) is an embellished variation of a dish we serve to dinner guests as an hors d'oeuvre of sorts all summer long. One taste of it brings thoughts of friends gathered in our kitchen, spreading brandade on croutons as Helen and I cook.

Some of the following recipes simply sum up the spirit of summer to me, namely a quartet of grilled dishes that are all relatively light but packed with potent flavors—a combination I find very appealing in the sweltering heat. These include a Grilled Yellowfin Tuna Salad with Anchovy Vinaigrette (page 97), Grilled Soft-Shell Crabs with Israeli Couscous and Summer Vegetable Sauté (page 105), Grilled Wild Striped Bass with Grilled Fennel, Tomatoes, and Picholine Olives (page 110), and Grilled Chicken Marinated in Cumin, Lemon, and Garlic (page 112). A fifth grilled dish takes me back to those family reunions in Canada—a variation on my father's Grilled, Marinated Rib-Eye Steak (page 113).

In accordance with this theme, I've also devoted two essays in this chapter to childhood summer staples: ice cream, which I can't get enough of at this time of year, and berries, which to me are the culinary counterparts of fireworks. In July, strawberries, raspberries, and blueberries are so ripe and juicy that they seem almost capable of bursting on their own. All the desserts in this chapter feature berries rather prominently—from the simple Strawberry Ice Cream (page 123) and White Angel Food Cake with Raspberries and Nectarines (page 117), to a Blueberry Crustade with Sweetened Mascarpone (page 119)—the intention being to allow you to end any July meal as you would a fireworks show—with a bang.

Brandade
with Radish, Red Onion, and Olive Salad

MAKES 6 APPETIZER SERVINGS

Salt cod was first embraced hundreds of years ago for the same reason as gravlax and other salted fish—preservation. While there are recipes that use this fish in many countries (Italy, Portugal, Spain), one of my favorite methods of cooking it is in a brandade, a name derived from the French word *brandar,* which means "to stir." It's made by puréeing salt cod, potatoes, and olive oil, transferring the mixture to a gratin dish, sprinkling the top with bread crumbs, and baking it in the oven. Despite the derivation of its name, today it's perfectly acceptable to purée the salt cod in a food processor.

Brandade is a wonderful party food that can be prepared largely in advance. When hosting people at our summer home, Helen and I serve it to friends lingering in the kitchen at the beginning of a dinner gathering.

If you've ever eaten a brandade, it probably seemed like a very simple dish, and in many respects it is.

THINKING AHEAD: The salt cod should be soaked for 3 days.

SALT COD

1¹/₂	pounds salt cod
2	cups water
2	tablespoons white wine vinegar
1	bay leaf
1	sprig fresh thyme
2 to 3	whole white peppercorns

In a large bowl, soak the salt cod in cold water to cover in the refrigerator for 72 hours. Change the water twice a day.

In a saucepan, combine the water, vinegar, bay leaf, thyme, and peppercorns and bring to a boil. Reduce the heat to medium and add the salt cod. Poach for 8 to 14 minutes, depending on the thickness of the salt cod, until the fish flakes easily when pierced with a fork.

Lift the fish from the poaching liquid and set it aside to cool slightly. Remove any bones, skin, and gray fat. Remove a third of the fish, flake it, and set it aside. Set aside the remaining two-thirds of the fish.

RADISH, RED ONION, AND OLIVE SALAD

2	ribs celery, peeled and cut into ¹/₄-inch dice
3	plum tomatoes, peeled, seeded, and cut into ¹/₄-inch dice
1	red onion, quartered lengthwise and thinly sliced
1	clove garlic, peeled and finely minced
1	cup thinly sliced red radishes
1	cup pitted and halved mixed olives, such as kalamata, niçoise, and picholine
6	tablespoons extra-virgin olive oil
1	tablespoon aged red wine vinegar
1	teaspoon chopped fresh thyme leaves
	Coarse salt and freshly ground white pepper to taste
1	heaping tablespoon finely minced fresh flat-leaf parsley

In a saucepan, cook the celery in boiling salted water over high heat for about 4 minutes. Drain and refresh under cold water. Set it aside to drain on paper towels.

In a bowl, toss together the tomatoes, onion, garlic, radishes, olives, and celery. Add the olive oil, vinegar, and thyme, and toss again. Taste and season with salt and pepper. The salad can be made to this point, covered, and refrigerated for several hours. Let the salad return to room temperature before serving.

Just before serving, toss with the parsley.

BRANDADE

2	pounds potatoes, peeled and diced
$^1/_2$	cup extra-virgin olive oil
2	teaspoons minced garlic
$^1/_2$	cup half-and-half
$^1/_4$	teaspoon cayenne pepper
	Freshly ground white pepper to taste

In a saucepan, cook the potatoes in boiling water over high heat for about 20 minutes until tender. Drain and rice or mash the potatoes. Transfer them to a bowl.

Put the larger portion of cod (not the flaked portion) in a food processor fitted with a metal blade. Add the olive oil and garlic, and purée until smooth. Scrape the purée into the bowl with the potatoes and fold together. Work in the half-and-half and cayenne until the mixture is creamy and fluffy and has the consistency of mashed potatoes. Season with pepper. Fold in the flaked salt cod to give the mixture texture. Taste and add a little more garlic and olive oil, if necessary.

ASSEMBLY

$^1/_2$	cup fresh white bread crumbs
1	teaspoon chopped flat-leaf parsley
1	teaspoon extra-virgin olive oil
1	clove garlic, peeled and minced
	Coarse salt and freshly ground white pepper to taste
18	$^1/_2$-inch-thick slices bread, cut from a baguette and lightly toasted

Preheat the oven to 350°F.

In a bowl, combine the bread crumbs, parsley, olive oil, and garlic, and mix with a fork until crumbly. Season with salt and pepper.

Spread the brandade in a 2$^1/_2$-quart gratin dish and sprinkle it evenly with the bread-crumb topping. Bake for 20 to 30 minutes, until the top is browned and the brandade is heated through. Serve with the radish salad and the toasted bread on the side.

WHAT TO DRINK. Serve this dish with a Manzanilla Sherry or Albariño.

ANCHOVY VINAIGRETTE

- 1   2-ounce tin anchovy fillets in oil, drained
- 1   clove garlic, peeled, sprinkled with coarse salt, and mashed to a paste
- 1/2   cup extra-virgin olive oil
- 1   tablespoon red wine vinegar
- 1   tablespoon fresh lemon juice
- 1   shallot, minced
- 1   tablespoon capers, drained and chopped
    Coarse salt and freshly ground white pepper to taste
- 1   tablespoon finely chopped flat-leaf parsley

In a food processor fitted with a metal blade, combine the anchovies and garlic and process until mixed. With the motor running, add the olive oil in a thin stream, scraping down the sides of the bowl after about half the oil has been added. Transfer the mixture to a stainless-steel bowl and whisk in the vinegar, lemon juice, shallot, and capers. Season with salt and pepper, and stir in the parsley just before serving.

ASSEMBLY

- 1   tablespoon canola oil, plus more for oiling grate
- 1 1/2   pounds sushi-quality yellowfin tuna, cut into 4- to 6-ounce steaks
    Coarse salt and freshly ground white pepper to taste
- 4   cups loosely packed salad greens, such as *frisée* (curly endive), red oak leaf and Lolla Rossa lettuce, and watercress, washed and carefully dried
- 1   tablespoon fresh lemon juice
- 3   tablespoons extra-virgin olive oil
- 2   ripe beefsteak tomatoes, cored and cut into thick wedges

Build a charcoal fire in a grill and let the coals burn until covered with white ash. Spread them out in the grill. Lightly oil a very clean grill grate.

Lightly oil the tuna with the canola oil and season it with salt and pepper. Grill, turning once, for about 3 minutes total for rare and 4 to 5 minutes for medium-rare. Transfer the tuna to a clean cutting board and carve it into thick slices. Arrange the slices on 4 individual plates.

In a large mixing bowl, toss the greens with the lemon juice,

Grilled Yellowfin Tuna Salad with Anchovy Vinaigrette

MAKES 4 SERVINGS

I'm not sure how it happened, but over the years the anchovy has developed an undeservedly bad reputation in the United States. Great animosity is directed toward this harmless, herringlike fish. "Anything but anchovies" is often the first decision reached when friends are trying to settle on a group pizza order, and many Caesar salad lovers ask that the anchovies be left off of theirs.

In this dish, the powerful flavor of anchovies provides the basis for a broken, or nonemulsified, vinaigrette that includes garlic, lemon juice, shallot, and capers, all of which complement the tuna exceptionally well and add a dramatic visual effect to the plate. In this company, the lettuces need only to be dressed with lemon and olive oil because they will take on the ambient flavors of the anchovy dressing.

olive oil, and salt and pepper. Arrange the greens and tomatoes on the plates. Drizzle the tuna and the plate with the anchovy vinaigrette and serve.

VARIATIONS: The anchovy vinaigrette is assertive enough to stand up to red meats; spoon some over steak for a unique change of pace. You can also substitute Lemon-Caper Vinaigrette (page 28) for the anchovy vinaigrette in this recipe.

THINKING AHEAD: Like most soups, this one can be made a day ahead, but it should be reheated gently to avoid toughening the clams or overcooking the fish.

Montauk Chowder with Clams, Wild Striped Bass, Tomatoes, and Yellow Finn Potatoes

MAKES 6 SERVINGS

CLAMS

2	tablespoons extra-virgin olive oil
1	medium onion, sliced
2	cloves garlic, peeled, sprinkled with coarse salt, and mashed to a paste
3	cups dry white wine
2	sprigs fresh thyme
3	dozen littleneck clams, well scrubbed

In a large stockpot, heat the oil over medium-high heat. Add the onion and garlic, and sauté for about 4 minutes, until the onion is translucent. Add the wine and thyme, and bring to a boil over high heat. Cook for about 8 minutes to reduce the wine by a third to cook off most of the alcohol, and integrate the flavors. Add the clams, cover the pot, and steam, stirring occasionally, for 10 to 12 minutes, or until the clams open.

Using tongs, lift the clams from the pot and spread them out on a pan to cool. Discard any that do not open. Strain the cooking broth through a fine-mesh sieve or a colander lined with cheese-cloth into a bowl; you should have about 2^{1}/$_{4}$ cups of broth. Cover and refrigerate until ready to use.

When the clams are cool enough to handle, remove the meat and discard the shells. You should have about 9 ounces of clam meat. Cover and refrigerate until ready to use.

CHOWDER

1	tablespoon extra-virgin olive oil
3	ounces slab bacon, diced
1	medium onion, diced
1	rib celery, diced
1	small head fennel, trimmed and diced
2	cloves garlic, peeled and minced
1	28-ounce can whole plum tomatoes with their juice
1	teaspoon chopped fresh thyme
^{1}/$_{4}$	teaspoon cayenne pepper, or to taste
1^{1}/$_{2}$	cups diced Yellow Finn potatoes, cut into ^{1}/$_{2}$-inch dice
12	ounces skinless, wild striped bass fillets, cut into 1-inch-thick pieces

This satisfying seafood dish is based on the classic Manhattan clam chowder—a tomato broth, redolent of garlic and thyme, to which potatoes and clams are added—but with one significant modification: Wild striped bass, cut into chunks and added to the broth during the final minutes of cooking, makes this a substantial dish that can, without a doubt, stand on its own for lunch or dinner.

Appropriately enough, it was inspired one July afternoon after my daughters, Olympia and Victoria, went clamming for the first time on Long Island. Armed with a shellfish permit and the necessary equipment from a local bait shop, their first foray into Napeague Bay brought in close to 80 clams in just 90 minutes. To put this abundance to use,

Helen and I began with the obvious and decided to make chowder for dinner that night. But later that morning, our next-door neighbor, returning from a chartered fishing expedition off Montauk, swung by with a freshly caught bass, presenting it to us as a surprise gift.

Soon enough, inspiration struck, and this "Montauk clam chowder" has become a summer staple at our home—one you can adapt freely to include the most appealing offering from the fish store on any given day. (See Variations for some ideal substitutions.)

WHAT TO DRINK: Serve this soup with an Oregon Pinot Gris or a Chablis.

Coarse salt and freshly ground white pepper to taste
Chopped fresh flat-leaf parsley for garnish

In a large stockpot, heat the oil over medium heat and cook the bacon until it is lightly browned and the fat is rendered. Stir in the onion, celery, and fennel, and sauté for about 5 minutes, until the onion is translucent. Add the garlic and cook about 2 minutes longer. Add the tomatoes and their juice, the reserved clam broth, thyme, and cayenne. Bring to a boil over high heat. Reduce the heat, cover, and simmer for about 20 minutes.

Meanwhile, cook the potatoes in lightly salted boiling water for about 8 minutes, until just tender. Drain and spread them on a plate to cool. Set aside.

Add the bass to the soup and poach it gently for 6 to 8 minutes, until the fish is just cooked through and opaque. Just before serving, add the reserved clam meat and the potatoes. Cook until just heated through. Season with salt and pepper, and serve it garnished with parsley.

VARIATIONS: Firm-fleshed fish like monkfish, red snapper, wolffish, and swordfish all make fine substitutions for the wild striped bass.

FLAVOR BUILDING: Combine some mussels with the clams to add another flavor to the pot.

THINKING AHEAD: The entire dish can be prepared several hours in advance. Reserve the components separately.

4	1¹/₄-pound live lobsters
1	tablespoon extra-virgin olive oil
1	large onion, sliced
3	whole heads garlic, halved
5	sprigs fresh thyme
2	bay leaves
2	tablespoons tomato paste
1¹/₄	cups dry red wine
2	28-ounce cans whole plum tomatoes, with their juice
¹/₂	teaspoon crushed red pepper flakes
1¹/₂	teaspoons black peppercorns
	Coarse salt and freshly ground white pepper to taste
	Cayenne pepper to taste

Using a large stockpot, bring salted water to a boil over high heat. Add the lobsters and cover the pot. Return to the boil and cook for about 6 minutes. Lift the lobsters from the pot with tongs and set them aside to drain and cool. The lobsters will not be fully cooked at this point. When cool enough to handle, crack the shells and remove the meat. Work over a bowl to catch the juices and set aside. Reserve the shells. Cut the meat into ¹/₂-inch-thick pieces. Transfer the meat to a clean bowl, cover, and refrigerate. Using a heavy knife, chop the lobster shells into coarse pieces.

In a stockpot, heat the oil over medium-high heat and cook the onion, stirring, for about 8 minutes, until softened but not colored. Add the garlic and cook about 4 minutes longer, stirring to prevent burning. Add the thyme and bay leaves, tomato paste, and chopped lobster shells. Cook, stirring often, for about 8 minutes. Add the wine and bring to a boil. Boil for about 5 minutes and add the reserved juice from the lobster, the tomatoes and their juice, red pepper flakes, and peppercorns. Bring to a boil, reduce the heat, and simmer for about 40 minutes, until richly flavored. Remove from the heat and set aside to cool for about 15 minutes.

Strain the sauce through a colander set over a bowl. Discard the large solids in the colander. Strain the sauce again through a mesh sieve into a saucepan, using a large spoon to press against the solids to extract as much liquid and flavor as possible. Season with salt, pepper, and cayenne.

Once in a while, the desire to re-create a memorable flavor can turn even the most reserved of chefs into a mad scientist.

That's what happened to me with this recipe, as I became consumed with re-creating and recording the steps required to make a haunting lobster and red wine sauce I had enjoyed in East Hampton one summer Saturday. The embarrassing irony is that I first enjoyed a version of this recipe in my own kitchen when an improvised dinner for my family turned out better than expected. Having neglected to pay sufficient attention to the measurements and timing that produced the sauce, it took several attempts to re-create it for this book. The key to its full dimension and body is the butter whisked in at the end.

(continued)

ASSEMBLY

- 1¹/₄ cups fresh shelled peas
- 8 tablespoons unsalted butter, cut into pieces
- Coarse salt and freshly ground white pepper to taste
- 1¹/₂ pounds dry angel hair pasta
- 1¹/₂ cups loosely packed pea shoots or watercress leaves
- 1 tablespoon finely chopped fresh flat-leaf parsley

In a small saucepan of boiling salted water, cook the peas over high heat for about 2 minutes. Drain and rinse them under cold water to set the color. Set aside.

Reheat the sauce over medium heat, if necessary. Reduce the heat to low and whisk in the butter, a piece at a time, to enrich and thicken the sauce. Add the reserved lobster meat and gently warm for about 4 minutes. Taste and season with salt and pepper, if necessary.

Meanwhile, bring a large pot of salted water to a boil over high heat and cook the pasta for 6 to 8 minutes, stirring occasionally, until al dente. Drain and divide the pasta among 6 individual bowls or transfer it to a large, warm serving bowl.

Toss the pasta with the peas and pea shoots, and season it with pepper. Spoon the sauce over the pasta, distribute the lobster meat equally among the bowls, garnish with the parsley, and serve.

WHAT TO DRINK: Since this recipe only calls for little more than a cup of red wine, select one of your favorites and drink the remaining wine with the pasta.

VARIATION: Although it will yield a very different effect, 1 cup lightly packed arugula can be substituted for the pea shoots.

Grilled Wild Striped Bass with Grilled Fennel, Tomatoes, and Picholine Olives

MAKES 4 SERVINGS

I recommend that you serve this stunning dish on a platter for a dramatic effect at the table. The Tomato and Picholine Olive Vinaigrette is the perfect foil for the sturdy fennel and the crisp-skinned bass.

TOMATO AND PICHOLINE OLIVE VINAIGRETTE

- 1 cup extra-virgin olive oil
- 1/2 cup peeled, seeded, diced tomatoes (1/4-inch dice)
- 1/3 cup pitted, halved picholine olives
- 2 tablespoons aged sherry vinegar
- 1 tablespoon minced shallot
- 1/2 teaspoon minced garlic
  Coarse salt and freshly ground white pepper to taste

In a bowl, combine the oil, tomatoes, olives, vinegar, shallot, and garlic. Season with salt and pepper.

GRILLED FENNEL

- 2 medium bulbs fennel, trimmed
- 2 tablespoons extra-virgin olive oil
  Coarse salt and freshly ground white pepper to taste

Build a charcoal fire in a grill and let the coals burn until covered with white ash. Spread them out in the grill. Lightly oil the grill grate.

Using a chef's knife, cut the fennel bulbs in half lengthwise. Slice each half lengthwise into 1/4-inch-thick slices. Keep each slice attached at the root end. Brush the fennel with olive oil and season it with salt and pepper.

Grill the fennel pieces for about 5 minutes on each side, or until they are softened and take on a pleasant, smoky flavor. Each side should have nice grill marks, as well. Remove and set them aside, covered to keep warm.

Clean and oil the grill grate again before cooking the bass fillets for assembly.

ASSEMBLY

- 4 6- to 7-ounce striped bass fillets
- 2 tablespoons canola oil
  Coarse salt and freshly ground white pepper to taste
- 2 tablespoons minced chives

Brush the fillets with oil and season them with salt and pepper. Grill the fish on a clean, oiled grill grate for about 4 minutes, then turn and cook it about 2 minutes longer, or until the fish is just done and barely opaque in the center.

Stack the grilled fennel on 4 individual plates or a serving platter. Top the fennel with a grilled bass fillet. Whisk the chives into the vinaigrette and spoon over and around the fish.

VARIATION: Snapper can be substituted for the bass.

Grilled Chicken Marinated in Cumin, Lemon, and Garlic

MAKES 4 SERVINGS

This Middle Eastern chicken recipe employs one of my favorite techniques for a marinade—making a paste of puréed vegetables. In this case, onion and garlic are combined in a food processor and the mixture is liquefied with oil. Toasted and ground coriander seeds, cumin, and cinnamon are added, creating a highly seasoned paste that is used to coat the chicken pieces. To ensure an intense penetration of flavors, the chicken is marinated overnight.

The following day, the excess marinade is scraped off, and the chicken is seasoned and grilled over charcoal. The result is a wonderful dialogue between the fresh acidity of the lemon, the smokiness of the grill, and the fragrant spices—a sublime contrast that welcomes the company of any number of grilled vegetables. (See Variations.)

This dish also provides delicious leftovers and will travel well for a picnic.

THINKING AHEAD: Ideally, the chicken should be marinated overnight.

1¹/₂	tablespoons cracked white peppercorns
2	teaspoons coarsely ground cumin
1	teaspoon coarsely cracked coriander seeds
¹/₂	teaspoon ground cinnamon
1	cup chopped onion
¹/₄	cup fresh lemon juice
¹/₄	cup canola oil
4	tablespoons chopped fresh flat-leaf parsley
2	tablespoons grated lemon zest
12	cloves garlic, peeled, mashed to a paste, and sprinkled with coarse salt
2	3-pound free-range chickens, quartered
	Coarse salt to taste

In a sauté pan, combine the peppercorns, cumin, coriander seeds, and cinnamon; toast the spices, shaking the pan gently, over medium heat for about 1 minute, until fragrant. Take care not to burn them. Transfer them to a food processor or spice grinder and pulse to blend.

In a stainless-steel mixing bowl, combine the onion, lemon juice, canola oil, parsley, lemon zest, and garlic. Season the chicken with the ground spices, then add the chicken pieces to the bowl with the marinade. Mix well. Put the chicken in a dish, cover, and refrigerate for at least 8 hours.

Build a charcoal fire in a grill and let the coals burn until covered with white ash. Spread them out in the grill. Lightly oil the grill grate.

Lift the chicken from the dish and scrape off the excess marinade. Season the chicken with salt, and grill it, turning the pieces several times, for 20 to 25 minutes, or until the chicken is cooked through and the thigh juices run clear when pricked with a small, sharp knife.

WHAT TO DRINK: Serve this dish with a high-quality microbrew, preferably an amber lager.

VARIATIONS: Serve the chicken with grilled eggplant or squash, and/or with spinach, fava beans, or couscous.

4   12-ounce rib-eye steaks, each about $1^1/4$ inches thick
3   tablespoons coarsely cracked black peppercorns
6   tablespoons extra-virgin olive oil
3   tablespoons aged red wine vinegar
2   tablespoons chopped fresh oregano, or 1 tablespoon dried oregano
1   tablespoon chopped fresh rosemary
3   cloves garlic, peeled and finely minced
     Coarse salt to taste

Season the steaks on both sides with the peppercorns, pressing them into the meat with your fingertips. Transfer the steaks to a shallow dish.

In a small bowl, combine the olive oil, vinegar, oregano, rosemary, and garlic. Stir well and pour the mixture over the steaks. Turn the steaks to coat both sides, cover, and marinate at room temperature for 30 minutes, or in the refrigerator for up to 2 hours. Remove from the refrigerator about 15 minutes before grilling.

Build a charcoal fire in a grill and let the coals burn until covered with white ash. Spread them out in the grill. Lightly oil the grill grate.

Lift the steaks from the marinade, reserving the marinade. Season both sides of the steaks with salt and grill them for about 4 minutes on each side for rare; 5 minutes on each side for medium-rare. During the first few minutes of grilling, baste the steaks with the marinade. Let the steaks rest for about 5 minutes before carving them into thick slices.

FLAVOR BUILDING: Serve this dish with Salad of Local Wax Beans, Shell Beans, and Mint (page 57) or Grilled Corn and Potatoes (page 74).

Grilled Marinated Rib-Eye Steak

MAKES 4 SERVINGS

We all have things we don't understand about our parents. I, for example, have no idea what in the world my father thought he was doing when he made the dish that inspired this recipe.

One weekend each July, my entire extended family would descend on our house on Crystal Beach. The central event was an Italian-American feast for which everyone would bring a dish.

My father would light up the charcoal, and while the coals were burning down, he mixed olive oil, red wine vinegar, salt, pepper, garlic salt (as opposed to fresh garlic), and dried oregano. But instead of dressing the salad with this, he marinated the steaks in it for 20 minutes, and then—while they were grilling—he basted them every so often with the remaining marinade.

I now understand that there are cultural precedents in cooking for this technique. Building on this encouraging observation, I've adjusted the recipe, using a great deal of fresh garlic, fresh oregano, black peppercorns, and a high-quality olive oil.

Berries

Berries are the ultimate summer fruit. During July, I can't get enough of our locally grown berries, which I pick up from roadside farm stands whenever possible. I find myself celebrating the days of July with berries, eating them for breakfast with a little sugar and cream, and ending each day with berry tarts and ice cream.

Berries are highly perishable and delicate, susceptible to bruising, mold, and over-ripening. When shopping for them, seek out the ones that have a healthy, robust appearance, a vibrant color, and no softness or mold. This last consideration is very important; if the berries are sold in cartons, check to be sure there are no stains on the box, which probably indicates that a berry has spoiled within. Look for mold, especially in the case of raspberries and blackberries, because even a small amount can impact the entire box.

PRESERVING:
Strawberry Preserves

MAKES 4¹/₂ TO 5 CUPS

During the summer, my wife and I spend most of our weekends in East Hampton, Long Island. Out in the country, there are strawberry farms marked with "U-Pick" signs that invite you to gather your own. Our daughters have a blast running through the fields picking berries, so much so that we usually end up with a surplus. To keep these incredible berries from going to waste, we make a lot of preserves and jam in July. Here's the recipe we use. It varies the traditional formula of equal parts fruit and sugar because I find that this yields an excessively sweet preserve.

5	pints ripe strawberries
1¹/₂	cups sugar
	Grated zest of ¹/₂ lemon (approximately ¹/₂ teaspoon)
1	tablespoon lemon juice

Gently wash the berries by dropping them into a sink full of cold water. Remove them by handfuls to a large colander and drain well. Using a small sharp paring knife, cut away the green tops. Halve the berries lengthwise and set them aside. In a large heavy-bottomed stainless-steel pot, combine the sugar and half the berries. Crush the fruit lightly with the back of a spoon to release some juice. Place the pan over low heat and stir occasionally until the sugar melts, approximately 5 minutes. Raise the heat to high and boil rapidly, stirring constantly for 12 to 15 minutes. Add the remaining berries, lower the heat and cook until the added berries have softened, approximately 15 minutes more. Remove the preserves from the heat and stir in the lemon zest and juice. Allow to cool slightly. Spoon the hot preserves into hot, sterilized canning jars (see note page 81), leaving about ¹/₄ inch of headroom. Screw on the lids. Let cool completely, and then store in a cool, dry place. The jars should not touch each other during cooling. Refrigerate after opening.

At home, take a moment to examine freshly purchased berries by carefully pouring them out and discarding any imperfect ones. Berries should be refrigerated between sheets of paper towels to keep moisture from collecting. For this same reason, they should not be washed before storage but, rather, cleaned in a colander under a gentle stream of running water just prior to serving. Gingerly pat them dry after rinsing.

There are too many varieties of berries to examine them all in detail here, but following are some observations on those used in this chapter:

Strawberries
The slightly grainy texture on the skin of this red heart-shaped fruit is actually the seeds, which are displayed on its exterior. Strawberries are best eaten fresh, but they will last about 48 hours in the refrigerator provided they are not overripe. As fellow tennis fans probably know from the annual coverage of "Breakfast at Wimbledon," strawberries have a great affinity for sugar and cream. I also enjoy making blended strawberry cocktails using hulled, frozen strawberries in place of ice.

When I was a kid, my mother would slice strawberries, sprinkle them with sugar, and refrigerate them, which produced a sweet, natural juice. While the addition of sugar will hold strawberries fresher longer, they should generally be eaten within one hour of preparation.

When I was cooking in France, I was introduced to the dainty little *fraises des bois*—small, dark red strawberries that I couldn't get enough of. Among their numerous charms is the fact that they do not need to be hulled. Unfortunately, *fraises des bois* are all but nonexistent in the United States. At the Gotham, we purchase Tri-star berries, a hybrid of *fraises des bois,* which do a noble job of approximating the qualities of the European fruit.

Raspberries
Raspberries actually have two seasons, one that begins in the late spring and runs through July, and another, briefer one in late summer. They are sweet and slightly acidic, and generally boast an attractive dark red color, although yellow and dark ruby varieties are not uncommon. Fresh raspberries should be firm and plump, but even the most superior specimens won't keep for long. Like strawberries, they are delicious with sugar or cream. They're also wonderful in any number of desserts, as well as jams, compotes, jellies, liqueurs, and brandy.

Blueberries

Blueberries' "bloom," a phantomlike coating, preserves their moisture and allows them to keep longer than other berries. Blueberries are perhaps the quintessential American berry, turning up in such national favorites as blueberry muffins and blueberry pancakes. I also love blueberry jam and am pleased to share my favorite recipe for it.

PRESERVING:
Helen Chardack's Blueberry Jam

MAKES THREE 8-OUNCE JARS

6	cups fresh blueberries
1¹/₂	cups sugar, or more to taste
	Juice of ¹/₂ lemon, or more to taste

In a large saucepan, bring the blueberries, sugar, and lemon juice to a boil over high heat. Crush the berries lightly to release their juices. Taste and adjust the sugar and lemon juice. Skim any foam from the surface. Return to a boil and cook for about 4 minutes.

Remove from the heat and perform a "gel test" by spooning a little of the blueberry mixture into a small cup. Cool in the refrigerator for 5 to 10 minutes, then check for consistency. If the jam does not hold together when cold, or if it looks too thin, return the pan to the heat and boil for 2 to 3 minutes longer.

Transfer to a dish to cool. Cover, refrigerate, and serve within a week.

For longer storage, pack the hot jam into sterilized canning jars (see note page 81), leaving about ¹/₄ inch of headroom. Screw on the lids. Let cool completely, and then store in a cool, dry place. The jars should not touch each other during cooling. Refrigerate after opening.

CAKE

6	tablespoons all-purpose flour
5	tablespoons almond flour
4	large egg whites
$3/4$	cup sugar

Preheat the oven to 350°F.

Sift the flours together.

In the bowl of an electric mixer, using the whip attachment, whip the egg whites on high speed for about 40 seconds until foamy. Add the sugar, a tablespoon at a time, beating for a few seconds after each addition. Whip until the egg whites form soft peaks.

Fold the flour into the meringue, using a rubber spatula and taking care not to overmix and deflate the egg whites.

Spoon the batter into 6 nonstick individual brioche molds to fill each one $3/4$ full. Set the molds in the center of the oven and bake for about 20 minutes or until the tops are lightly browned and the sides begin to pull away from the molds. Let the cakes cool on a wire rack. When completely cool, run a small knife around the edges of the molds, taking care not to tear the cakes. Invert the molds and let the cakes unmold. Turn them right side up.

SAUCE

4	ripe nectarines, peeled, pitted, and chopped
$1/2$	cup water
1	teaspoon fresh lemon juice
	Sugar to taste

In a saucepan, combine the nectarines, water, and lemon juice. Bring to a boil over high heat. Reduce the heat and simmer for 10 to 15 minutes, until slightly thickened. Cool slightly.

Transfer the sauce to a blender or a food processor fitted with a metal blade and purée until smooth. Strain through a mesh sieve into a bowl. Stir in the sugar until pleasingly sweet. The amount of the sugar will depend on the sweetness of the nectarines.

ASSEMBLY

2	ripe nectarines, peeled, pitted, and sliced into thin wedges
1	pint raspberries
	Confectioners' sugar, for garnish

White Angel Food Cake with Raspberries and Nectarines

MAKES 6 SERVINGS

This is my variation on one of the desserts my godmother made for my birthday when I was growing up. The nectarine sauce takes a traditional white cake in an unexpected direction.

Fan the nectarine slices on the sides of 6 dessert plates. Spoon the sauce on the plate next to the nectarines. Set the angel food cakes on the plates and garnish with the raspberries and confectioners' sugar.

PASTRY DOUGH

2	cups all-purpose flour
1/2	teaspoon salt
1 1/2	cups unsalted butter, cut into pieces and chilled
	About 1/2 cup heavy cream, chilled

In the bowl of a food processor fitted with the metal blade, combine the flour and salt. Add about half (3/4 cup) of the butter and process until well combined. With the motor running, add the remaining butter and pulse only until it forms pea-sized pieces. Turn off the motor and sprinkle the dough with a few tablespoons of cream, tossing it with a fork until it is just lightly mixed and starts to pull together. Add more cream as necessary. (This is easier to do if you remove the metal blade or transfer the mixture to another bowl.)

Spread 2 sheets of plastic wrap side by side on the countertop, overlapping slightly lengthwise, forming one sheet about 20 inches square. Scrape the dough onto the center of the plastic wrap. Fold the sides of the plastic wrap over the dough and press it into a flat disk. Refrigerate for at least 20 minutes before proceeding.

CRISP TOPPING

1/2	cup all-purpose flour
1/2	cup sugar
1/4	cup crushed amaretti, biscotti, or granola
1/2	teaspoon baking powder
1	large egg yolk
1/4	cup unsalted butter, melted and cooled

In a bowl, whisk together the flour, sugar, crushed amaretti, and baking powder.

Add the egg yolk to the melted butter and whisk to mix. Add the egg mixture to the flour and mix with a fork until combined but crumbly. Set aside.

ASSEMBLY

4	pints fresh blueberries
1/4	cup sugar
1	teaspoon grated lemon zest
2 to 3	tablespoons heavy cream, for brushing
	Sweetened Mascarpone (page 120)

Blueberry Croustade with Sweetened Mascarpone

MAKES 6 TO 8 SERVINGS

In this relatively free-form, rustic pastry, the dough frames the fruit, which is finished with a crumb topping. The recipe can easily be adapted to use other berries.

Preheat the oven to 425°F. Line a baking sheet with parchment paper. Remove the pastry disk from the refrigerator and set it on the countertop. Unfold the plastic and smooth it on the countertop so that the disk is sitting on it. Spread a fresh sheet of plastic over the dough, using the overlapping technique described above. Roll the dough out between the plastic into a disk about 16 to 18 inches in diameter and $^{1}/_{4}$ inch thick. Slide it with the plastic wrap onto the prepared baking sheet and refrigerate it for at least 30 minutes, or until firm. Peel off the bottom and top sheets of plastic wrap and let the dough come up to room temperature to prevent it from cracking when folded.

Spoon the blueberries into the center of the pastry, spreading them out but leaving a generous border all around. Sprinkle the berries with about 3 tablespoons of the sugar and all the lemon zest.

Fold the edges of the dough over and around the berries to frame them but not to cover them completely. Crumble the topping over the berries. Brush the pastry lightly with a little cream. Sprinkle the remaining tablespoon of sugar over the edge of the pastry.

Bake the crustade in the bottom third of the preheated oven for about 45 minutes, or until the crust is browned and the blueberries are swollen but not bursting. Check the crustade after 20 minutes. If the topping is browned and crisp, float a piece of aluminum foil over it and reduce the oven temperature to 375°F. Keep a close watch on the crustade during the final 20 to 25 minutes of baking.

NOTE: The mascarpone can be flavored with a splash of kirsch, rum, or vanilla extract.

Remove the crustade from the oven and cool it for at least 40 minutes, sitting on the baking sheet. Cut it into wedges and serve with sweetened mascarpone.

Sweetened Mascarpone

MAKES ABOUT 1 $^{1}/_{2}$ CUPS

$^{1}/_{2}$ cup heavy cream
2   tablespoons sugar
1   cup mascarpone cheese

In a small mixing bowl, using an electric mixer or wire whisk, whisk the cream and sugar until soft peaks form. With a spatula, gently fold the mascarpone into the whipped cream. Use immediately; the cheese does not hold up for very long.

Ice Cream

The common foundation of almost any ice cream is a base, or custard, that is flavored with extracts, fruits, or other ingredients. There are countless variations in the recipe for custard, but two principal factors affect the richness or butterfat content: the number of egg yolks and the amount of cream. In certain classic French cookbooks, there are recipes with quantities of egg yolks that would horrify most Americans, but the ice cream they produce is rich beyond your wildest dreams.

Perhaps it's because the French produce such fantastic ice creams that they have created so many classic sundaes (*coupes glacées*) through the ages. Until I began studying food, I had always assumed that sundaes were an American invention; who else could have conceived such indulgent dessert fantasies as the banana split or the hot fudge sundae? But there are dozens of French sundaes—many with formal-sounding names like Belle Hélène—that are every bit as irresistible and satisfying as their American counterparts.

When I was a kid, making ice cream seemed like a big production, one that called for such antiquated and unfamiliar equipment as a wooden bucket set into a cylinder that was fitted with a hand crank and rotated in a bed of ice and rock salt. But today, charming little home machines enable anyone to make ice cream, and many of them produce very respectable results. Some feature a freezing unit and electric dasher, while others have an actual cooling unit that is kept in the freezer until the moment of preparation.

I think of making ice cream at home as an irresistible proposition, especially for people who have children. Accordingly, I've included several recipes for ice cream in this book. But I hasten to add that there are numerous premium brands on the market these days, and while they are expensive, I firmly believe they are well worth it. If you're not inclined to make your own ice cream, by all means purchase one for use in any dish that calls for ice cream. (One tip: If your freezer turns your ice cream hard as a rock, do not defrost it in a microwave or on the countertop; instead, leave the ice cream in the refrigerator for ten minutes to attain the perfect consistency before serving.)

At the Gotham, our machine runs constantly as we make five to eight flavors of ice cream every day. We also make chocolate and fruit sorbets, although sorbet aficionados will no doubt notice that there are only two in this book. This is intentional. Because fruit sorbets derive much of their sweetness from the sugar in the fruit itself, a certain instinct and level of experience are required to adjust for the variance that occurs from one variety of fruit to another, or even within one variety as it goes through its annual changes.

There's also a bit of artistry involved in making sorbet soft and creamy. At the Gotham, we use inverted sugar (a heavy syrup made from equal parts fructose and sucrose) rather than granulated to keep ice crystals from forming in the sorbet, and we churn our sorbets twice daily, just before lunch and just before dinner, to ensure the proper consistency when they are served. (Some four-star restaurants have even begun using high-tech machines that churn sorbets to order.) Having said all of this, there are plenty of sorbet recipes out there to try. If you choose to pursue them, I'd invest in a sugar-density meter, a device that floats in the sorbet liquid and tells you the sugar level. For most sorbets, a reading of 12 to 14 degrees is optimal.

THINKING AHEAD: You can prepare the mixture as many as 2 days in advance and refrigerate it.

2 cups heavy cream
2 cups milk
1 cup sugar
14 large egg yolks
4 pints strawberries, hulled and roughly chopped

In a large saucepan, combine the cream, milk, and $1/2$ cup of sugar. Bring to a simmer over low heat, stirring occasionally to help the sugar dissolve.

In a bowl, whisk the egg yolks with the remaining sugar. Measure about 1 cup of the hot cream mixture into the beaten egg yolks, whisking to mix. Add this mixture to the saucepan, whisking well to combine. Cook over low heat for 6 to 7 minutes, stirring constantly until the custard is thick enough to lightly coat the back of a wooden spoon. Strain the custard through a mesh sieve into a stainless-steel bowl.

Set the bowl in a larger bowl filled with ice and water, and let it stand for about 40 minutes, stirring occasionally, until chilled.

In a food processor fitted with a metal blade, purée the strawberries until smooth. Strain the purée through a mesh sieve into a bowl, pressing against the solids to extract as much liquid as possible. You should have about 2 cups of purée. Stir the purée into the custard.

Pour the custard into the container of an ice-cream machine and freeze according to the manufacturer's directions. Transfer to a covered container and freeze for at least 4 hours or overnight, until firm.

VARIATION: For chunky strawberry ice cream, sauté an additional 2 pints of hulled and quartered strawberries with 1 cup of sugar over low heat until soft. Set aside to cool and then refrigerate or chill in an ice-water bath. Fold the berries into the custard just before transferring it to the ice-cream machine.

Strawberry
Ice Cream
MAKES ABOUT 2 QUARTS

Most people picture candle-covered cakes when they reminisce about childhood birthdays, but my mind races to the memory of freshly churned strawberry ice cream eaten right out of the bucket. In the suburb where I grew up, Aunt Teresa and Uncle Russell, who also happened to be my godparents and our next-door neighbors, made ice cream the old-fashioned way. They owned a hand-crank machine in which an old wooden bucket was rotated raspingly within a cylinder full of rock salt and ice. Strawberry ice cream was my favorite frozen treat, and Aunt Teresa prepared it for my birthday on several occasions, allowing me to attack the machine with a spoon and eat to my heart's content.

Most ice-cream recipes, including mine, suggest that you allow the finished product to harden in the freezer for several hours after making it. But there's nothing wrong with a family, or a group of friends, eating it out of the maker—it's softer and less formed than what we're used to, but the flavors are so fresh, and the cream so eager to melt in your mouth, that it's a very sensuous and satisfying experience.

Ginger-Berry Lemonade

**MAKES FOURTEEN 8-OUNCE SERVINGS;
ABOUT 3 1/2 QUARTS**

Lemonade is one of those things—like ice cream and popsicles—that appeals to the child in everyone. A few years ago, on a particularly hot day in New York City, I found myself craving a lemonade while working at the Gotham, so I set about designing this adult version. The secret of its success is the ginger syrup; it provides a buoyancy that keeps the mixture from becoming watery, and a backdrop that's as flavorful and textured as the berries themselves.

8	cups water
3	cups sugar
1 1/4	cups coarsely chopped fresh ginger
1	pint fresh raspberries
4	cups fresh lemon juice (about 22 lemons)
	Lemon slices, for garnish
	Fresh mint sprigs, for garnish

In a large saucepan, combine the water, sugar, and ginger, and bring to a boil over high heat. Boil for about 15 minutes, stirring occasionally, until the sugar dissolves and the liquid is hot and aromatic. Cool for about 15 minutes and then strain the liquid. Discard the solids and let the liquid cool completely. Refrigerate it for at least 2 hours until well chilled.

Reserve about a third of the raspberries to use for garnish. Put the remaining berries in a blender or the bowl of a food processor fitted with a metal blade. Process until smooth. Strain the purée through a mesh sieve, pressing on the berries to extract as much liquid as possible.

In a large bowl, combine the ginger-flavored water, the strained raspberries, and the lemon juice. Taste and add water, if necessary. Strain into a large pitcher and serve over ice, garnished with the reserved raspberries, lemon slices, and mint sprigs.

Summer Dinner Party

Both these menus can be served indoors or out. In both cases, the main course is prepared on the grill.

CANAPÉ

GRILLED POTATO, ROQUEFORT CHEESE, RED ONION,
AND SMOKED BACON SANDWICHES **(page 143)**

MENU 1

PASTA WITH SUMMER VEGETABLES AND
PECORINO ROMANO **(page 145)**

DUCK WITH ROASTED PEACHES AND BABY TURNIPS **(page 147)**

WHITE ANGEL FOOD CAKE WITH RASPBERRIES
AND NECTARINES **(page 117)**

MENU 2

MONTAUK CHOWDER WITH CLAMS, WILD STRIPED BASS, TOMATOES,
AND YELLOW FINN POTATOES **(page 99)**

GRILLED, MARINATED RIB-EYE STEAK **(page 113)**

BLACKBERRY AND PEACH COBBLER **(page 157)**

Tuna Carpaccio with Mizuna and Yuzu Dressing

Baba Ghanoush

Tomatoes

Heirloom Tomato Salad with Shaved Fennel and Gorgonzola

Two *Bruschettas:*

Bruschetta of Cherry Tomatoes, Fava Beans, and Pecorino Toscano

Grilled Tomato *Bruschetta* with Lemon Thyme

Chilled Tomato Soup with Basil and Goat Cheese Croutons

Grilled Potato, Roquefort Cheese, Red Onion, and Smoked Bacon Sandwiches

Pasta with Summer Vegetables and Pecorino Romano

Duck with Roasted Peaches and Baby Turnips

Grilled Squab with Grilled Radicchio, Endive, and Black Mission Figs

Grilled Tenderloin of Beef with Corn, Chanterelles, and Chervil

Blackberry and Peach Cobbler

Raspberry Tart

Mediterranean Dinner Party

AUGUST

SEIZE THE DAY

August is like a gentle, extended version of that moment in life when you become aware of your own mortality. As soon as this month arrives, fall suddenly seems to be looming on the horizon, reminding us of everything we love about summer, and of how little time we have left to enjoy it. You might say that August is the time when the mortality of the year registers for the first time.

There are two ways to respond to this realization. One is to slip into a deepening depression over the finite nature of all good things. The other, far more appealing approach—in August, as in life—is to make the most of every day, to leave the air conditioning behind for the sun-dappled outdoors, and to savor every last grain of sand in summer's hourglass.

One of the ways my family and I seize the precious days of August is by spending as much time as we can outside. We spend most of our extended weekends outdoors—from breakfast in the garden to dinner beside the grill. When we go to the beach, it becomes an all-day affair, with an ice chest full of home-cooked foods to last until sunset. We do almost as much entertaining in August as we do during the winter holidays, albeit in a much more casual manner. And potluck dinners, often coordinated on the spur of the moment, become a part of the everyday fabric of the month.

If you have children, you probably also tend to eat lighter and later as their days fill up with summer activities and they try to remain outside as long as possible.

To facilitate the flexibility August inspires, this chapter features a number of recipes that can be prepared with a minimum of planning. The Grilled Potato, Roquefort Cheese, Red Onion, and Smoked Bacon Sandwiches (page 143), for example, may become a favorite last-minute lunch or the contribution that your friends insist you bring to every potluck gathering. And the Tuna Carpaccio with Mizuna and Yuzu Dressing (page 130) makes a fantastic main-course salad as well as an appetizing first course.

Sophisticated grilled dishes are also provided, including Duck with Roasted Peaches and Baby Turnips (page 147), Grilled Squab with Grilled Radicchio, Endive, and Black Mission Figs (page 154), and Grilled Tenderloin of Beef with Corn, Chanterelles, and Chervil (page 151).

August marks the arrival of some fabulous seasonal vegetables. Tomatoes, in every conceivable shape and size, are so intense and dependable in August that many people have written entire books on how to make the most of them. While I would love to do the same, for the moment I've put down some notes in an essay on tomatoes. There's also a range of recipes for them here, including an Heirloom Tomato Salad with Shaved Fennel and Gorgonzola (page 138), Chilled Tomato Soup with Basil and Goat Cheese Croutons (page 141), and Two *Bruschettas* (page 135).

Eggplant, too, is at its best in August and is put to use here in the Pasta with Summer Vegetables and Pecorino Romano (page 145) and a traditional Arabic Baba Ghanoush (page 131).

Finally, two desserts, Blackberry and Peach Cobbler (page 157) and Raspberry Tart (page 159), promise to end any meal with a sweet simplicity that strikes just the right final chord for these precious, waning days of summer.

Tuna Carpaccio

with Mizuna and Yuzu Dressing

MAKES 4 SERVINGS

The key to this salad's success is the vibrant flavor of the dressing, which owes a lot to the inclusion of yuzu juice. (Look for this juice, bottled, in Japanese markets, where you might also find fresh yuzu fruit.) In the event that you cannot obtain yuzu juice, an alternate dressing is provided, using sesame seeds, lime, and orange juice to approximate its flavors.

This presentation differs from that of the traditional carpaccio in that the tuna is sliced thin and fanned out on the plate rather than covering it in a single, unified layer.

YUZU DRESSING

2	tablespoons canola oil
2	tablespoons tamarind or regular soy sauce
2	tablespoons yuzu juice
2	teaspoons Ginger Juice (page 65)
$1/4$	teaspoon minced garlic
$1/4$	teaspoon cayenne pepper

In a small bowl, mix together all the ingredients.

CARPACCIO AND ASSEMBLY

12	ounces sushi-quality yellowfin tuna, chilled
	Coarse salt and freshly ground white pepper to taste
4	scallions, white parts only, thinly sliced
2	tablespoons finely chopped cilantro
3	tablespoons grape-seed or canola oil
1	tablespoon fresh lemon juice
4	cups loosely packed mizuna or other salad greens

On an impeccably clean cutting board and using a sharp thin-bladed knife, slice the tuna in half and then cut these pieces into very thin slices, each only 2 to 3 inches long. Fan the tuna at the bottoms of 4 chilled salad plates.

Season the tuna lightly with salt and pepper, and scatter the scallions and cilantro over it. Drizzle $1^1/2$ tablespoons of either the yuzu or the citrus-ginger dressing (see sidebar) over each serving.

In a small bowl, whisk together the oil and lemon juice. Season the mixture with salt and pepper, and toss it with the salad greens. Divide the greens equally among the plates, arranging them so that they are above the fans of tuna. Serve immediately.

ALTERNATE DRESSING:

Citrus-Ginger Dressing

2	tablespoons canola oil
1	tablespoon tamarind or regular soy sauce
1	tablespoon fresh lime juice
1	tablespoon fresh orange juice
1	tablespoon sesame seeds
2	teaspoons Ginger Juice (page 65)
1	teaspoon sesame oil
1	teaspoon mirin (optional)
$1/4$	teaspoon minced garlic

In a small bowl, mix together all the ingredients.

1   1½-pound eggplant
¼   cup extra-virgin olive oil, plus more for drizzling
3   tablespoons fresh lemon juice, or to taste
2   tablespoons tahini
½   teaspoon minced garlic
     Coarse salt and freshly ground white pepper to taste
     Lightly toasted bread or pita bread

Char the eggplant over a gas burner turned to medium heat or under a broiler, turning it as it blackens on all sides and until the inside is soft and takes on a nice smoky flavor. This will take about 40 minutes. Use large tongs or long-handled forks to handle the eggplant. Let the eggplant cool. Peel the skin, which should pull right off.

Quarter the eggplant lengthwise and try to scoop out most of the seeds. You will have about a pound of eggplant flesh. Transfer it to the bowl of a food processor fitted with a metal blade and pulse several times to chop. Add the olive oil, lemon juice, tahini, and garlic. Process until smooth. Season with salt and pepper, and add more lemon juice, if desired. Pulse again to mix.

Spoon into a serving dish and drizzle with a little more olive oil. Serve with the toasted bread or pita.

Baba Ghanoush

MAKES 4 SERVINGS

When I started at the Gotham, one of the things on my menu was an eggplant caviar, based on a recipe I had learned to love in France, comprising charred roasted eggplant, extra-virgin olive oil, and garlic. This recipe starts in much the same way—charring eggplant over an open flame and peeling off the skin—but departs from the other in that it's puréed, resulting in a much finer texture. Lemon juice and tahini are added to round out the flavors. This is a very easy, delicious dish and makes a convenient canapé. Set it out with grilled bread to welcome summer guests to your home.

Tomatoes

We as a nation can't seem to get enough of tomatoes. They appear in many of the most popular dishes in the country, from basic pasta sauces to tomato soup, chili to salsa, used as a garnish in sandwiches and as one of the principal ingredients in almost any salad as well as the brunch-time favorite Bloody Mary.

Despite their popularity, I tend to feature tomatoes as a principal ingredient on my menu only during the late summer months. It's also during this time that I use them at home compulsively, making fresh tomato soups, sauces, and salads. In August, I make up for lost time the rest of the year by really focusing on tomatoes, featuring them in a variety of dishes that take full advantage of their intense flavor.

One of the developments that's been most pleasing to me in American agriculture over the past ten years is the focus on heirloom varieties, which in many ways is a response to the heavy genetic engineering that took place in the late 1970s in an attempt to create tomatoes that would ship without bruising. The casualty of this experiment was that much of the flavor was bred out of them. To counteract this sad phenomenon, small farms, cottages, and independent organic farmers began bringing back old varieties of heirloom tomatoes with great names like Brandywine and Zebra.

The four principal categories of tomatoes are beefsteak, plum, cherry, and medium-sized. They should be stored at room temperature (not in the refrigerator), out of direct sunlight, with the stem end up.

When tomatoes are out of season and I'm cooking a recipe that calls for them, I'll often turn to high-quality imported canned tomatoes, such as Maranzano from Italy, which are actually quite satisfactory, with a strong flavor and low salt content. Another solution in nonseasonal months is to oven-roast tomatoes into a confit that summons up their flavor.

You'll also notice that I use diced plum tomatoes as a garnish year-round. This is more of a restaurant concern than anything else, born of my cooking-school upbringing and time in France. I select the best plum tomatoes, which have a high ratio of flesh to seed. I always peel and seed tomatoes for this use, but you don't need to do this at home.

Two *Bruschettas*

In today's restaurant world, there are few dishes taken for granted as much as the *bruschetta.* Even the most humble mom-and-pop Italian eatery is likely to present an assortment as a welcome when you're seated. Classically, a *bruschetta* is a slice of grilled bread spread with a garlic paste and drizzled with olive oil. But it has been adapted in so many ways that you might see a *bruschetta* with a wide variety of toppings.

Here are two *bruschettas* that I love. They both feature grilled bread and tomatoes, but some key differences make them more distinct than this might suggest. When it came time to pick one for the book, I couldn't make up my mind. I ultimately decided that both would be welcome additions to your repertoire, and, in this tomato-haven of a month, you should have ample opportunity to make them several times.

Bruschetta of Cherry Tomatoes, Fava Beans, and Pecorino Toscano

MAKES 6 SERVINGS

This recipe grew out of my love for the foundation on which *bruschetta* is built—grilled bread, garlic, tomatoes, and extra-virgin olive oil. Looking for a way to turn the *bruschetta* into a knife-and-fork affair, I first decided to use a flavorful rosemary *ciabatta,* and spread it with an aioli. I topped this with a towering pyramid of halved red, green, yellow, orange, and striped heirloom tomatoes.

But real inspiration struck on a trip to Italy, where I sampled the time-honored dynamic duo of *Pecorino Toscano e Fagioli,* or fresh sheep's milk cheese and fava beans, and knew they were the complements I was seeking for this recipe.

The dressing is mostly extra-virgin olive oil, with just 1 tablespoon of vinegar, intended to peak the flavors and meet the expectations of acidity.

THINKING AHEAD: The tomatoes should be marinated for about an hour.

1	pound assorted heirloom cherry tomatoes of varying size and color
1/4	cup finely chopped shallot
1	clove garlic, peeled and finely minced
1	bunch purple basil (about 2 ounces)
6	tablespoons extra-virgin olive oil
2	teaspoons red wine vinegar
1	teaspoon balsamic vinegar
	Coarse salt and freshly ground white pepper

6   $^1/_2$-inch-thick slices country bread, such as rosemary *ciabatta*
$^1/_4$ cup Lemon Aioli (page 65)
$^1/_2$ cup cooked, peeled fava beans
4   ounces Pecorino Toscano cheese, crumbled

Using a sharp knife, cut the larger tomatoes in half and leave the small ones whole. Transfer them to a bowl, add the shallot and garlic, and toss gently. Remove 12 of the best-looking basil leaves from the bunch and set them aside. Finely chop the remaining basil and add it to the bowl. Add the oil and vinegars, and season with salt and pepper. Toss to mix and set aside to marinate at room temperature for 30 minutes to 1 hour.

Lightly grill or toast the bread slices. Cool slightly and spread with the aioli. Set a slice in the center of each serving plate or arrange them all on a serving platter.

Add the beans to the tomatoes, taste, and adjust the seasoning if necessary. Spoon the tomato-bean mixture on the bread and garnish the *bruschettas* with the crumbled cheese and reserved basil leaves. Spoon any remaining marinade over the *bruschetta* and serve.

VARIATIONS: I love this dish with cherry tomatoes, but any combination of cut-up ripe tomatoes will work fine. Also, other cheeses such as *ricotta salata,* crumbled Roquefort or Stilton, or Herbed Goat Cheese (page 141) can be substituted for the Pecorino Toscano.

Grilled Tomato *Bruschetta* with Lemon Thyme

MAKES 8 APPETIZER SERVINGS OR 6 MAIN-COURSE SERVINGS

This is a buffet-style *bruschetta* based on one made by my East Hampton neighbor, David Gibbons. Big red tomatoes are peeled, halved, and seeded, then marinated in extra-virgin olive oil and garlic. They are cooked on the grill and basted with the marinade, which includes the herbaceous lemon thyme. When finished, they are loaded with smoky flavor and so loose that they must be removed from the grill with a spatula. Present them on a platter, sprinkled with fresh herbs, and invite your guests to make their own *bruschettas* by serving toasted bread on the side.

TOMATOES
6   large ripe beefsteak tomatoes, peeled, halved, and seeded
$^1/_3$ cup extra-virgin olive oil
2   cloves garlic, peeled, mashed to a paste, and sprinkled with coarse salt
2   shallots, finely minced
1   teaspoon fresh lemon thyme leaves or English thyme leaves
$^1/_2$ teaspoon finely chopped fresh rosemary
Coarse salt and freshly ground white pepper to taste

In a large bowl, combine the tomatoes, olive oil, garlic, shallots, thyme, and rosemary. Season lightly with salt and generously with pepper. Toss to combine and set aside to marinate at room temperature for about 30 minutes.

ASSEMBLY

12 to 16 slices country bread, such as rosemary *ciabatta* or a baguette, about $^1/_2$ inch thick
3 to 4 tablespoons extra-virgin olive oil
Coarse salt to taste
4 large fresh basil leaves, cut into a chiffonade
1 tablespoon finely minced chives

Build a charcoal fire in a grill and let the coals burn until they are covered with white ash and the heat is about medium intensity. Spread the coals out in the grill. Lightly oil the grill grate.

Lift the tomatoes from the marinade and reserve the marinade. Place the tomatoes on the grill cut side down and grill them for 10 to 11 minutes, turning them once, until they are lightly charred, soft, and have a nice smoky flavor. During the last 5 or 6 minutes of grilling, brush the tomatoes with the reserved marinade. Using a spatula, transfer the tomatoes to a platter to cool to warm room temperature or cooler. Slice the largest tomato halves in half again or into thirds.

Meanwhile, drizzle the bread slices with olive oil. Grill the bread for about 2 minutes on each side until golden brown. Transfer it to the platter.

Season the tomatoes with salt and sprinkle them with the basil and chives. Serve from the platter, with the warm bread on the side.

VARIATIONS: Substitute basil or parsley for the lemon thyme.

FLAVOR BUILDING: Add olives, Anchovy Vinaigrette (page 97), crumbled Roquefort cheese and/or crumbled aged goat cheese to the buffet to allow for more flavor combinations.

Heirloom Tomato Salad with Shaved Fennel and Gorgonzola

MAKES 6 SERVINGS

We eat a variation of this salad at home almost every day in August, and it's a favorite at the Gotham as well. It seems especially appropriate to the last days of summer because its ease of preparation allows for flexibility. A study in the art of balance, the salad harmonizes the peppery flavor of arugula with the assertive Gorgonzola cheese, the sweetness of red onion, and the acidity of the tomato.

The trick to the success of this dish is keeping the acidity in check. The vinaigrette combines extra-virgin olive oil, red wine and balsamic vinegars, and garlic to provide just a touch of acidity that unites the dish. Depending on what type of tomatoes you're using—yellow tomatoes, for instance, are low in acidity—you may need to add some more vinegar. If, on the other hand, the vinaigrette seems too strong, thin it with a bit of tomato water.

1	small head fennel, trimmed
1/2	cup extra-virgin olive oil
1	tablespoon aged red wine vinegar
1	tablespoon aged balsamic vinegar
3	pounds assorted heirloom tomatoes of varying size and color
	Coarse salt and freshly ground white pepper to taste
1/2	cup finely chopped red onion
1	clove garlic, peeled, mashed to a paste, and sprinkled with coarse salt
2	teaspoons fresh thyme leaves
1/4	pound haricots verts, trimmed
2	tablespoons finely minced chives
2	cups loosely packed baby or regular arugula
5 1/2	ounces Gorgonzola cheese, crumbled

Slice the fennel into 1/8-inch-thick slices. Immediately put it into a bowl of ice water and refrigerate for about 1 hour, until crisped and curled. Drain just before using.

In a small bowl, whisk together the oil and vinegars.

Cut the tomatoes into wedges, slices, or halves, depending on the size and shape of the tomato. Put the tomatoes in a bowl and season them with salt and pepper. Add the onion, garlic, and thyme, and spoon the vinaigrette over the tomatoes, whisking the dressing as you pour it. Set the bowl aside to let the tomatoes marinate for about 15 minutes.

In a small saucepan of lightly salted boiling water set over high heat, blanch the haricots verts for 4 to 5 minutes, or until bright green. Drain and immediately plunge them in ice water to set the color. Drain again and set aside.

Add the chives to the tomatoes and toss gently. Lift the tomatoes and onions from the bowl with a slotted spoon, reserving the vinaigrette left in the bowl. Stack the tomatoes and onions in the centers of 6 salad plates or on a serving platter. Carefully arrange the haricots verts and fennel curls on top of the tomatoes, garnish with a bouquet of arugula, and scatter with the Gorgonzola. Spoon the remaining vinaigrette over the salad and serve immediately.

NOTE: A Japanese-style mandoline works well to slice the fennel.

VARIATIONS: Feel free to change the cheese, using a different blue (such as Danish blue or Roquefort), *ricotta salata,* or aged goat cheese.

FLAVOR BUILDING: If you have the grill fired up, grilling the onions will add a smoky-sweet dimension to the dish. If you choose to do this, slice the onions into rounds rather than chopping them.

The flavors and textures are rounded out with haricots verts and raw fennel. I recommend serving it on a platter with coarse salt on the side.

SOUP

2	tablespoons extra-virgin olive oil
2	cups coarsely chopped onions
5	cloves garlic, peeled and thinly sliced
4	pounds ripe plum tomatoes, halved, seeded, and coarsely chopped
1/4	cup loosely packed fresh basil leaves
2	sprigs fresh thyme
1	46-ounce can tomato juice, preferably organic
	Coarse salt and freshly ground white pepper to taste

In a stockpot, heat the olive oil over medium heat. Add the onions and cook, stirring often, for about 5 minutes, until softened. Add the garlic and cook about 2 minutes longer. Add the tomatoes, basil, and thyme, and cook for about 6 minutes, stirring, until the tomatoes begin to soften and release their juices.

Add the tomato juice and bring the soup to a boil. Reduce the heat and simmer for about 30 minutes, uncovered, until the flavors have intensified. Remove and discard the thyme sprigs. Season with salt and pepper.

Transfer the soup to a blender or the bowl of a food processor fitted with a metal blade and purée until smooth. You may have to work in batches. Strain the soup through a fine-mesh sieve into a bowl, pressing on the solids to extract as much liquid as possible. Discard the solids. Cover the bowl with plastic wrap and refrigerate the soup for at least 2 hours, or until well chilled.

HERBED GOAT CHEESE AND ASSEMBLY

6	ounces fresh goat cheese, at room temperature
2	teaspoons extra-virgin olive oil
2	teaspoons finely minced fresh chives
1/4	teaspoon finely minced garlic
	Coarse salt and coarsely ground white pepper
12	1/4-inch-thick slices bread cut from a baguette

In a small bowl, mash the goat cheese with a fork. Add the oil, chives, and garlic, and mix well. Season with salt and pepper and set aside.

Chilled Tomato Soup with Basil and Goat Cheese Croutons

MAKES 6 SERVINGS

Bring the garden to the table with this late-summer soup that unlocks all the irrepressible delights of an August tomato—its alluring scent and luscious flavor.

If you're used to slow-cooking tomatoes for use in a tomato sauce or soup, this recipe will be a pleasant change. In order to retain as much of their character as possible, this soup's relatively short cooking time keeps the flavor fresh. After cooking, it's puréed together with the basil, which is also at its prime in the year's eighth month.

Fresh herbed goat cheese is compelling enough on its own, but played off the tomato soup it's truly startling. Each of the two components bring out the best in the other, making for an experience that adds up to more than the sum of its deceptively simple parts.

(continued)

About 15 minutes before serving, take the soup from the refrigerator and let it sit at room temperature. Taste and adjust the seasonings.

Lightly toast the bread slices. Spread them with the herbed goat cheese. Ladle the soup into bowls and garnish each bowl with a crouton. Pass the remaining croutons on the side.

VARIATIONS: The recipe calls for plum tomatoes, but you can substitute heirloom Brandywine or beefsteaks if you prefer them or have them on hand. For a dramatically different result, make this with 6 pounds of yellow and orange beefsteak tomatoes, omit the can of tomato juice and the $1/4$ cup of basil, and sprinkle each serving with 2 tablespoons of finely chopped basil.

1	pound small new potatoes, about 2 inches in diameter
4	teaspoons extra-virgin olive oil
	Coarse salt and freshly ground white pepper to taste
2	small red onions, sliced thick
4	$^{1}/_{2}$-inch-thick slices country bread, such as *ciabatta*
8	ounces thick-sliced bacon
$^{1}/_{4}$	cup mayonnaise, preferably homemade (page 420)
1	cup loosely packed arugula leaves
4	ounces Roquefort cheese, crumbled

Build a charcoal fire in a grill and let the coals burn until they are covered with white ash. Spread them out in the grill. Lightly oil the grill grate.

Preheat the oven to 400°F.

In a bowl, toss the potatoes with 2 teaspoons of the oil and season them with salt and pepper. Lay the potatoes on the grill grate or arrange them in a single layer in a mesh grill basket. Grill for 20 to 25 minutes, turning them frequently, until tender. (If the potatoes are very small—1$^{1}/_{2}$ inches in diameter or smaller—they will cook in about 15 minutes.) Transfer the potatoes to a bowl and, using the tines of a fork or a potato masher, lightly crush them. Set aside and keep warm.

Meanwhile, drizzle the onions with the remaining 2 teaspoons of oil and season them with salt and pepper. Grill for 8 to 10 minutes total, turning once, until lightly browned and softened. Set aside.

Grill the bread slices until lightly toasted.

While the potatoes and onions are grilling, lay the bacon in an ovenproof sauté pan and roast it in the oven for about 20 minutes, until browned and crisp. Lift it from the pan and drain it on paper towels. Crumble the bacon when cool.

Spread each slice of bread with mayonnaise and top with a few arugula leaves. Divide the warm potatoes evenly among the slices of toast. Top with crumbled cheese, grilled onion, and crumbled bacon.

VARIATIONS: Use rosemary *ciabatta* or black-olive bread. Substitute thick tomato slices, grilled, for the potato, and add lettuce for a twist on the BLT. (See method for grilling tomatoes in the *bruschetta* recipe on page 136.)

Grilled Potato, Roquefort Cheese, Red Onion, and Smoked Bacon Sandwiches

MAKES 4 SANDWICHES

This sandwich will delight anyone who loves the effects created by a grill. Cooking the potato, country-style bread, and onion over a flame attaches to them a level of flavor that goes well beyond what most diners expect from these seemingly ordinary ingredients.

To make the sandwich, the grilled potatoes are crushed, spread over the bread, and topped with the red onion and bacon. The heat given off by the grilled ingredients melts the soft, blue-veined Roquefort cheese just enough for it to meld with the other flavors.

This open-faced sandwich is best served from a platter as part of a barbecue buffet. Or, in a small format, it can become a *bruschetta*-sized canapé at an August party.

THINKING AHEAD: The sauce can be prepared a day ahead of time. Reheat slowly over a medium fire, stirring occasionally.

SAUCE

3	tablespoons extra-virgin olive oil
3	cloves garlic, peeled and minced
4	pounds ripe plum tomatoes, peeled, seeded, and coarsely chopped
1/2	cup loosely packed fresh basil leaves
2	sprigs fresh thyme, leaves picked and chopped
1	tablespoon sugar
	Coarse salt and freshly ground white pepper to taste

In a stockpot, heat 1 tablespoon of the oil over medium heat. Add the garlic and cook, stirring, for about 2 minutes. Add the tomatoes and use a fork or potato masher to break them up as they cook. Stir in the basil and thyme. Season with sugar, salt, and pepper. Raise the heat and bring to a boil. Reduce the heat to medium-low and simmer for about 20 minutes. Adjust the seasonings.

Transfer the soup to the bowl of a food processor fitted with a metal blade or use an immersion blender and purée until smooth. During the puréeing, add the remaining 2 tablespoons of oil in a thin stream. Set the sauce aside, covered, to keep warm.

SUMMER VEGETABLES

4	tablespoons extra-virgin olive oil
1	medium zucchini, cut into 1-inch dice
1	medium yellow squash, cut into 1-inch dice
1	red bell pepper, seeded and cut into 1-inch dice
1	yellow bell pepper, seeded and cut into 1-inch dice
1/2	small eggplant or 2 baby eggplants, cut into 1-inch dice
1	large onion, peeled, halved, and sliced 1/4 inch thick
3	large ripe plum tomatoes, halved, seeded, and coarsely chopped
1	clove garlic, peeled and minced
1	sprig fresh thyme, leaves picked and chopped
	Coarse salt and freshly ground white pepper to taste

Preheat the oven to 400°F.

Set a large sauté pan over high heat, and when the pan is hot, add about 1 tablespoon of the oil. Sauté the zucchini and

Pasta with Summer Vegetables and Pecorino Romano

MAKES 6 APPETIZER SERVINGS OR 4 MAIN-COURSE SERVINGS

This recipe beautifully illustrates the compound value of cooking with in-season ingredients—eggplant, zucchini, yellow squash, tomatoes, and red and yellow peppers. Not only are they at their least expensive when in season, but they're also at their peak of flavor. At the Gotham Bar and Grill, this dish becomes an August selection on our famously inexpensive, prix-fixe lunch menu, allowing us to pass the savings along to our customers without skimping on quality.

The technique that produces the sauce for this pasta is a study in the benefits of cooking major components separately. Rather than sautéing the vegetables together—an approach that can cause the flavors to overlap—they are sautéed separately and added at the last minute to the fresh tomato sauce. The result is that each vegetable's individual texture and taste stands out in the finished dish.

(continued)

The salty olives and herbaceous basil leaves round out the Mediterranean allure of this late summer recipe, and super-sharp Pecorino Romano—a quintessential Italian grating cheese—is shaved over the bowl. One taste of it in this context and you'll understand why Italians love it with vegetables and pasta.

yellow squash for about 5 minutes, until slightly softened. Transfer to a shallow baking dish. Sauté the peppers in the same pan for about 3 minutes, until slightly softened, adding more oil as necessary, and then transfer them to the baking dish. Add the eggplant and onion to the pan and sauté for 8 to 10 minutes, until they begin to soften. Add more oil as needed. Transfer to the baking dish. Cook the tomatoes for 3 to 4 minutes, until just warmed, and then transfer them to the baking dish.

Add the garlic and thyme to the vegetables and season with salt and pepper. Bake the vegetables for about 10 minutes, stirring occasionally, until the flavors just meld. Remove them from the oven, cover with foil, and set aside to keep warm.

ASSEMBLY

1	pound dry spaghetti
1/2	bunch fresh basil, leaves picked and chopped
1/2	cup pitted and quartered lengthwise kalamata or niçoise olives
5	ounces Pecorino Romano cheese, freshly grated

In a large pot of lightly salted boiling water, cook the pasta for about 8 to 10 minutes, until al dente. Drain. Toss the pasta with the warm vegetables and sauce. (Mix the vegetables with the sauce and warm them, if necessary, before adding them.) Spoon the pasta onto a warmed serving platter and garnish with the basil leaves, olives, and cheese. Serve immediately.

SAUCE

Trimmings, necks, carcasses, wing tips, and giblets (no livers) from 2 Muscovy ducks, including drumsticks (reserve breasts and thigh pieces for sautéing)

2	tablespoons canola oil
1	small onion, chopped
1	small rib celery, chopped
1	small leek, washed and chopped
1¹/₂	cups dry red wine
1¹/₂	quarts water, or as needed
1	whole head garlic, halved crosswise
¹/₂	teaspoon whole black peppercorns
¹/₄	teaspoon caraway seeds
5	sprigs fresh thyme
1	bay leaf

Preheat the oven to 400°F.

Using a heavy cleaver or knife, coarsely chop the necks and carcasses. Spread the duck parts in a large roasting pan and roast, stirring several times, for 30 to 40 minutes, or until lightly browned.

Meanwhile, in a large stockpot, heat the oil over medium heat. Cook the onion, celery, and leek for 7 to 10 minutes, stirring occasionally, until nicely browned. Remove from the heat.

Transfer the duck bones and trimmings into the stockpot. Discard any fat in the roasting pan. Put the roasting pan on top of the stove, add the wine, and bring to a boil over medium-high heat. Using a wooden spoon, scrape up any browned bits on the bottom of the pan and then pour the mixture into the stockpot.

Add enough cold water to the stockpot to cover the solids by 2 inches. Bring to a boil over high heat, skimming any foam that rises to the surface. Add the garlic, peppercorns, caraway seeds, thyme, and bay leaf. Reduce the heat to low and simmer gently for at least 2¹/₂ hours and for up to 6 hours—the longer the better. Add water to the stockpot if the water level evaporates below the surface of the ingredients.

Strain the stock through a colander into a large bowl or pot, pressing on the solids to extract as much flavor as possible. Let the stock stand for about 5 minutes, until the fat rises to the surface. Skim off and discard the fat. You should have about 1¹/₂ quarts of stock.

In a medium saucepan, bring the stock to a boil over high heat

Duck with Roasted Peaches and Baby Turnips

MAKES 4 SERVINGS

Here in the United States, the mention of a backyard grill triggers images of hamburgers, hot dogs, and chicken. But there's no reason to limit ourselves to these options. This recipe is a loose, summer-vacation variation on the classic *Duck à la Pêche.* Traditionally, a whole roasted duck is brushed with a sauce made by deglazing its pan drippings with peach liqueur. The finished bird is served with poached peaches, and the essential lesson of the recipe is that the sweet fruit acts as a foil for the fatty quality of the duck.

Here, the peaches are roasted with just a bit of sugar. Much of their liquid cooks off and they begin to caramelize, intensifying the essence of the peach and allowing the skin to slip right off, revealing a delicate blush color.

Turnips are a traditional accompaniment that I see no need to modify. Serve them on a platter with the duck sliced in long, thin slices.

and cook until it reduces to $1^1/_2$ to 2 cups and has a rich, thick consistency. Set aside, covered, to keep warm.

ROASTED PEACHES AND BABY TURNIPS

$1^1/_2$	pounds medium ripe peaches (about 3 peaches)
$^1/_4$	cup sugar
12 to 14	baby turnips
2	tablespoons unsalted butter
	Coarse salt and freshly ground white pepper to taste

Preheat the oven to 400°F.

Halve and pit the peaches. Arrange them cut sides down in a stainless-steel roasting pan or on a low-sided baking sheet. Sprinkle with the sugar. Roast for 20 to 30 minutes, depending on the ripeness of the peaches, until they are tender. As they roast, the released juices will combine with the sugar to caramelize. Lift the peaches from the pan, peel, and transfer them to a bowl. The skins will slip off easily. Pour the caramelized juices over the peaches and set them aside, covered, to keep warm. Reduce the oven temperature to 325°F.

Do not peel the turnips, but trim them, leaving $^1/_4$ inch of the green tops.

In a saucepan of boiling salted water, cook the turnips for 12 to 15 minutes, or until tender when pierced with the tip of a knife. (If the green tops fall off during cooking, the turnips are overcooked.) Drain and rinse them under cool water to stop the cooking. Using a clean, damp kitchen towel, gently rub the skins from the turnips, leaving the green tops in place. Work at the sink under running water to make the job easier.

Put the turnips in a saucepan and add enough cold water to come about 1 inch up the sides. Add the butter and season with salt and pepper. Bring to a boil over medium-high heat and cook for about 2 minutes, until the turnips are heated through. Cover to keep warm.

DUCK BREAST

> Reserved duck breasts and thigh pieces
> Coarse salt and freshly ground white pepper to taste

Trim any excess fat and excess skin from the duck breasts and thigh pieces. With a sharp knife, score the skin in a cross-hatch pattern but do not cut into the flesh. This will help render the fat and allow the skin to crisp nicely. Season the breasts and thigh pieces with salt and pepper.

In a nonstick sauté pan, arrange the thigh pieces skin side down. Set over medium-high heat. Cook, rendering the fat and crisping and browning the skin, 8 to 10 minutes. Turn and continue cooking until the duck is slightly pink at the bone when pierced, another 8 to 10 minutes. Remove from heat and cover loosely with foil to keep warm.

Meanwhile, in another nonstick sauté pan, arrange the duck breasts in a single layer. Set them over high heat and cook for about 8 minutes, until nicely browned and crisp on one side. Turn and cook about 4 minutes longer, until medium-rare. Remove and cover them to keep warm.

NOTE: If you choose not to bone the ducks yourself, ask the butcher if any duck bones and trimmings are available to use for the sauce. Otherwise, substitute the trimmings, necks, carcasses, wing tips, and giblets (no livers) from 2 chickens.

ASSEMBLY

> $1/4$ cup unsalted butter, cut into pieces
> Coarse salt and freshly ground white pepper to taste
> Fresh thyme, for garnish

Reheat the peaches, if necessary, in the 325°F oven. Slice them into thick wedges.

Heat the sauce over medium-high heat, whisking in the butter one piece at a time to enrich and thicken the sauce. Season with salt and pepper. Remove and discard bones from thigh pieces and thinly slice.

Slice the duck breasts on the diagonal into $1/4$-inch-thick pieces. Arrange slices on a serving platter and garnish with the turnips and peaches. Spoon a little sauce over the duck and serve the remaining sauce on the side. Garnish the dish with fresh thyme.

VARIATION: You can substitute fresh figs for the peaches, presenting them as they are with the squab on page 154.

TENDERLOIN AND POTATOES

1¹/₂	pounds small new potatoes, about 2 inches in diameter
¹/₄	cup extra-virgin olive oil
	Coarse salt and freshly ground white pepper to taste
1	2¹/₂-pound tenderloin of beef

Build a charcoal fire in a grill and let the coals burn until covered with white ash. Spread them out in the grill. Lightly oil the grill grate.

In a bowl, toss the potatoes with 3 tablespoons of the oil and season with salt and pepper. Lay the potatoes on the grill grate or arrange them in a single layer in a mesh grill basket. Grill for 20 to 25 minutes, turning frequently, until tender. (If the potatoes are very small—1¹/₂ inches in diameter or smaller—they will cook in about 15 minutes.)

Rub the meat with the remaining oil and season it on both sides with salt and pepper. Grill, turning often, until the meat develops a nice crust on the outside. For rare meat, grill for 18 to 20 minutes; for medium-rare, grill for 20 to 25 minutes. Let the meat rest for about 10 minutes before serving.

CORN AND CHANTERELLES

1	tablespoon canola oil
1¹/₂	pounds chanterelles, cleaned and stemmed
2	tablespoons minced shallot
1	tablespoon minced garlic
1	cup fresh corn kernels, preferably cut from the cob
	Coarse salt and freshly ground white pepper to taste
2	tablespoons unsalted butter

While the tenderloin and potatoes are cooking, in a large sauté pan, heat the oil over medium heat. Add the chanterelles and sauté for about 1 minute. Reduce the heat to low, add the shallot and garlic, and sauté about 4 minutes longer, until the mushrooms begin to release their juices.

Add the corn and sauté for 3 to 4 minutes, or until the corn is tender. Season with salt and pepper. Swirl the butter into the pan to enrichen the mixture. Cover and keep warm.

(continued)

Grilled Tenderloin of Beef with Corn, Chanterelles, and Chervil

MAKES 4 TO 6 SERVINGS

This dish was developed with one mission in mind—to give in to the irresistible notion of whole, grilled filet mignon, which is actually very easy to cook in this manner with excellent results.

Sweet corn and chanterelles are a fantastic combination, both casual and refined. Here, the mushrooms are sautéed and the corn is cut fresh from the cob—their flavors mingle thanks to some butter added to the pan, creating an intense sauce for this versatile side dish.

ASSEMBLY

    2   tablespoons chopped fresh chervil

    1   tablespoon chopped fresh chives

If necessary, reheat the corn and chanterelles. Add the chervil and chives and stir to combine. Carve the tenderloin into $3/4$-inch slices. Arrange on a large platter, surround with grilled potatoes, and pass the corn and chanterelles in a separate serving bowl.

VARIATIONS: This dish can also be served cold, with a mayonnaise (page 420) or aioli (page 65).

FLAVOR BUILDING: Shave 2 ounces of summer truffles over the corn and chanterelles. Before grilling, marinate the filet in a few tablespoons of extra-virgin olive oil combined with 4 cloves of thinly sliced garlic, rosemary, thyme, and a tablespoon of cracked peppercorns.

Grilled Squab with Grilled Radicchio, Endive, and Black Mission Figs

MAKES 4 SERVINGS

The first time I tasted squab with figs was about 25 years ago, in the hilltop town of St. Paul de Vence, a Provençal community overlooking Nice. One day, I had lunch at a restaurant just inside the perimeter that boasted an informal art gallery with works by Calder, Picasso, and Miró—painters and sculptors who used to live nearby and had bartered their art for food.

The walled-in courtyard was set off by an ancient wooden door and was appointed with heavy tables and chairs that leant the whole scene a vaguely medieval quality.

The view from the restaurant was unforgettable—situated on a cliff, it seemed to hover over the region, looking out on all of Provence and the Mediterranean beyond. And yet, the most potent sensory memory I have of that afternoon is of the huge fig trees that hung like a canopy over the tables, perfuming the air

GRILLED RADICCHIO AND ENDIVE

1   large head radicchio
2   large Belgian endive, halved lengthwise
1/4   cup extra-virgin olive oil
      Coarse salt and freshly ground white pepper to taste

Build a charcoal fire in a grill and let the coals burn until covered with white ash. Spread them out in the grill, leaving a portion of the grill free of coals for indirect cooking. Lightly oil the grill grate.

Cut the radicchio lengthwise into 8 wedges. Rinse it under cold water and dry briefly in a kitchen towel, so that the radicchio retains a little moisture and will steam slightly on the grill. This will prevent it from burning.

Put the radicchio and endive on a platter and brush with most of the olive oil. Season with salt and pepper. Grill the vegetables away from direct heat, turning often, until nicely browned, softened, and cooked through. The time will vary, but for the radicchio it should take about 12 minutes, and for the endive, 15 to 20 minutes. Remove the vegetables from the grill and arrange them in the center of a warmed serving platter. Drizzle with the remaining olive oil and cover to keep warm.

SQUAB AND FIGS

4   whole squab, each about 18 ounces
2   tablespoons extra-virgin olive oil
    Coarse salt and freshly ground white pepper to taste
2   tablespoons chopped fresh flat-leaf parsley
12   ripe Mission figs

Build a charcoal fire in a grill and let the coals burn until covered with white ash. Spread them out in the grill. Lightly oil the grill grate. (The grill may already be fired from grilling the vegetables.)

Using a sharp knife, cut the wing tips off the squabs. Cut down each side of the backbones and remove. Place the squabs, breast side up, on the work surface. Press down on the breast with the heel of your hand to crack the breast keel bone. Turn the squabs over and pull out the keel bone.

Brush the squabs with olive oil and season with salt and pepper. Grill over medium-high heat, skin side down, for about 8 minutes, until the skin is nicely browned and crisp. Turn and cook about 4 minutes longer for medium-rare.

Arrange the squabs on top of the grilled radicchio and endive, and sprinkle with the parsley. Cut the figs in half, arrange them around the outside of the platter, and serve.

VARIATIONS: Replace the figs with the peaches from Duck with Roasted Peaches and Baby Turnips (page 149), or in the fall, combine this squab with the pear recipe on page 230.

with their sweet fragrance. To a young man just out of cooking school and visiting France for the first time, the trees—decorated with an abundance of fruit set against pale green leaves—made quite an impression, one that was only rein-forced by our simple lunch, which included roast squab with warm figs that were splashed with port wine.

I am reminded of this experience whenever I look out at the fig tree that resides in our backyard. Though it's bare at winter's end, we eagerly monitor its growth every summer as it gradually begins to offer us its magnificent bounty once again. By August, it's in full fruit, and I make this dish as soon as possible, re-creating, as best I can, that midday meal savored long ago and high above Provence.

Blackberry
and Peach
Cobbler

MAKES 8 SERVINGS

These quaint, little individual cobblers are as simple as they are rewarding. The peaches are stoned, sliced, macerated with vanilla bean and sugar, and put in dishes with the berries.

PEACHES

10	medium ripe peaches, peeled, pitted, and chopped
1	Tahitian vanilla bean, split lengthwise
$^1/_2$	cup sugar, or to taste

In a bowl, combine the peaches and vanilla bean and enough sugar to sweeten. Cover and refrigerate for at least 8 hours or overnight.

ASSEMBLY

$1^1/_2$	cups all-purpose flour
$^1/_2$	cup sugar
$^1/_2$	teaspoon baking powder
$^1/_2$	teaspoon salt
$^3/_4$	cup unsalted butter, softened
$^1/_3$	cup plus 1 tablespoon buttermilk
2	pints blackberries
	Vanilla Bean Ice Cream (page 84)

Preheat the oven to 350°F. Have ready 8 ramekins, each about 5 inches in diameter.

In the bowl of an electric mixer fitted with the paddle attachment, combine the flour, sugar, baking powder, and salt, and whisk to combine. Add the butter and mix on medium-high speed, until the mixture is just crumbly. Add the buttermilk and mix until combined.

Remove the vanilla bean from the peaches and discard it. Fill each ramekin with peaches and blackberries, distributing the fruit equally. Top each with batter, crumbling it over the fruit. Bake for about 35 minutes, until the crust is golden brown and the fruit is bubbling. Cool slightly on wire racks and serve warm with a scoop of vanilla bean ice cream.

WHAT TO DRINK: Savor this dessert with a sweet Hungarian Tokaji.

THINKING AHEAD: The dough can be made a day in advance and kept covered in the refrigerator.

TART DOUGH

10	tablespoons unsalted butter, softened
1/3	cup granulated sugar
1	tablespoon confectioners' sugar
1	tablespoon almond flour
2	tablespoons milk
1	large egg yolk
1 1/2	cups all-purpose flour
1/2	teaspoon salt

In the bowl of an electric mixer set on medium-high speed, cream the butter, granulated sugar, confectioners' sugar, and almond flour for about 5 minutes, until light and fluffy. Add the milk and egg yolk, and beat until mixed.

Reduce the speed to medium and add the flour and salt. Mix until just smooth. Scrape the dough onto a sheet of plastic wrap or wax paper, wrap it well, and refrigerate for at least 1 hour, or until well chilled.

LEMON FILLING

1/2	cup fresh lemon juice
5	tablespoons sugar
2	large eggs
1	large egg yolk
1/2	cup heavy cream or crème fraîche
	Grated zest of 3 lemons

Preheat the oven to 350°F.

In a bowl, combine the lemon juice and sugar, and stir until the sugar dissolves. Add the eggs, egg yolk, and cream, and whisk until smooth. Strain through a sieve into another bowl. Stir in the zest and then pour into a shallow, ungreased 8-by-4-inch or 8-by-5-inch pan.

Set the pan in a larger roasting or baking pan set on the oven rack. Pour enough hot water into the larger pan to come about halfway up the sides of the smaller pan. Bake for about 20 minutes, until firm. Set the pan on a wire rack and let the filling cool.

The key to this dessert is the lemon curd, which is lightened with Chantilly cream before being poured into the shell, making a creamy, tart bed for the fresh raspberries.

Making the sugar crust, or *pâte sucrée,* is a versatile technique to master because it can be filled with a wide variety of fresh fruits—such as peaches, apricots, or berries—or even flavored whipped cream. I love painting the bottom of the shell with a thin layer of jam or preserves before adding the cream.

(continued)

ASSEMBLY

2   tablespoons raspberry jam

1   cup heavy cream, whipped to soft peaks

2   pints raspberries

Preheat the oven to 400°F. Lightly spray an 8-inch tart pan with a removable bottom with vegetable oil.

On a lightly floured surface, roll the chilled dough into a circle about $^1/_4$ inch thick and about 3 inches larger in diameter than the tart pan. (If the dough cracks, it is too cold. Let it stand for a few minutes to soften and then try rolling it again.) Roll the dough around the rolling pin. Place the pin over the tart pan and unroll the pastry over the pan. Ease the dough into the pan, pressing gently against the sides and bottom to fit it securely. Smooth out any cracks. Trim the dough flush with the top edge of the pan. Prick the dough all over with the tines of a fork. If the dough seems soft, firm it in the freezer for a few minutes. Bake for 15 to 20 minutes, until golden brown. Press down any swelling or bubbles in the crust. Allow to cool completely on a wire rack.

Spread the raspberry jam inside the tart shell. Fold the whipped cream into the cooled lemon filling. Smooth the filling over the jam. Arrange the raspberries in concentric circles, working from the center outward, on top of the filling, pressing them into it very gently. Serve.

VARIATION: For a true indulgence, you might also cover the bottom of the tart shell with melted bitter chocolate and top it with whipped cream and sliced bananas instead of the berries, topping the whole thing with grated chocolate.

Mediterranean Dinner Party

These menus bring together the flavors and traditions of my favorite warm-weather region—the Mediterranean. If possible, enjoy these outdoors.

CANAPÉS

EITHER OF THE TWO *BRUSCHETTAS* **(page 135)**

BABA GHANOUSH **(page 131)**

MENU 1

BRANDADE WITH RADISH, RED ONION, AND OLIVE SALAD **(page 94)**

GRILLED WILD STRIPED BASS WITH GRILLED FENNEL, TOMATOES, AND PICHOLINE OLIVES **(page 110)**

RASPBERRY TART **(page 159)**

MENU 2

SOUPE DE POISSON **(page 58)**

GRILLED SQUAB WITH GRILLED RADICCHIO, ENDIVE, AND BLACK MISSION FIGS **(page 154)**

BLUEBERRY CRUSTADE WITH SWEETENED MASCARPONE **(page 119)**

Leek and Roquefort Salad with Mimosa Vinaigrette

Salt Cod Salad, Roasted Pepper, and Kalamata Olives

Atlantic Salmon Carpaccio with Arugula and Cremini Mushroom Salad

Sandwiches

Prosciutto, Pear, Arugula, and Honey Mustard Sandwich

Orecchiette with Chicken, Swiss Chard, and Parmigiano-Reggiano

Cremini Mushroom Pasta with Wilted Arugula, Goat Cheese, and Extra-Virgin Olive Oil

Pan Sauces

Seared Halibut with Haricots Verts, Scallions, and White Wine Sauce

Chicken Breasts with Rosemary and Chanterelles

Gotham Profiteroles with Chocolate Sauce

Peanut Butter Coupe

Last-Minute Dinner Party

SEPTEMBER

RECIPES FOR BUSY TIMES

There's an unavoidable irony to Labor Day. This supposed gift to working men and women takes place at the end of the summer and—in cities like New York—actually defines the unofficial end of that season. It usually falls at the beginning of September and ranks among the most surreally silent days of the year in Manhattan. (In fact, we often close the Gotham on Labor Day and make cosmetic changes such as renovating the bar or repainting the dining room.)

The days immediately following this holiday can be fatiguing as we acclimate to the taxing pace of "normal" life—not unlike the first days back to the gym after a period of inactivity. In the city, the volume of traffic picks up almost overnight. The streets and sidewalks, too, are more crowded as everyone returns from their August respites. I'm actually convinced that on the Tuesday after Labor Day, at about 8:15 A.M., water must spill over the edges of Manhattan as the island sinks with the weight of millions of returning New Yorkers.

But, wherever you live, the upshot is that there's precious little free time in September. And, while one of the premiums of cooking may be time itself, this doesn't mean you have to turn to dining out and ordering in for sustenance. The following pages contain some of the less complicated recipes in this book, intended to supply solutions and inspiration for satisfying dining in the busy weeks following Labor Day.

Given this buildup, you won't be surprised to find several salads here. The Leek and Roquefort Salad with Mimosa Vinaigrette (page 166) adapts a classic French preparation, while the Salt Cod Salad, Roasted Pepper, and Kalamata Olives (page 168) varies another one—brandade—in a pleasing and less complicated recipe. A similar offering is made by the Atlantic Salmon Carpaccio with Arugula and Cremini Mushroom Salad (page 170). All of these can be served either as starters or as light meals in their own right on particularly demanding days.

Sandwiches, too, are reliably swift. Looking forward to autumn, I've included the Prosciutto, Pear, Arugula, and Honey Mustard Sandwich (page 174), but more importantly, I've also provided several notes on sandwich-making that should inspire your own creations in this often undervalued category.

You won't find many dishes here that call for roasting, braising, or stewing since they require longer cooking. This is a time for seeking out dishes that avail themselves of the stove-top. There are two satisfying ones here: Seared Halibut with Haricots Verts, Scallions, and White

Wine Sauce (page 181), in which a pan sauce is created in seconds by deglazing the pan in which the fish was seared, then adding additional ingredients. Another, Chicken Breasts with Rosemary and Chanterelles (page 183) uses a similar technique. Here, too, I've included some notes on pan sauces that will enable you to create your own dishes using this convenient method.

Pasta warrants consideration when time is scarce because the ingredients often can be prepared while the water is boiling and the pasta cooking. I've included two in this chapter, and each is designed with a dual purpose in mind. Cremini Mushroom Pasta with Wilted Arugula, Goat Cheese, and Extra-Virgin Olive Oil (page 178) offers a lesson in how to use an abundance of basic ingredients to produce a simple, sumptuous meal. The other, Orecchiette with

Chicken, Swiss Chard, and Parmigiano-Reggiano (page 175), is designed to enable you, in one focused cooking session, to prepare many high-quality components that will last the entire week.

Finally, there are two decadent but simply made desserts—Gotham Profiteroles with Chocolate Sauce (page 186) and Peanut Butter Coupe (page 188). You might think that in such a busy month the easiest thing would be to forgo the sweets, but I've always believed in making time for the important things in life, and dessert definitely makes the list.

Leek and Roquefort Salad with Mimosa Vinaigrette

MAKES 4 SERVINGS

From the first time I made leeks vinaigrette in cooking school, I've loved this classic recipe, especially the sieved hard-boiled eggs (textbook French), which are officially referred to as mimosa, salted capers, and *moutarde de Meaux* (whole-grain mustard). We're so accustomed to slicing leeks into rings or julienning them to accessorize other ingredients that several whole leeks taking center stage can be quite impressive. Cooked until tender in boiling salted water, they take on a greater-than-natural heft, and a full, soft mouth-feel. This salad also works as a satisfying small meal thanks in part to the croutons, which are spread with a rich and creamy Roquefort cheese. (See Flavor Building for more thoughts on enriching this salad.)

THINKING AHEAD: The leeks can be cooked in the morning, then cooled, covered, and refrigerated. The vinaigrette can be prepared as many as 24 hours in advance and kept refrigerated in a sealed container.

LEEKS AND POTATOES

12	small creamer potatoes, scrubbed
1¼	pounds leeks, root ends trimmed

Put the potatoes in a saucepan and add enough cold water to cover. Salt the water and bring to a boil over high heat. Reduce the heat and simmer for about 12 minutes, or until tender when pierced with a sharp knife. Drain, transfer to a small bowl, and set aside.

Wash the leeks and trim about 2 inches off the green ends, leaving some of the tender green leaf. In a saucepan of boiling salted water, cook the leeks for about 10 minutes, or until tender when pierced with a sharp knife. Drain and submerge them in a bowl of ice water until completely cool.

Lift the leeks from the water bath, pat them dry with a clean kitchen towel, and, using your hands, squeeze out the excess water. Beginning at the white ends, cut the leeks into 3-inch lengths. Slice each length in half lengthwise, place them on a shallow plate, and set aside.

VINAIGRETTE

2	tablespoons fresh lemon juice
1	tablespoon whole-grain Dijon mustard
2	teaspoons red wine vinegar
¾	cup extra-virgin olive oil
	Coarse salt and freshly ground white pepper to taste
1	hard-boiled egg
2	tablespoons chopped fresh flat-leaf parsley
1	tablespoon capers, rinsed and coarsely chopped

In a small bowl, whisk together the lemon juice, mustard, and vinegar. Slowly add the olive oil, whisking continuously, until emulsified. Season with salt and pepper. Pour off ¼ cup of the vinaigrette and set it aside.

Separate the egg yolk from the white. Press the white through a fine sieve and then press the yolk through the sieve. Stir the whites and yolks into the remaining $^3/_4$ cup of vinaigrette. Stir in the parsley and capers.

ASSEMBLY

4   cups loosely packed mesclun salad greens
4   ounces Roquefort cheese, at room temperature
4    $^1/_2$-inch-thick slices bread, cut from a baguette, toasted

Spoon a few tablespoons of mimosa vinaigrette over the potatoes and season them with salt and pepper. Spoon a little mimosa vinaigrette over the leeks, rolling them in the dressing until well coated. Season them with salt and pepper. Arrange the potatoes and leeks in the centers of 4 salad plates or on a serving platter. Drizzle with any remaining vinaigrette.

In a bowl, toss the mesclun with the reserved $^1/_4$ cup of plain vinaigrette and season it with salt and pepper. Arrange the lettuce with the leeks and potatoes. Spread the cheese on the croutons and serve with the salad.

VARIATION: Goat cheese can be substituted for the Roquefort.

FLAVOR BUILDING: Substitute Lemon Vinaigrette (page 169) for the mimosa vinaigrette and shower each serving with black truffle slices. Or eliminate the Roquefort crouton and toss some cold poached lobster or shrimp with the greens.

Salt Cod Salad, Roasted Pepper, and Kalamata Olives

MAKES 6 SERVINGS

This colorful salad serves equally well as a starter or a light main course and travels well for a picnic. It's one of two recipes in the book for salt cod, the other being a brandade (page 94) in which salt cod is whipped with potatoes and extra-virgin olive oil and baked.

Here, the fish is poached and flaked, then accompanied with roasted red pepper, olives, capers, and parsley.

My fondness for salt cod was sparked by my wife, who grew up spending summers in the Algarve in Portugal, where she came to love dishes that feature it. This is one of my favorite recipes in her repertoire, and happily, she makes it all the time.

It's worth noting that there's great disagreement over how long to soak salt cod. My personal point of view is that there's not one right answer, but rather the correct time changes somewhat from piece to piece,

THINKING AHEAD: The cod must be soaked for at least 3 days prior to making the salad.

1	pound salt cod
1/4	cup white wine vinegar
1	bay leaf
1/2	teaspoon black peppercorns
1	medium red bell pepper
1	pound fingerling potatoes
1	clove garlic, peeled, mashed to a paste, and sprinkled with coarse salt
2	tablespoons minced shallot
2	tablespoons extra-virgin olive oil
1/2	cup pitted, halved kalamata olives
2	teaspoons capers, rinsed and drained
1	tablespoon chopped fresh flat-leaf parsley
	Coarse salt and freshly ground white pepper to taste
6	cups mixed salad greens
1	cup Lemon Vinaigrette (page 169)

In a large bowl, soak the salt cod in cold water to cover in the refrigerator for 72 hours. Change the water twice a day. When ready to cook, remove cod and discard soaking liquid.

In a small saucepan, combine 3 cups water, vinegar, bay leaf, and peppercorns, and bring to a boil over high heat. Reduce the heat and simmer for about 5 minutes. Add the cod, return to a simmer, and poach for about 6 minutes, until the cod is barely cooked through. Drain and set it aside to cool slightly. Flake the cooled fish into large pieces.

Char the pepper over a gas burner turned to medium heat or under a broiler, turning as it blackens on all sides and until it is soft on the inside and takes on a nice smoky flavor. This will take about 15 minutes. Use large tongs or long-handled forks to handle the pepper. Transfer the pepper to a bowl and cover it tightly with plastic wrap to steam as it cools. Peel the skin, which should pull right off. Scrape out the seeds and dice the pepper.

Meanwhile, put the potatoes in a saucepan and add cold salted water to cover. Bring to a boil, reduce the heat, and simmer for 7 to 10 minutes, until just tender. Drain and set the potatoes aside. When just cool enough to handle, slice the potatoes into 1/2-inch-thick rounds.

In a salad bowl, combine the still-warm cod with the potatoes.

Add the garlic, shallot, and olive oil, and toss to combine. Toss in the olives, capers, parsley, and roasted red pepper, and season with a little salt and pepper.

Dress the salad greens with lemon vinaigrette and season with salt and pepper. Serve alongside the cod salad.

Lemon Vinaigrette

MAKES ABOUT 1 CUP

1½   tablespoons fresh lemon juice
1½   tablespoons red wine vinegar
½   teaspoon Dijon mustard
12   tablespoons extra-virgin olive oil
       Coarse salt and freshly ground white pepper to taste

In a small bowl, whisk together the lemon juice, vinegar, and mustard. Gradually whisk in the oil. Season with salt and pepper. Whisk again before using.

largely due to variations in the thickness of the fish. That said, most people agree that 3 days, with 2 changes of water per day, will get the salt out. If you're not sure you've soaked yours enough, it's best to fall back on the obvious, slicing off a piece and tasting it. If it seems too salty, it's not ready.

Atlantic Salmon Carpaccio
with Arugula and Cremini Mushroom Salad

MAKES 4 SERVINGS

This recipe uses the full, rich flavor of salmon as the base for an arugula and mushroom salad that would be satisfying on its own. Together, the two components are visually stunning and wonderfully complex.

When slicing the salmon, be certain that your hands and the work surface are impeccably clean and the fish is well chilled. Use a hollow-ground or thin-bladed knife and cut the fish as thin as possible. You may find this difficult at first, but hang in there—it gets easier after the first plate.

Be careful not to overlap the salmon slices; instead, you want to push them together, not unlike the states on a map, creating a unified surface that covers the plate. Use the "foot" of one plate to cut a perfect circle in the one beneath, as explained in the recipe.

THINKING AHEAD: You can plate the salmon as many as 4 hours in advance. Cover the plates with plastic wrap, and stack them, inverting every other plate, in the refrigerator. (The salmon will adhere to the plate, even if it's turned upside-down.)

SALMON

1 pound Atlantic salmon fillet, chilled

On an impeccably clean cutting board and using a sharp, thin-bladed knife, slice the salmon across the top of the fillet as thin as possible to make sheets, as you would with smoked salmon. Wipe the blade with a clean, dry kitchen towel after each slice. The first few tries will be difficult, but it will get easier as you progress.

Lay the salmon on a chilled dinner plate without overlapping the slices. Use smaller slices to fill in any gaps so that the plate is covered with a sheet of salmon. Cover the plate entirely with a sheet of plastic wrap, making sure the plastic touches the salmon. Set a second plate on top and press down on it while rotating it a quarter turn, moving it back and forth a few times. Lift the plate. The foot, or base, of the plate will have trimmed the carpaccio into a perfect circle. Refrigerate and continue with the remaining salmon to make 4 plates of carpaccio.

ASSEMBLY

4 tablespoons plus 1 teaspoon extra-virgin olive oil
2 tablespoons plus 1 teaspoon fresh lime juice
   Coarse salt and freshly ground white pepper to taste
2 cups stemmed arugula leaves
4 ounces cremini mushrooms, trimmed and thinly sliced
1 tablespoon finely minced chives
1 teaspoon cracked coriander seeds

In a small bowl, whisk together 3 tablespoons of the olive oil and 1 tablespoon of the lime juice. Season with salt and pepper. Toss the arugula and mushrooms in another bowl and drizzle with the vinaigrette. Adjust the seasoning again with salt and pepper.

Remove the plastic wrap from the plates of carpaccio and drizzle each plate with the remaining lime juice and then the remaining olive oil. Sprinkle the surface with the chives and cracked coriander seeds, and season with salt and pepper. Garnish the center of each carpaccio with a bouquet of arugula and cremini mushroom salad and serve.

WHAT TO DRINK: Serve this dish with a Savennières or Chenin Blanc.

VARIATIONS: Striped bass makes a wonderful alternate for the salmon here, or—for a special occasion—prepare half of each dish with salmon and the other with bass.

Dress the carpaccio with scallions, dill, basil, chervil, or lemon juice (instead of the lime juice).

FLAVOR BUILDING: Scatter salmon roe or flying-fish roe over the surface of each salad.

Sandwiches

Because of its reputation as the quintessential quick fix, the sandwich is often undervalued as a medium for sophisticated creativity. But the virtually endless possibilities that the deceptively simple structure of a sandwich invites can, and should, be explored as part of any serious cook's culinary development. Following a few simple guidelines can produce deeply gratifying results.

The one constant in all sandwiches is, of course, the bread, which should not be a casual decision—forgetting the very notion of mass-produced, presliced white bread will start you down the road to sandwich success. If making sandwiches in advance (as for a picnic), grilling or lightly toasting the bread will help keep it from getting soggy. But this is also a technique you can use when eating the sandwich immediately. Be creative with your choice of breads—experiment with, say, a *ciabatta,* a raisin or olive loaf, or a bread with herbs such as rosemary baked into it. Even a bagel can sometimes be a fine choice for a sandwich.

It's important to be sensitive to the thickness of the bread in relation to the amount of sandwich "filling." There are many schools of thought on this. In France, for example, you might see a section of baguette with a thin slice of ham, while in New York, if you order a sandwich at institutions like the Carnegie

PRESERVING:
Spicy Garlic Pickles

MAKES 3 QUARTS

I came to the Gotham one year after it opened and was charged with changing the entire menu, with one notable exception—one of my partners, Jerry Kretchmer, insisted that we keep a hamburger on the lunch menu. I set out to create the best burger possible, grinding my own beef, searching out the best roll in town, and even making my own pickles and pickled vegetables. This was the pickle recipe I used 16 years ago. It's very spicy, with lots of garlic and a few jalapeños thrown in to heighten the effect.

PICKLES
4	pounds Kirby cucumbers
12	large cloves garlic, peeled
3	jalapeño peppers, split in half
12	sprigs fresh dill
3	bay leaves

In 3 sterilized quart canning jars (see page 81 for sterilizing instructions), layer the ingredients, dividing them equally among the jars.

BRINE AND SPICES
6	cups water
1/3	cup cider or white wine vinegar

Deli or the Second Avenue Deli, you're likely to be served a Dagwood-style tower that would require a detachable jaw to attack. Find your own happy medium and, when you do, remember it the next time you make a sandwich.

There are so many fine cheeses out there that, as with bread, my advice would be to steer clear of the predictable such as Cheddar and Swiss. Any number of soft cheeses, such as blue-veined or goat varieties can be great in this context. Similarly, if you usually use iceberg lettuce out of habit, try some different greens, such as watercress, radicchio, or arugula. For extra flavor and texture, sprouts behave very well in sandwiches. With this same thought in mind, don't omit leftover vegetables from consideration. Cold spinach, for example, can itself be the basis for a memorable sandwich, combined with nothing more than coarse salt, aioli, and extra-virgin olive oil. Wilted greens can also provide similar results.

Condiments in a sandwich act much the same way a sauce does on a plate, tying together the ingredients and unifying the flavors. For this reason, being too conservative with a simple mustard or mayonnaise can actually lower the quality of the sandwich. Free your mind and explore other possibilities such as pesto, or olive, artichoke, or mushroom pastes. Or doctor up a store-bought mayonnaise with herbs, a few drops of lemon juice, extra-virgin olive oil, or even lemon zest or crushed garlic. One of my favorite tricks when making a sandwich with chicken, steak, or lamb leftovers is to reserve the pan juices from those meats and mix them into a mayonnaise.

1/3	cup coarse or kosher salt
1/3	cup sugar
1	teaspoon whole mustard seeds
1	teaspoon whole coriander seeds
1	teaspoon celery seeds
1	teaspoon whole black peppercorns
1/2	teaspoon whole allspice

In a saucepan, combine the water, vinegar, salt, and sugar. Add the mustard seeds, coriander seeds, celery seeds, peppercorns, and allspice. Bring to a boil over high heat. Reduce the heat and simmer for about 5 minutes. Strain the brine into a bowl. Reserve the spices.

Pour the brine over the cucumbers, garlic, jalapeños, and herbs, leaving about 1 inch of headroom. Distribute the reserved spices equally among the sterilized jars.

Screw the lids on the jars. Submerge the jars in a large canning pot of boiling water. Use a canning basket if possible to submerge and lift the jars from the water. The basket prevents the jars from knocking into each other during processing. When the water returns to the boil, process the pickles for about 6 minutes. Lift from the water bath.

Let cool completely in a dark, well-ventilated area, and then store in a cool, dry place. The jars should not touch each other during cooling. Store in a cool, dark place for months. Refrigerate the pickles after opening.

Prosciutto, Pear, Arugula, and Honey Mustard Sandwich

MAKES 4 SERVINGS

This uniquely delicious combination of sweet pear, salty prosciutto, and tangy mustard will haunt your taste memory for a good long while. Inspired by the classic combination of prosciutto and melon, this open-faced sandwich is a worthy canapé for all but the most formal affairs and is perfect for lunch as well. Fortunately for Americans, the laws on importation changed a few years ago, so we can now get *prosciutto di Parma* here at home. It costs a few dollars more but is worth every penny. I suggest making your own honey mustard by stirring some honey into a strong Dijon. The flavor will be much fresher and sharper than in any ready-made brand.

2	tablespoons Dijon mustard
1	tablespoon honey
3	ripe Bosc pears, halved, cored, and cut into $1/2$-inch-thick slices
8	ounces prosciutto, thinly sliced
4	slices country-style bread, lightly toasted
2	cups loosely packed arugula
2	tablespoons extra-virgin olive oil
	Coarse salt and freshly ground white pepper to taste

In a small bowl, whisk together the mustard and honey.

Build the sandwiches by layering the pears and prosciutto on the toasted bread. Spread the prosciutto with a little honey mustard.

In a small bowl, toss the arugula with the olive oil and season it with salt and pepper. Top each sandwich with the dressed arugula leaves and arrange on a platter for serving.

THINKING AHEAD: The entire dish can be made as many as 24 hours in advance, covered in the refrigerator, and reheated gently, stirring occasionally. The white beans must be soaked overnight.

HERB SACHET

1	head garlic, split in half
2	sprigs fresh thyme
2	sprigs fresh rosemary
1	bay leaf
1	teaspoon black peppercorns

Wrap the garlic, herbs, and peppercorns in a large piece of cheesecloth and tie it with kitchen twine. Set aside.

CHICKEN

2	tablespoons extra-virgin olive oil
1	2-pound chicken, legs, thighs, and breasts separated, backbone cut in half
	Coarse salt and freshly ground white pepper to taste
1	small carrot, coarsely chopped
1	rib celery, coarsely chopped
1	small onion, coarsely chopped
3	quarts White Chicken Stock (page 421)

In a medium sauté pan, heat the oil over high heat until hot but not smoking. Season the chicken pieces with salt and pepper, and add them to the pan. Cook for 4 to 5 minutes, turning the pieces several times, until lightly browned. Add the carrots, celery, and onion, and continue cooking for 5 to 6 minutes longer, until the vegetables are lightly browned. Transfer the chicken and vegetables to a stockpot.

Deglaze the pan with $1/2$ cup of chicken stock, scraping up the browned bits on the bottom. Pour the deglazing liquid into the pot along with the rest of the chicken stock. Add the herb sachet. Bring to a boil over high heat. Reduce the heat to medium-low and simmer, skimming the surface several times, until the chicken pieces are tender. Using a slotted spoon, remove the breast pieces from the stock after 30 to 40 minutes, when they are just cooked; remove the legs and thighs when the meat is loose on the bone, about 1 hour. Set the chicken aside.

(continued)

Orecchiette
with Chicken, Swiss Chard, and Parmigiano-Reggiano
MAKES 6 SERVINGS

If you do the cooking for a family, or find yourself expecting a houseful of weekend guests, planning ahead can save time and stress. An adaptation of the classic *pasta e fagioli*, this recipe combines chicken, pasta, broth, and shaved cheese in a meal that—after it's cooked—will leave you with versatile, intentional left-overs. Not only can it be made a day in advance, but if you increase the quantity of chicken (see Variations), the extra poached chicken can be used later in the week for a chicken-salad or club sandwich. Note that the pasta dish itself relies on a few well-chosen ingredients; a great extra-virgin olive oil and high-quality cheese are essential to its success.

Strain the stock, reserving the vegetables but discarding the herb sachet. Skim the surface of the stock, removing any foam and fat. There should be about 2 quarts of stock. Return the stock to the pot and bring it to a boil over high heat. Cook for about 30 minutes, until reduced to 1 quart.

Remove the meat from the chicken bones, discarding the bones and skin. Add the meat and reserved vegetables to the stock. Cover to keep warm.

ASSEMBLY

1/4	pound white beans, soaked overnight
1	quart water
	Coarse salt and freshly ground white pepper to taste
1	pound dry orecchiette pasta
2	cups roughly chopped Swiss chard leaves
6	tablespoons extra-virgin olive oil
1/4	cup freshly grated Parmigiano-Reggiano cheese
6	teaspoons finely minced chives

Drain the beans and transfer them to a large pot. Add the water and season with salt and pepper. Bring to a boil over high heat. Reduce the heat and simmer for about 1 hour and 15 minutes, or until the beans are tender but not too soft. They should hold their shape. Drain and add to the stockpot with the chicken and vegetables.

In a saucepan of boiling salted water, cook the orecchiette for 8 to 10 minutes, until al dente. Drain and add to the stock. Add the Swiss chard leaves, and stir to mix and wilt the leaves. Ladle the soup into bowls and garnish each serving with a drizzle of olive oil, freshly grated cheese, and minced chives.

VARIATIONS: Increase the stock by 1 quart and the chicken to a 4 1/2- or 5-pound bird to yield extra poached chicken.

Turkey can be substituted for the chicken. Kale, spinach, or escarole can be substituted for the Swiss chard.

FLAVOR BUILDING: Stir a heaping teaspoon of Pesto (page 106) into each bowl before serving.

Cremini Mushroom Pasta with Wilted Arugula, Goat Cheese, and Extra-Virgin Olive Oil

**MAKES 6 APPETIZER SERVINGS
OR 4 MAIN-COURSE SERVINGS**

I've never been a fan of spontaneity in the professional kitchen for the simple reason that I can't bring myself to think of paying customers as guinea pigs for new concepts. Consequently, we don't post nightly specials at the Gotham but, rather, work out new dishes behind the scenes, unveiling them only when they've been thoroughly fine-tuned. At home, on the other hand, I do enjoy experimenting with new ideas, often with little or no planning, and sometimes the results are worth recording.

This is a recipe I fashioned out of found ingredients in my refrigerator. It is included here to give a sense of how you might think about using some cooking staples to make a simple and spontaneous dish. In this case, the ingredients in question

THINKING AHEAD: Keep the next day in mind when shopping; a little extra of one or two ingredients you need for dinner can go a long way in another recipe.

1	pound dry spaghetti
1/2	cup plus 2 teaspoons extra-virgin olive oil
2	pounds cremini mushrooms, trimmed and thinly sliced
	Coarse salt and freshly ground white pepper to taste
2	tablespoons finely minced garlic
3	cups tightly packed arugula, cut into a fine chiffonade
12	ounces fresh goat cheese, crumbled and softened to room temperature
4	tablespoons chopped fresh flat-leaf parsley

In a large pot of boiling salted water set over high heat, cook the spaghetti for 8 to 10 minutes, until al dente. Scoop out and reserve a generous 1/2 cup of cooking water. Drain the pasta.

While the pasta is cooking, heat 1 teaspoon of the oil in a 12–inch nonstick sauté pan over high heat. Add half the mushrooms, season them with salt and pepper, and cook, stirring often, for about 3 minutes, until they begin to release their liquid and soften. Add 1 tablespoon of the garlic and cook about 3 minutes longer, until the garlic is fragrant. Transfer the mushrooms to a bowl and cover to keep warm. Add another teaspoon of oil to the pan and repeat the cooking process with the remaining pound of mushrooms and tablespoon of garlic. Transfer them to the bowl and set aside, covered, to keep warm.

Return the drained, hot pasta to the pot. Add the mushrooms, the remaining 1/2 cup of oil, the arugula, goat cheese, and parsley. Toss until the arugula wilts and the goat cheese melts, adding the reserved cooking water a little at a time until the sauce is rich and creamy. Adjust the seasoning with salt and pepper, and serve.

VARIATIONS: Instead of using arugula, cook a bunch of broccoli rabe in boiling salted water until tender, about 5 minutes, and toss it into the pasta. Other mushrooms will work well here, especially chanterelles. A combination of ricotta cheese and some grated pecorino would be a fine substitute for the goat cheese. Aged goat cheese will also provide a delicious result.

FLAVOR BUILDING: At the Gotham Bar and Grill, I serve this pasta drizzled with white truffle oil.

were goat cheese, cremini mushrooms, and arugula—an assortment you might have available for lunch after making, say, a salad the previous night.

Making this recipe takes exactly as much time as it does to boil the pasta water and cook the spaghetti. While this is happening, you sauté the mushrooms. Then all the ingredients are tossed together with a cup or so of reserved pasta liquid, which melts the cheese into a rich, creamy emulsion.

Obviously, this is not a September-only proposition. You can apply this time-saving technique year-round.

Pan Sauces

One of the many differences between the demands on a home cook and those on a professional chef is that the home cook has little need to fret over consistency, and this is nowhere more apparent than in the preparation of sauces.

One of the fantasies I entertained all the way through cooking school was that the great three-star French chefs made their sauces *à la minute*. But when I had the opportunity to work in France, I discovered that the great restaurants actually employ a saucier who makes all the sauces, slowly reducing stocks, enriching them with butter, and passing them through a strainer until perfectly clear, at which point they are seasoned. And this is all done *before* service. This is how we do it at the Gotham. And the reason is consistency.

It would be tempting for a chef to make every sauce *à la minute* because the concept of doing so is very romantic. But even the best chef, at the height of service, when he or she is preoccupied with the minutiae of hundreds of dishes, would end up with a repertoire of sauces that came out differently every time they were prepared. Regular customers, who have been ordering the same dish for years, won't stand for this. And they shouldn't be expected to.

But in a home setting, this is no problem. And a pan sauce can be a great way to take advantage of the informality of home cooking. After cooking chicken, veal, or steak, the *fonds* (the flavorful bits cooked onto the bottom of the pan) are released with a quick deglazing, usually using the wine you'll be drinking with dinner. As the *fonds* are loosened, structure, roundness, and acidity are provided. Water or chicken broth are added to increase the volume, and butter is usually swirled in to enrich the sauce, depending on the quality of the drippings.

How much liquid you add and how much you reduce it depends on the amount and quality of the *fonds,* and on how much sauce you require. While you can usually hope to get no more than a few tablespoons per person, if you happen to have some Brown Chicken Stock (page 422) on hand, you can extend the quantity dramatically.

If cooking fish, keep in mind that you may not be left with any *fonds*. When you're cooking fish and making a pan sauce, generally you're deglazing with a fair amount of wine or lemon juice, which provides some structure and important acidity for the fish pan sauces. You might also add clam juice or even a light chicken stock, but generally I think of these fish pan sauces as a sort of quick *beurre blanc,* in which white wine is poured into the pan, quickly reduced, and enriched with a generous amount of butter. For Basic *Beurre Blanc,* see page 30.

1	pound haricots verts or young green or wax beans
4	7-ounce halibut fillets, each approximately 1 inch thick
	Coarse salt and freshly ground white pepper to taste
2	tablespoons canola oil
$^1/_4$	cup Sauvignon Blanc or other dry white wine
2	tablespoons fresh lemon juice, or to taste
$^1/_2$	cup unsalted butter
5	scallions, white part only, finely sliced on the bias
1	tablespoon capers, drained and rinsed
1	large, ripe tomato, peeled, seeded, and cut into $^1/_4$-inch dice

Seared Halibut with Haricots Verts, Scallions, and White Wine Sauce

MAKES 4 SERVINGS

In a pot of boiling salted water set over high heat, cook the haricots verts for 3 to 4 minutes, until tender. Drain and place them in the center of a large, warm serving platter. Cover to keep warm.

Season the halibut on both sides with salt and pepper. In a 12-inch sauté pan, heat the oil over medium-high heat. Cook the fish for about 3 minutes, until lightly browned. Turn, reduce the heat to medium, and cook about 4 minutes longer, until the fish is opaque in the center and browned on both sides. Put the fish on the platter with the beans and cover to keep warm.

Pour off any oil in the pan and add the wine and lemon juice. Raise the heat to high and deglaze the pan by scraping up any browned bits with a wooden spoon. Cook until the sauce reduces by half, about 2 minutes. Reduce the heat and stir in the butter, a piece at a time, to enrich and flavor the sauce. Add the scallions, capers, and tomato. Season with salt and pepper, and pour over the fish on the platter. Serve immediately.

VARIATION: You can substitute any white-fleshed fish, such as cod or grouper, for the halibut.

FLAVOR BUILDING: Puréed Potatoes (page 337) or Israeli Couscous (page 105)—both of which will have an affinity for the white wine sauce—can be added to this dish.

Here's a dish I used to cook for myself on the job at an intimate San Francisco restaurant, where I worked early in my career.

This recipe offers a prime example of cooking *à la minute* because the entire dish can be prepared and executed very quickly. (It also uses few enough ingredients that you could purchase all of them in the express lane of your local supermarket on the way home from work.) After sautéing the halibut, the fish is removed from the pan, which is then deglazed with white wine and fresh lemon juice. Butter is swirled in gradually to yield a rich, flavorful sauce—punctuated by scallions, capers, and diced tomato—that is simply poured over the fish; its pleasing citric acidity and buttery richness make it a perfect foil for the halibut.

ROASTED GARLIC POTATOES

1¼	pounds small Red Bliss potatoes, well scrubbed
2	heads garlic, separated into unpeeled cloves
¼	cup olive oil
	Coarse salt and freshly ground black pepper

Preheat oven to 375°F. Place a roasting pan in the oven for 5 minutes to preheat. In a mixing bowl, combine the potatoes, garlic, and olive oil and stir to coat the potatoes and garlic. Season generously with salt and pepper. Transfer to the roasting pan and roast, stirring occasionally until potatoes are soft when pierced with the tip of a knife and the garlic cloves are very soft and sweet in flavor, about 40 minutes. Remove from oven and keep warm.

MUSHROOMS

2	tablespoons unsalted butter
1	shallot, minced
2	cloves garlic, peeled and minced
1	pound fresh chanterelle mushrooms, trimmed, cleaned, and cut if large
2	sprigs fresh thyme, leaves picked and chopped
2	cups White Chicken Stock (page 421)

In a 12-inch sauté pan, heat the butter over medium heat. Add the shallot and cook for about 3 minutes, until softened. Add the garlic and cook about 1 minute longer. Add the mushrooms and thyme. Cover the pan and cook for 7 to 10 minutes, until the mushrooms are tender and have released their juices. If the mushrooms seem dry during cooking, add about ¼ cup of the chicken stock.

When the mushrooms are soft, add the rest of the chicken stock, raise the heat to high, and cook until the liquid is reduced by half, about 6 minutes. There will be quite a bit of liquid in the mushrooms. Remove them from the heat, cover, and set aside to keep warm.

CHICKEN

2	teaspoons canola oil
¼	cup unsalted butter
4	boneless chicken breast halves, skin on
	Coarse salt and freshly ground white pepper to taste
1	sprig rosemary, about 6 inches long, coarsely chopped
¼	cup dry white wine

Chicken Breasts with Rosemary and Chanterelles

MAKES 4 SERVINGS

In the previous recipe, I mentioned the tradition of the restaurant "family meal." Here's a recipe born of that tradition. If you happen to be the cook saddled with the task of making dinner for the crew, the best thing to do is choose a dish that is very fast to prepare and can be made with inexpensive ingredients—small portions of fish, chicken, or meat and lots of vegetables and/or starch. The potato recipe featured here was part of a family meal I used to make when I had that job. In fact, I cooked it so often that I could prep it in five minutes, after which it required just an occasional stirring in the oven. The temperature of the pan is very important in this dish; the heat must be high enough to cook the meat without burning the *fonds*.

2   tablespoons Cognac
1¹/₂ cups White Chicken Stock (page 421)
¹/₄   cup finely minced fresh chives

Heat the oil and 1 tablespoon of the butter in a 12-inch sauté pan over medium–high heat. Season the chicken breasts with salt and pepper. Place the chicken breasts in the pan, skin side down. Cook for about 6 minutes, until golden brown. Turn and cook until the juices run clear when pierced with the tip of a knife, about 6 more minutes. Add the rosemary and cook, basting frequently, for 6 to 8 minutes longer, until the chicken is cooked through and nicely browned. Transfer the chicken to a serving platter and set it aside, covered, to keep warm.

Pour off any oil in the pan and add the wine and Cognac. Raise the heat to high and deglaze the pan by scraping up any browned bits with a wooden spoon. Add the stock and cook until the sauce is reduced nearly by half or thickened and richly flavored, about 4 minutes. Remove the pan from the heat and swirl in the remaining 3 tablespoons of butter. Season with the chives, salt, and pepper. Spoon the sauce over the chicken and serve, passing the mushrooms and potatoes on the side.

WHAT TO DRINK: Serve this dish with a Grand Cru Beaujolais, such as a Moulin-à-Vent or Brouilly.

VARIATIONS: Replace the roast potatoes with Puréed Potatoes (page 337). Replace the chanterelles with thickly sliced portobello mushrooms. The chicken can be replaced with half-inch-thick veal medallions (6 ounces per person) cooked 3 to 4 minutes on each side for medium-rare.

Gotham Profiteroles with Chocolate Sauce

MAKES 8 SERVINGS

I've simply never overcome my childhood addiction to hot fudge sundaes (My preference: Vanilla Ice Cream, no whipped cream, and no maraschino cherry.) I've been known to eat more than one at a single sitting. For all my culinary education, travels, and experience, I'd happily end just about any meal with one.

In the early 1980s, I was fortunate enough to live a short time in Paris, where, at the famous brasserie La Coupole, I enjoyed my first taste of profiteroles—a French hot fudge sundae if ever I saw one, or close enough.

When I took over the kitchen of the Gotham Bar and Grill in 1985, I was set on putting profiteroles on the menu. To make ours unique, I replaced the simple chocolate sauce that the French pour over theirs with a more unrestrained, rich and thick hot fudge—a paean to the sundaes I remember so fondly. The *choux* pastry is easy to make,

CHOUX PASTRY

1/2 cup milk
1/2 cup water
7 tablespoons unsalted butter
1 cup plus 2 tablespoons all-purpose flour
1 teaspoon sugar
 Pinch of salt
5 large eggs
 Vanilla Bean Ice Cream (page 84)
 Chocolate Sauce (page 187)

Preheat the oven to 450°F. Lightly spray 2 baking sheets with vegetable oil and line them with parchment paper. Lightly spray the paper.

In a saucepan, combine the milk, water, and butter, and bring to a boil over high heat. Cook, stirring with a wooden spoon, for about 3 minutes. Add the flour, sugar, and salt, and cook about 2 minutes longer, stirring, until the mixture pulls away from the sides and bottom of the pan.

Transfer the mixture to the bowl of an electric mixer. With the mixer set on low speed, add the eggs one at a time. Make sure each egg is incorporated before adding the next. Mix until all the eggs are added and the dough is lukewarm.

Spoon the dough into a pastry bag fitted with a large, plain tip. Pipe 1-inch rounds onto the baking sheet, leaving about 1 1/2 inches between them. Bake for 20 to 22 minutes, or until the rounds are nicely browned and still soft on the inside. Transfer to wire racks to cool completely.

Split each round in half horizontally. Arrange 3 on each of 8 dessert plates. Put a small scoop of ice cream in the bottom half of each round and top with the other half. Spoon the chocolate sauce over the profiteroles and serve.

VARIATIONS: Feel free to substitute your favorite premium store-bought ice cream for the vanilla.

and while it's fun to make your own ice cream, you should feel free to save time this month by buying a super-premium brand at the market.

Chocolate Sauce

MAKES ABOUT 4 1/2 CUPS

$^1/_2$ cup heavy cream
$^1/_2$ cup light corn syrup
$^1/_4$ cup canola oil
  1   pound extra-bittersweet chocolate, such as Valrhona, finely chopped
$^1/_2$ cup milk

In a saucepan, combine $^1/_4$ cup of the cream, the corn syrup, and oil. Bring to a boil over high heat.

Put the chocolate in a bowl. Pour the hot cream mixture over the chocolate and stir until smooth and thoroughly blended. Combine the remaining cup of cream and the milk. Slowly pour into the chocolate, whisking well.

Peanut Butter
Coupe
MAKES 4 SERVINGS

If you're a dessert lover, this one pushes all the right buttons by combining ingredients that are close to the heart of anyone with a bona fide sweet tooth. With peanut butter, chocolate fudge, whipped cream, praline ice cream, and chocolate sorbet, it's difficult to go wrong, especially when they are presented as here, in a restrained balance, providing layer after layer of sweet pleasure.

THINKING AHEAD: The chocolate sorbet must be made at least 4 hours in advance.

CHOCOLATE SORBET

8	ounces extra-bittersweet chocolate, such as Valrhona, coarsely chopped
1 1/2	cups sugar
2	cups water

Put the chopped chocolate and sugar in a bowl. In a saucepan, heat the water until almost boiling. It should be about 180°F. Pour the water over the chocolate and stir until the chocolate melts and the sugar dissolves. While still warm, pour the mixture into the container of an ice-cream machine and freeze according to the manufacturer's directions. Transfer it to a covered container and freeze until firm, at least 4 hours or overnight.

ASSEMBLY

1	cup heavy cream, chilled
1 to 1 1/4	cups Chocolate Sauce (page 187)
1/2	cup unsalted peanuts
	Praline Ice Cream (page 189)
1/2	cup creamy or chunky peanut butter

In the bowl of an electric mixer set on high speed, whip the cream to stiff peaks. Spoon the cream into a pastry bag fitted with a large plain tip. Layer the ingredients in the following way: Pipe about a 1-inch layer of cream into 4 chilled pilsner glasses. Top the cream in each glass with a scoop of sorbet.

Pour about a tablespoon of chocolate sauce over the sorbet in each glass and top with about 2 tablespoons of nuts. Add a scoop of praline ice cream to each glass and more nuts.

Repeat the layering, but finish the coupe by spooning a thick layer of peanut butter over the top, the chocolate sauce, then scoops of praline ice cream. Serve immediately.

Praline Ice Cream

MAKES ABOUT 1 1/2 QUARTS

1	cup hazelnuts
2	cups heavy cream
1	cup milk
10	tablespoons sugar
8	large egg yolks

Preheat oven to 350°F.

Spread nuts onto a baking sheet. Roast in the oven, stirring often until lightly browned and fragrant, about 6 minutes. Remove from oven and cool completely. In a blender or food processor fitted with the metal blade, grind nuts into a thick paste. Scrape into a small bowl and set aside.

In a large saucepan, combine the cream, milk, and 5 tablespoons of the sugar and the nut paste. Slowly bring to a boil over medium heat, stirring occasionally to help the sugar dissolve. Remove from heat, cover and allow to steep for 10 minutes.

In a bowl, whisk the egg yolks with the remaining 5 tablespoons of sugar. Slowly drizzle about 1 cup of the hot cream mixture into the beaten egg yolks, whisking to combine. Add this mixture to the saucepan, whisking well to combine. Cook over low heat for 4 to 6 minutes, stirring constantly until the custard is thick enough to lightly coat the back of a wooden spoon. Remove from the heat. Strain the mixture through a mesh sieve into a stainless-steel bowl.

Set the bowl in a larger bowl filled with ice and water, and let it stand for about 40 minutes, stirring occasionally, until chilled and richly flavored.

Pour the custard into the container of an ice-cream machine and freeze according to the manufacturer's directions. Transfer to a covered container and freeze until firm, at least 4 hours or overnight.

VARIATIONS: This sundae will be almost as decadent if you use chocolate ice cream instead of sorbet, and if you substitute vanilla ice cream for the praline.

Concord Grape Jam

MAKES 2 1/2 CUPS

8 1/2   cups or 3 quarts Concord grapes
3/4   cup sugar

Wash the grapes under cold running water. Transfer them to a colander and allow them to drain. Stem the grapes and discard any green underripe ones. Place the grapes in a large nonreactive saucepan. Crush them with the back of a spoon or a potato masher to release their juice. Bring them to a boil quickly over a high flame and boil for approximately 10 minutes. Remove them from the heat and, using a wooden spoon, push them through a wire strainer. Try and extract as much juice and flavor as possible but do not crush the seeds (which would effect the flavor). Discard the skins and seeds. Return the strained grapes to a clean saucepan and bring to a boil quickly over high heat. Add the sugar and stir until it dissolves. Boil rapidly for approximately 15 minutes. Remove from the heat.

To test the jam's consistency (gel test), spoon some of the mixture into a small saucer. Chill quickly in the refrigerator. If the mixture is too thin and loose, return the mixture to the stove and cook a little longer. If you have overcooked the jam and it becomes hard, return it to the stove and thin the mixture with a few tablespoons of water or fruit juice.

Spoon the hot jam into hot, sterilized canning jars (see note page 81), leaving about 1/4 inch of headroom. Screw on the lids. Let cool completely and then store in a cool, dry place. The jars should not touch each other during cooling. Refrigerate after opening.

TECHNICAL NOTE: This type of grape is rich in pectin, so be careful not to overcook it, which will harden it.

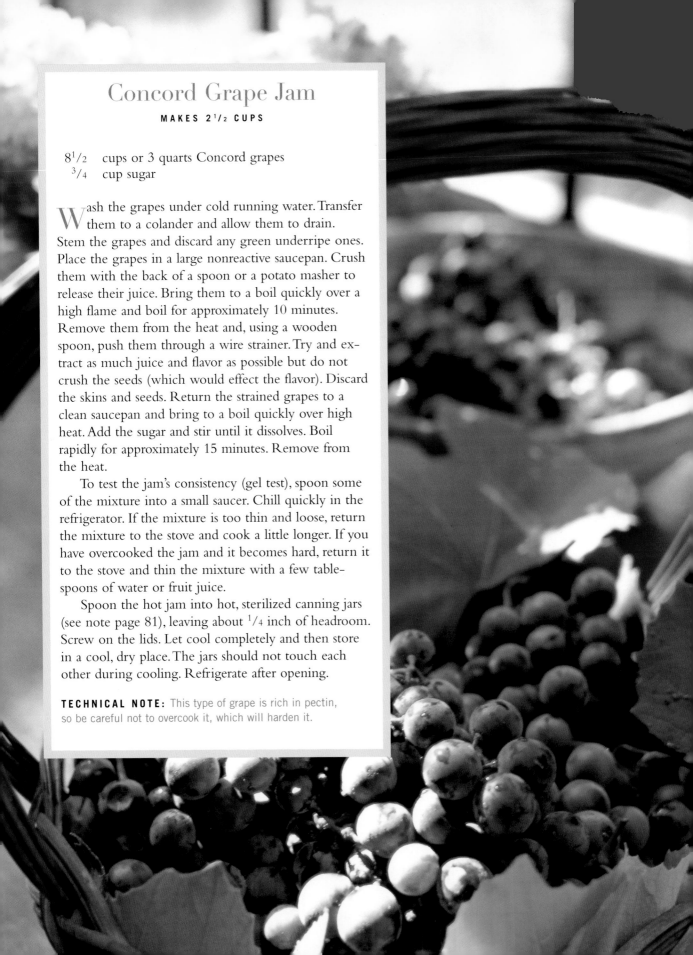

Last-Minute Dinner Party

These menus can be prepared on short notice. They involve relatively short ingredient lists and cooking times and do not require any unusual or complicated techniques.

CANAPÉ

PROSCIUTTO, PEAR, ARUGULA, AND HONEY MUSTARD SANDWICH **(page 174)**

MENU 1

WILD MUSHROOM RISOTTO **(page 202)**

SEARED HALIBUT WITH HARICOTS VERTS, SCALLIONS,
AND WHITE WINE SAUCE **(page 181)**

PEANUT BUTTER COUPE **(page 188)**

MENU 2

LEEK AND ROQUEFORT SALAD WITH MIMOSA
VINAIGRETTE **(page 166)**

CHICKEN BREASTS WITH ROSEMARY AND CHANTERELLES **(page 183)**

CLASSIC CRÈME BRÛLÉE **(variation page 215)**

Squash

Butternut Squash Soup with Spiced Crème Fraîche

Potato and Butternut Squash Gratin with Gruyère

Seared Foie Gras with Poached Quince, Tangerine, and Pomegranate Juice

Wild Mushroom Risotto

Ricotta Ravioli with Cremini Mushroom Broth and Parmigiano-Reggiano

Salmon with Black Trumpet Mushrooms, Brussels Sprout Leaves, and Fingerling Potatoes

Whole Roasted Chicken with Rosemary and Root Vegetables

Pear Tart Tatin

Maple Crème Brûlée

Apples

Warm Apple Strudel with Ginger Ice Cream

First Fall Dinner

OCTOBER

SWEATER WEATHER

October is the bridge between the last warm days of September and the coming frigid months. It is when we recognize that the end of the year is in sight and may even learn for the first time the number of shopping days left until Christmas. We are reminded of the forces of nature as our breath becomes visible and we slow down a bit, donning thicker clothing against a more and more persistent chill. As the skies darken earlier, the brisk romanticism of the month may give way to an unavoidable melancholy. But we'll adjust soon enough; we do every year.

One of the things that eases us into the coming season is the warm, comforting fall palette—earth tones of yellow, orange, and brown—that transforms October leaves, as well as the fruits and vegetables of the season. The colors, shapes, and textures that emerge during this month make for wonderful decoration. In fact, we dress up the reception area of the Gotham Bar and Grill at this time of year much as my family adorns our home—with huge, cornucopialike baskets of gourds, pumpkins, Indian corn, and apples, as well as the fallen leaves that my daughters gather in the country and preserve by ironing them between sheets of wax paper.

These are just some of the foods that flourish in October. Others are ripe pears, versatile harbingers of autumn, equally at home in savory and sweet dishes; firm, densely textured root vegetables, a sweetness lurking within their tough exteriors; and wild mushrooms, boasting abstract shapes and more pronounced flavors than their more common, cultivated cousins. These raw ingredients, coupled with the shift in the weather, inspire an approach to cooking that sets the tone for the rest of the year—a natural gravitation to slow-cooked, restorative "comfort foods," soul-warming dishes that provide the perfect antidote to the weather.

I can't think of anything that fits this description more than Butternut Squash Soup with Spiced Crème Fraîche (page 197) or Whole Roasted Chicken with Rosemary and Root Vegetables (page 209). Both find familiar and reassuring ensembles elevated by a complementary ingredient—the squash by the spiced crème fraîche and the chicken by the bold rusticity of whole, roasted garlic cloves. Another dish in the same vein is Salmon with Black Trumpet Mushrooms, Brussels Sprout Leaves, and Fingerling Potatoes (page 207).

For my family, apples are the inspiration for an October ritual. We take to suburban orchards to pick our own, enjoying the outdoors during that brief time when the cool air is more invigorating than forbidding. Back at home, we snack on them or turn them into pies, tarts, and applesauce. My daughter Victoria has her own favorite preparation—cutting apples into wedges and sprinkling them with cinnamon and sugar. This chapter includes one of our favorite apple recipes, Warm Apple Strudel with Ginger Ice Cream (page 218).

Pears and quince, too, reach their prime in the tenth month. They are represented here in such dishes as Seared Foie Gras with Poached Quince, Tangerine, and Pomegranate Juice (page 200) and Pear Tart Tatin (page 213).

But the most alluring October arrivals are wild mushrooms—chanterelle, black trumpet, hedgehog, cremini, and pleurote. Boasting distinct, unpredictable shapes, they contribute an untamed elegance and woodsy flavor, especially when enhanced with luxurious, fragrant, white truffle oil. You'll find them here in such dishes as Ricotta Ravioli with Cremini Mushroom Broth and Parmigiano-Reggiano (page 204) and Wild Mushroom Risotto (page 202).

Once you've settled into October, you'll no doubt want to celebrate the advent of autumn. Accordingly, a menu is provided for a First Fall Dinner that unites many of the classic autumn ingredients described above into a memorable meal for you to savor with friends and loved ones on your first special occasion of the fall, perhaps for an adult Halloween supper on the last day of this transitional month.

Squash

Squash are part of the gourd family— a large and diverse clan that also includes cucumbers and eggplant. Within the squash category, there are two primary types: summer squash (such as yellow squash, zucchini, and pattypan) and winter squash (such as acorn, butternut, hubbard, pumpkin, and spaghetti).

The season for winter squash is October through March, and within these months the quality is fairly consistent, though it should be noted that all squash are better after the first cold snap and a few weeks of storage, placing the true peak season at about October through January.

When purchasing squash, look for one that feels heavy for its size, which indicates a small seed cavity and more usable flesh. Most winter squash look somewhat similar: the outside color varies greatly from species to species, but you should generally seek out the ones with no bruises or blemishes. Subtle differences between species include starch and sugar content, and the level of moisture and fiber. Most recipes allow you the freedom to use your favorite squash, which is a personal decision. My favorites are butternut, delicata, acorn, buttercup, turban, and sugar pumpkins.

Ideal uses vary from species to species as well. Acorn, butternut, and hubbard are generally baked, puréed (as in a soup) or glazed with honey or maple syrup; pumpkin can be used the same way but is more often found in pies or breads, and the spaghetti squash, named for its stringy flesh, is generally steamed or roasted and served with some kind of simple sauce.

Butternut Squash Soup with Spiced Crème Fraîche

THINKING AHEAD: The soup and the crème fraîche can be made a day in advance; if you do this, do not enrich the soup with butter until reheating the next day.

SOUP

1/4	cup unsalted butter
4	pounds fresh butternut squash, peeled, seeded, and diced into 1-inch cubes
	Coarse salt and freshly ground white pepper to taste
2	shallots, peeled and sliced
2	cloves garlic, peeled and sliced
2	sprigs fresh thyme
1	bay leaf
2	cups White Chicken Stock (page 421)

In a 12-inch sauté pan, heat 1 tablespoon of the butter over medium-high heat. Add the squash and season it with salt and pepper. Cook for 15 to 20 minutes, stirring occasionally, until nicely caramelized but still firm.

When the squash is nearly cooked, heat 1 more tablespoon of butter in a soup pot over medium-high heat. Add the shallots and cook for about 2 minutes, stirring, until translucent. Add the garlic, thyme sprigs, and bay leaf, and stir for about a minute. Add the squash and chicken stock.

Raise the heat to high and bring to a boil. Reduce the heat and simmer, partially covered, for 20 to 25 minutes, or until the squash is tender. Using a slotted spoon, remove and discard the thyme and bay leaf. Transfer the soup to a blender or food processor fitted with a metal blade, and purée until smooth.

Return the soup to the pot to keep warm. Stir in the last 2 tablespoons of butter to enrich and thicken the soup. Ladle it into bowls and garnish each serving with a swirl of crème fraîche.

VARIATIONS: You can vary the squash, using buttercup or sugar pumpkin if you prefer their flavor.

The porridgelike consistency of this soup preserves all the distinguishing characteristics of butternut squash, to which hints of nutmeg, allspice, and cinnamon are added for a soul-warming autumnal starter that's as comforting and nurturing as an evening in front of a roaring fire.

To coax out as much flavor as possible, the squash is first cut into cubes that are heated slowly in butter until thoroughly caramelized and just beginning to break down around the edges. When shopping, look for a butternut squash with a long neck and pick it up to gauge its weight: if it feels heavy for its size, it will have a small seedbed, which means more usable flesh inside.

The crème fraîche behaves almost like a condiment here; swirl it in, or let it rest decoratively on top.

(continued)

SPICED CRÈME FRAÎCHE

$^1/_3$ cup crème fraîche
$^1/_8$ teaspoon ground cinnamon
$^1/_8$ teaspoon ground allspice
$^1/_8$ teaspoon ground nutmeg
      Coarse salt and freshly ground white pepper to taste

SQUASH: Avoid acorn squash in recipes that call for peeling and dicing; its deep ridges make this task almost impossible. Instead, use acorn squash for roasting, after which the pulp can be easily scooped out.

In a stainless-steel bowl, whisk together the crème fraîche, cinnamon, allspice, and nutmeg. Season with salt and pepper. Serve immediately or cover and refrigerate for up to 1 hour. Whisk again before serving.

FLAVOR BUILDING: Stir in pieces of duck confit (page 233) to add gamey punctuation, or top the soup with chopped, roasted chestnuts.

Potato and Butternut Squash Gratin
with Gruyère

MAKES 6 SERVINGS

2 pounds butternut squash

3 large russet potatoes

1 teaspoon chopped fresh thyme

1 teaspoon chopped fresh marjoram

1 teaspoon chopped fresh sage

Coarse salt and freshly ground white pepper to taste

3 cloves garlic, peeled and minced

About 2 cups heavy cream

4 ounces Gruyère cheese, coarsely grated

Potato gratins can be enormously satisfying, especially as rich accompaniments to steaks, but they are also rather one-dimensional. In this recipe, the modest investment of adding butternut squash, and suffusing the cream with thyme and marjoram, pays huge dividends as the gratin assumes a more compelling and complex character with virtually no additional work.

Preheat the oven to 375°F. Generously butter a 9-by-12-inch gratin dish.

Peel the squash and trim the top and bottom. Cut off the seed-filled bottom, halve it, and remove and discard the seeds. Slice the neck of the squash into $^1/_8$-inch-thick rounds and slice the base into $^1/_8$-inch-thick half circles. Peel the potatoes and cut them into $^1/_8$-inch-thick slices. (A French or Japanese mandoline works very well for this.)

In a small bowl, combine the thyme, marjoram, and sage.

Beginning with the half circles of squash (reserve the more attractive rounds for the top layers), layer about $^1/_3$ of the squash slices in the gratin dish. Sprinkle with some of the herbs and season with salt and pepper. Layer $^1/_2$ the potato slices over the squash layer. Sprinkle with some of the herbs and $^1/_2$ of the minced garlic. Season with salt and pepper.

Spread another third of the squash slices on the potatoes. Sprinkle with some of the herbs and season with salt and pepper. Spread the remaining potatoes in another layer over the squash and sprinkle some of the herbs and the rest of the garlic. Top with the remaining squash and herbs, and season with salt and pepper.

While firmly pressing down on the squash and potatoes with a large spoon, spatula, or your fingers, slowly pour the cream over the top and down the sides of the dish. Add enough to just barely cover the vegetables when pressed. Too much cream will result in a soupy gratin. Too little cream will make it dry.

Cover the dish with foil and bake the gratin for 45 to 50 minutes. Remove the foil and sprinkle with the Gruyère. Continue to bake, uncovered, for 25 to 30 minutes, or until the vegetables are tender, the cream is nearly absorbed, and the top of the gratin is lightly browned. Let the gratin rest for about 10 minutes to absorb all the cream before serving.

Seared Foie Gras
with Poached Quince, Tangerine, and Pomegranate Juice

MAKES 6 SERVINGS

Seared foie gras tastes delicious with just about anything, but it's especially good with compositions of sweetness and acidity that balance the richness of the foie. This is just such a recipe, comprising quince, pomegranate, and tangerine. That trio of flavors may sound painfully eclectic, but there's actually a culinary precedent for it: quince and pomegranates are native Persian fruits, and tangerines are a common ingredient in Persian cuisine.

If you don't love quince, it may be because you've never had a ripe one. Once known as "love apples," these fruits were invested with mystical powers in Greek and Roman lore. Personally, I find their exotic, musky fragrance positively intoxicating and often keep a bowl of them in the kitchen, savoring their perfume until they turn yellow. (Ripe quince are

THINKING AHEAD: The quince can be cooked as many as 2 days in advance and stored in their own juice. The pomegranate juice can be cooked 1 day in advance. Both should be reheated gently before serving.

FOIE GRAS
1^1/$_2$ pounds foie gras, chilled

Separate the 2 lobes of the foie gras and cut away any excess fat at the points of separation. Using a sharp, thin-bladed knife dipped in hot water and then wiped dry, cut the foie gras crosswise into ^{1}/$_2$-inch-thick slices. Cover it with plastic wrap and refrigerate until well chilled. About 15 minutes before assembling the dish, remove the foie gras from the refrigerator and let it sit at room temperature.

POACHED QUINCE
3   medium ripe yellow quince (about 1^1/$_2$ pounds)
2   cups water
^{1}/$_2$ cup sugar
    Peel of 1 tangerine
    Juice of 2 tangerines (about ^{1}/$_3$ cup)
4   whole cloves
2   tablespoons peeled and chopped fresh ginger
1   cinnamon stick

Slice the ends from the quince and peel the fruit with a sharp knife or a vegetable peeler. Cut the quince in half lengthwise and remove the tough core with a small sharp knife or a small scoop. Cut the quince lengthwise into 1-inch-thick wedges. Put the wedges in a medium, nonreactive saucepan.

Add the water, sugar, tangerine peel, juice, cloves, ginger, and cinnamon stick. Bring to a boil over medium-high heat. Reduce the heat and simmer for 8 to 10 minutes, until the quince are tender. Remove from the heat.

Using a slotted spoon, lift the quince pieces and tangerine peel from the poaching liquid and set them aside. Strain the poaching liquid through a fine sieve and discard the solids.

Cut the tangerine peel into julienne. Return the julienned peel and the quince pieces to the poaching liquid and cover to keep warm.

POMEGRANATE JUICE

1 large red pomegranate
¼ cup red wine vinegar
2 tablespoons sugar

Cut the pomegranate in half and remove the seeds. Reserve 2 heaping tablespoons of seeds to use as garnish.

In a nonreactive saucepan, combine the remaining seeds, the vinegar, and sugar. Bring to a boil over high heat. Reduce the heat and simmer for 6 to 7 minutes. Transfer the mixture to a blender and purée until smooth. Strain the purée through a fine sieve, pressing gently against the seeds to extract as much liquid as possible.

ASSEMBLY

Coarse salt and freshly ground white pepper to taste
6 sprigs fresh thyme
6 sprigs fresh chervil
2 tablespoons pomegranate seeds

Heat a 12-inch sauté pan over medium-high heat. Season the foie gras slices with salt and pepper and sear them for about 1 minute. Turn and sear about 1 minute longer. The foie gras should be nicely browned on the outside and rare in the middle. If necessary, cook the foie gras in batches but work steadily and quickly.

Gently heat the poached quince in its sauce, if necessary. Arrange the quince in the centers of 6 plates. Top with the foie gras slices. Drizzle the pomegranate juice around the foie gras and garnish with the herbs, pomegranate seeds, and the julienne of tangerine peel.

WHAT TO DRINK: Serve this dish with a Sauternes or a late-harvest Riesling from Germany, Australia, or Canada.

VARIATION: Rather than making your own pomegranate juice, you can purchase pomegranate syrup from Middle Eastern specialty shops.

yellow, not green as is commonly thought.) Because they're so hard, quince can be difficult to core, but a melon baller or Parisian scoop works well for this task. In this same regard, be sure to remove the core completely because it will not soften when cooked and will discolor the beautiful ruby red transformation that occurs. I especially like to use quince in a recipe like this because it takes full advantage of the fruit's resiliency—unlike an apple, you can cook, poach, or sauté quince until quite tender, but it will always retain its basic shape.

Here, quince is poached in a broth of spices, ginger, tangerine juice, and tangerine peel. The confluence of these vibrant ingredients creates dazzling colors, especially with the addition of pomegranate sauce, which—properly executed—is as arresting as a sunset.

There are two methods of extracting pomegranate juice: One is to cook the seeds briefly, then purée and strain them. The other is simply to cut the fruit in half and press it in a juicer. Keep in mind that the white pith is extremely tannic and should be avoided entirely by not using excessive pressure.

Be sure to reserve some pomegranate seeds, which can be scattered around the plate like jewels—an apt finishing touch for this exotic and regal recipe.

Wild Mushroom Risotto

MAKES 6 APPETIZER SERVINGS
OR 4 MAIN-COURSE SERVINGS

Risotto has a reputation as a complicated dish, but—in reality—it doesn't take longer to make than most meals because the prep work for a basic risotto is fairly simple and short. Here, the stock is infused with dried porcini or morels in order to transmit a deep mushroom flavor throughout the dish. The mushrooms are simply sautéed separately, then folded into the risotto at the end.

I usually like to enhance a risotto with an herbed or compound butter of some kind, but I have forsaken that step here. If, however, you would like to augment the flavor, see Flavor Building below.

While I generally eschew the use of cheese in risotto, a carefully measured amount of Parmesan really piques the flavors in this dish.

THINKING AHEAD: See page 339 for notes on making a risotto in advance.

MUSHROOM BROTH

2	quarts White Chicken Stock (page 421)
8	ounces sliced cremini mushrooms
1	ounce dried mushrooms, such as morels, porcini, or black trumpets, or an assortment
	Coarse salt and freshly ground white pepper to taste

In a stockpot, combine the stock, cremini mushrooms, and dried mushrooms. Bring to a boil over high heat, reduce the heat, and simmer, covered, for about 30 minutes, until the flavors have infused. Strain through a fine-mesh sieve, pressing on the solids to extract as much flavor as possible. Discard the solids. Return the strained stock to the pot, cover, season with salt and pepper, and keep at a simmer over low heat.

RISOTTO

5	tablespoons unsalted butter
1	pound assorted wild mushrooms, such as chanterelle, hedgehog, pleurote, and black trumpet, cleaned and sliced
	Coarse salt and freshly ground white pepper to taste
1	tablespoon extra-virgin olive oil
2	shallots, peeled and minced
2	cloves garlic, peeled and minced
1	pound rice, preferably *vialone nano* or arborio
1	teaspoon chopped fresh thyme leaves
1/2	cup dry white wine
1/4	cup freshly grated Parmesan cheese, or more to taste

In a large sauté pan, heat 1 tablespoon of the butter over high heat. Add the mushrooms and season with salt and pepper. Cook, stirring occasionally, for 1 to 2 minutes, or until the mushrooms have softened. Set aside.

In a large stockpot, heat 2 more tablespoons of the butter and the olive oil over medium-high heat until the butter melts. Sauté the shallots for 1 to 2 minutes, until softened. Add the garlic and cook about 2 minutes longer. Add the rice and cook, stirring with a wooden spoon, for 7 to 10 minutes, until it turns milky white and opaque, and begins to stick to the bottom of the pan. Add the thyme and continue stirring.

Add the wine and stir for about 2 minutes, until nearly absorbed. Ladle about 1 cup of the simmering stock into the rice. Cook for about 2 minutes, stirring often, until the stock is almost completely absorbed. Add more stock, a cup at a time, stirring gently, until the broth is absorbed by the rice before adding the next cup. After about 15 minutes, begin tasting the rice. At this point, add the stock judiciously. The rice should be firm, yet cooked through in 18 to 20 minutes total cooking time.

Stir in the sautéed mushrooms, the Parmesan, and the remaining 2 tablespoons of butter. Season with salt and pepper, and serve.

VARIATIONS: Feel free to use any type of fresh mushrooms you have access to, or concentrate exclusively on one mushroom. Reconstituted dried shiitakes can also be used.

FLAVOR BUILDING: Top each serving with some white truffle butter or drizzle each one with white truffle oil. Or you might shave an ounce or two of fresh or flash-frozen black Périgord truffles over each serving. Using a 14-ounce can of black truffle juice in place of the last addition of stock will also deepen the flavor considerably.

Ricotta Ravioli with Cremini Mushroom Broth and Parmigiano-Reggiano

MAKES 6 APPETIZER SERVINGS OR 4 TO 5 MAIN-COURSE SERVINGS; ABOUT 48 RAVIOLI

My mother, a wonderful Italian-American home cook, makes cheese ravioli so creamy and delicious that, when we were kids, my brother, sister, and I would actually count the quantity on one another's plates to ensure pasta-equity. In those days, my mother would make large batches and freeze them on sheet pans, breaking them out for just a few special occasions throughout the year.

Like many big-city residents, we were fortunate to have a few Italian neighborhoods in town. My favorite stores were the family-owned markets there. I can still remember the aroma of freshly baked Italian bread, pungent cheeses, and barrels of olives that wafted through the air, and what it was like browsing shelves lined with tins, bottles, and boxes of olive oils, tomatoes,

THINKING AHEAD: The ravioli can be made and frozen several weeks in advance following the Thinking Ahead note on page 361.

RAVIOLI

1	pound ricotta cheese
1	large egg
1	large egg yolk
2	tablespoons mascarpone cheese
1	tablespoon finely grated fresh Parmesan cheese
$^1/_4$	teaspoon minced garlic
	Coarse salt and freshly ground white pepper to taste
$^1/_2$	recipe Semolina Pasta Dough (page 364)
1	large egg beaten with 1 tablespoon water

Line a colander with cheesecloth. Spoon the ricotta into the colander and set it over a bowl. Refrigerate for 8 hours or overnight to drain. Gather the cheesecloth around the cheese and lift it from the colander. Gently squeeze the cheese wrapped in the cheesecloth to extract any excess liquid. Discard the drained liquid.

In the bowl of an electric mixer fitted with a paddle, combine the drained cheese with the egg, egg yolk, mascarpone cheese, Parmesan cheese, and garlic, and mix until smooth. Taste and season with salt and pepper. You can also mix this by hand using a rubber spatula. Transfer the mixture to a pastry bag fitted with a #5 plain tip.

Roll out a quarter of the dough at a time. Place the pasta dough sheet on a lightly floured work surface. Brush off any excess flour from the dough. Cut off the irregularly shaped ends, making a long rectangle, and then cut the sheet in half to make 2 equal-sized rectangles.

About 1 inch from the top of one rectangle, pipe out mounds of filling about $1^1/_2$ inches apart. The mounds should be about $^3/_4$ inch wide. Pipe out another row of mounds parallel to the first, about 1 inch from the bottom of the dough. Brush the second rectangle with the egg wash and place it over the piped sheet, brushed side down. Using your fingers, gently press around each mound of filling to seal. Using a fluted pastry wheel, cut out ravioli about $1^1/_2$ inches square, trimming away the excess dough as necessary. Put the ravioli on a semolina-dusted baking sheet. Repeat the procedure with the remaining dough and filling, using more baking sheets as needed. Refrigerate until ready to cook.

SAUCE AND ASSEMBLY

2 tablespoons extra-virgin olive oil
1 1/2 pounds cremini mushrooms, stems trimmed, sliced into
1/8-inch-thick slices
Coarse salt and freshly ground white pepper to taste
2 cloves garlic, peeled and finely minced
2 shallots, peeled and finely minced
3 sprigs fresh thyme
3 cups White Chicken Stock (page 421)
2 tablespoons unsalted butter
1/2 cup freshly grated Parmesan cheese
2 tablespoons chopped fresh chives

In a large sauté pan, heat the oil over high heat. Add the mushrooms and season with salt and pepper. Cook, stirring, for about 5 minutes. Add the garlic and shallots, and cook about 2 minutes longer, until they soften. Add the thyme and then the chicken stock and bring to a boil. Reduce the heat and simmer for 6 to 8 minutes, or until the liquid is reduced to about 2 cups and is deeply flavored. Cover and set aside to keep warm.

Bring a large pot of salted water to a boil over high heat. Add the prepared ravioli and cook for about 3 minutes, until tender. Carefully drain in a colander.

Spoon the ravioli into deep, warmed pasta bowls. Reheat the mushroom sauce if necessary. When hot, set it over very low heat and stir in the butter to soften and enrich the flavors. Season with salt and pepper. Spoon the mushroom sauce over the ravioli. Sprinkle with the cheese and chives.

VARIATIONS: If you're fortunate enough to encounter an Italian market that makes its own cheese, they probably also sell freshly made ravioli. By all means avail yourself of this option, and enjoy them with this mushroom broth instead of a standard red sauce. Conversely, if you don't happen to have such a shop in your city or town from which to buy fresh ricotta, don't despair—add some mascarpone and grated pecorino cheese to supermarket-brand ricotta to improve its texture and flavor.

FLAVOR BUILDING: Drizzle truffle oil over each serving.

and pastas. Many of the proprietors made their own mozzarella and ricotta cheeses, so when it was time to make ravioli, my mother had a great resource.

To help compensate for the time-consuming process of making ravioli, this dish uses a relatively simple one-pan method in which the sauce is produced from the essence of the mushrooms that remains after they've been sautéed. (See Pan Sauces, page 180, for more on this technique.) This method is useful for creating a quick fix the next time you find yourself craving mushrooms during their October peak.

THINKING AHEAD: The Brussels sprouts can be made the morning you serve this dish. Blanch them, shock them in ice water, drain, and refrigerate.

POTATOES AND BRUSSELS SPROUTS

1	pound fingerling potatoes
1	carrot, peeled and cut into $1/4$-inch dice
6	ounces pearl onions, cut into $1/4$-inch slices (5 or 6 onions)
8	ounces fresh Brussels sprouts, cored and separated into leaves
1	cup White Chicken Stock (page 421)
$1/2$	cup heavy cream
$1/4$	cup unsalted butter
	Coarse salt and freshly ground white pepper to taste
2	teaspoons fresh lime juice

In a large saucepan of lightly salted boiling water, cook the potatoes for 10 to 15 minutes over medium-high heat, until tender when pierced with the tip of a sharp knife. Drain and set them aside to cool.

At the same time, bring another pot of salted water to a boil over medium-high heat. Cook the carrot for about 2 minutes, until just barely tender. Remove with a slotted spoon or strainer and set aside. Add the onions to the same pot of boiling water and cook for about 2 minutes until barely tender. Remove and set aside. Cook the Brussels sprout leaves in the boiling water for 2 to 3 minutes, until barely tender. Drain and plunge them into a bowl of ice water. Drain again. Squeeze out as much excess water as possible from the leaves and pat them dry with kitchen towels.

Cut the cooled potatoes into $1/2$-inch-thick rounds. Set aside.

In a large saucepan, combine the stock and cream and bring to a boil over high heat. Cook for 7 to 8 minutes, until reduced by $1/3$ and thickened. Whisk in the butter, a piece at a time, until the sauce is thickened and enriched. Add the potatoes, carrot, onions, and Brussels sprout leaves. Reduce the heat to low and simmer gently for about 5 minutes. Season with salt and pepper. Remove from the heat and stir in the lime juice. Cover and keep warm.

(continued)

Salmon
with Black Trumpet Mushrooms, Brussels Sprout Leaves, and Fingerling Potatoes

MAKES 4 SERVINGS

This dish demonstrates the fiscal benefits of buying in-season ingredients, Brussels sprouts in this case. I made it as the main course when the program *CBS Saturday Morning* challenged me to make dinner for four on a budget of $20 as part of their regular "Chef on a Shoestring" segment. If not for the seasonally priced Brussels sprouts, I would have failed the test, as my meal came in just shy of the limit at $19.93.

If Brussels sprouts bring to mind the image of wincing children angling for a shortcut to dessert, you're not alone. The problem, of course, is that when cooked whole, all of the flavor is sacrificed. But if you core the sprouts and cook the leaves in boiling salted water, they will retain their appealing pale green color, and their sweet flavor will be a revelation.

ASSEMBLY

- 1 tablespoon unsalted butter
- 6 ounces fresh black trumpet mushrooms, trimmed
- 4 7-ounce salmon fillets
  Coarse salt and freshly ground white pepper to taste
- 3 tablespoons canola oil
- 3 tablespoons finely minced fresh chives

In a large sauté pan, heat the butter over medium heat. Add the mushrooms and cook for 5 to 7 minutes, until they begin to release their liquid and soften. Remove from the heat and set aside.

Season the salmon with salt and pepper on both sides. Heat the oil in a 12-inch sauté pan over medium-high heat. Cook the salmon for about 3 minutes, until lightly browned. Turn and cook for about 3 minutes longer. Reduce the heat and cook about 3 minutes longer, until the salmon is opaque in the center.

Stir the chives into the vegetables and sauce. Using a slotted spoon, lift about $2/3$ of the vegetables from the sauce and arrange them on individual plates or a serving platter. Top with the salmon fillets. Spoon the remaining vegetables over the salmon and then top with the mushrooms. Spoon any sauce remaining in the pan over the vegetables and salmon.

VARIATIONS: Halibut, grouper, or cod will work well with the vegetables in this dish. The vegetables also pair well with game, such as duck breast or squab. You can also substitute hedgehog, chanterelle, hen-of-the-woods, or cremini mushrooms for the black trumpet mushrooms.

Whole Roasted Chicken
with Rosemary and Root Vegetables

MAKES 4 SERVINGS

There are a handful of reliable standbys that even people who don't have a vast repertoire seem to know how to cook, and roast chicken is certainly one of them. In my version, the chicken cavity is massaged with olive oil, fresh lemon juice, and herbs before being seasoned with pepper, crushed garlic cloves, and lemon zest. It is cooked at high heat and basted frequently.

CHICKEN

4	sprigs fresh thyme
4	sprigs fresh marjoram
4	sprigs fresh sage
2	sprigs fresh rosemary
$1/4$	cup extra-virgin olive oil
	Zest and juice of 1 lemon
1	$4^1/_2$- to 5-pound chicken
	Freshly ground white pepper to taste
6	cloves garlic, peeled and crushed
	Coarse salt to taste
3	tablespoons unsalted butter, melted, for basting

Pick the leaves from the sprigs of fresh herbs. Chop the leaves. You should have about $1/4$ cup packed, chopped fresh herb leaves. Transfer them to a small bowl, add the olive oil and lemon juice (reserve the zest), and whisk to mix. Rub the chicken inside and out with the herb mixture.

Season the chicken inside and out with a generous amount of pepper. Combine the garlic cloves and lemon zest. Stuff this mixture into the cavity of the chicken. Truss the chicken with kitchen twine and put it in a shallow glass bowl or dish. Cover it with plastic wrap and refrigerate for at least 4 hours or overnight.

Preheat the oven to 425°F.

Remove the chicken from the refrigerator about 15 minutes before roasting and scrape off any excess marinade, being sure to leave a thin coating. Set the chicken on a rack in a roasting pan and season it with salt. Roast for 20 minutes. Reduce the oven temperature to 375°F and roast the chicken for about 1 hour, or until cooked through. Baste the chicken frequently with melted butter and any marinade remaining in the glass dish. Remove chicken from roasting pan, tent with foil and let rest on a plate for 10 to 15 minutes before carving.

(continued)

ROASTED VEGETABLES

³/₄	pound carrots, peeled and cut into 2-inch pieces
³/₄	pound red potatoes, halved or quartered if large
2	onions, peeled and quartered
2	heads garlic, separated into cloves and peeled (approximately 20 cloves)
1	tablespoon olive oil
	Coarse salt and freshly ground white pepper to taste

Preheat the oven to 425°F. Put a roasting pan in the oven—preferably a nonstick pan.

In a bowl, toss the vegetables with the olive oil and season with salt and pepper. Transfer them to the hot roasting pan and roast for about 40 minutes, stirring occasionally, until soft and caramelized. Serve hot.

PAN SAUCE AND ASSEMBLY

¹/₂	cup white wine
2	cups White Chicken Stock (page 421)
2	tablespoons unsalted butter
	Coarse salt and freshly ground white pepper to taste
2	tablespoons finely chopped flat-leaf parsley, optional

Pour off the fat from the chicken roasting pan, reserving the pan juices. Set the roasting pan over medium-high heat and add the wine. Deglaze the pan, scraping up the browned bits on the bottom. Cook until nearly all the wine is evaporated, about 4 minutes. Add the chicken stock and any juices that have accumulated from the resting chicken.

Transfer the liquid to a saucepan and cook it over high heat for 15 to 20 minutes, until the stock is reduced by about half and is slightly thickened and richly flavored. Add any collected juices from the chicken platter to the sauce. Swirl the butter into the sauce to enrich it. Season with salt and pepper, then stir in the parsley, if using.

Cut and remove the string from the chicken using a very sharp knife, and transfer the whole chicken to the center of a large platter. Spoon the roasted vegetables around the outside of the platter. Serve the pan sauce on the side.

WHAT TO DRINK: Serve this dish with a French Burgundy such as Nuits-St.-Georges or Vosne-Romanée.

THINKING AHEAD: The pastry dough must be made 1 to 2 hours in advance and stored in the refrigerator.

QUICK PUFF PASTRY

4^1/$_2$	cups all-purpose flour
1	tablespoon coarse salt
2^1/$_2$	cups unsalted butter, cut into pieces and chilled
^{1}/$_2$	cup cold water

In a mixing bowl, whisk together the flour and salt. Add the butter and, using your fingertips or 2 forks, work the butter into the flour until the mixture resembles coarse crumbs. Do not overmix. Add the water all at once and stir to just combine. There will be small chunks of butter in the dough.

Turn the dough out onto a lightly floured surface and, using a lightly floured rolling pin, roll it into a large rectangle approximately ^{1}/$_2$ inch thick. Fold one side of the dough into the center and then fold the other side over it, so that the rectangle is folded in thirds, like a letter. Roll the dough into another ^{1}/$_2$-inch-thick rectangle and fold it again in a similar fashion. Repeat the rolling and folding process 4 times. Doing so will form buttery, flaky layers in the baked crust. Wrap the dough in plastic and refrigerate it for 1 to 2 hours.

Remove the chilled dough from the refrigerator. On a lightly floured surface, roll the dough out to about ^{1}/$_4$ inch thick. Using a 10-inch round cake pan as a guide, cut the dough into a 10-inch circle. Put the circle on an ungreased baking sheet and prick it all over with a fork. Cover and refrigerate until ready to bake.

PEARS AND ASSEMBLY

1	tablespoon vegetable oil
1	cup sugar
2	tablespoons water
7	firm Bosc pears, not overripe
3	tablespoons unsalted butter, cut into slices
^{1}/$_2$	cup crème fraîche

Preheat the oven to 350°F. Brush a 10-inch-round cake pan with the oil.

In a small saucepan, combine the sugar and water, and cook over medium heat for 10 to 15 minutes without stirring, until the

The classic tart Tatin dates back to the early 1900s and is an "upside down" tart in which apples, covered with pastry, are baked in a pan, which is then inverted to great effect, revealing beautifully caramelized fruit atop a piping hot crust. This dessert is a variation that substitutes pears for apples.

Years ago, my wife, Helen, and I sampled a Pear Tart Tatin at a food, wine, and ski festival in Vail, Colorado. Subsequently, we have made this dish for guests countless times, and the unveiling of the finished dessert from under an overturned pan never fails to elicit an appreciative response. The recipe presented here departs from the textbook one because the pears and crust are cooked separately and then assembled moments before serving. In a restaurant, where all preparation is done in advance, this method is essential; the dessert becomes soggy if not consumed immediately after baking. At home, it allows you to monitor the doneness of the pears, greatly reducing the chances of over- or under-cooking them. (It's also a great convenience that the pastry bakes in exactly as much time as it takes the pears to cool.)

The delicate quality of the pears suits this preparation very well: Their pale coloring, set aglow by a coat of caramel, adds to the golden aura of this timeless dessert. The sweet aroma of the fruit, and its succulent feel on the palate, are two of the culinary sensations I associate most closely with fall. Serve the Pear Tart Tatin with a glass of sherry or a tawny port for a warm, semisweet conclusion to a chilly October evening.

WHAT TO DRINK: Serve this dessert with amontillado sherry or a tawny port.

sugar turns an amber color. Pour the hot sugar into the cake pan. Be careful and stand back because the sugar is very hot.

Peel and halve the pears. Quarter any that are very large. Core the pears. Arrange them in the cake pan, rounded sides down and points toward the center. Dot with the butter and bake for about 30 minutes, or until tender. Remove the pears from the oven and pour off enough liquid to leave about a $1/2$-inch depth in the pan. Discard the excess liquid. Press on the pears with a spatula to form a firm layer. Do not turn off the oven.

Remove the dough circle from the refrigerator and bake it for about 10 minutes, until lightly puffed and golden. Put the baked circle on top of the pears. Carefully invert the tart onto a serving plate. Serve warm, with a few tablespoons of crème fraîche spooned over each serving. Pass the remaining crème fraîche on the side.

VARIATION: To create a classic tart Tatin, substitute Granny Smith apples for the pears.

FLAVOR BUILDING: Praline Ice Cream (page 189) and Sweetened Mascarpone (page 120) also complement the flavors in this dessert.

Maple
Crème Brûlée

MAKES 8 SERVINGS

THINKING AHEAD: These crème brûlées can be made as many as 2 days in advance.

BRÛLÉE SUGAR

1	cup light brown sugar
1/2	cup granulated sugar

Preheat the oven to 250°F.
Combine the sugars, mixing well to integrate evenly. Spread the mixture on a baking sheet and dry it in the oven for about 1 hour. Transfer to a blender and process to a fine powder. Set aside, covered, and store in a cool dry place at room temperature for up to a week.

CUSTARDS

3 3/4	cups heavy cream
1 1/4	cups pure maple syrup
10	large egg yolks, lightly beaten

Preheat the oven to 350°F.
In a bowl, combine the cream, maple syrup, and egg yolks, and whisk until smooth. Strain through a fine-mesh sieve. Pour into eight 5-ounce ramekins. Set the ramekins in a shallow roasting pan or baking pan and put them in the oven. Pour enough hot water into the pan to come halfway up the sides of the ramekins. Bake for about 45 minutes, until the custards are set around the edges but still a little shaky in the center.

Carefully remove the pan from the oven. Let the custards cool in the water bath to room temperature. Remove from water bath, cover with plastic wrap, and refrigerate for at least 8 hours or overnight.

ASSEMBLY

Preheat the broiler or, better yet, use a small propane torch designed for kitchen use.

Remove the plastic wrap and sprinkle each custard with brulée sugar. Broil for 30 to 60 seconds, until the sugar caramelizes, or hold the torch over the sugar to caramelize it. Serve at once.

In New York City, Nature doles out precious few of its more poetic touches. If you've lived elsewhere, this can be a frustrating element of life in this, or any, big city. One of the natural rites I miss the most each year is the changing of the leaves—the brown and orange piles that collected across the landscape are among my most vivid memories of growing up in upstate New York.

In Manhattan, the closest experience available is the blur of fall colors on a cab ride through Central Park. But I was reminded of those upstate days a few years ago during a Columbus Day weekend getaway to a Vermont maple farm. In addition to purchasing jars of their superior, sweet syrup, each member of my family indulged in their extraordinary homemade maple ice-cream cones—which inspired this crème brûlée. Maple syrup may be tapped in the spring, but its flavor is an autumn favorite. Keep this dessert in mind for that evening when you realize—perhaps due to the first frost or the first whiff of chimney smoke in the air—that you've entered the twilight of the year.

(continued)

VARIATION: On restaurant menus, classic crème brûlée refers to vanilla custard, which can be made by omitting the maple syrup from this recipe, replacing it with 2 vanilla beans (split lengthwise) and 1 cup of granulated sugar. In a medium saucepan, bring the cream, vanilla bean, and sugar to a simmer over medium heat. Remove the custard from the heat, cover, and allow the flavors to infuse for 10 minutes. Meanwhile, place the egg yolks in a stainless-steel mixing bowl and whisk to combine. Slowly pour the warm cream mixture into the eggs, whisking constantly. Strain the mixture, discard the vanilla beans, and proceed with the recipe from this point, filling the ramekins and cooking the dessert.

Apples

During the days of September, when the air begins to turn cold, home cooks may find themselves thinking about apples for the first time in the year. I know I do. As soon as the first cool weekend rolls around, I can't wait to make an apple tart. But the same restriction stops me in my tracks year after year—early in September, you can only find mealy, stored varieties that don't lend themselves to baking.

But in October, when the first crop of apples materializes, it's an incredible treat. Owing to the growing sophistication and discerning taste of the American palate, many heirloom varieties have worked their way into the supermarket, and at farm stands and gourmet markets, the selection can be breath taking. At the Union Square Green Market in New York City, the incredible range of varieties is represented by a sea of reds and greens flowing from booth to booth across the park.

There are expansive orchards in upstate New York and Long Island where my family goes apple picking every October. If you do the same, keep in mind that, though they all look very similar, different varieties are good for different purposes. For example, crabapples make wonderful sauces and relishes, while McIntosh apples are ideal in sauces and ciders. Many of the more familiar varieties such as Golden Delicious, Granny Smith, and Rome Beauty are all-purpose apples, as good for eating on their own as anything else. Among the best baking apples are Greening, Northern Spy, and Winesap.

This last group is a valuable one to know. While it's generally a good idea to experiment with different varieties of any fruit or vegetable, cooking with apples is a rare case where I actually encourage people not to stray too far from what they know. Identify a few varieties that you like for baking and stick to them. The simple truth is that most apples don't hold up in the oven, and the wrong one in a pie or tart Tatin will disintegrate, no matter how high your skill level.

Warm Apple Strudel

with Ginger Ice Cream

MAKES 8 SERVINGS

When the powerful aroma of this strudel—comprising apples, cinnamon, dried cranberries, and toasted walnuts—permeates your home, you'll know that fall has arrived. This is a convenient recipe to bear in mind if you're pressed for time or don't do much baking, because it uses phyllo (or filo) dough, which can be purchased from any supermarket.

GINGER ICE CREAM

2	cups heavy cream
1	cup milk
10	tablespoons sugar
1	tablespoon peeled, chopped fresh ginger
8	large egg yolks

In a large saucepan, combine the cream, milk, 5 tablespoons of the sugar, and the ginger. Bring to a simmer over low heat, stirring occasionally to help the sugar dissolve. Remove the pan from the heat, cover, and let stand for about 10 minutes.

In a bowl, whisk the egg yolks with the remaining 5 tablespoons of sugar. Pour about 1 cup of the hot cream mixture into the beaten egg yolks to temper them, whisking constantly to prevent the eggs from curdling. Add the tempered eggs to the saucepan, whisking well to combine. Cook over low heat for 4 to 6 minutes, stirring constantly until the custard is thick enough to lightly coat the back of a wooden spoon. Strain through a sieve into a stainless-steel bowl. Set into a larger bowl filled with ice and water. Let it stand for about 40 minutes, stirring occasionally, until the custard is chilled.

Pour the custard into the container of an ice-cream machine and freeze according to the manufacturer's directions. Transfer to a covered container and freeze for at least 4 hours or overnight.

PASTRY CREAM

1/2	cup milk
2	tablespoons sugar
1/2	Tahitian vanilla bean, split lengthwise
2	tablespoons cornstarch
2	large egg yolks
2	teaspoons unsalted butter

In a saucepan, combine the milk, 1 tablespoon of the sugar, and the vanilla bean. Cook over medium-high heat for about 5 minutes, stirring, until the milk boils and the sugar dissolves. Remove from heat.

Sift together the remaining tablespoon of sugar and the cornstarch.

In a small bowl, lightly whisk the egg yolks. Add the cornstarch mixture and whisk to mix. Add 2 to 3 tablespoons of the hot milk mixture into the yolks to temper them, whisking constantly to keep the eggs from curdling. Return the saucepan to the stove over very low heat. Add the tempered egg yolks to the saucepan and cook, stirring, for 4 to 6 minutes, until hot and smooth. Take care to keep the heat very low to prevent the eggs from scrambling.

Remove the pastry cream from the heat and stir in the butter until incorporated. Set aside to cool completely.

APPLE FILLING

6	firm, tart apples, peeled, cored, and cut into $1/4$-inch pieces (about 6 cups), such as McIntosh, Rome, or Cortland
1	cup dried cranberries
$1/2$	cup sugar
$1/4$	cup unsalted butter
1	cinnamon stick
$1/2$	teaspoon freshly grated nutmeg
2	cups toasted chopped walnuts

In a large sauté pan, combine the apples, cranberries, sugar, butter, cinnamon stick, and nutmeg. Cook over high heat for 10 to 12 minutes, stirring, until the apples are soft and the mixture is well blended. Stir in the walnuts. Set aside to cool.

STRUDEL AND ASSEMBLY

10	sheets phyllo pastry
	About $1/2$ cup unsalted butter, melted

Preheat the oven to 400°F. Line a baking sheet with parchment paper.

Separate 5 sheets of phyllo from the stack and set them aside, covered with a well-wrung, damp kitchen towel while working with the other 5 sheets.

Stack the 5 phyllo sheets, brushing each with about 2 teaspoons of the melted butter. Spread half the filling over the stack and then top with half of the pastry cream. Leave about a $1/2$-inch-wide border around the edge of the pastry. Beginning on the long side, roll the strudel into a cylinder. Place the roll seam-side down on the baking sheet. Repeat with the remaining 5 sheets of phyllo, melted butter, apple filling, and pastry cream. Brush the top of each roll with the remaining melted butter. Bake for 25 to 30 minutes, until the phyllo is golden brown and the apples are hot and bubbling.

Slice each strudel into 4 pieces. Place 1 slice on each of 8 dessert plates. Scoop some ice cream next to each slice.

VARIATIONS: You might also serve this dessert with Vanilla Bean Ice Cream (page 84) or a store-bought or homemade ice cream of your choice.

FLAVOR BUILDING: Add dried cherries, diced dried apricots, or golden raisins (plumped up in rum or Cognac) to this strudel.

First Fall Dinner

Both these menus include several of the foods most closely associated with the fall. Serve either of them on one of the first cold nights of the year.

MENU 1

RICOTTA RAVIOLI WITH CREMINI MUSHROOM BROTH
AND PARMIGIANO-REGGIANO **(page 204)**

FENNEL-AND-GARLIC-CRUSTED PORK ROAST
WITH WARM QUINCE AND APPLE COMPOTE **(page 285)**

PEAR TART TATIN **(page 213)**

MENU 2

BUTTERNUT SQUASH SOUP WITH SPICED CRÈME FRAÎCHE **(page 197)**

WHOLE ROASTED CHICKEN WITH ROSEMARY
AND ROOT VEGETABLES **(page 209)**

WARM APPLE STRUDEL WITH GINGER ICE CREAM **(page 218)**

Pumpkin and Sweet Garlic Custards

Pears

Seared Foie Gras and Pears Caramelized with Honey
and Rosemary

Duck Confit and Sweet Turnip Risotto

Potatoes

Lobster with Savoy Cabbage, Flageolets, and Roasted Garlic

Chicken Poached with Savoy Cabbage and
Black Truffle

Squab Roasted with Potatoes, Pancetta, and Sage

Wild Roast Turkey with Cornbread Stuffing

Red Wine Poached Pears with Mascarpone and
Pistachio Nuts

Pumpkin Crème Brûlée

Cranberry-Ginger Sorbet

Thanksgiving Menus

NOVEMBER

GIVING THANKS

When you stop to think about it, Thanksgiving might just be one of the two or three most anticipated days in the United States each year. And with good reason, for what more American celebration is there? Memorial Day and the Fourth of July are more noble, patriotic occasions to be sure. And there's no minimizing the importance of Easter and Christmas, as well as the special allure they hold for children. Labor Day? New Year's Eve? Valentine's Day? They're all fine holidays, no doubt about it.

But Thanksgiving is something else altogether: a day when subtle spirituality meets with sanctioned slothfulness, when lounging around the house, watching football, and cooking at a leisurely pace is what you're actually supposed to be doing—until you come together with the most important people in your life to enjoy a meal like no other, stopping everything, if only for a few hours, for the sole, simple purpose of appreciating all that you have.

As if that weren't enough, there are beautiful rituals of giving that have become a part of the Thanksgiving tradition; even the most Scrooge-like among us are apt to take a moment to help the less fortunate at this time of year. Our daughters' school conducts various drives, and at the Gotham Bar and Grill, we encourage Thanksgiving diners to donate a can of food, which we then deliver to neighborhood shelters and churches.

Thanksgiving is such an American ritual that I'm inclined to wonder what marketing executive, at what company, could have devised a more well-timed, more appealing, more perfect spectacle.

But wait, there's more! Since it always falls on a Thursday, Thanksgiving is also the only holiday that, for most people, promises four days off, year after year, without fail. The three days that follow Turkey Day are a well-placed opportunity to settle into the rhythm of the holidays without any distractions. The more ambitious among us might seize the opportunity to start shopping for Christmas presents, while most of us are content to eat leftovers and line up for the first of Hollywood's holiday movies. There are, after all, still nearly four weeks until Christmas.

Having shared all this, you won't be surprised to learn that it's not just on Thanksgiving that my family and I look forward to the familiar sanctuary of the dinner table; we actually spend the entire month in this state. It's like the slow, giddy crawl up a roller coaster's incline, with the exhilaration of the holidays waiting on the downward slope.

Maybe it's also because I'm a chef, and Thanksgiving is the only American holiday officially centered around a meal. Accordingly, I thought it would be fun to devote a chapter to this holiday, offering some unexpected variations on the obligatory ingredients. While there's certainly nothing wrong with the traditional feast of turkey, stuffing, cranberry sauce, sweet potatoes, and pumpkin pie, you might be pleasantly surprised by how many liberties you can take to make these elements new and exciting.

The pumpkin, closely associated with Thanksgiving, is represented here in the Pumpkin and Sweet Garlic Custards (page 227). Another accompaniment well suited to a variety of contexts is the potato and pancetta recipe that figures prominently in Squab Roasted with Potatoes, Pancetta, and Sage (page 245). And pears, one of the most autumnal of fruits, are put to dramatic effect in Seared Foie Gras and Pears Caramelized with Honey and Rosemary (page 230).

Of course, the requisite main course in any Thanksgiving feast is turkey. Here, I've presented an unusual Wild Roast Turkey with Cornbread Stuffing (page 247), and for those seeking a less traditional Thanksgiving poultry, Chicken Poached with Savoy Cabbage and Black Truffle (page 242) and Duck Confit and Sweet Turnip Risotto (page 233). For variety's sake, there's also a seafood dish that's appropriate to November, Lobster with Savoy Cabbage, Flageolets, and Roasted Garlic (page 239).

While your menu might include a cranberry relish or compote of some kind, why not return to cranberries at the end of the meal with a Cranberry-Ginger Sorbet (page 254), or conclude with two of the other quintessential ingredients of November as in Red Wine Poached Pears with Mascarpone and Pistachio Nuts (page 250) or Pumpkin Crème Brûlée (page 252)—an audacious answer to the traditional pumpkin pie that will leave your guests very thankful indeed.

Pumpkin and Sweet Garlic Custards

MAKES 8 SERVINGS

THINKING AHEAD: The entire recipe can be made a day ahead of time and gently reheated in a water bath in a 350°F oven for 10 minutes.

2	heads garlic, separated into cloves but not peeled (approximately 20 cloves)
1	3-pound sugar pumpkin or butternut squash, peeled, seeded, and cut into 1-inch cubes
2	tablespoons unsalted butter
4	large eggs
2	cups heavy cream
2	teaspoons finely chopped fresh marjoram leaves
$1/4$	teaspoon freshly grated nutmeg
	Coarse salt and freshly ground white pepper to taste
8	small sprigs fresh marjoram, for garnish

Put the garlic cloves in a small saucepan. Add enough cold salted water to cover and bring to a boil over high heat. Drain, discarding the water. Return the garlic cloves to the pan, add more water and salt, and repeat twice more. When the water comes to a boil for the third time, reduce the heat and simmer for about 12 minutes, until the cloves are tender. Drain, and set aside 8 cloves for garnish. Peel the remaining cloves.

Meanwhile, put the pumpkin in a 2½-quart saucepan. Add enough cold salted water to cover, and bring to a boil over high heat. Reduce the heat and simmer for about 6 to 8 minutes, or until tender when pierced with the tip of a small, sharp knife. Drain.

In a 12-inch sauté pan, heat the butter over medium-high heat. Add the squash and peeled garlic cloves, and cook for 5 to 10 minutes, stirring often to avoid scorching, until the excess moisture evaporates. Remove from the heat to cool to room temperature.

Preheat the oven to 350°F.

Transfer the squash and garlic to a blender or a food processor fitted with the metal blade and process until smooth. Add the eggs, cream, marjoram, and nutmeg. Season with salt and pepper, and pulse to combine. Ladle the custard into eight 4-ounce ramekins.

Set the ramekins in a shallow roasting pan or baking pan, cover loosely with a sheet of foil, and put the pan in the oven. Pour enough hot water into the pan to come halfway up the sides of the ramekins. Bake for 35 to 40 minutes, until the custards are set

For me, pumpkins evoke the cornucopia that symbolizes Thanksgiving, so I believe that these versatile custards will make a wonderful addition to your November repertoire. The pumpkin is deeply caramelized to activate its complex flavors while, in contrast, the garlic is slow-roasted to a sweet, fragrant softness. In addition to turkey, this savory combination complements a variety of other meats and fowl at this time of year, including roast pork and roast chicken.

When making this dish be sure you periodically peek under the foil to ensure that the custards don't "soufflé"; instead, you want a soft, silky, elegant quality. You might also use this recipe as the model for any number of vegetable custards of your own design. (See Variations.)

around the edges but still a little shaky in the center. Check the custards after about 15 minutes in the oven. If they are puffing up and resembling soufflés, reduce the oven temperature to 325°F.

Carefully remove the pan from the oven. If not serving right away, let the heat escape from the oven and, at the same time, reduce the temperature to its lowest setting (between 180° and 200°F). Let the custards cool slightly in the water bath, then lift the ramekins from the water and serve immediately or return them to the oven to keep warm. Serve the custards in the ramekins or unmolded, inverted onto a plate. To serve, garnish each custard with a reserved unpeeled clove of garlic and a sprig of marjoram.

NOTE: If making well in advance, remove the ramekins from the water bath and allow to cool to room temperature. Cover the ramekins with plastic wrap and refrigerate them. To reheat, place the custards, still covered with plastic wrap, in a large sauté pan and add enough water to come about ½ inch up the sides of the ramekins. Bring to a simmer over low heat for about 30 minutes, or until the custards are warmed through. Off the heat, the custards will keep warm in the water bath for up to 30 minutes.

VARIATIONS: This recipe can be used to make custards with vegetables that have low fiber and water content, such as cauliflower, carrots, parsnips, and turnips. If using a more fibrous vegetable such as peas or asparagus, you must first sieve them.

Pears

I don't know exactly why the pear is such a perfect autumn fruit. Maybe it's simply because its season so closely tracks that of the year's colder months. Pears show up in late October and November, are with us all winter long, and by the time spring arrives, have quietly slipped away.

Pears generally ripen off the tree. They lend themselves to a multitude of preparations including grilling, roasting, or sautéing. The mildly granular flesh contrasted with their sweet, syrupy juice make pears ideal for snacking, as well as for one of my personal favorite ways to enjoy them—with cheese, especially the blue-veined ones.

While there are countless varieties of pears available from local farm stands around the country, three or four primary selections—most of them grown in California, Oregon, and Washington state—dominate.

The most popular is the Bartlett, a large, bell-shaped pear—predominantly yellow, though some red variations exist. Because it maintains its shape when cooked, it is ideal for poaching. The Bartlett is also used in making the eau-de-vie, Poire William, which I love at the end of a meal. If you've ever seen a bottle of Poire William with an actual pear preserved inside of it, that pear is a Bartlett. (In fact, the French name for Bartlett is "Williams," though it should be noted that the best Poire William comes from Switzerland.)

Anjou pears are green-yellow in color, short and squat in shape, and are good for snacking. In sharp contrast, Bosc pears are tall, thin, and often exquisitely shaped with relatively long necks. They show a pleasant brown skin and are exceptionally crisp and sweet. A reliable variety, Boscs lend themselves to cooking and eating fresh. They also hold up well in storage, so keep them in mind when using pears outside of the peak season.

Among the other popular varieties are Forelle and Seckel pears, both wonderful dual-purpose fruits; their firm-but-not-too-firm texture makes them as reliable for snacking as for poaching.

I use all these pears frequently, but to my taste, the most beautiful of this lovely fruit's varieties is the Comice, with its yellow coloring, brown spots, and brush of red—it's the pear you might associate with Monet still-life paintings. And this is one case where looks are not deceiving—Comice pears are luscious and supersweet, with a powerful pear fragrance—the ultimate expression of all of this fruit's considerable charms.

Seared Foie Gras and Pears Caramelized with Honey and Rosemary

MAKES 6 SERVINGS

Ask most home cooks if they've ever made foie gras and, if they're being truthful, nine out of ten will tell you they're afraid it will melt away in the pan—a concern that has dissuaded even the most intrepid cooks from trying to make this luxurious delicacy. If you've found yourself similarly intimidated by the idea of cooking foie gras, you may find this recipe therapeutic.

I myself have gone through a bit of a learning curve with foie gras. After graduating from cooking school, I discovered that I was operating under the misconception that foie gras had to be cooked in a superhot pan, when in fact this threatens to ruin its fragile delicacy, browning it quickly on both sides but leaving the middle raw and cold.

Try this method instead: Remove the foie gras from the refrigerator, slice it cold using a warm knife, and allow the slices to sit for 15 minutes

THINKING AHEAD: You can slice the foie gras and return it to the refrigerator as many as 4 hours in advance, but wrap each slice individually in plastic wrap. The pears can be cooked 4 hours in advance, kept at room temperature, and then reheated in a hot oven for about 5 minutes.

FOIE GRAS
$1^1/_2$ pounds foie gras, chilled

Separate the 2 lobes of the foie gras and cut away any excess fat at the points of separation. Using a sharp, thin-bladed knife dipped in hot water and then wiped dry, cut the foie gras crosswise into $^1/_2$-inch-thick slices. Cover with plastic wrap and refrigerate until well chilled. About 15 minutes before assembling the dish, remove the foie gras from the refrigerator and let it sit at room temperature.

CARAMELIZED PEARS
2   tablespoons canola oil
3   large, firm Bosc pears, peeled, halved, and cored
$^1/_2$ cup honey
3   large sprigs rosemary, cut in half
$^1/_4$ cup white or red port wine

Preheat the oven to 450°F.
In an ovenproof 12-inch sauté pan, heat the oil over high heat until very hot but not smoking. Add the pears and roast in the oven for 8 to 10 minutes, turning them often, until the pears begin to caramelize. Add the honey and rosemary, and roast for 6 to 8 minutes longer, until the pears are nicely caramelized and golden but still hold their shape.

Remove the pan from the oven. Leaving the pears in the pan, create a little sauce by deglazing the pan with the port over high heat, scraping the bottom of the pan with a wooden spoon. Toss the pears with the deglazing liquid until they are nicely coated. Remove and reserve the rosemary. Cover the pears to keep warm.

ASSEMBLY

    Coarse salt and freshly ground white pepper to taste
2   tablespoons Balsamico Tradizionale vinegar

Heat a 12-inch sauté pan over medium-high heat. Season the foie gras slices with salt and pepper, and sear them for about 1 minute. Turn and sear them about 1 minute longer. The foie gras should be nicely browned on the outside and rare in the middle. If necessary, cook the foie gras in batches but work steadily and quickly.

Place a pear half in the center of each of 6 warmed plates. Next, arrange the foie gras slices on the plates. Spoon a little of the pear sauce around the pears and foie gras, drizzle with balsamic vinegar, and garnish with the reserved rosemary. Serve immediately.

VARIATIONS: This is a versatile dish because you can change the accompaniments with the season. The best guideline is to use a soft fruit with a touch of sweetness and acidity (peaches in the summer, for example). If you don't have any 25-year-old balsamic vinegar in the house (which most people don't), cook down a "regular" balsamic vinegar to concentrate its flavors.

The pear and rosemary accompaniment is also delicious on its own or as a side dish with game, duck, or squab.

to come to room temperature. Then sear the slices in a hot pan for just about 20 seconds on each side. You'll be amazed at the world-class results you'll get with this technique. It's important to note that, even if you're doing it right, the foie gras will throw a lot of smoke. Don't panic; in fact, take a moment to savor that heady, delicious aroma.

As good as foie gras is, I think the real star of this dish is the combination of pears and rosemary, a recipe you should keep in mind for other culinary scenarios. The fruit is roasted with honey and rosemary, balancing the sweetness with a surprising savory counterpoint. A quick deglazing of the pan with port wine creates a lovely, sweet pan sauce that has a great affinity for the rich foie gras.

THINKING AHEAD: The confit must be started 3 days in advance but can be preserved in the refrigerator in its fat for several weeks. To prepare a risotto in advance, follow the instructions on page 339.

Duck Confit and Sweet Turnip Risotto

MAKES 6 APPETIZER SERVINGS OR 4 MAIN-COURSE SERVINGS

DUCK CONFIT

1	shallot, sliced
6	cloves garlic, thinly sliced
3	bay leaves
3	sprigs thyme
1	teaspoon crushed black pepper
1	tablespoon coarse salt
4	duck legs
3	pounds duck fat

In a dish large enough to hold the duck legs in a single layer, sprinkle half the shallot, garlic, bay leaves, thyme, pepper, and salt. Lay the duck legs on top and sprinkle them with the remaining herbs and spices. Cover the dish tightly with plastic wrap and refrigerate for 24 to 48 hours to marinate.

In a medium pot, melt the duck fat over low heat. You will have about 7 cups.

Remove the duck legs from the marinade and place them in a deep casserole or 4-quart stockpot. Ladle in enough melted duck fat to cover the duck legs completely. Cook over low heat for 3 1/2 to 4 hours, taking care the fat does not boil but remains just below a simmer. It should barely bubble, and the temperature, gauged with a deep-fat thermometer, should register around 185°F.

When the meat is very tender, nearly falling off the bone, transfer the legs to a dish. Strain the duck fat over the duck, adding any additional fat you did not use for cooking. Set aside to cool. When cool, cover and refrigerate until ready to use.

TURNIPS

1	tablespoon unsalted butter
1	tablespoon canola oil
4	medium white turnips, peeled and cut into 1/2-inch dice
1	tablespoon sugar
	Coarse salt and freshly ground white pepper to taste
1/2	head savoy cabbage, cored, leaves separated and roughly chopped

You probably don't expect to find duck confit and sweet, caramelized turnips in a risotto, but this classic French pairing works as well in this Italian context as it does anywhere else. The richness of the ingredients calls for a comparably assertive backdrop, which is created here by first cooking the rice with smoked bacon and then finishing the dish with a heady garlic butter.

I created this recipe as an outlet for my love of duck confit, which mystified me a bit in my younger years. But when I found myself cooking in confit country in the southwest of France, I had many opportunities to sample the best duck confit in the world and learned that they all share a few key traits, namely a crackling, ultracrisp skin and soft, shredding meat underneath.

The technique for the turnips in this recipe is unusual because they are cut into large dice and cooked in butter and sugar, creating a sweet confit effect even as they retain their shape.

When these ingredients, not to mention the pale, crunchy cabbage, are folded into the rice, the juxtaposition of flavors and textures is unique and beguiling. It's a dish that initially may seem unfamiliar, but it will feel tried and true by the time you finish your first serving.

In a medium sauté pan, heat the butter and oil over medium heat. Add the turnip cubes and cook for 2 to 3 minutes, until lightly browned. Sprinkle them with the sugar and season with salt and pepper. Continue cooking, tossing, for 8 to 10 minutes, or until the turnips are browned on all sides and are tender and nicely caramelized. Remove the pan from the heat and set it aside.

In a saucepan of boiling salted water, blanch the cabbage for 2 to 3 minutes. Drain and plunge it in ice water. Drain and set aside.

RISOTTO AND ASSEMBLY

2 quarts Double Turkey Stock (page 424) or White Chicken Stock (page 421)
2 tablespoons canola oil
2 ounces slab bacon, cut into $1/8$-inch dice
1 cup minced onion
1 pound rice, preferably *vialone nano* or arborio
1 teaspoon fresh thyme leaves
$1/2$ cup white wine
2 tablespoons Garlic Butter (page 235)
2 tablespoons chopped fresh chives
Coarse salt and freshly ground white pepper to taste

Preheat the oven to 400°F.

Remove the duck legs from the refrigerator. Measure 1 cup of fat from the dish and heat it in an ovenproof, 12-inch skillet over medium-high heat until melted. Lift the duck legs from the remaining fat and lay them in the hot fat, skin side down. The fat should come about $1/3$ inch up the sides of the legs. If not, add more fat. Raise the heat and cook for about 6 minutes, until the skin turns brown. Do not turn the legs over.

Put the skillet in the oven and roast the duck legs for about 15 minutes, until the skin is crisp and the meat is heated through. Remove the legs from the pan and transfer them to a cutting board.

When cool enough to handle, pull the meat from the bones. They should separate easily. Cut the meat and crispy skin into large pieces. Place them on a small plate and cover to keep warm.

Meanwhile, bring the stock to a boil over high heat. Reduce the heat and simmer the stock gently.

In a large stockpot, heat the oil over medium heat. Cook the bacon for 3 to 5 minutes, until lightly browned. Add the onion and cook about 3 minutes longer. Stir in the rice and cook, stirring with a wooden spoon, for 7 to 10 minutes, until the rice turns milky white and opaque and begins to stick to the bottom of the pan. Add the thyme and stir.

Add the wine and stir for about 2 minutes, until nearly absorbed. Ladle about 1 cup of the simmering stock into the rice. Cook for about 2 minutes, stirring often, until the stock is almost completely absorbed. Add more stock, a cup at a time, stirring gently until it is absorbed by the rice before adding the next cup. After about 15 minutes, begin tasting the rice. At this point, add the stock judiciously. The rice should be firm yet cooked through in 18 to 20 minutes total cooking time. When the risotto is done, it will be creamy but still firm to the bite.

Add the turnips and cabbage to the risotto and heat through. Add the duck meat and duck skin, stir in the butter and chives, and adjust the seasonings with salt and pepper. Serve immediately.

VARIATIONS: This recipe works very well with simple roasted duck pieces, especially legs. You can also purchase confit from the mail-order source on page 426. Roasted chicken legs, though not as rich, also make a viable substitute.

Garlic Butter

MAKES ABOUT 4 CUPS

1	pound unsalted butter, softened
2	tablespoons minced garlic
2	tablespoons fresh lemon juice
1/2	tablespoon chopped fresh thyme
1/2	tablespoon freshly ground black pepper
	Coarse salt to taste

THINKING AHEAD: This butter can be frozen, wrapped tightly in plastic wrap, for up to 2 weeks.

In the bowl of an electric mixer fitted with the paddle and set on medium speed, beat the butter until smooth. Add the garlic, lemon juice, thyme, pepper, and salt. Beat until well blended. Cover and refrigerate until ready to use.

Potatoes

There are few vegetables that enjoy the dubious compliment of assumed simplicity more than the potato. As the phrase "meat and potatoes" reflects, these tubers have a reputation for unfailing straightforwardness, which is easy to understand given their imperfect shapes and dirty brown skins.

But potatoes should not be underestimated. They exist in a number of varieties, and knowing the characteristics of each is a prerequisite to cooking effectively with potatoes. They also happen to be one of the most utilized vegetables, appearing with great frequency in high and low cuisine the world over.

Potatoes are a member of the nightshade family, with a season that runs from early summer to early winter, at which point they are stored. Here in New York City, we get most of our potatoes from upstate New York and Long Island.

When purchasing potatoes, examine them to ensure that they do not have any sprouts. They should never be stored in the refrigerator, but rather in a cool place that approximates cellar conditions.

Among my favorite potatoes are fingerlings, named for their long, crooked shape. Five or six years ago, fingerling potatoes were not commercially available. In fact, they were so scarce that several restaurants in New York, the Gotham included, found themselves vying for the same supply. In the end, I took care of our needs by agreeing to buy 5,000 pounds in advance from my supplier at the start of the season. The farmer would hold them for us once the Union Square Green Market closed in October or November and deliver them to the restaurant in installments throughout the winter.

Today, fingerlings are more popular, and farmers have taken the cue by growing them in much greater volume. There are about a dozen varieties including Ratte, which is starchy, and Banana, Ruby Crescent, and Rose, all of which are waxy. The uses for each variety are very well defined, and the best way to determine which ones work best for you is with a little trial and error to see which ones suit your personal taste and hold their shape well enough for their intended purpose.

New potatoes are thin-skinned and hard as stones. Most potatoes are harvested after the vines have shriveled, but new potatoes are harvested when the vines still have leaves and the plants are green. When they're pulled out of the ground, you can still see the root structure. They are best cooked whole and simply, perhaps steamed and dressed with a little olive oil and coarse salt.

The best potatoes for mashing or puréeing are Yellow Finns or Yukon Golds, which are fine-grained and yield a silky purée.

Red Bliss are small, red-skinned, white potatoes that are good when potatoes need to hold their shape, as when roasting, slicing, sautéing, or making a potato salad.

Idaho and russet potatoes are good, all-purpose potatoes, starchy and ideal for baking, mashing, or frying. Both have thick brown skin and are also the best potatoes for French frying because the starch can be rinsed off successfully. In case you've ever wondered, the difference between an Idaho and a russet is simply that the former is a russet grown in Idaho, where the conditions produce superior results—a small but important distinction that illustrates the hidden depths and quiet complexities of the humble potato.

CABBAGE AND FLAGEOLETS

1	head Savoy cabbage, cored, stemmed, leaves separated
12	medium fingerling potatoes
1	cup flageolets, soaked overnight and drained
1^1/$_2$	cups White Chicken Stock (page 421)
1	cup water
1	small onion, halved
1	small head garlic, split in half
2	sprigs fresh thyme
	Coarse salt and freshly ground white pepper to taste

In a saucepan of boiling salted water, blanch the cabbage leaves for 3 to 4 minutes. Drain and plunge them in ice water. Drain again and reserve.

In a saucepan of boiling salted water, cook the potatoes for 15 to 20 minutes, until tender. Drain and set them aside to cool. When cool, cut them in half lengthwise.

In a pot, combine the flageolets, stock, water, onion, garlic, and thyme. Bring to a boil over high heat. Reduce the heat and simmer for 20 to 25 minutes. Season the beans with salt and pepper, and cook them 30 to 40 minutes longer, until they are tender. Remove the pot from the heat and let the beans cool in their cooking liquid.

LOBSTER SAUCE

6	1^1/$_4$-pound live lobsters
^{1}/$_4$	cup canola oil
6	plum tomatoes, roughly chopped
2	ribs celery, roughly chopped
2	heads garlic, split in half
1	medium Spanish onion, roughly chopped
1	large carrot, roughly chopped
^{1}/$_2$	bunch flat-leaf parsley
6	sprigs fresh thyme
2	bay leaves
2	tablespoons black peppercorns
1^1/$_2$	cups white wine
3	cups White Chicken Stock (page 421)
^{1}/$_4$	cup heavy cream
1	cup unsalted butter, cut into pieces
^{1}/$_4$	teaspoon cayenne pepper, or to taste
	Coarse salt and freshly ground white pepper to taste

Lobster
with Savoy Cabbage, Flageolets, and Roasted Garlic

MAKES 4 SERVINGS

A lot of seafood restaurants offer you a choice of steamed or broiled when you order a lobster. Though I usually prefer them steamed, this is my take on broiled lobster. The recipe employs a time-saving technique that allows some of the messy lobster preparation to be done ahead of time. Because it's rich, owing to the use of a lot of butter and the effect of the creamy flageolets (those regal dry beans from France) this is an ideal dinner for a cold-weather month like November.

THINKING AHEAD: The flageolets must be soaked overnight. The lobster can be prepared the morning of the day you are making this dish.

Bring a large pot of salted water to a boil over high heat. Add the lobsters, cover, and cook for 2 to 3 minutes, or until the lobsters stop moving. This kills the lobsters and sets the meat. Transfer the lobsters to a work surface.

Remove the claws from the lobsters and separate the tails from the heads. Split the tails in half lengthwise and crack the claws. Cover and refrigerate until ready to use.

With a heavy kitchen knife or cleaver, coarsely chop the heads. In a large stockpot, heat the oil over medium heat until very hot and just beginning to smoke. Add the lobster heads and cook for about 20 minutes, turning occasionally, until browned. Take care the lobster does not burn. Add the tomatoes and cook for about 4 minutes. Add the celery, garlic, onion, carrot, parsley, thyme, bay leaves, and peppercorns. Cook for 2 to 3 minutes longer.

Add the wine and cook for about 15 minutes, until the wine is reduced by three-quarters. Add the stock. Bring to a boil, reduce the heat, and simmer about 1 hour.

Strain the liquid through a fine sieve into a bowl, pressing on the solids with the back of a spoon to extract as much liquid as possible. Discard the solids. You will have about 4 cups of liquid.

Transfer the liquid to a saucepan and cook it over high heat for about 30 minutes, until it is reduced by half and the flavors intensify. Add the cream and bring to a boil. Reduce the heat to low.

Whisk the butter into the sauce to thicken and enrich it. Season with cayenne pepper, salt, and pepper, and set aside. You will have about 2 1/2 cups of sauce.

LOBSTER AND ASSEMBLY

16	cloves garlic, separated but not peeled
1/4	cup extra-virgin olive oil
1	tablespoon water
	Coarse salt and freshly ground white pepper to taste
1/4	cup canola oil
2	tablespoons finely minced fresh chives

Preheat the oven to 350°F.

Put the garlic cloves in a small baking dish. Add the olive oil and water, and season with salt and pepper. Cover tightly with aluminum foil and bake for 20 to 25 minutes, until the cloves are soft. Remove the pan from the oven and set aside. Do not turn off the oven.

Season the lobster tails and claws with salt and pepper. In 2 large, ovenproof sauté pans over high heat, heat the canola oil, dividing it equally between the pans. Add the lobster tails, flesh side down, claws, and fingerling potatoes. Cook for 2 to 3 minutes, until browned. Turn each piece in the pan. Add the roasted garlic cloves, distributing them evenly between the pans. Put the pans in the oven and cook for 2 to 3 minutes longer, or until the lobster is bright red and cooked through, and the potatoes are browned.

In a sauté pan, combine the cabbage leaves and 1/2 cup of the sauce and heat gently.

Drain the cooled beans, add them to the remaining lobster sauce, and heat gently. Arrange the lobster, potatoes, garlic cloves, and cabbage leaves on serving plates. Spoon the beans and sauce over the vegetables and lobster. Garnish with the chives and serve immediately.

VARIATIONS: Replacing the flageolets with fresh shell beans—such as limas, peas, or favas—and the cabbage with Swiss chard will allow this recipe to work in a summer context. Because the components are so flavorful, the rather complicated sauce can be replaced with just a squeeze of lemon, and the dish will still be delicious.

WHAT TO DRINK: Serve this with a big, fat Chardonnay, either from the central coast of California or from Australia.

FLAVOR BUILDING: Top each serving with an ounce of Sevruga caviar.

Chicken
Poached with Savoy Cabbage and Black Truffle

MAKES 4 SERVINGS

As a culinary student, I went through a period when I was prone to day-dreaming about the classic French dish *Poulet Demi-Deuil,* and I wasn't alone—this recipe has been highly romanticized by countless cookbook writers over the years. *Demi-Deuil* literally means "in half-mourning," and in *Poulet Demi-Deuil,* black truffles are stuffed under the skin of a chicken, covering the breast, and the bird's cavity is filled with black truffles before it is poached and then served with the root vegetables from its cooking liquid. At the time, I had never seen, smelled, or tasted black truffles, but I was obsessed with the concept of a plump chicken stuffed with them and poached in an intensely flavored broth teeming with root vegetables.

A few years ago, we paid tribute to this extravagant dish at the Gotham, using pheasant instead of chicken and modernizing the vegetable mix in the poaching liquid. Creating and serving a dish based on *Poulet Demi-Deuil* stirred

THINKING AHEAD: The double chicken broth can be made several days in advance and refrigerated or frozen for up to 2 weeks.

CHICKEN AND STOCK

2	3^1/$_2$-pound chickens
2	teaspoons canola oil
2	cloves garlic, peeled and sliced
1	shallot, sliced
2	bay leaves
2	sprigs fresh thyme
1^1/$_2$	quarts White Chicken Stock (page 421)

Begin preparing the chickens by removing and reserving the neck and giblets and discarding the liver. Cut off the wing tips, cut out and reserve the backbone. Split the breasts in half and re-move the leg and thigh pieces. You should have 4 breast halves and 4 leg-thigh pieces. Cover and refrigerate until ready to use.

In a stockpot, heat the oil over medium-high heat. Add the chicken wingtips, neck, giblets, and backbone and cook for about 10 minutes, until nicely browned. Stir in the garlic and shallot, and sauté until translucent, about 4 minutes. Add the bay leaves and thyme, and cook for about 1 minute. Add the chicken stock, bring to a boil, reduce the heat, and simmer for about 30 minutes. Strain the stock through a fine sieve into a bowl. You should have about 1 quart. Discard the solids. Set the stock aside.

VEGETABLES

6	fingerling potatoes
6	large Savoy cabbage leaves
2	salsify, peeled and cut into 2-inch lengths
^{1}/$_2$	lemon
1	turnip, peeled and cut into 8 pieces, or 8 baby turnips
12	baby carrots, peeled

In a saucepan of boiling salted water, cook the potatoes for 15 to 20 minutes, until tender. Drain and set aside to cool. When cool, cut them in half lengthwise.

In a saucepan of boiling salted water, blanch the cabbage leaves for 3 to 4 minutes. Drain and plunge them in ice water. Drain again and reserve.

Put the salsify in a saucepan and cover it with cold salted

water. Squeeze the juice from the lemon half into the water and then drop the lemon half in, too. Bring to a boil, reduce the heat, and simmer for about 20 minutes, until the salsify is quite tender. Drain and reserve the salsify.

In a saucepan of boiling salted water, cook the turnip and carrots for about 3 minutes. Drain and plunge them in ice water. Drain again and reserve.

ASSEMBLY

    Coarse salt and freshly ground white pepper to taste
1   1-ounce black truffle, sliced
    Fresh chervil sprigs, for garnish
    Coarse sea salt

Remove the chicken from the refrigerator and season it well with salt and pepper. Put the reserved stock in a large pot and bring it to a boil over high heat. Reduce the heat to a simmer and add the chicken leg-thigh pieces. When the stock returns to a low simmer, cover, and poach the chicken for about 15 minutes. Add the breasts and cook at a low simmer about 12 minutes longer, or until done. The chicken leg-thigh pieces will be very tender when pierced at the joint with a sharp knife and will almost be falling from the bone. The chicken breasts are done when still barely pink in the center.

Add the vegetables, and when the stock returns to a simmer, cook for about 4 minutes, until the chicken is cooked through. Add the sliced truffle and remove the pot from the heat.

Remove the chicken from the pot. Taste the broth and adjust the seasoning.

Divide half of the vegetables and broth among 4 oversized, rimmed soup plates. Top each serving with 1 breast half and 1 leg-thigh piece. Top with the remaining vegetables, taking care to distribute the truffle slices evenly. Garnish with chervil and sprinkle each serving with sea salt.

an emotion like that I imagine recording artists feel when performing a cover version of a teenage favorite. Part of the secret of this recipe's success is that before straining the liquid to use as a sauce, it is boiled to concentrate the flavors, and the whole thing is perfumed with a handful of thinly sliced black truffle.

Poaching pheasant can be tricky because, unlike chicken, it threatens to dry out when cooked, so I've returned to the original here and was delighted to do so. It was, after all, good enough to become the stuff of legend.

1   tablespoon extra-virgin olive oil
1   head garlic, separated into cloves but not peeled (about
    12 to 14 cloves)
3   ounces pancetta, sliced into $^1/_8$-inch-thick slices
16 fingerling or creamer potatoes (1 to $1^1/_4$ pounds)
1   teaspoon chopped fresh sage
1   teaspoon chopped fresh thyme
    Coarse salt and freshly ground black pepper to taste
4   whole squab, each about 18 ounces
1   tablespoon canola oil
2   tablespoons unsalted butter
$^1/_4$ cup red wine
1   cup White Chicken Stock (page 421)
2   teaspoons chopped fresh flat-leaf parsley

In a 12-inch sauté pan, heat the oil over low heat. Add the garlic cloves and sauté for about 12 minutes, until softened.

Meanwhile, cut the pancetta slices into $^1/_2$-inch dice. Add the pancetta to the sauté pan and cook for 6 to 8 minutes, stirring occasionally, until browned.

Slice the potatoes into $^1/_8$-inch-thick slices. Add them to the sauté pan, raise the heat to medium-high, and cook for about 30 minutes, tossing occasionally, until the potatoes are lightly browned and cooked through. When the potatoes are nearly done, after about 25 minutes, season them with the sage, thyme, salt, and pepper, and toss gently. When done, remove the pan from the heat and cover to keep warm.

While the potatoes cook, season the squab with salt and pepper. Heat the canola oil in a 12-inch sauté pan over high heat. Cook the squab, skin side down, until the skin browns, about 8 minutes. Turn the birds and add 1 tablespoon of the butter to the pan. Cook about 8 minutes longer, basting the squab with the buttery pan juices, until done. Remove the squab from the pan and set them aside covered to keep warm.

Pour the fat from the pan. Add the wine, raise the heat to high, and deglaze the pan, using a wooden spoon to scrape the brown bits from the bottom. Add the chicken stock and cook for about 5 minutes, until reduced to $^1/_3$ to $^1/_4$ cup. Remove the pan from the heat and swirl in the remaining tablespoon of butter to enrich and flavor the sauce. Season with salt and pepper.

Divide half the potatoes among 4 plates. Place a squab on top of the mounded potatoes. Top with the remaining potatoes and

Squab
Roasted with Potatoes, Pancetta, and Sage
MAKES 4 SERVINGS

A plump squab, pan-roasted in butter, coated with a simple pan sauce, and accompanied by a bottle of good red Burgundy is a meal that I love. But the truth is that I've included this dish in here as a means of sharing the recipe for the rich, rustic pancetta-potato accompaniment. Cooked together, these ingredients yield a heavenly hash, and the whole, unpeeled garlic cloves, sage, and thyme impart a powerful aromatic quality that is perfect for just about any autumn feast.

NOTE: A Japanese-style
mandoline works very well to
slice the potatoes. The garlic cloves
are served with their skins left on.
The squab can be cooked in
batches in smaller pans if you have
only one 12-inch sauté pan.

spoon the pan sauce over the squab and potatoes. If you prefer, strain the sauce through a fine sieve before spooning it over the plates. Sprinkle with the parsley and serve.

VARIATIONS: Chicken breasts or poussin can be substituted for the squab.

FLAVOR BUILDING: Slice your favorite mushrooms thin, sauté them, then add them to the potatoes during the last 5 minutes of cooking.

The cornbread can be made a day in advance. The stuffing should be made the morning of the day you will serve this and allowed to cool, then covered and refrigerated.

Wild Roast Turkey with Cornbread Stuffing

MAKES 6 TO 8 SERVINGS

CORNBREAD

1	cup white or yellow cornmeal
1	cup all-purpose flour
2	tablespoons sugar
1	tablespoon baking powder
$1/4$	teaspoon baking soda
$1/4$	teaspoon coarse salt
$1^1/4$	cups buttermilk or whole milk
$1/4$	cup unsalted butter, melted
$1/4$	cup vegetable oil
1	large egg

Preheat the oven to 350°F. Butter an 8-inch-square baking pan. In a large bowl, whisk together the cornmeal, flour, sugar, baking powder, baking soda, and salt.

In another bowl, whisk together the buttermilk, melted butter, oil, and egg until smooth. Stir the wet into the dry ingredients, and when smooth and well mixed, scrape the batter into the prepared pan. Bake for 35 to 40 minutes, until a toothpick inserted near the center comes out clean, the cornbread begins to pull away from the sides of the pan, and the top is golden brown. Cool in the pan set on a wire rack. When cool, crumble into large pieces.

CORNBREAD STUFFING

8	ounces stale white bread, cut into 1-inch cubes
2 to 3	cups Double Turkey Stock (page 424)
2	tablespoons vegetable oil
3	ribs celery, cut into small dice
1	small onion, cut into small dice
2	cloves garlic, peeled and finely minced
	Coarse salt and freshly ground white pepper to taste
1	pound sweet Italian sausage, casing removed
$1/3$	cup golden raisins
3	tablespoons toasted pine nuts
$1/4$	cup coarsely chopped fresh flat-leaf parsley
1	tablespoon chopped fresh sage
1	teaspoon fresh thyme leaves

Wild turkeys are unusual tasting and difficult to come by, although they can be obtained from some butchers and by mail order (see page 426). Because they actually have to be called in, even many veteran hunters have never managed to see one. My experience is that they generally weigh about 12 to 14 pounds, so they're not necessarily big enough for a large crowd of people. (Fourteen pounds is the minimum for a farm-raised turkey.)

The difference between a wild turkey and a farm-raised turkey is not unlike that between a pheasant and a chicken—the meat is a little firmer, tougher, and leaner—but the willingness to forgive these flaws rewards you with a more pronounced, gamey flavor. You have to closely monitor the cooking and basting of a wild turkey because there is a greater risk of this variety drying out in the oven.

The cornbread-and-sausage stuffing included here is the one we developed at the Gotham the first time we opened the restaurant for

Thanksgiving. We generally make it with venison sausage, but this recipe calls for a more common sweet sausage. What makes the stuffing memorable is the inclusion of raisins and toasted pine nuts, which add sweetness and crunch to the cornbread.

WHAT TO DRINK: Serve this with a fine, French red Burgundy, perhaps a Richebourg or an Echézeaux.

In a large bowl, combine the cornbread and white-bread cubes and set aside. In a large saucepan, bring the stock to a boil over high heat. Remove from the heat and set aside.

In a large sauté pan, heat 1 tablespoon of the oil over medium-high heat. Add the celery and onion, and cook for 2 to 3 minutes, stirring often. Add the garlic and cook about 3 minutes longer, until the vegetables begin to soften. Season with salt and pepper, and transfer to the bowl with the bread.

Heat the remaining oil in the sauté pan over medium-high heat. Add the sausage and cook for 6 to 8 minutes, breaking it apart with a fork, until lightly browned. Drain the fat and add the sausage to the bowl with the bread and vegetables. Stir the raisins, pine nuts, parsley, sage, and thyme into the bowl. Begin adding the hot stock, stirring gently, until the stuffing is quite wet (even a little soupy). Season with salt and pepper and set aside to cool at room temperature.

ROAST TURKEY

1 12- to 14-pound wild turkey, wing tips, neck, and giblets reserved

2 tablespoons vegetable oil

2 tablespoons unsalted butter, softened
   Coarse salt and freshly ground white pepper to taste

3 cups Double Turkey Stock, plus about $^1/_2$ cup for basting the stuffing (page 424)

Preheat the oven to 400°F. Generously butter a 2-quart casserole dish.

Loosely stuff the turkey with the cornbread stuffing. Spoon the remaining stuffing into the buttered casserole, cover, and refrigerate. Truss or skewer the turkey closed. Rub the turkey with the oil and the softened butter, and season it with salt and pepper. Transfer the turkey to a large roasting pan fitted with a wire rack.

Put the roasting pan in the oven and add 2 cups of the stock. Reduce the oven temperature to 325°F and roast the turkey for 20 minutes per pound, or for 4 to $4^1/_2$ hours, basting with the pan drippings every 15 to 20 minutes and adding more stock, as necessary. The basting will turn the skin mahogany. When the turkey is done, a meat thermometer inserted in the thickest part of the thigh should read 175°F. During the last 45 minutes to 1 hour of roasting, tent the turkey with aluminum foil to prevent it from overbrowning. When done, lift the turkey from the pan and transfer it to a platter. Do not turn off the oven. Tent the turkey with foil to keep it warm, and let it rest for 20 to 30 minutes to allow the juices to distribute before carving.

Take the casserole of stuffing from the refrigerator and bake it, uncovered, for about 20 minutes, until golden brown and heated through. Baste the stuffing several times during baking with the reserved turkey stock.

TURKEY SAUCE AND ASSEMBLY

      Turkey wing tips, neck, and giblets, reserved from the turkey
8   cups Double Turkey Stock (page 424)
1   sprig fresh rosemary
1   tablespoon cornstarch stirred into 2 tablespoons cold water, if needed
      Coarse salt and freshly ground white pepper to taste
$^1/_4$ cup unsalted butter, cut into pieces

Chop the turkey neck into large pieces. Transfer the neck pieces to a large, heavy saucepan and add the giblets, wing tips, and stock. Bring to a boil over medium-high heat, skimming any impurities that rise to the surface. Reduce the heat to low and simmer for 3 hours.

Strain the stock through a strainer into a bowl. Chop the meat from the neck and the giblets and transfer it to a small bowl. Cover and refrigerate. Discard the bones.

Pour the pan drippings from the turkey into a bowl. Skim off and discard the fat that rises to the surface and set the drippings aside.

Set the roasting pan over 2 burners and add 2 cups of the strained turkey stock. Bring to a boil and use a wooden spoon to scrape up any browned bits sticking to the bottom of the pan. Transfer the stock to a saucepan and add the reserved pan drippings, remaining stock, and rosemary. Bring to a boil over high heat and cook until reduced to about 4 cups and the sauce is richly flavored. Whisk in the cornstarch mixture, if necessary, to thicken. Cook for about 2 minutes. Add the reserved meat and giblets, and season with salt and pepper. Whisk in the butter to enrich the sauce.

Carve the turkey and serve with the stuffing and sauce passed on the side.

VARIATIONS: You can, of course, use a farm-raised turkey and vary the cooking time accordingly by poundage. (You might also make more stuffing in that case.) Dried raisins are very important to this recipe, but you could substitute dried apricots, dried figs, or 1 cup of diced, cooked quince.

Red Wine Poached Pears with Mascarpone and Pistachio Nuts

MAKES 4 SERVINGS

In the early 1980s, I worked at Comptoir Gourmand—a gourmet carryout shop located in midtown Manhattan's Bloomingdale's department store. One of the desserts we sold was pears poached in red wine, which I thought were the most satisfying, stunning, and simple things in the world.

It's not an exaggeration to say that anyone can poach pears, regardless of their pastry-making acumen. Serve them on Thanksgiving, or with any November meal, to take advantage of this month's pears, which are at their annual prime.

Not only can the pears be poached a day in advance, but they'll actually benefit from the extra time, soaking up their liquid and deepening in color and flavor.

THINKING AHEAD: The pears can be poached up to 2 days in advance and stored in their liquid in the refrigerator.

PEARS AND GRANITÉ

$3^3/_4$	cups (one 750-ml bottle) Cabernet Sauvignon wine
1	tablespoon grated orange zest
$1^1/_2$	cups fresh orange juice
1	cup sugar
$^1/_2$	tablespoon grated lemon zest
$^1/_2$	vanilla bean
1	cinnamon stick
2	firm Bartlett pears, peeled, halved, and cored

In a saucepan, combine the wine, orange zest and juice, sugar, lemon zest, vanilla bean, and cinnamon stick. Bring to a boil over high heat and reduce the heat to a simmer. Add the pears and poach for about 1 hour, until tender when pierced with the tip of a sharp knife. Lift the pears from the pan.

Strain the poaching liquid through a fine-mesh sieve into a bowl. Reserve $^1/_2$ cup of the liquid and pour it over the pears. Cover and refrigerate.

Pour the remaining liquid into a shallow, metal pan and set it aside to cool. When cool, freeze for about 1 hour, or until the mixture is partially frozen and icy around the edges. Using a large spoon, break up the icy edges and stir them into the center. Freeze about 1 hour longer and repeat the process.

Let the granité freeze for about 2 hours or overnight. Before serving, scrape it into large crystals with a fork.

ASSEMBLY

$^1/_2$	cup mascarpone cheese
1	tablespoon sugar
2	tablespoons plus 2 teaspoons coarsely chopped, toasted pistachio nuts
	Fresh mint leaves for garnish

In a small bowl, whisk together the mascarpone cheese and sugar. Spoon the sweetened cheese into a pastry bag fitted with a #3 plain tip.

Remove the pears from the refrigerator and place each pear half in a shallow soup plate. Pipe a little of the sweetened mascarpone into the cored space in the pears. Spoon a little of the reserved poaching liquid around the pears. Sprinkle with chopped pistachios and garnish with mint leaves. The granité can be served on the side or enjoyed by itself another time.

VARIATIONS: Feel free to experiment with different pears such as Bosc or Anjou. In the summer months, make this recipe with peaches, and use the liquid to make "adult" popsicles or as the base for a memorable sangria.

This recipe requires more wine than the pears can absorb. If you like, use the leftover liquid to make a pear and wine granité by following the steps on page 250, or freeze it in an ice-cube tray and use it to add an unusual accent to cocktails.

Pumpkin
Crème Brûlée

MAKES 8 SERVINGS

While pumpkin pie deserves great respect as a Thanksgiving dessert, it's fun to shake up tradition and impress your friends with this sophisticated variation. The burnt sugar top tastes especially delicious with the sweetly spiced pumpkin cream.

THINKING AHEAD: These custards can be made a day in advance.

BRULÉE SUGAR

1	cup light brown sugar
1/2	cup granulated sugar

Preheat the oven to 250°F.

Combine the sugars, mixing well to integrate evenly. Spread on a baking sheet and dry in the oven for about 1 hour. Transfer to a blender and process to a fine powder. Set aside, covered, and store in a cool dry place at room temperature for up to a week.

CUSTARDS

2	cups milk
2	cups heavy cream
10	tablespoons sugar
1	cinnamon stick
1/2	teaspoon allspice
1/4	teaspoon ground cloves
1/4	teaspoon freshly grated nutmeg
9	large egg yolks
3/4	cup unseasoned canned pumpkin purée

Preheat the oven to 350°F.

In a saucepan, combine the milk, cream, sugar, cinnamon, allspice, cloves, and nutmeg over medium heat until hot but not boiling. Remove from the heat and set aside to cool slightly. Cover and refrigerate for about 30 minutes.

Remove the cinnamon stick. Whisk in the egg yolks, mixing until smooth. Add the pumpkin purée, whisking until well blended. Strain the custard through a fine-mesh sieve into a bowl.

Pour the custard into eight 4-ounce ramekins. Set the ramekins in a shallow roasting pan or baking pan and put in the oven. Pour enough hot water into the pan to come halfway up the sides of the ramekins. Bake for 25 to 30 minutes, until the custards are set around the edges but still a little shaky in the center.

Carefully remove the pan from the oven. Remove ramekins from the water bath and let the custards cool to room temperature. Cover with plastic wrap and refrigerate for at least 8 hours or overnight.

Preheat the broiler, or better yet, use a small propane torch designed for kitchen use.

Remove the plastic wrap and sprinkle each custard with brulée sugar. Broil for 30 to 60 seconds, until the sugar caramelizes, or hold the torch over the sugar to caramelize it. Serve immediately.

VARIATIONS: Acorn, butternut squash, and sweet potatoes make fine substitutes for the pumpkin purée.

Cranberry-Ginger Sorbet

MAKES 6 TO 8 SERVINGS

When my wife, Helen, and I were students at the Culinary Institute of America together, many food corporations sponsored contests seeking new uses for their products. This recipe is based on Helen's winning entry in an Ocean Spray Cranberry competition for which she created a cranberry-ginger sorbet, which was rather innovative at the time. The result is an adult sorbet with complex flavors and a compelling tartness. Try serving it to wake up the palate before a rich course, or as a "first dessert course" before moving on to a more decadent finale.

4   cups fresh cranberries
3   cups water
1¹/₂   cups sugar
2   tablespoons grated fresh ginger (about one 2-inch knob)

In a saucepan, combine the cranberries, water, sugar, and ginger, and bring to a boil. Boil for about 15 minutes, or until the cranberries are very soft. Set aside to cool slightly.

Using a hand-held electric mixer, purée the mixture until smooth. Or transfer to a blender and purée. Cover and refrigerate for about 2 hours, until chilled.

Pour the cranberry purée into the container of an ice-cream machine and freeze according to the manufacturer's directions. Transfer to a covered container and freeze for at least 4 hours or overnight, until firm.

WHAT TO DRINK:
Beaujolais Kir

Every November, French viniculture meets the American susceptibility to marketing when the new Beaujolais hits the United States and wine-store windows are cluttered with signs announcing *Le Beaujolais Nouveau Est Arrivé!* I enjoy using this wine to make a variation on a kir (white wine and cassis), adding a splash of Grand Marnier. Each glass should be prepared according to the following recipe:

4¹/₂   ounces Beaujolais Nouveau
¹/₂   ounce cassis
Splash of Grand Marnier

Thanksgiving Menus

Two Thanksgiving menus are offered here. The first is a very traditional buffet-style feast. The second, which substitutes lobster for turkey, is more unusual, but the components of the main course can be served family-style and passed around your table.

TRADITIONAL

CAULIFLOWER VICHYSSOISE (page 305)

WILD ROAST TURKEY WITH CORNBREAD STUFFING (page 247)

PUMPKIN AND SWEET GARLIC CUSTARDS (page 227)

POTATO AND WILD MUSHROOM GRATIN (page 410)

CRANBERRY-GINGER SORBET (page 254)

PEAR TART TATIN (page 213)

NONTRADITIONAL

SEARED FOIE GRAS WITH POACHED QUINCE, TANGERINE, AND POMEGRANATE JUICE (page 200)

LOBSTER WITH SAVOY CABBAGE, FLAGEOLETS, AND ROASTED GARLIC (page 239)

PUMPKIN CRÈME BRÛLÉE (page 252)

Champagne Cocktails

Luxury Ingredients

Canapés

Warm Bluepoint Oysters with Leeks and Osetra Caviar
Foie Gras with Sour Cherry Chutney
Terrine of Foie Gras
Salmon Rillette
Diver Scallops and Sevruga Caviar Tartare

Warm Potato and Smoked Eel Salad

Garbure

Roast Cod with Savoy Cabbage, White Beans, and Black Truffle

Linguine with White Truffles

Lamb Chops with Swiss Chard and Truffled Mashed Potatoes

Fennel-and-Garlic-Crusted Pork Roast with Warm Quince and Apple Compote

Chestnut Tiramisu

Walnut Tart

The Gift of Food

Chocolate Cocoa Christmas Cookies
Chocolate Hazelnut Biscotti
Fig Cookies

Christmas Eve Dinner

New Year's Eve Dinner

DECEMBER

CELEBRATIONS

Every December, something strange happens deep in the concrete canyons of midtown Manhattan. Paunchy, gray-bearded men in velvety red and white suits take their places among the more purposeful, properly attired Masters of the Universe; the smoky-sweet aroma of roasting chestnuts freshens the more unfortunate, everyday bouquet of the street; and gargantuan shopping bags become more prevalent than briefcases. When the holidays descend on New York City, they transform the entire metropolis into a virtual fantasia of the most cheerful sights, sounds, and tastes in the world.

I love the glory of December in Manhattan. But, for me, the holidays are also a touchstone. They cast me back to the snowy suburbs of Buffalo, New York, and the storybook December evenings of my first fifteen years. When I think of Christmas Eve upstate, I remember the silent syncopation of Christmas lights on neighboring houses, the plastic reindeer dashing across their lawns, and the Norman Rockwellian image of small children unself-consciously asleep in church pews during midnight mass.

The Christmas season began for my family the first day the trees went on sale. My father and I would visit the local nursery and return home with an evergreen, carrying it between us onto the front porch and into our house where—it seems through the romanticizing lens of memory—my mother was already busy making her first batch of cookies for the season.

All of my most vivid holiday memories are of food. On Christmas Eve, Christmas Day, and December 26, which happens to be my sister's birthday, we engaged in a series of feasts that, in recollection, are difficult to pry apart from one another. On each of these days, thirty or so family members showed up at one house or another, and like the Three Wise Men, we all showed up bearing gifts. But ours were gifts of food. Uncles might arrive with a roasted venison or turkey personally hunted with a bow and arrow in the wilds of Buffalo, my grandfather with bottles of his homemade wine under each arm, and my aunts with cookies and pastries—stuffed fig cookies, pizzelle, cannoli, and my mother with her melt-in-your-mouth cocoa cookies—that they had made themselves from secret family recipes. How secret? Put it this way: the Portales didn't discuss cookies outside our family the way the Corleones didn't discuss "business" outside of theirs.

Cookies weren't the only Christmas pastime we took seriously—we took *everything* about Christmas seriously. Though my extended family of Sicilian grandparents, aunts, uncles, and cousins saw each other at least once a week, there was a different tenor to our late December get-togethers. For the children, it was one of those first times when, donning a sportcoat and granted permission to sip wine, you felt grown up and important, but also more than a little excited by the prospect of finally discovering what was waiting for you under the tree.

Of the three holiday dinners, the most sacred was the Christmas Eve *Cena della Vigilia,* or "dinner of the vigil," which was eaten before Midnight Mass. In a Catholic home, Christmas Eve dinner is supposed to be penitential, to purify the body before Christmas Day. But, although we ate a meatless supper, there was nothing purifying about it; in fact, it was an unabashed feast.

The *Cena della Vigilia* is by tradition a multicourse affair, though opinions abound as to how many courses are appropriate. Some Catholics prepare seven dishes (representing the sacraments), some twelve (the number of apostles), and some thirteen (one for each apostle, plus one for Jesus). I don't think anyone in my family paid much attention to the number of courses, but I know we had far more than seven, and probably exceeded thirteen on more than one occasion.

We always began with shrimp cocktail, and there was usually a dish featuring cod, the most traditional Christmas fish. Occasionally, salt cod—soaked a day or two in advance—would be served with potatoes, or with onions and a thin tomato sauce. There was smoked eel salad, as well as my father's annual contribution of baked clams with pancetta and bread crumbs, which I loved.

There was also an endless parade of side dishes, including braised fennel and dandelion greens, which my grandfather harvested from roadsides in the fall, blanched, and froze in batches. And, of course, there were bowls brimming with pasta and seafood, including calamari and octopus, which I now love but could barely stand the sight of in those days.

Then there was my grandmother, who delighted in playing the same trick on the youngest children every year: She'd serve us a dish of pasta with sardines, a Sicilian favorite that was met with disdain by her American grandchildren. To entice us to eat the whole thing, she'd tell us there was a surprise waiting for us at the bottom of the bowl. We'd shovel our way down there . . . only to find a painted flower mocking us.

Dishes that didn't require such subterfuge were my mother's manicotti, lasagna, and pasta with canned tuna. My grandmother also made focaccia with anchovies but saved some anchovy-free dough and fried it up like doughnuts for the children. One bite of that light, fluffy bread and the painted flower scandal was forgiven.

Christmas Day itself culminated at my grandfather's home, and it always ended with the spectacle of old Italian men gathered in the den, speaking in the language of their homeland and washing down roasted chestnuts with grappa while the women sat talking in the kitchen.

The holidays are one of the few times in New York that I'm reminded of small-town life. When I see young couples and roommates carrying trees home, it takes me right back to the time when my father and I would try to find a tree to please everyone at our house.

I've physically returned to Buffalo a few times for Christmas as well, but nobody in my family celebrates the way they used to. Even my parents have whittled down their dinner to champagne, shrimp cocktail, and one fish dish, but I have such fond memories of those days that, in some ways, I've tried to replicate elements of it for my family in New York City. After my grandfather's tradition, we festoon the front door with red foil, jingle bells, and a wreath we make ourselves. We also carry on his tradition of hanging stockings, although we fill ours with carefully chosen gifts while he filled his at the last minute with walnuts and tangerines straight from the kitchen table.

For us, ornaments are also a big part of the celebration. While we have some very elaborate, antique ornaments, there was a time—when Helen and I were first together—that we had no ornaments. In those days, we covered the tree with little red bows that we twisted on wire and saved over the years. As precious as they are to us, there are only five left because, somehow, a few get lost every Christmas. We also created ornaments to commemorate our tradition of drinking champagne on Christmas Eve, writing dates and messages on the corks and then hanging them on the tree. These days, the messages feature our daughters' names, and this particular cluster of decorations evokes almost two decade's worth of memories.

When the time comes to buy our tree every year, we bring our ornaments out of storage, unpack them, and reminisce about each one—where we bought it or who gave it to us. Though the dialogue is often the same, it's an important family time and a tradition that I hope our daughters will carry on with their families.

To make room for these ornaments, we always purchase a grand Christmas tree and make a big production of decorating it, beginning in the center and working our way out. In addition to the ornaments, we also illuminate it with hundreds of lights that blaze away in the apartment.

Every year, we also have Christmas dinner together, regardless of where we actually spend the holiday. We begin with champagne, move on to shrimp cocktail (though we make ours with a lemony aioli), baked clams, smoked eel salad, and cod with beans and savoy cabbage.

We also keep the cookie tradition alive and well. Helen makes great quantities of pizzelle, which we give as gifts, and our daughters love making gingerbread cookies.

In this chapter I'll share some of our favorite holiday recipes, intended to help fulfill your full range of December needs.

Here, you'll find luxurious cocktail party canapés including Warm Bluepoint Oysters with Leeks and Osetra Caviar (page 266), Foie Gras with Sour Cherry Chutney, (page 268) Salmon Rillette (page 271), and Diver Scallops and Sevruga Caviar Tartare (page 273). I'll also share some notes on champagne cocktails.

As the 25th and 31st grow closer, you'll find some of the most elegant dishes in the book, including a Warm Potato and Smoked Eel Salad (page 274), Roast Cod with Savoy Cabbage, White Beans, and Black Truffles (page 278), and Lamb Chops with Swiss Chard and Truffled Mashed Potatoes (page 281). There's also Garbure (page 276) and Fennel-and-Garlic-Crusted Pork Rib Roast with Warm Quince and Apple Compote (page 285).

Keep in mind that food can also make a deeply personal gift. To that end, I've included recipes for Cocoa Cookies (page 292) and Chocolate Hazelnut Biscotti (page 293). As much fun as it is to shop for presents, it's often more satisfying to spend an afternoon in the kitchen, listening to holiday music and baking for family and friends—taking a productive culinary respite from the festive bustle of the season.

Champagne Cocktails
Pousse Rapier

1	glass champagne
$^1/_4$	ounce Grand Marnier
3 to 4	drops Cognac or Armagnac
3	drops cassis
2	cherries preserved in brandy or Cognac

Pimm's Cup

1	glass champagne
1	ounce Pimm's No. 1

Passionfruit Cocktail

2	ripe passionfruit, halved
8	drops Cognac
4	glasses champagne

Spoon some passionfruit pulp into each of 4 champagne glasses. Place 2 drops of cognac into each glass and fill each glass with champagne.

VARIATION: You may substitute 1 ounce of Alize, a passionfruit liqueur, for the passionfruit. If you do this, omit the Cognac.

Luxury Ingredients

While caviar, foie gras, and truffles appear throughout this book, they are so prominent in this celebratory month that a few words about each seemed in order.

Caviar

The three principal types of caviar are Sevruga, Osetra, and Beluga. All come from sturgeons, but from sturgeons of varying weights, which in turn produce variances in color and size of the grain. (It should also be noted that there are hundreds of species of sturgeon.) Of the three forenamed varieties, Beluga are the largest eggs, followed by Osetra and Sevruga.

Beluga caviar is large-grained and varies in color from gray to black; Osetra is pale golden to amber in color; and Sevruga eggs are black and the saltiest of the three. Though the least expensive, Sevruga is not necessarily low in quality. Rather, this is a nod to supply and demand, as these are the most plentiful sturgeon in the sea. Osetra, which happens to be my favorite, costs just a bit more than Sevruga but significantly less than Beluga. I love it with warm toast and a bit of crème fraîche and maybe some chives, or atop the classic warm blini.

When purchasing caviar, check to be sure the tins are securely vacuum-sealed. The caviar within should have an oily sheen, and the individual eggs should be well defined and somewhat firm, smelling faintly of sea spray. (As with fresh fish, they should not smell at all fishy.) Caviar will keep well in the refrigerator for about three weeks unopened.

Personally, I think that cooking with caviar, when it isn't the center of attention, is a wonderful way to add a touch of opulence to a dish. As for serving caviar on its own, there are few more festive social gestures. Contrary to popular belief, serving caviar doesn't necessarily require an ornate serving dish. When offering caviar with champagne or iced vodka, I place the tin itself in a small bowl filled with crushed ice—a pleasing and informal presentation. Caviar is available in 125- and 500-gram tins. The smaller size serves 4 people comfortably. The larger, 500-gram tins look fabulous and will usually leave you with some leftover caviar, which is not a bad thing.

Apart from caviar, which refers to sturgeon eggs only, there are many fish eggs that are commonly eaten, such as those from flying fish and salmon, many of which are worth trying, if for no other reason than to expand your own culinary horizons.

Foie Gras

Fresh foie gras comes from ducks and geese that are specially raised on a high-calorie diet to produce plump livers with a decadent texture and flavor. In the United States, foie gras is primarily produced in the New York Hudson Valley from Moulard ducks, a hybrid of Muscovy and Pekin (Long Island). (See page 365 for notes on ducks.) The finer butchers may stock fresh foie gras or be able to procure it for you. (See page 426 for a direct mail-order source.) Be sure to request fresh foie gras, or you might find yourself purchasing canned foie gras or a terrine or pâté.

In the early 1980s, when I worked at Bloomingdale's, there was no fresh foie gras in the United States. You could only purchase it cooked, and it often tasted like something approaching dog food. When, later in the decade, production began in upstate New York and California, it was a wonderful turning point for American cuisine.

Purchase the highest grade, Grade A, which is free of bruises and easiest to clean. Let it stand unopened at room temperature before cleaning and deveining. If you attempt to manipulate it while it's too cold, it's apt to crack.

White Truffles

As famously expensive as foie gras and caviar are, there's perhaps no luxury that requires more of an investment than white truffles. The expense is almost justified, however, not only by the intense flavor and aroma of truffles, but also by the legendary method by which they are located—specially trained truffle hounds sniff them out in Italy's Alba. What could be more romantic and exciting?

Despite their high price tag, white truffles are currently so popular that they are now being allocated to certain restaurants, like cult California cabernets, and so are very hard to come by. In New York, they do turn up in gourmet markets. If you're lucky enough to be able to both encounter and purchase one, be very careful about quality. If the purveyor allows you to inspect it, the truffle should be firm and round, with a powerful fragrance. There are, however, other ways of experiencing the flavor of a white truffle. One is white truffle oil, which is also quite expensive, but a little of it goes a long way. Another is white-truffle butter.

Black Truffles

Black truffles from Umbria don't really have any flavor, although black Perigord truffles are highly prized and boast an intense flavor and intoxicating aroma. French summer truffles are relatively inexpensive and exude a pleasing flavor and perfume; at least the best of them do. Black truffles are sold in a variety of forms. At the Gotham, we get both fresh truffles and flash-frozen truffles, which can be of a very high quality. When I worked in France, I was taught that black truffles should be cooked briefly in truffle juice to release their flavor. But today you are apt to see chefs shaving them raw into dishes, as though they were as precious as white truffles. You can purchase truffle peelings, truffle juice, and canned truffles, but the quality may vary. Although high-quality canned truffles can be procured in France, the varieties sent to the United States aren't as flavorful, due to the sterilization laws here.

A truffle slicer can be an expensive investment, which leads many people to wonder why they can't simply use a knife. To my mind, the difference is that a slicer allows you to obtain paper-thin slices, giving you more slices from each truffle, which—given the expense of this ingredient—allows the slicer to pay for itself.

Warm Bluepoint Oysters with Leeks and Osetra Caviar

MAKES 4 SERVINGS

When it comes to oysters, I'm an unabashed purist, preferring them on the half-shell with no adornment except perhaps a few drops of *mignonette*, the classic sauce of vinegar with pepper and minced shallots, because I really want to taste and enjoy the differences between the types of oysters. Having said this, I do love a few recipes using cooked oysters. One is the risotto featured on page 348 and the other is this one, in which the oysters are very briefly poached, just enough to firm them up, then sauced extravagantly with butter and caviar. This recipe is very much in the style of French cooking of the 1970s and 1980s and is based on the signature dish of L'Ambroisie, a three-star restaurant in Paris.

4	leeks, white parts only, sliced into $1/4$-inch rounds
1	tablespoon canola oil
1	tablespoon finely minced shallot
1	cup white wine
$1/2$	cup heavy cream
$3/4$	cup unsalted butter, cut into pieces
	Pinch of cayenne pepper
	Coarse salt and freshly ground white pepper to taste
20	bluepoint oysters, or substitute Wellfleet, Kumamoto, or Malpeque oysters
1	heaping tablespoon finely minced chives
2	ounces Osetra caviar
	Fresh chervil sprigs for garnish
	Seaweed or coarse sea salt, for serving

In a saucepan of boiling salted water, cook the leeks for about 6 minutes, until very tender. Drain and plunge them into ice water. Drain again and set aside.

In a small sauté pan, heat the oil over medium-high heat and cook the shallot for about 4 minutes, until softened. Add the wine and cook for about 6 minutes, until nearly evaporated. Add the cream and bring to a boil. Cook for a few minutes until the cream reduces slightly. Reduce the heat to low and whisk in the butter, a piece at a time, until the sauce is rich and slightly thickened. Season with cayenne, salt, and pepper. Cover and set aside to keep warm.

Working over a bowl to catch the juices, hold oyster firmly in the palm of your hand using a towel to protect your palm. Insert an oyster knife into the hinge at the pointed end of the oyster. Work it in using steady, even pressure. Pop open the shell, then run the blade around until you cut the muscle that attaches the top of the shell to the oyster. Remove the top shell. Slide knife under the oyster, finding where it is attached to the bottom shell, and cut through. Add the oysters to the escaped oyster liquor in the bowl. Reserve the deep bottom shell and discard the top shell. Wash and dry the reserved shells.

Add the reserved leeks to the cream sauce and cook over medium heat for about 2 minutes. Add the oysters and reserved liquor, and cook for about 1 minute, until just heated through. Stir in the chives.

Using a slotted spoon, spoon some leeks onto the clean, dry

shells. Set an oyster on top of the leeks and spoon a little more sauce over the oysters. Garnish each with a few grains of caviar and a sprig of chervil.

Spread the seaweed or coarse sea salt on a platter. Arrange the oyster shells on the platter, anchored on the seaweed or salt to prevent slipping and tipping. Serve immediately.

Foie Gras with Sour Cherry Chutney

MAKES 24 CANAPÉS

In this recipe, a terrine of foie gras is used to make a generous number of canapés. Though the chutney is by no means necessary, its sweet and sour notes are a perfect foil for the rich and creamy foie gras. (If serving a Sauternes with this canapé, leave the chutney out as the wine will fulfill the same purpose.)

SOUR CHERRY CHUTNEY

1	cup dried sour cherries
3/4	cup water
6	tablespoons sugar
1/2	clove garlic, peeled and finely minced
1/2	teaspoon ground ginger

In a nonreactive saucepan, combine the cherries, water, sugar, garlic, and ginger, and cook over low heat, stirring occasionally to prevent scorching, for about 1 hour or until thickened. Cool completely before serving.

ASSEMBLY

1	Terrine of Foie Gras (page 269)
1	baguette, cut into 24 thin slices, toasted
1	small bunch chervil, for garnish

Spread the foie gras on the toast slices, or place a thin slice on each one. Garnish each canapé with about 1 teaspoon of chutney and a sprig of chervil.

THINKING AHEAD: The foie gras must marinate overnight (for up to 36 hours), and the terrine itself must be refrigerated overnight.

FOIE GRAS

1	23-ounce foie gras
1¹/₂	teaspoons fine salt
¹/₂	teaspoon freshly ground white pepper
¹/₂	teaspoon sugar
¹/₄	teaspoon cognac

Take the foie gras from the refrigerator and rinse it under cold, running water, then pat it dry with paper or kitchen towels. Let the lobes soften up at room temperature for 5 to 10 minutes before working.

Carefully pull apart the lobes. Use a small knife to cut away any fat at the point of separation. Place the lobes on a work surface with the inner sides facing up. Work with the smaller lobe first. Use the edge of a teaspoon to scrape away the surface and expose the large vein that runs horizontally through the center. Carefully remove this vein with the tip of a knife. Remove any small veins that branch from it. Repeat with the larger lobe; it contains a more complicated but similar network of veins. Do not worry about getting all of them or making a mistake. You cannot. It's more important to work with a gentle touch and to keep the lobes intact. The entire process of cleaning one lobe should take no more than 8 to 10 minutes. If they begin to feel warm, it's important to refrigerate them to firm them up.

Place the clean foie gras in a glass or enameled dish. Combine the salt, pepper, and sugar, and sprinkle the mixture evenly over the foie gras. Sprinkle evenly with the Cognac. Press a piece of plastic wrap onto the surface of the foie gras to keep it as airtight as possible. Tightly wrap the dish with plastic wrap and refrigerate it overnight.

Preheat the oven to 275°F.

Remove the foie gras from the refrigerator and pack it into a terrine mold. Because of the irregular shapes of the lobes, you may have to cut the liver into large pieces to get them to fit tightly in the terrine. The terrine will not be full, which is fine. Press down on the liver with your fingertips to create an even layer. The foie gras will behave somewhat like putty and will mold to the shape

SPECIAL EQUIPMENT: Large (11¹/₂-by-3¹/₂-by-2¹/₂-inch) ceramic or enameled cast-iron terrine mold (do not use an uncoated metal mold); plastic wrap; large roasting pan to hold the terrine mold; an instant-read thermometer; 3 pieces of thick cardboard cut to fit the inside of the terrine, stacked and wrapped together with a double thickness of plastic wrap; 3-pound weight or its equivalent.

of the terrine. Tightly wrap the entire mold with a double thickness of plastic wrap. (The plastic will not melt in the oven.)

Put the terrine mold in a large roasting pan and pour enough hot water into the roasting pan to come about $1^1/2$ inches up the sides of the terrine. The water will insulate the terrine and evenly diffuse the heat. Bake for 30 to 40 minutes, or until an instant-read thermometer reads 118°F when inserted in the center of the terrine. Insert the thermometer through the plastic directly into the liver. If you do not have a thermometer, unwrap the terrine and stick your finger into the soft foie gras. If it feels cool, return it to the oven; if it feels warm (a little warmer than body temperature), it is probably about 118°F. Remove it from the oven. If it feels hot, you have left it in the oven too long. Because you do not want to overcook the foie gras, begin checking it after 20 minutes of baking.

Remove the mold from the roasting pan and pour out the water. Return the terrine to the empty pan and insert the prepared cardboard into the terrine. Weight it evenly, using 3 cans of food or other weights. When the terrine is weighted, its juices may overflow into the roasting pan. Refrigerate the terrine overnight.

To unmold, run a sharp knife around the inside of the mold to release the terrine. Invert the terrine onto a serving platter and gently tap the bottom of the mold. The foie gras should slide right out. Cut it into thick slices using a thin-bladed slicing knife that is dipped in hot water and wiped dry between each slice.

THINKING AHEAD: The rillette must be refrigerated for at least 2 hours, and can be refrigerated for as many as 8 hours.

POACHING LIQUID

$1/4$	cup dry white wine
1	tablespoon champagne vinegar or white wine vinegar
1	shallot, finely minced
1	bay leaf
1	cup water
	Coarse salt and freshly ground white pepper to taste

In an 8-inch sauté pan or a medium saucepan, combine the wine, vinegar, shallot, and bay leaf, and bring to a boil over high heat. Cook for about 4 minutes, until reduced by half. Add the water, season to taste with salt and pepper, and lower to a simmer.

SALMON

$1/2$	pound fresh salmon
	Coarse salt and freshly ground white pepper to taste
$1/2$	pound smoked salmon
$1/4$	cup unsalted butter, softened at room temperature
2	tablespoons mayonnaise
	Grated zest of 1 lemon
	Juice of $1/2$ lemon, or more as needed
1	bunch fresh dill, tops picked and reserved for garnish, remaining dill chopped (about 1 tablespoon chopped dill)
1	tablespoon finely minced fresh chives

Season the fresh salmon with salt and pepper. Put it in the simmering, poaching liquid, reduce the heat, and poach gently for 6 to 8 minutes, until cooked through. Lift the salmon from the poaching liquid and set it aside to cool. When cool, flake it into small pieces. Discard the poaching liquid.

In a food processor fitted with the metal blade, purée the smoked salmon until just smooth. Scrape it into a mixing bowl and fold in the butter. (If you mix the smoked salmon and butter in the food processor, the mixture may become too warm and break.) When the butter is combined, carefully fold in the flaked salmon, mayonnaise, lemon zest, lemon juice, chopped dill, and minced chives. Do not overmix; there should be texture to this. Taste and

We often serve this dish when entertaining, especially during the holidays, when the fact that it can be made in advance is particularly appealing.

A rillette is a potted meat, traditionally a mixture of highly seasoned pork, which is cooked down, served in a crock, and spread over thick slices of lightly toasted bread. When I apprenticed in a charcuterie shop in New York City, and later worked as a line cook in France, I came to love the creaminess and pronounced flavor of a rillette. In this modernized variation, fresh poached salmon and fresh herbs (most noticeably dill) are folded into a purée of smoked salmon.

adjust the seasonings with salt, pepper, and lemon juice if necessary. Cover and refrigerate for at least 2 hours or for up to 8 hours.

ASSEMBLY

1   loaf *pain ficelle* or baguette, sliced on the bias into 48 small slices
4   ounces salmon roe
     Fresh chervil sprigs for garnish, optional

Lightly toast the bread slices. Spread each toast with some of the rillette. Garnish each canapé with a few grains of salmon roe and a sprig of the reserved dill, or if you prefer, a chervil sprig. Arrange on a platter and serve.

Diver Scallops and Sevruga Caviar Tartare

MAKES 4 SERVINGS

$3/4$	pound Maine diver scallops, chilled
$2^1/2$	tablespoons crème fraîche
1	tablespoon fresh lemon juice, or more as needed
1	teaspoon grated lemon zest
$1/4$	teaspoon cayenne pepper
	Coarse salt and freshly ground white pepper to taste
$2^1/2$	tablespoons finely minced fresh chives
2 to 4	ounces Sevruga caviar
8	sprigs fresh chervil
16	toast points, each about $1^1/2$ inches wide at the base

Begin with well-chilled scallops. To make sure the scallops are cold enough, put them in the freezer for 10 minutes. On an impeccably clean cutting board and using a small sharp knife, slice the scallops and then cut the slices into $1/4$-inch dice. Transfer them to a mixing bowl, cover, and refrigerate for about 15 minutes, until cold again or until ready to serve.

In a small bowl, combine the crème fraîche, lemon juice, and lemon zest, and season with cayenne, salt, and pepper.

Remove the scallops from the refrigerator and add a spoonful of the crème fraîche dressing, gently mixing it with the scallops. Add only enough dressing to nicely dress the scallops. Add the chives and mix gently. Taste and then adjust the seasoning with salt and pepper and a gentle squeeze of lemon juice, if desired.

Divide the scallop tartare among 4 small, chilled appetizer plates, mounding it in the center. Spoon some caviar on top of each mound, using only as much as you like. Garnish with chervil. Serve the warm toast points on the side.

Save this dapper little canapé for the most elegant occasion of the season, perhaps a black-tie affair, where the stark contrast of the scallops and caviar will echo the sartorial motif. Because this recipe is so simple—voluptuous, creamy scallops set off by the intense sea-spray flavor of the caviar—its success relies even more than most recipes on using the very best ingredients. (In fact, if you can't get diver scallops, save this for some other time.) You might also combine the ingredients in more ways than one, opening the door to a number of presentations. For instance, serve the tartare in the scallop's shell, atop a pyramid of crushed ice, or serve it from a terrine with warm toasted bread or brioche. Be sure to dress it with the lemon juice; do this at the last minute to keep the acid from "cooking" the scallop.

WHAT TO DRINK: Accompany this canapé with a Blanc de Blancs champagne.

Warm Potato and Smoked Eel Salad

MAKES 6 SERVINGS

Eel plays an important part in Christmas and New Year's celebrations in Italian American families, as it has in Italian culture for ages, because of its resemblance to the Biblical serpent.

My personal experience with eel dates back about 25 years to the Christmas Eve dinners my wife Helen's family had in Buffalo. Each year, the dinner began with a spread of smoked eel, sturgeon, caviar, and other luxury seafoods that weren't as easy to obtain in the suburbs as they are today. In the weeks leading up to Christmas, Helen's father would make the necessary phone calls to procure these foods from New York City, asking friends and business acquaintances to ship them to Buffalo. It was one of the first times I came to appreciate how much effort it sometimes takes to put your hands on rare ingredients, an effort for which I've developed a healthy respect as a professional chef.

Eel tastes like a very rich cross between smoked trout and smoked sturgeon, but it has a firmer texture

2	pounds smoked eel
2	pounds fingerling or baby white potatoes
6	tablespoons extra-virgin olive oil
2	small cloves garlic, peeled, mashed to a paste, and sprinkled with coarse salt
2	tablespoons chopped shallots
2	tablespoons coarsely chopped fresh flat-leaf parsley
	Coarse salt and freshly ground white pepper to taste

Clean the eel. Start on one side of the belly and peel the skin up and around the body, peeling it off in one piece. It will come off easily. Scrape off any fat and gray flesh. Slice the eel in half lengthwise, separating the two fillets from the backbone. If you feel any pin bones, pull them out with tweezers. Cut the fillets across the grain into $1/2$-inch-thick pieces. Set aside.

In a saucepan of boiling salted water, cook the potatoes for 15 to 20 minutes, until tender. Drain and set aside. When still quite warm but cool enough to handle, cut them into $1/2$-inch rounds.

In a bowl, combine the warm potatoes, eel, olive oil, garlic, shallots, and parsley. Season to taste with salt and pepper. Toss gently to combine. Mound the salad in a serving bowl and serve while still warm.

VARIATION: You can substitute smoked trout for the eel.

than either of them. This recipe offers an uncomplicated technique for making a warm eel salad: potatoes are steamed, then tossed hot with the eel, extra-virgin olive oil, minced shallots, garlic, and parsley. Try it once and you may find that it becomes a December tradition for your family as well.

Garbure

MAKES 6 SERVINGS

This recipe is based on that for a classic garbure—which is a hearty cross between a stew and a soup—but is made here with chicken legs rather than the traditional goose. It's markedly different from chicken soup because the chicken is first browned, which lends the broth a golden tint. While this recipe does cook the beans in the soup itself, after the classic fashion, the Brussels sprout leaves are incorporated at the last minute, allowing them to maintain their essential character.

THINKING AHEAD: The white beans must be soaked overnight.

BROTH

4	chicken leg-and-thigh pieces
	Coarse salt and freshly ground white pepper
4	pounds chicken bones or wings
2	heads garlic, split in half
1	small onion, roughly chopped
1	rib celery, roughly chopped
1	small carrot, roughly chopped
6	sprigs fresh flat-leaf parsley
2	sprigs fresh thyme
1	bay leaf
1	tablespoon black peppercorns
3	quarts White Chicken Stock (page 421)

Preheat the oven to 450°F.

Season the chicken leg-and-thigh pieces on both sides with salt and pepper. Spread them, the chicken bones, and the garlic heads in a roasting pan and roast for approximately 30 minutes, or until the bones are golden brown and the garlic is soft. Stir occasionally. Transfer the leg-and-thigh pieces and chicken bones to a large stockpot. Reserve the grease in the roasting pan.

Squeeze the softened garlic from the garlic heads. Put the garlic in a small bowl and mash to a purée. Set aside. Put the garlic heads in the stockpot.

Pour the grease from the roasting pan. Set the pan on the burners on top of the stove. Add 1 cup of boiling water to the pan and deglaze it over high heat by scraping up the browned bits on the bottom. Add the deglazing liquid to the stockpot.

Add the onion, celery, carrot, parsley, thyme, bay leaf, and peppercorns to the stockpot and stir to mix with the bones. Add the stock and bring to a boil over high heat. Reduce the heat, skim the surface of any foam, and simmer gently for about 30 minutes. Using tongs or a slotted spoon, remove the leg-and-thigh pieces from the pot. Continue cooking the stock for another 30 minutes. Meanwhile, pick the meat from the leg-and-thigh pieces, discard the bones, and coarsely chop the chicken meat. Reserve. Strain the broth through a mesh sieve into a bowl and skim any fat from the surface. You should have approximately 2 quarts of golden brown, richly flavored broth.

SOUP

2 tablespoons canola oil

2 ounces salt pork, cut into small dice

3 carrots, peeled and cut into small dice

3 small leeks, cut into small dice

2 ribs celery, cut into small dice

2 russet potatoes, peeled and cut into small dice

4 ounces dry white beans, soaked overnight in cold water to cover and drained
 Coarse salt and freshly ground white pepper to taste

1 pound of Brussels sprouts, cored and separated into leaves

2 sprigs fresh savory or marjoram

2 tablespoons chopped flat-leaf parsley

In a stockpot, heat the oil over medium heat and cook the salt pork until the fat is rendered. Add the carrots, leeks, celery, and potatoes, and cook for about 2 minutes, until the vegetables just begin to release moisture. Add the beans and reserved chicken broth, and season with salt and pepper. Bring to a boil over high heat. Reduce the heat and simmer for 40 to 50 minutes, or until the beans are tender but still firm enough to hold their shape.

Add the Brussels sprout leaves, reserved garlic purée, and savory reserved chicken meat. Stir and simmer about 10 minutes longer, until the flavors develop and the soup is rich and full bodied. Ladle it into bowls and garnish with the parsley.

Roast Cod
with Savoy Cabbage, White Beans, and Black Truffle

MAKES 4 SERVINGS

I've written of salt cod twice in this book (pages 94, 168), so it seems only fair to include one dish featuring cod itself, especially in December because this fish is the most traditional of all Christmas selections. While the dried and salted variety enjoys greater culinary celebrity, the original has become increasingly popular in recent years. I find that its relatively mild flavor can be a very effective and enjoyable base on which to build recipes in a variety of styles.

This one is as notable for its range of textures as for its assemblage of flavors. The Savoy cabbage provides a crucial counterpoint to the soft, flaky fish, and the same is true of the white runners—an heirloom variety of Italian *gigante* beans that I happen to love. Their huge size and creamy mouth-feel register on the palate not unlike mashed potatoes. It's unusual to serve black truffles with Christmas cod, but here

THINKING AHEAD: The beans must be soaked overnight.

CABBAGE AND BEAN RAGOUT

$^2/_3$	cup dry white runners (*cannellini* beans may be substituted), soaked overnight in cold water to cover and drained
1	small onion, quartered
3	cloves garlic, peeled and crushed
2	sprigs fresh thyme
	Coarse salt and freshly ground white pepper to taste
1	small head Savoy cabbage (about 1 pound), cut into $^1/_2$-inch-wide shreds
1	small carrot, peeled and cut into $^1/_4$-inch dice
$^1/_4$	cup heavy cream
$^1/_4$	cup unsalted butter, cut into pieces
1	ounce black truffle, very thinly sliced

In a medium saucepan, combine the beans, onion, garlic, and thyme. Add enough cold water to cover by about 2 inches. Bring to a boil over high heat. Reduce the heat to medium and simmer for about 20 minutes. Season with salt and continue cooking about 20 minutes longer, until the beans are tender but still firm. Drain, reserving 1 cup of the cooking liquid. The cooking time will depend on the dryness of the beans before they were cooked.

Meanwhile, in a saucepan of boiling salted water, cook the cabbage for 3 to 4 minutes, until barely tender. Drain and plunge it into ice water. Drain again and, using your hands, squeeze out the excess water.

In a saucepan of boiling salted water, cook the carrot for about 2 minutes, until tender. Drain and set aside.

Transfer the reserved cooking liquid to a saucepan and bring it to a boil over high heat. Add the cream and bring to a simmer. Cook gently for about 5 minutes, until slightly thickened. Stir in the butter, piece by piece, to enrich the sauce. Season with salt and pepper.

Reduce the heat to low. Add the cooked beans, cabbage, and carrot to the saucepan. Stir in the truffle and cook for about 6 minutes, until the ragout is heated through and infused with the earthy flavor of the truffle. Cover and set aside to keep warm.

COD AND ASSEMBLY

    2   tablespoons canola oil
    4   cod fillets, each weighing 6 to 7 ounces
         Coarse salt and freshly ground white pepper to taste
    2   tablespoons finely minced fresh chives

In a 10-inch sauté pan, heat the oil over medium–high heat. Season both sides of the cod with salt and pepper, and cook for about 3 minutes, until golden. Turn and cook about 4 minutes longer, until golden brown on both sides and opaque in the center.

Using a slotted spoon, spoon some ragout into the center of a warmed serving platter. Arrange the cod fillets on top and spoon the remaining sauce and ragout over the fish. Garnish with the chives and serve.

Linguine with White Truffles

Years ago, my wife, Helen, and I shared a farmhouse overlooking the town of Siena in the Tuscan countryside south of Florence. Like many visitors to this increasingly popular destination, we treated our temporary residence as a base from which to make day trips—culinary pilgrimages to restaurants, markets, *gelaterias,* and vineyards. Since we were there at the height of truffle season, on our first night out to dinner we ordered pasta with truffles to begin our meal. It was so transcendent that we canceled our main-course orders, requesting a second helping of the pasta instead.

Unlike most pasta and truffle dishes, this one had virtually no sauce but was lightly coated with an intense mushroom cream. You might also toss the pasta with butter and then truffles, which will yield excellent results, especially if you're using truffle oil instead of the more extravagant, and expensive, raw ingredient. (See Variation, right.)

$1^1/_4$	cups water
1	ounce dried porcini mushrooms
2	tablespoons extra-virgin olive oil
4	medium shallots, peeled and thinly sliced
3	cloves garlic, peeled and thinly sliced
$1^1/_2$	cups White Chicken Stock (page 421)
3	sprigs fresh thyme
$^1/_4$	cup heavy cream
3	tablespoons unsalted butter
	Salt and freshly ground white pepper to taste
1	pound dry linguine
3	tablespoons chopped fresh flat-leaf parsley
$1^1/_2$ to 2	ounces white truffle

In a saucepan, bring the water to a boil over high heat. Add the mushrooms and remove the pan from the heat. Set aside for about 20 minutes to allow any sediment to sink to the bottom of the pan. Using a slotted spoon, carefully remove the mushrooms and set them aside. Pour the soaking liquid into a small bowl, taking care to leave the sediment in the pan. Discard the sediment. You should have about $^3/_4$ cup of flavorful porcini stock. Set it aside.

In a large saucepan, heat the oil over medium heat. Add the shallots and garlic, and cook gently for about 4 minutes, until softened but not browned. Add the reserved porcini and cook gently about 3 minutes longer, taking care the vegetables do not brown. Add the reserved porcini stock, the chicken stock, and the thyme. Bring to a boil and cook for 8 to 10 minutes, or until reduced by about half.

Reduce the heat and add the cream. Simmer for 5 to 6 minutes, or until the sauce is thick enough to coat the back of a spoon. Strain it through a fine chinois or fine-mesh sieve into a bowl, pressing on the solids to extract as much sauce as possible. Return the sauce to the pan. Over medium heat, add the butter, a tablespoon at a time, swirling it into the sauce to enrich it. Season with salt and pepper. Cover and set aside to keep warm.

In a large pot of boiling salted water, cook the linguine for about 8 minutes, until al dente. Drain and then add it to the warm sauce. Stir in the chopped parsley and spoon the pasta into 4 bowls. Shave the truffle over the top and serve immediately.

VARIATION: You can omit the white truffles and drizzle each serving with white-truffle oil instead.

TRUFFLED POTATOES

2³/₄	pounds Yellow Finn or russet potatoes, peeled and cut into uniform pieces (about 2 inches wide)
³/₄	cup unsalted butter, cut into pieces
¹/₄ to ¹/₃	cup half-and-half
2	ounces black truffle, thinly sliced
	Coarse salt and freshly ground white pepper to taste

Put the potatoes in a large saucepan and add enough cold water to cover. Salt the water and bring to a boil over high heat. Reduce the heat and simmer for about 15 minutes, or until the potatoes are tender when pierced with a sharp knife. Drain and return them to the pan.

Set the pan over low heat and cook for about 3 minutes, stirring constantly, until the excess moisture evaporates. Rice the potatoes in a food mill or ricer into a bowl, or simply put them in a bowl and mash them with a potato masher. Add the butter, working it into the potatoes until blended.

In a small saucepan, bring the half-and-half and sliced truffles to a boil over medium heat, infusing the cream with a powerful truffle flavor. Add the mixture to the potatoes, stirring gently, until the desired consistency. Do not overmix the potatoes. Season with salt and pepper, cover, and set aside to keep warm.

VEGETABLES

1	bunch baby carrots (about 12 carrots), peeled
2	tablespoons unsalted butter
4	ounces pearl onions (about 20 onions), peeled
	Coarse salt and freshly ground white pepper to taste

In a saucepan, cook the carrots in boiling salted water over high heat for about 6 minutes, until tender. Using a slotted spoon, remove the carrots and set them aside. Reserve 2 cups of the cooking water.

Set the saucepan with the reserved cooking liquid over high heat and add the butter. Bring to a boil. Add the onions, reduce the heat, and simmer for about 10 minutes, until the onions are almost tender. Return the carrots to the pan and mix. Remove from the heat, season with salt and pepper, cover, and set aside to keep warm.

Lamb Chops with Swiss Chard and Truffled Mashed Potatoes

MAKES 4 SERVINGS

This is the dish that I served at the Gotham Bar and Grill for the millennial New Year's Eve. Years earlier, we made a version of it with a loin of lamb, but for the biggest celebration of the century, I shifted to chops for a more decadent steakhouse effect. In this recipe, I use double-cut lamb chops in which the loin is split and sawed through the bone to resemble a miniature Porterhouse steak. This lamb is wonderful, but bear in mind that it's more difficult to cook than "normal" lamb because leaving the bone in prevents the heat from being transmitted evenly. Paired with the truffled mashed potatoes, this is a dish that's perfect for ending any year, or beginning a new one, with something truly special.

WHAT TO DRINK: Serve this with a northern Rhône such as Cornas or Hermitage.

SWISS CHARD

2 cups water
2 tablespoons unsalted butter
1¹/₂ pounds Swiss chard, washed and stemmed
Coarse salt and freshly ground white pepper to taste

In a large saucepan, bring the water and butter to a boil over high heat. Add the chard and season it with salt and pepper. Cook, stirring, for about 4 minutes, or until the chard just wilts and is tender. Drain, pressing out the excess water. Return the chard to the hot pan, cover, and set it aside to keep warm.

LAMB CHOPS AND ASSEMBLY

4 double-cut loin lamb chops
Coarse salt and freshly ground white pepper to taste
2 tablespoons canola oil
¹/₄ cup unsalted butter
1 large sprig fresh rosemary, cut into ¹/₂-inch lengths
1 large shallot, peeled and finely minced
1 clove garlic, peeled and thinly sliced
³/₄ cup dry red wine
³/₄ cup Brown Chicken Stock (page 422)

Preheat the oven to 400°F.

Season the chops with salt and pepper. In an ovenproof 12-inch sauté pan, heat the oil over high heat until very hot but not smoking. Add the chops and cook for about 4 minutes, until nicely seared on 1 side. Turn and sear the other side for about 4 minutes.

Remove the pan from the heat and add 2 tablespoons of the butter and the rosemary. Put the pan in the oven and roast for 4 to 6 minutes, basting the chops often with the melted butter. Lift the chops from the pan and set them aside on a plate, covered loosely with foil, to keep warm.

Pour off all but 1 tablespoon of fat from the pan. Set the pan over medium-high heat and add the shallot. Cook, stirring, for about 3 minutes. Add the garlic and cook, stirring, about 2 minutes longer. Add the wine and deglaze, scraping up any browned bits from the bottom of the pan, for about 6 minutes, until the wine is reduced to about ¹/₄ cup. Add the stock and any collected juices from the plate holding the chops. Bring to a simmer, reduce the heat, and simmer for about 4 minutes to concentrate the flavors. Strain the sauce through a fine-mesh sieve into a clean saucepan. Over medium heat, swirl in the remaining 2 tablespoons of butter and season with salt and pepper.

Spoon the potatoes onto 4 warmed dinner plates. Mound the Swiss chard next to the potatoes and set a chop on top of the chard. Using a slotted spoon, arrange the carrots and onions around the outside of the plate. Spoon a little sauce around the chops and pass the remaining sauce in a warm sauceboat.

VARIATIONS: You can, of course, serve this lamb with puréed potatoes (page 337) or no potatoes at all.

The pork must marinate for 1 to 8 hours.

1	small head fennel with 2 inches of fronds attached, coarsely chopped
$1/2$	cup coarsely chopped onion
6	cloves garlic, peeled and sliced
2	teaspoons finely chopped fresh thyme
2	teaspoons finely chopped fresh rosemary
2	teaspoons finely chopped fresh sage
2	teaspoons finely chopped fresh oregano
2	teaspoons fennel seeds
$1^1/2$	teaspoons coarsely ground white pepper
1	$4^1/2$-pound pork rib roast, tied
	Coarse salt to taste
	Warm Quince and Apple Compote (page 286)

In a food processor fitted with the metal blade, combine the fennel and fennel fronds, onion, and garlic, and process to a paste. Add the thyme, rosemary, sage, oregano, fennel seeds, and pepper, and pulse to combine.

With a small, sharp knife, make shallow crosshatch cuts in the skin of the pork roast. Season it all over with salt, rubbing it in well. Rub the fennel-garlic paste over the roast to cover it with a layer about $1/4$ inch thick. Cover and refrigerate for at least 1 hour and up to 8 hours.

Preheat the oven to 350°F.

About 20 minutes before cooking, remove the roast from the refrigerator and let it sit at room temperature. Transfer the pork to a roasting pan and roast for about 1 hour and 15 minutes, or until the internal temperature in the thickest section of meat is 150°F. Remove the roast from the oven and cover it loosely with foil. Let it rest for 15 to 20 minutes before removing the butcher twine and slicing it into thick chops. Serve with the compote.

Fennel- and Garlic- Crusted Pork Roast with Warm Quince and Apple Compote

MAKES 6 SERVINGS

Many years ago, on a trip to Italy, I found myself in a quintessential outdoor market that brought to colorful life all the images I'd seen in cookbooks over the years: booth after booth where local vendors sold everything from pecorino cheese to whole roasted pigs to their own brands of olive oil and preserves. To a lover of Italian food, it was a spiritual homecoming of sorts.

One purveyor sold roasted pork seasoned with a selection of herbs that was so powerfully aromatic I not only bought several pounds to use in sandwiches, but also convinced him to write down the combination and proportions of herbs for me. Sometime before returning to New York, I managed to misplace it, but my taste memory was almost like a carbon copy; I was able to re-create the recipe, along with the blend of fennel, onion, and garlic that are puréed to act as a vehicle for the herbs.

The Quince and Apple Compote is a grown-up version of applesauce, a favorite pork-chop accompaniment. The apples break down when cooked, but the diced quince retain their shape, providing a wonderful texture and a floral taste that marries very well with the apples' sweetness.

Warm Quince and Apple Compote

MAKES 6 SERVINGS

2   large tart, firm apples, such as McIntosh, Rome, or Cortland (about $3/4$ pound)
2   large quince (about $3/4$ pound)
2   tablespoons unsalted butter
2   tablespoons sugar
$1/2$ cup apple cider
1   teaspoon fresh lemon juice
$1/2$ teaspoon ground ginger
     Coarse salt to taste

Peel, core, and dice the apples and quince into $1/2$-inch dice. In a 10-inch sauté pan, heat the butter over low heat. Sprinkle the sugar over the melted butter. Raise the heat to medium and cook, occasionally stirring or swirling the pan, for about 3 minutes, until the sugar melts and caramelizes.

Add the quince and apples, and cook, tossing occasionally, for 10 to 12 minutes, or until the fruit is lightly browned and the apples have softened. The quince dice will retain their shape.

Add the cider and lemon juice, and cook for about 2 minutes, until reduced but not evaporated. Season with the ginger and salt. Serve warm.

Chestnut
Tiramisu
MAKES 8 SERVINGS

When my wife, Helen, worked as the pastry chef at the Gotham Bar and Grill, she delighted in changing the menu constantly, exploring new ideas, often on a daily basis. There were many times when I arrived at the restaurant not knowing what desserts would be on the menu that night. That December, she created this tiramisu, presenting it in a martini glass garnished with candied chestnuts. Note that it's not made with ladyfingers, but rather with cake layers that have a similar flavor.

LADYFINGER LAYER

1	cup bleached all-purpose flour
3/4	cup cornstarch
6	large eggs, separated
3/4	cup sugar

Preheat the oven to 350°F. Butter two 10-inch-round cake pans or spray them with vegetable oil. Line the bottoms of the pans with a parchment paper round. Butter or spray the paper.

Sift together the flour and cornstarch. Set aside.

In the bowl of an electric mixer set on high speed, beat the egg yolks with $^1/_4$ cup of the sugar until light and fluffy. Set aside.

In another bowl with the electric mixer set on medium speed and the beaters thoroughly cleaned and dried, beat the egg whites until foamy. Increase the speed to high and beat until soft peaks form. Gradually add the remaining $^1/_2$ cup of sugar and continue beating until the sugar dissolves and the whites form semistiff peaks.

Using a rubber spatula, alternately fold the beaten whites and the flour-cornstarch mixture into the egg yolk mixture until well incorporated. Take care not to overwork the batter. Scrape the batter into the prepared pans and bake for about 15 minutes, until the top is golden brown and the edges begin to pull away from the sides of the pans. Invert onto wire racks to cool.

FLOURLESS SHEET CAKE

5	ounces extra-bittersweet chocolate, such as Valrhona, coarsely chopped
3	tablespoons unsalted butter
1/4	cup plus 3 tablespoons sugar
2	large egg yolks
2	tablespoons warm water
4	large egg whites

Preheat the oven to 350°F. Butter a 10-inch-round cake pan or spray it with vegetable oil. Line the bottom of the pan with a parchment or wax-paper round. Butter or spray the paper.

In the top of a double boiler, combine the chocolate,

the butter, and $^1/_4$ cup of the sugar, and heat over barely simmering water, stirring occasionally, until melted and smooth. Set aside.

In a bowl, whisk together the egg yolks and water until smooth. Set aside.

In another bowl, with the electric mixer set on medium speed, beat the egg whites until foamy. Increase the speed to high and beat until soft peaks form. Gradually add the remaining 3 tablespoons of sugar and continue beating until the sugar dissolves and the whites form semi-stiff peaks.

Using a rubber spatula, fold the chocolate into the yolks. Then fold half the whites into the chocolate-yolk mixture. When combined, fold in the remaining whites. Take care not to overwork the batter. Scrape the batter into the prepared pan and bake for 20 to 25 minutes, until the top is browned and the edges begin to pull away from the sides of the pan. Remove from the oven and while still warm, flatten the layer by gently pressing on it with a smaller cake pan, a stiff cardboard round, or a saucepan. Invert the cake onto a wire rack to cool.

CHESTNUT FILLING AND ASSEMBLY

10	candied chestnuts in syrup
1	cup unsweetened chestnut paste
4	cups heavy cream
2	cups mascarpone cheese
1	cup Kahlua
$2^1/_2$	tablespoons sugar
	Cocoa powder, for garnish

Drain the chestnuts, reserving $^1/_4$ cup of the syrup. Combine the chestnuts, reserved syrup, and chestnut paste in the bowl of a food processor fitted with a metal blade and process until puréed. Transfer the purée to the bowl of an electric mixer, add 2 cups of the cream and the mascarpone. Beat on medium-high speed until thick and smooth. Spoon the mixture into a pastry bag fitted with a #3 plain tip.

Line a 10-inch-round pan with a parchment or wax-paper round. Put one of the ladyfinger layers in the pan. Brush it with enough Kahlua to soak it. Pipe half the filling over the ladyfinger layer. Press the flourless cake layer over the filling and drizzle Kahlua over the layer. Pipe the remaining filling over the flourless cake layer. Gently press the remaining ladyfinger layer onto the filling. Brush with enough Kahlua to soak. Wrap the cake pan with plastic wrap and refrigerate it for at least 8 hours or overnight.

Unwrap the cake pan. Dip the bottom of the pan in warm water to loosen the torte. Invert it onto a platter or cardboard round and lift off the cake pan. Peel off the paper.

In the bowl of an electric mixer set at high speed, whip the remaining 2 cups of cream with the sugar to soft peaks. Spread the whipped cream over the sides and top of the torte. Sift the cocoa powder over the top of the torte. If you choose, pipe a whipped cream border around the outside of the torte. Slice the tiramisu and serve it on cocoa-dusted dessert plates.

Walnut Tart

The character and contents of tarts change throughout the year. In the summer months, a fruit tart celebrates the life-giving nourishment of the sun with the vibrant colors and flavors of strawberries, cherries, plums, and other summer favorites. We're eased into fall with the more muted charms of apple and pear tarts, and—come winter—the shift is profound as we move on to other fillings, primarily nuts. Here, dry, ground walnuts are bound together with caramelized sugar—a technique that can also be used with hazelnuts and almonds. Another crucial difference in the winter is that this tart must be eaten warm.

THINKING AHEAD: The pastry dough can be made in advance and held in the refrigerator.

TART SHELL

$1/3$	cup chopped hazelnuts
$1/2$	cup plus 2 teaspoons sugar
$1/4$	cup plus $1/2$ tablespoon almond flour
$3/4$	cup unsalted butter
1	large egg
$1^1/2$	cups all-purpose flour
$1^1/2$	tablespoons ground cinnamon
2	teaspoons baking powder

Preheat the oven to 400°F. Spread the nuts in a single layer in a shallow baking pan and toast them in the oven for about 6 minutes, until lightly browned and fragrant. Shake the pan or stir the nuts several times during toasting. Transfer the nuts to a plate to cool completely. Do not turn off oven.

Lightly spray a 10-inch tart pan with a removable bottom with vegetable oil.

In the bowl of an electric mixer set on medium-high speed, cream the sugar, almond flour, and butter for 3 to 5 minutes, until smooth and light colored. Add the egg and mix to just combine.

In another bowl, whisk together the flour, toasted hazelnuts, cinnamon, and baking powder. Reduce the speed to medium-low and gradually add the dry ingredients to the dough. Mix until just incorporated.

On a lightly floured surface, roll the dough to a circle about 13 inches in diameter and $1/4$ inch thick. Roll the dough around the rolling pin. Place the pin over the tart pan and unroll the pastry over the pan. Ease the dough into the pan, pressing gently against the sides and bottom to fit securely. Smooth out any cracks. Trim the dough flush with the top edge of the pan. Prick the dough all over with the tines of a fork. Bake for about 10 minutes. Press down any swelling or bubbles in the crust. Remove the partially baked pastry from the oven. Set it on a wire rack to cool slightly.

FILLING AND ASSEMBLY

$2^1/2$	cups walnut halves
1	cup packed light brown sugar
$1/4$	cup light corn syrup

¹/₄   cup molasses
   3   tablespoons heavy cream
   2   tablespoons bourbon
¹/₂   teaspoon salt
   1   tablespoon unsalted butter, melted

Preheat the oven to 400°F.
   Spread the nuts in a single layer in a shallow baking pan and toast them in the oven for about 6 minutes, until lightly browned and fragrant. Shake the pan or stir the nuts several times during toasting. Transfer the nuts to a plate to cool slightly. Reduce the oven temperature to 350°F.

   In a bowl, stir together the sugar, corn syrup, molasses, cream, bourbon, and salt. When combined, stir in the butter and nuts.

   Scrape the filling into the partially baked tart shell. Bake for 35 to 40 minutes, or until the filling is set. Allow to cool slightly on a wire rack at room temperature. Serve warm.

Chocolate
Cocoa
Christmas
Cookies

This is my variation on the Italian Christmas cookies I grew up with. When I began work on this book, I asked my mother for the recipe that produces these sinfully rich and chocolately indulgences. As soon as it arrived at our home, we made a batch, and after more than 30 years, one bite unleashed a flood of memories.

3	sticks butter
1¼	cups sugar
2	eggs
6	ounces apricot jam
2	teaspoons ground cinnamon
1	teaspoon freshly ground nutmeg
1	teaspoon ground cloves
½	teaspoon salt
¼	cup milk, warmed
1	teaspoon vanilla extract
4	cups flour
4½	teaspoons baking powder
1½	cup raisins, coarsely chopped
1	tablespoon orange juice
1½	cups chopped toasted walnuts
1	recipe Sugar Icing (recipe follows)

In the bowl of a heavy duty electric mixer fitted with the paddle attachment and set on speed one, cream the butter and sugar. When incorporated, add the eggs, one at a time, then add the jam, spices, salt, warm milk, and vanilla and mix.

Add flour and baking powder and combine. "Plump" the raisins in the orange juice for about 10 minutes. Fold in the raisins along with the chopped nuts. Cover and refrigerate the cookie dough until firm, at least 2 hours.

Preheat oven to 350°. Form walnut-sized rounds of dough and place them one inch apart, on a nonstick baking pan. Bake 10 to 12 minutes.

Remove them to a wire rack to cool. While still slightly warm, glaze the cookies by dipping the tops in the sugar icing.

SUGAR ICING
½	cup confectioners' sugar
1½	teaspoons water
1½	teaspoons lemon juice

Combine all the ingredients in a bowl. Then, if necessary, thin with a few more drops of water.

Chocolate
Hazelnut
Biscotti

MAKES 4 ¹/₂ DOZEN BISCOTTI

As much as I love traditional Italian biscotti, hard and nutty, I also have a fondness for these softer, chocolate biscotti. Fill a tin with them for a perfect holiday gift.

1¹/₄	cups hazelnuts
1	stick (4 ounces) butter
³/₄	cup sugar
1	tablespoon ground espresso
3	eggs
1³/₄	cups flour
6	tablespoons cocoa
1	pinch salt
1	teaspoon baking soda
³/₄	cup Valrhona chocolate, chopped

reheat the oven at 350°F. Place the hazelnuts on a baking sheet
fragrant and just beginning to brown, approxi-
then coarsely chop. In the
a paddle and set at a medium
gar, and ground espresso until
ites. Slowly add the eggs, then
g soda and mix until the mix-
ugh. Add the chopped chocolate
ly into the dough. Scrape the
p. Wrap it tightly and chill it in
y 1 hour. Line 2 baking sheets
ne chilled dough into thirds. On
inch logs, separating the logs by at
ing dough into one 12-inch log on
witching the position of the baking
the logs feel firm and are lightly
inutes. Cool them slightly on the
ven temperature to 325°. Remove the
g a serrated knife, cut them on a slight
es. Arrange the slices flat on the baking
the oven. Bake, turning the biscotti over
p, approximately 10 to 15 minutes.

Fig Cookies

MAKES 30 TO 40 COOKIES

THINKING AHEAD: The filling can be made as many as 3 days in advance.

FILLING

8	ounces dried figs
2	ounces dates
2	ounces golden raisins
2	ounces dried cherries
2	ounces dried apricots
2	ounces fresh pineapple
2	ounces toasted walnuts
$1/4$	orange, unpeeled
1	tablespoon water
$1/4$	teaspoon ground cinnamon
$1/4$	teaspoon ground nutmeg
1	tablespoon brandy

As is the case with tomato sauce, every Italian mother seems to have her own fig cookie recipe. When I was a kid, I would help my mother make these using a grinder clamped to the kitchen table, because she had a chronic sore shoulder. The biggest chore is icing each one. I've adjusted her recipe, using pistachios instead of walnuts. These will keep for quite a while in an airtight tin, making them a perfect holiday gift.

In a large bowl, combine the fruits and nuts. Chop the mixture coarsely with a large, heavy knife, push it through a hand grinder, or put it in the bowl of a food processor fitted with a metal blade and pulse until just coarsely chopped. Do not purée; the mixture should be chunky.

Transfer the chopped fruits and nuts to a large saucepan and add the water, cinnamon, and nutmeg. Cook over low heat, stirring often, for about 30 minutes, until thick.

Remove from the heat and stir in the brandy. Set aside to cool to room temperature. Cover and refrigerate for at least 1 hour, until chilled.

COOKIE DOUGH

$1/2$	cup unsalted butter, softened
$1/2$	cup vegetable shortening, such as Crisco
$1/2$	cup sugar
4	cups all-purpose flour
$1^1/2$	teaspoons baking powder
2	small eggs, lightly beaten
$1/2$	teaspoon fresh lemon juice

In an electric mixer set on medium speed, cream the butter, vegetable shortening, and sugar until light and fluffy. Add the flour and baking powder, and mix until just incorporated. Add the eggs and lemon juice, and mix until just blended. Remove the bowl

(continued)

from the mixer and stir the dough by hand with a wooden spoon. When well mixed, cover the bowl and refrigerate the dough for at least 1 hour, until chilled.

Preheat the oven to 350°F. Line 2 baking sheets with parchment paper.

On a lightly floured surface, roll the dough out into a rectangular shape to a thickness of approximately $1/4$ inch. Divide the dough into shapes that measure $5^1/2$ inches wide by approximately 10 to 12 inches long. Spoon filling down the center of each rectangle, mounding it about an inch high. Make sure there is enough dough on either side of the filling to enclose it. Fold the dough up over the filling and seal where the two ends meet. Gently flatten the roll and turn so that the roll is seam side down on the work surface.

Using a sharp, thin-bladed knife, cut the rolls on a slight bias into $1/2$-inch-thick pieces. Set the pieces seam side down on the parchment-lined baking sheets and bake for about 15 minutes, or until golden brown. Cool on wire racks.

ASSEMBLY

1 recipe Sugar Icing (page 292)
1 cup chopped pistachios

When cookies have cooled, dip each cookie in icing, then in chopped pistachios to cover.

Christmas Eve Dinner

This is a fish and seafood affair, modeled after those on which I was raised.

SALMON RILLETTE (page 271)

DIVER SCALLOPS AND SEVRUGA CAVIAR TARTARE (page 273)

WARM POTATO AND SMOKED EEL SALAD (page 274)

SHELLFISH RISOTTO (page 67)

ROAST COD WITH SAVOY CABBAGE, WHITE BEANS,
AND BLACK TRUFFLE (page 278)

WALNUT TART (page 290)

COCOA COOKIES (page 292)

New Year's Eve Dinner

This extravagant meal is perfect for New Year's Eve or for any formal winter celebration.

FOIE GRAS WITH SOUR CHERRY CHUTNEY (page 268)

LINGUINE WITH WHITE TRUFFLES (page 280)

SALMON WITH BLACK TRUMPET MUSHROOMS, BRUSSELS SPROUT LEAVES,
AND FINGERLING POTATOES (page 207)

LAMB CHOPS WITH SWISS CHARD AND TRUFFLED
MASHED POTATOES (page 281)

CHESTNUT TIRAMISU (page 287)

Puréed Soups

Artichoke Heart Soup

Cauliflower Vichyssoise

Bosc Pear Carpaccio with Microgreens, Pecorino Romano, and 25-Year-Old Balsamico Tradizionale

Cured Salmon Salad with White Beans, Green Lentils, and Quail Eggs

Stock-Based Vinaigrettes

Sole Chablis

Halibut with Steamed Spinach and Portobello Mushroom Vinaigrette

Trout Wrapped in Bacon with Braised Escarole, Green Lentils, Sage, and Sherry Vinaigrette

Meyer Lemon Granité

Candied Grapefruit Rinds

Super Bowl Party

JANUARY

A FRESH START

If the calendar year were compressed into just one week, New Year's Eve would be the last stop on the social Saturday night of December, and January would be the sleepy, silent Sunday morning after.

In fact, regardless of when New Year's Day falls, it always has the feel of a Sunday about it. The world seems to shut down, and we pause to anticipate the coming twelve months the same way one does a work week—leaving the holidays behind and bracing for a return to reality. The calendar's coming full-circle to January 1 inspires a lot of soul-searching and goal-setting. For me, it's a time to evaluate the year that just ended and determine how to attack the next twelve months.

Gastronomically speaking, January is also a time of reckoning and readjustment. Many of us emerge on January 1 to the realization that the festivities and feasts of the preceding weeks have taken their toll, and the final night of the year may have been the one of greatest excess. The same voice seems to whisper to many of us on New Year's Day, urging some restraint and suggesting that we rearrange our dietary priorities.

For gourmands, this is an annual turning point. The unabashed feeding frenzy that defines December looms in one's memory as a nirvana of sorts, but the need to rein it in is indisputable come the New Year. The obvious problem is that it's challenging to eat healthfully without giving in to the bland.

Challenging. But not impossible. In this chapter I'll share some of my thoughts for attaining satisfying flavors without pouring on the butter and cream.

In two of the dishes that follow, you'll learn about puréed soups—Artichoke Heart Soup (page 303) and Cauliflower Vichyssoise (page 305)—that cheat caloric fate by liquefying vegetables and enriching them with nondairy supplements. To build on them, I've also included an essay on this type of soup-making. After reading it, and trying one or both of these recipes, you should be able to successfully create a variety of soups using your favorite vegetables year-round.

For a vegetarian option, there's the Bosc Pear Carpaccio with Microgreens, Pecorino Romano, and 25-Year-Old Balsamico Tradizionale (page 307), a satisfying small meal.

It's no secret that seafood is a popular source of protein among the health-conscious. Here, I've included a variety of fish and cooking methods, from the Cured Salmon Salad with White Beans, Lentils, and Quail Eggs (page 309) to the Sole Chablis (page 313) which is steamed in white wine, to the pan-roasted Trout Wrapped in Bacon with Braised Escarole, Green Lentils, Sage, and Sherry Vinaigrette (page 317) and Halibut with Steamed Spinach and Portobello Mushroom Vinaigrette (page 315).

The trickiest category in this month of resolutions is desserts. I've kept things very simple on this front with a Meyer Lemon Granité (page 320) and Candied Grapefruit Rinds (page 322), two recipes that pack a sweet little punch thanks to the natural sugars in the raw ingredients themselves.

There is one day in January when dietary restraint goes right out the window—Super Bowl Sunday. For many Americans, this is a chance to indulge in so-called "junk food" and beer. Included here is a way to do this, Gotham-style, with a menu comprising Tuna Burgers, Slow-Cooked Lamb Shoulder, and Peanut Butter Coupe, which I find especially appropriate since my family and I watch the big game at the restaurant's Super Bowl party every year. Because the holiday schedule at the Gotham is so taxing, we have taken to postponing our Christmas party until January, when we throw a celebration for the staff complete with large-screen televisions and our own half-time show (last year, one of the waiters dressed in drag and serenaded my hometown's Buffalo Bills). It's our way of sneaking in one last holiday gathering long after the official season has come and gone.

Puréed Soups

Puréed soups focus on the essence of one primary ingredient (usually a vegetable), basically transforming that ingredient into the very soup itself rather than floating it in a broth. Other ingredients are blended into puréed soups to add depth of flavor, and potatoes or bread might be used to create thickness or creamy richness, but the flavor of the theme vegetable will always dominate.

In making a puréed soup, you don't need to cut vegetables to the same shape because they will ultimately be milled together, but it's a good idea to keep all of them about the same size to facilitate even cooking. When cooking the vegetables for such a soup, pay close attention to heating them until soft, without taking them so far that you boil the life and flavor out of them.

A foolproof method of modulating the thickness of a puréed soup and obtaining a smooth, silken result is to strain out the solids and purée them first, with just a ladleful of liquid. Then add the rest of the liquid back into the purée either by whisking or using a blender. This will guarantee a fine-textured purée and give you a feeling of great control over the soup's consistency, allowing you to adjust it to suit your own taste.

While you may not want to avail yourself of this option in January, stirring cream, milk, crème fraîche, butter, or olive oil into a puréed soup is a method of lending it extra body and making it more substantial and rich.

It's also important to note that, while most soups can be made ahead and frozen, puréed soups don't freeze very well, though they will generally hold in the refrigerator for up to three days.

3 tablespoons fresh lemon juice
3 cups cold water
4 pounds large artichokes (5 or 6 artichokes)
2 quarts White Chicken Stock (page 421)
   Coarse salt and freshly ground white pepper to taste
1/4 cup extra-virgin olive oil
1 large onion, chopped
1 rib celery, chopped
3 cloves garlic, peeled and minced
1/2 cup dry white wine
1 bay leaf

In a medium bowl, combine 2 tablespoons of the lemon juice with the water.

Using a sharp paring knife, pare off the thick green skin at the base of one artichoke. Remove the thick, dark outer leaves to reveal the light yellow center. Reserve the outer leaves. Trim the leaf tips just above the "choke" (the fuzzy center of the heart). Using a small spoon, scrape out the choke. Put the artichoke heart in the acidulated water to prevent discoloring. Repeat with the remaining artichokes.

In a stockpot, combine the reserved artichoke leaves and the chicken stock. Bring to a boil over high heat. Reduce the heat to medium and simmer gently for about 15 minutes. Remove the pot from the heat and let the soup stand for about 10 minutes to give the flavors time to develop.

Strain the stock through a fine-mesh sieve into a bowl, pressing on the artichoke leaves to extract as much flavor as possible. Discard the leaves. Season the stock with salt and pepper. You should have approximately 1 1/2 quarts of rich-tasting stock. Keep warm over very low heat.

In a large saucepan, heat 1 tablespoon of olive oil over medium-high heat. Cook the onion and celery, stirring, for about 6 minutes, until softened. Add the garlic and cook, stirring, for about 2 minutes, until softened.

Working quickly so they don't turn brown, remove the artichoke hearts from the acidulated water one at a time and cut them into thick slices. Add the slices to the pan and season lightly with salt and pepper. When all the hearts are sliced and in the pan, cook for about 4 minutes, stirring. Add the wine and bring to a boil. Cook for about 3 minutes, until the wine is nearly evaporated. Add

Artichoke
Heart Soup
MAKES 4 SERVINGS

This dish uses all parts of the artichoke to create a richly flavored soup. First, the edible hearts are separated from the leaves, which are very flavorful but inedible. These trimmings are used to make an artichoke stock, while the hearts are simmered in a white *mirepoix* of leeks, onions, and garlic. The two components are combined and then puréed to a silky white, creamy soup into which a fair dose of extra-virgin olive oil is emulsified, contributing additional flavor and richness.

the bay leaf and the reserved artichoke stock. Bring to a simmer and cook for 15 to 20 minutes, or until the artichoke hearts are tender.

Strain the soup through a fine-mesh sieve into another pot. Discard the bay leaf. Working in batches, purée the vegetables in a blender or food processor fitted with the metal blade until smooth. Transfer the puréed vegetables to a saucepan. Stir in the remaining 3 tablespoons of the olive oil.

Add the strained liquid to the purée, or enough of it to reach the desired consistency. Season with salt and pepper and as much of the remaining tablespoon of lemon juice as needed to lift the flavor. Heat gently, if necessary, to serve hot.

FLAVOR BUILDING: Serve this soup with croutons spread with tapenade and/or sprinkle it with freshly grated Parmesan cheese.

4 teaspoons canola oil
2 medium leeks, white parts only, sliced (about 1½ cups)
1 medium onion, diced (about 1 cup)
1 large head cauliflower, cut into florets (4 to 5 packed cups)
4 cups White Chicken Stock (page 421)
  Coarse salt and freshly ground white pepper to taste
¼ cup extra-virgin olive oil
1 tablespoon finely minced chives

In a large soup pot, heat 1 tablespoon (3 teaspoons) of the oil over medium-high heat. Cook the leeks and onion for 3 to 4 minutes, stirring, until translucent but not browned. Add the cauliflower and stock, and bring to a boil. Reduce the heat and simmer for 2 to 3 minutes. Using a slotted spoon, remove 3 of the largest florets and set them aside to cool.

When cool, cut the cauliflower florets into lengthwise slices about ⅛ inch thick. You will need 8 to 12 nicely shaped slices to garnish the soup. Return any cauliflower scraps to the soup pot. Set the slices aside.

Continue to simmer the soup for about 18 minutes, until the cauliflower is tender. Season it with salt and pepper. Transfer the soup to a blender or food processor fitted with the metal blade and purée until smooth. Return the soup to the pot to keep warm.

In a small nonstick sauté pan, heat the remaining 1 teaspoon of

Sautéed Scallops

2 tablespoons vegetable oil
4 large sea scallops, preferably diver-harvested, small muscle flaps removed
  Coarse salt
  Freshly ground white pepper

In a 12-inch nonstick sauté pan, heat the oil over high heat until very hot but not smoking. Season the scallops with salt and pepper. Cook the scallops until golden brown, about 3 minutes. Using kitchen tongs, turn the scallops and reduce the heat to medium. Cook until the other side is browned and the scallops are on the rare side, about 2 minutes.

Cauliflower
Vichyssoise
MAKES 4 SERVINGS

In the early 1980s, I spent some time working at a spa in France that used vegetable purées, including cauliflower, as a thickening agent in place of cream or butter. This culinary sleight-of-hand was especially handy in soups and sauces. (Another technique was to emulsify olive oil into a stock to thicken it; see the recipe for Artichoke Heart Soup, page 303.)

Years later, it occurred to me to create a soup that celebrated this underrated vegetable. Though often dismissed as one of the usual suspects in a *crudité* lineup, I've always found that cauliflower can be quite satisfying in its own right. Determined to put its clean flavor and full texture front and center, I returned to the technique for making vichyssoise, replacing potatoes with cauliflower. To bolster the overall flavor of the soup with a stronger cauliflower presence, I caramelized some cauliflower florets; floating on the surface of this creamy and visually anonymous soup, the florets proudly announce the identity of the vegetable within.

oil over medium–high heat. Sauté the reserved cauliflower slices for 2 to 3 minutes, or until lightly browned on both sides. Sprinkle with salt and pepper, and set them aside.

If necessary, gently reheat the soup for 1 to 2 minutes. Ladle the soup into bowls and garnish each with several slices of browned cauliflower. Drizzle the surface of the soup with olive oil, sprinkle with chives, and serve.

FLAVOR BUILDING: Upgrade this soup with diver scallops and Osetra caviar. Place a few florets in the center of each bowl and a sautéed scallop (see sidebar, previous page) on top. Ladle in the soup, and adorn the scallop with 1 to 1^1/$_2$ ounces of caviar, dispersed over the four bowls. (If you do this, encourage your guests to stir their caviar into the soup as opposed to eating it off the top in one fell swoop.)

Watercress, too, would be a flavorful addition; remove and discard the stems from one bunch, and purée the watercress into the soup at the end for a stunning, pale green variation.

VARIATION: Like its namesake, this soup is also delicious cold.

SPECIAL EQUIPMENT: Mandoline-type slicer

2   ripe Bosc pears
$^1/_4$ cup extra-virgin olive oil
4   teaspoons 25-year-old Balsamico Tradizionale vinegar
       Coarse salt and freshly ground white pepper to taste
4   cups loosely packed microgreens
1   tablespoon fresh lemon juice
4   ounces Pecorino Romano cheese, in one piece

Halve the pears lengthwise and remove the core with a small scoop. Using a thin-bladed knife or a Japanese-style mandoline, slice the pear halves $^1/_8$ inch thick. Fan each pear half on a chilled dinner plate.

Drizzle the pears with 1 tablespoon of the olive oil and the balsamic vinegar. Season them lightly with salt and pepper.

In a small bowl, toss the greens with the remaining 3 tablespoons of olive oil and the lemon juice. Season them with salt and pepper. Arrange a bouquet of greens on top of each pear half. Using a vegetable peeler, finish each plate with curls of Pecorino Romano. Serve immediately.

VARIATIONS: A blue cheese, such as Roquefort or Gorgonzola, will work brilliantly here in place of the Pecorino Romano. The sweetness of the pears and the balsamic vinegar will match the saltiness of the cheese bite for bite. Also, while Bosc pears are recommended for their crispness and reliability, other pears, such as Bartlett and Anjou, will work well, too.

If you're not using balsamic vinegar, substitute a mixture of 1 teaspoon red wine vinegar and 3 teaspoons extra-virgin olive oil, which will soften the vinegar, taking the edge off its acidity.

FLAVOR BUILDING: Thinly sliced *prosciutto di Parma* (4 ounces), toasted walnut halves, or Duck Confit (page 233), all complement the flavors of this dish.

If you love the combination of pears and cheese, here's a chance to put them center stage rather than relegating them to a supporting role. This dish was devised for a 10-course vegetarian tasting menu we prepared at the Gotham some years back. A decade later, it remains an unusual, successful salad course.

The recipe calls for aged balsamic vinegar, a potent elixir that delivers a complex range of sweetness and acidity and should be used sparingly because of its power and its value. When purchasing balsamic vinegar, be sure the label bears the full designation, *Aceto Balsamico Tradizionale di Modena*. (This means it is produced in the town of Modena, the home of balsamic vinegar, though a few are also produced in the vicinity of Reggio.) A different, or abbreviated name usually indicates a lesser-quality vinegar with sugar or caramel added to imitate the effects of the real thing. Some producers even heat the vinegar with oak chips to imitate aging in wood. You could prepare the salad with one of these, but buy the best quality you can find. If you don't have any balsamic on hand, use a good, high-quality red wine vinegar, following the instructions in Variations, previous page.

Cured Salmon Salad with White Beans, Green Lentils, and Quail Eggs

MAKES ABOUT TWELVE 4-OUNCE SERVINGS OR EIGHT 4-OUNCE SERVINGS, DEPENDING ON CHOSEN QUANTITIES

THINKING AHEAD: The cure requires 48 hours. The white beans must be soaked overnight.

FOR 12 SERVINGS

2   tablespoons fresh lime juice
2   tablespoons extra-virgin olive oil
2   tablespoons aquavit
1   3$^{1}/_{2}$-pound fillet of Atlantic salmon, skin on
4   bunches fresh dill (about 5 ounces), stemmed and chopped
8   tablespoons sugar
5   tablespoons fine table salt
10 tablespoons crushed white pepper

FOR 4–6 SERVINGS

1   tablespoon fresh lime juice
1   tablespoon extra-virgin olive oil
1   tablespoon aquavit
1   2-pound fillet of Atlantic salmon, skin on
2   bunches fresh dill (about 2$^{1}/_{2}$ ounces), stemmed and chopped
5   tablespoons sugar
4   tablespoons fine table salt
5   tablespoons crushed white pepper

In a bowl, combine the lime juice, olive oil, and aquavit. Rub the mixture over the salmon, making sure it covers the fish evenly on both sides.

In a bowl, combine the dill, sugar, salt, and pepper. On a baking tray or a platter large enough to hold the salmon fillet flat, spread about half the dill mixture in an even layer. Lay the salmon, skin side down, on top of the dill mixture. Spread the remaining dill mixture evenly over the salmon. Wrap the baking tray or platter with plastic wrap. Lay another baking sheet or a large, heavy piece of cardboard over the salmon and place 12 pounds of weight (such as cans of food) on top, distributing it evenly along the length of the fish. Refrigerate for 2 days. After the first day, pour off any accumulated liquid and return the salmon, wrapped and weighted, to the refrigerator.

After the second day, unwrap the salmon and scrape off the dill mixture with the back of a knife. Rewrap the salmon and keep it refrigerated until ready to serve.

Smoked salmon is to New York City what apple pie is to the rest of America. All manner of smoked fish are available here and have been since what feels like the dawn of time. But cold-smoking fish at home requires far more expertise and equipment than even most lifelong New Yorkers possess. Gravlax, or cured salmon, on the other hand, is relatively simple and fun to make, and is one of those recipes that, because most people don't make their own, tends to impress.

Gravlax coated with dill and served with sweet mustard sauce (see page 311) is a classic, but if you are like most contemporary chefs, rarely content to simply roll with tradition, you can create your own formulas by altering the aromat-

(continued)

ics in this recipe, creating a variety of gravlax that can stand on its own (that is, with no need of sauce), or with other accompaniments.

This recipe is my favorite. It involves two "rubs": one dry (dill, salt, sugar, and crushed white pepper) and one liquid (lime juice, extra-virgin olive oil, and aquavit).

The rest of the preparation is textbook: A weight is placed atop the treated fish (to quicken the penetration of the salt) which is then placed in the refrigerator, where its flake gradually softens and the salmon metamorphoses into a silky, buttery luxury that is easy to slice and work with, and is richly satisfying.

The recipe below is for a *salade composée,* but gravlax on its own makes a perfect buffet offering. During January, for example, it's ideal at a New Year's Day brunch.

Normally, gravlax recipes are designed to cure an entire side of salmon, but for those of you thinking on a smaller scale, I have provided a recipe for a 2-pound cut of fish that will be perfect for 4 to 6 people. If there's any left over, it will keep well refrigerated for several days, but why wait? You might, as New Yorkers have been known to do, just slap it on a bagel and treat yourself to something special for breakfast the very next morning.

WHITE BEAN AND GREEN LENTIL SALAD

1	cup dry white runner beans or Great Northern beans, soaked overnight and drained
1	small carrot, halved
1	rib celery, halved
1	small onion, halved
2	bay leaves
	Coarse salt and freshly ground white pepper to taste
$1/4$	cup French green lentils
3 to 4	tablespoons Basic Vinaigrette (page 420)
$1/4$	cup finely sliced scallions
1	tablespoon chopped fresh tarragon

In a medium saucepan, combine the beans with half the carrot, celery, and onion, and 1 bay leaf. Add enough cold water to cover and bring to a boil over high heat. Reduce the heat to low and simmer for 20 minutes. Season with salt and pepper, and simmer for about 1 hour longer, or until the beans are tender. The time will depend on the age and dryness of the beans. Drain well and discard the vegetables and bay leaf.

Meanwhile, in another saucepan, combine the lentils and the remaining halves of the carrot, celery, onion, and 1 bay leaf, and season with salt and pepper. Add enough cold water to cover and bring to a boil over high heat. Reduce the heat to low and simmer for about 25 minutes, or until the lentils are tender. Drain well and discard the vegetables and bay leaf.

In a bowl, combine the beans and lentils. Dress well with vinaigrette and season with salt and pepper. Stir in the scallions and tarragon.

ASSEMBLY

12	quail eggs
4	cups mixed salad greens
	About $1/2$ cup Basic Vinaigrette (page 420)
	Coarse salt and freshly ground white pepper to taste
	Sweet Mustard Sauce (page 311)

In a small saucepan, cover the eggs with cold salted water and bring to a boil over high heat. Boil for about 4 minutes. Drain and set aside to cool. When cool enough to handle, carefully peel the eggs and set them aside.

Remove the gravlax from the refrigerator and unwrap it. Slice it thin and arrange the slices on a serving platter.

In a bowl, dress the greens with the vinaigrette and season with salt and pepper. Serve the greens, quail eggs, and bean-and-lentil salad in separate bowls. Pass the mustard sauce on the side.

VARIATIONS: Once you've mastered the basic gravlax technique, feel free to experiment. Star anise, coriander seed, fennel seed, and caraway seed work particularly well with salmon. You might also try flavored vodka and gin or mix up the herbs with tarragon and chervil, or even add fresh ginger to the spices.

FLAVOR BUILDING: Pair gravlax and Salmon Rillette (page 271) and top with caviar.

FROM GRAVLAX TO LOX:
Lox is derived from the word for "salmon" in the Germanic languages, but what we today refer to as "lox" in the United States is a U.S. market name for Pacific salmon that has been cured in a heavily salted brine bolstered with sugar.

Sweet Mustard Sauce

This is the classic accompaniment to gravlax.

THINKING AHEAD: This sauce may be made as many as 3 days in advance and kept covered in the refrigerator.

2	tablespoons dry mustard
1	tablespoon fresh lemon juice
¹/₄	cup Dijon mustard
3	tablespoons honey
1	tablespoon extra-virgin olive oil
	Coarse salt and freshly ground white pepper to taste

In a small, nonreactive bowl, combine the dry mustard with the lemon juice, stirring to make a paste. Stir in the Dijon mustard and honey, and then whisk in the oil. Season with salt and pepper.

Sole Chablis

2   pounds lemon sole fillet
6 to 8 tablespoons unsalted butter, cut into pieces, at room
        temperature
1   teaspoon crushed coriander seed
        Coarse salt and freshly ground white pepper to taste
2   cups white wine, such as Chablis
1/4   cup extra-virgin olive oil
1   tablespoon fresh lemon juice
4   teaspoons chopped fresh chives

Preheat the oven to 400°F. Generously butter 2 shallow baking dishes, each large enough to hold half the fish in 6-inch-diameter circles.

Using a thin-bladed knife, slice the fillets crosswise into thin slices, similar to how you slice smoked salmon, but at a more severe angle, creating a somewhat abrupt cut. Arrange some of the slices in 2 circles approximately 6 inches in diameter in the bottom of each baking dish. Continue arranging the slices in concentric circles on top of each other for a petaled effect. Dot each circle with butter and season them with coriander seed, salt, and pepper. Pour 1 cup of the wine into each dish, cover with aluminum foil, and bake on 2 oven racks for 3 to 4 minutes, or until the fish turns opaque on the surface.

Carefully remove the dishes from the oven and remove the foil. Tilt the baking dishes one at a time and pour the cooking juices into a small saucepan. Cover the fish again with the foil and set aside to keep warm. When cooked, the petals of fish will adhere to one another, allowing for an easy transfer from baking dish to plate.

Set the saucepan over high heat and bring the juices to a boil. Boil for about 3 minutes to concentrate the flavors.

Using a spatula, transfer the fish circles to the centers of 4 warmed dinner plates. Whisk the olive oil and lemon juice into the sauce. Season with salt and pepper, stir in the chives, and spoon the sauce over the fish.

WHAT TO DRINK: Premier Cru or Grand Cru Chablis works perfectly with this dish, as the names might suggest.

In the highly organized, structured, and formal French kitchen, a *poissonnier* is in charge of all manner of fish and shellfish, and their *commis* (apprentices) attend to all of the scaling, gutting, and portioning of the fish. One of my most vivid memories of working as a *poissonnier* in France is of preparing the elegant, delicious, and beautiful recipe, *Pétales de Bar* or "petals of sea bass." Here I've substituted sole, or flounder, a flat fish that is a relative of the turbot, which we sometimes used in France as well.

The fragrant sauce of fresh herbs and extra-virgin olive oil takes literally seconds to make. Use the time this buys you to carefully arrange the petals on each plate (as pictured on the opposite page) for a stunning presentation.

Stock-Based Vinaigrettes

Most people think of vinaigrette as little more than a mixture of oil and vinegar used to dress greens or cooked vegetables. While this type of vinaigrette is too assertive and heavy-handed to be used as a sauce, I love using warm, stock-based vinaigrettes to sauce many dishes, especially seafood, for a number of reasons.

Vinaigrettes are a healthful, natural way to enhance or finish a dish and a lighter alternative to a reduction of cream and butter. Warm vinaigrettes are especially appropriate finishing touches in this month when we're trying to eat lightly.

On a practical level, these vinaigrettes are very simple to make. You might even use a tinned broth or bottled clam juice because there's no reducing of the liquid, which would unpleasantly concentrate the excessive salt in these products.

In a stock-based vinaigrette, oil (extra-virgin, or something even lighter perhaps) and an acid (vinegar, reduced white wine, sherry, or lemon juice) are combined and the mixture is softened with stock. Minced shallot, garlic, and ground crushed spices are added, and an abundance of fresh herbs are tossed in at the last minute. These vinaigrettes should be served warm, not hot, or the acidity level will be adversely affected.

PORTOBELLO MUSHROOM VINAIGRETTE

¹/₄ cup extra-virgin olive oil
1 pound portobello mushrooms, stemmed and cut into thick slices
1 cup White Chicken Stock (page 421)
1 tablespoon aged sherry vinegar
1 tablespoon aged balsamic vinegar
1 tablespoon finely minced shallot
¹/₄ teaspoon finely minced garlic
Coarse salt and freshly ground white pepper to taste

In a sauté pan, heat 1 tablespoon of the oil over medium–high heat until very hot but not smoking. Add the mushrooms and cook for about 5 minutes, until slightly softened. Add the stock, reduce the heat to medium, and braise the mushrooms about 5 minutes longer, until softened but still holding their shape. Using a slotted spoon or spatula, remove the mushroom slices and set them aside, covered to keep warm.

Measure the liquid in the pan. You should have 6 tablespoons. If you have more, reduce the liquid over high heat until it measures 6 tablespoons. Set aside to cool to room temperature.

Stir in the remaining olive oil, the sherry vinegar, balsamic vinegar, shallot, and garlic. Season to taste with salt and pepper. Reserve.

STEAMED SPINACH

2 cups water
2 tablespoons unsalted butter
1¹/₂ pounds fresh spinach, washed and stemmed
Coarse salt and freshly ground white pepper to taste

In a large saucepan, bring the water and butter to a boil over high heat. Add the spinach and season with salt and pepper. Cook, stirring, for 2 to 3 minutes, or until the spinach wilts. Drain well. Return the spinach to the saucepan and set aside, covered, to keep warm.

HALIBUT AND ASSEMBLY

2 tablespoons extra-virgin olive oil
4 halibut fillets, each weighing about 6 ounces and cut about 1¹/₄ inches thick
Coarse salt and freshly ground white pepper to taste
Fresh chervil sprigs, for garnish

Halibut with Steamed Spinach and Portobello Mushroom Vinaigrette

MAKES 4 SERVINGS

I sometimes find that grilling or sautéing portobello mushrooms can turn their flavor bitter. But braising them eliminates this problem. Here, these meaty mushrooms are braised quickly with a little stock to create a dark, mushroomy liquid. The mushrooms provide a toothsome contrast to the flaky fish, while the braising liquid is cooled and combined with vinegar, extra-virgin olive oil, and minced shallot to make a great, simple sauce.

WHAT TO DRINK: Serve this dish with a white Bordeaux.

In a large sauté pan, heat the oil over medium-high heat until very hot but not smoking. Season the halibut on both sides with salt and pepper. Cook for about 4 minutes, until golden brown. Turn and cook about 3 minutes longer, just until the fish is opaque in the center.

Mound the spinach in 4 oversized bowls. Set a halibut fillet on top of the spinach. Garnish with sliced mushrooms and 2 to 3 tablespoons of the warm vinaigrette. Garnish with the chervil sprigs and serve immediately.

VARIATIONS: The vinaigrette works well with other white fish and with skate.

Trout
Wrapped in
Bacon with
Braised
Escarole,
Green
Lentils, Sage,
and Sherry
Vinaigrette

MAKES 4 SERVINGS

THINKING AHEAD: The trout can be prepared a day in advance and allowed to marinate overnight. The vinaigrette should be prepared a few hours in advance, if possible, to allow its flavors to develop.

ROAST GARLIC PURÉE

 1   head garlic, separated into cloves
 1   tablespoon extra-virgin olive oil
 1   tablespoon water
      Coarse salt and freshly ground black pepper to taste

Preheat the oven to 325°F.
In a small baking dish, combine the garlic cloves, olive oil, and water. Season with salt and pepper. Cover the dish with aluminum foil and bake for about 30 minutes, or until the garlic is tender (squeeze a clove to determine when the garlic is done). Set the garlic aside until cool enough to handle.

Remove half the garlic and squeeze the cloves from their skins into a small bowl. Mash with a fork until puréed and set aside. Leave the other cloves and oil in the dish. Set aside. Do not turn off the oven.

LENTILS

 1   carrot, peeled
 2^1/$_4$ cups water
 ^{1}/$_2$ cup French green lentils
 2   ribs celery, sliced
 ^{1}/$_4$ medium onion
 1   bay leaf
      Coarse salt and freshly ground white pepper to taste
 1   tablespoon extra-virgin olive oil

Slice half the carrot into rounds. Cut the remaining carrot half into very small dice, called a *brunoise*. These should be about ^{1}/$_8$ inch square.

In a saucepan, combine the carrot rounds, the water, the lentils, celery, onion, and bay leaf. Bring to a boil over medium-high heat. Reduce the heat and simmer for about 30 minutes, or until the lentils are al dente. Remove the carrot rounds, celery, onion, and bay leaf from the pan and discard. Season the lentils with salt and pepper. Stir in the carrot *brunoise* and the olive oil, cover, and keep warm.

(continued)

At the time of this writing, trout scarcely figures in the thought process of the American home cook wondering, "What kind of fish should I make tonight?" Though it might not win a popularity contest, trout does offer something valuable to cooks of all levels: simplicity. They are usually sold partially boned, with only a few bones remaining in the dorsal fin. A related benefit is that, due to its compact size, trout can be cooked through in a relatively short amount of time.

But it might be said that what the trout offers in convenience, it lacks in flavor; or, rather, its flavor is a bit more shy than that of other white fish such as halibut or bass. Here, the trout's character is drawn out by opening the fish and rubbing the inside with a roast-garlic paste and placing fresh sage and thyme leaves in its cavity. Two strips of bacon are wrapped around the fish to lock in these ingredients during cooking and intensify them with an alluring smokiness.

Originally, we made this dish at the Gotham with a rich red-wine reduction finished with butter, but in keeping with our New Year's theme of moderation, it's presented here with a warm, aromatic sherry vinaigrette. With the exception of the bacon, this dish is very healthful, piled high with vegetables and lentils and using just a modicum of olive oil.

One caveat regarding trout: Great trout is hard to come by. Even trout fishermen today release them as a nod to preservationist concerns. All commercial trout is farmed, but not all farmed trout is created equal. More ambitious farmers raise it in a simulated natural habitat, the other extreme being a sterile hatchery, which produces bland, generic trout. Find out where your fishmonger's trout originated and only settle for those hailing from a natural habitat.

BRAISED ESCAROLE

1   large head escarole

Bring a saucepan of salted water to a boil over high heat. Set a bowl of ice water next to the stove.

Cut the escarole in half lengthwise. Slice the halves lengthwise into $1^1/2$-inch-thick wedges. Blanch them in the rapidly boiling water for about 15 seconds. Immediately plunge them in the ice water to set the color. When cool, remove the escarole and squeeze out the excess water. Set aside.

SHERRY VINAIGRETTE

2   tablespoons aged sherry wine vinegar
$1/4$ cup Clam Broth (page 349) or bottled clam juice
1   small clove garlic, peeled and minced
1   small shallot, peeled and minced
   Coarse salt and freshly ground white pepper to taste
$1/4$ cup extra-virgin olive oil

In a small bowl, combine the vinegar and clam broth. Stir in the garlic and shallot, and season with salt and pepper. Whisk in the olive oil. Set aside. Whisk again before using.

POTATOES

12   fingerling potatoes, sliced in half lengthwise

In a saucepan of boiling salted water, cook the potatoes for 5 to 7 minutes, or until just tender. Remove the pan from the stove but let the potatoes sit in the hot water until ready to serve. Do not cook them until you are ready to cook the trout.

TROUT AND ASSEMBLY

1   bunch fresh sage
4   brook trout, each about 14 ounces, cleaned (head removed, back and pin bones removed)
   Coarse salt and freshly ground white pepper to taste
1   sprig fresh thyme, leaves picked and chopped
8   thin-sliced strips bacon
1   tablespoon canola oil
2   tablespoons extra-virgin olive oil

R aise the oven temperature to 375°F.

Pick the leaves from the sage, reserving half of the biggest leaves. Mince the other leaves.

On an impeccably clean cutting board, lay the trout, opening them to expose their cavities. Rub the reserved garlic purée in the cavities and season with salt and pepper. Sprinkle the chopped sage leaves and thyme leaves in the cavities.

Working with 1 trout at a time, lay 2 strips of bacon on the cutting board, arranging them at 45° angles so that they overlap slightly. Lay a large sage leaf in the center of the strips. Close one of the trout and place it in the middle of the bacon. Lay a second sage leaf on top of the fish. Carefully wrap the trout with the bacon strips, securing them as tightly as possible. Repeat with the remaining bacon, sage, and trout.

Preheat a 10-inch sauté pan. Heat the canola oil over medium-high heat. Sauté 2 of the fish at a time for about 4 minutes, until lightly browned on both sides. Use 2 pans if you have them so that you can cook all 4 fish at the same time. Transfer the fish to a shallow roasting pan and roast them for about 6 minutes, until cooked through and opaque.

In a sauté pan, heat the olive oil over medium-high heat. Add the reserved escarole and whole roasted garlic cloves, season with salt and pepper, and cook, tossing, for about 4 minutes, until heated through.

Divide the escarole among 4 plates. Using a slotted spoon, spoon the lentils on top of the escarole. Lift the potatoes from their cooking water with a slotted spoon and layer them on top of the lentils. Finally, set a trout next to the mounded vegetables. Whisk the vinaigrette and drizzle it over the plates. Serve immediately.

VARIATIONS: You can omit the bacon and tie the fish together in three or four places with kitchen string. These accompaniments also work very well with cod, striped bass, and snapper.

Meyer Lemon
Granité

Meyer lemons are generally available from October through January and are worth seeking out for their strong lemon flavor, mild tartness, and moderate acidity. These qualities make them ideal for desserts, though you could substitute regular lemon juice in this recipe and it would still be delicious. Many satisfying desserts conjure some memory of childhood, and this one may leave you with thoughts of the lemon ices of yours.

$1^1/_2$ cups fresh Meyer lemon juice or any fresh lemon juice
$1^1/_2$ cups sugar
$1^1/_4$ cups water

Place a 9-by-13-inch nonreactive metal pan in the freezer to chill.

In a nonreactive medium saucepan, combine the lemon juice, sugar, and water. (If substituting regular lemon juice, you might want to adjust sugar quantity to taste.) Cook over medium heat, stirring constantly, until the sugar is dissolved. Pour into a medium bowl. Place in a larger bowl filled with ice water and let stand, stirring often, until cooled.

Pour into the chilled pan and freeze for about 1 hour, or until the mixture is partially frozen and icy around the edges. Using a large spoon, break up the icy edges and stir them into the center. Freeze for about 1 hour longer and repeat the process.

Let the granité freeze for about 2 hours or overnight. Before serving, scrape it with a fork into large crystals. Mound it into chilled glasses and serve.

Candied
Grapefruit
Rinds

MAKES 40 PIECES

This is my version of the candied fruits we served at the end of every meal at the Troisgros brothers' renowned restaurant in Roanne, France.

THINKING AHEAD: This dessert must be made about 48 hours in advance. The rinds may be stored tightly covered in a cool, dry place, but not in the refrigerator, for as long as a week.

2   large grapefruits
6   cups sugar
2   cups water
     Juice of 1 lemon
3   ounces bittersweet chocolate, such as Valrhona, coarsely chopped

Slice both ends off one of the grapefruits just enough to reveal the fruit within. Using a paring knife, start at one cut end of the grapefruit and make an incision just through the peel, running the knife down through the peel to the other end. Repeat on the other side of the grapefruit, opposite the first incision, then, using your fingers, remove the skin in two large sections.

Trim the white pith to an even thickness of about $1/4$ inch. Slice the rind into $1/4$-inch-wide strips. Wrap the grapefruit in plastic wrap and refrigerate for another time. Repeat all steps with the other grapefruit.

In a saucepan of boiling water, blanch the rind for about 4 minutes. Drain and bring more water to the boil over high heat. Repeat so that the rind is blanched and drained 5 times in all.

In a large saucepan, combine 4 cups of the sugar, the 2 cups of water, and the lemon juice, and bring to a boil over high heat. When the sugar dissolves, add the rinds. Reduce the heat to low and cook for about 20 minutes. Remove from the heat and let the rinds cool in the syrup. Cover and refrigerate for 2 days. The rinds will become soft during this preserving time.

Take the rinds from the refrigerator and, using a fork, lift the rinds from their syrup. Lay them on wire racks to dry at room temperature for about 8 hours.

Spread the remaining 2 cups of sugar in a shallow bowl. Roll the rinds in the sugar and set them aside.

In the top of a double boiler set over hot (not simmering) water, melt the chocolate, stirring until smooth. Remove the melted chocolate from the heat and dip the grapefruit rinds in the chocolate so that about half of each one is covered. Lay them on a wax-paper-lined baking tray and refrigerate until the chocolate is firm and they are ready to serve.

Super Bowl Party

Here are two menus made up of casual dishes to be enjoyed while watching the big game. Most involve minimal preparation and can be readied in advance.

MENU 1

BLACK BEAN SOUP WITH TOMATO-AVOCADO SALSA **(page 333)**

SEARED YELLOWFIN TUNA BURGERS WITH LEMON AIOLI **(page 64)**

SLOW-COOKED LAMB SHOULDER **(page 375)**

POTATO AND BUTTERNUT SQUASH GRATIN WITH GRUYÈRE **(page 199)**

PEANUT BUTTER COUPE **(page 188)**

MENU 2

STEAMED MUSSELS WITH FENNEL, SAFFRON,
AND WHITE WINE **(page 331)**

CHICKEN WITH GINGER, JUNIPER BERRIES, RED CABBAGE,
AND POTATO PURÉE **(page 336)**

WALNUT TART **(page 290)**

Oranges

Curly Endive, Blood Orange, and Tangerine Salad with Citrus Vinaigrette

Steamed Mussels with Fennel, Saffron, and White Wine

Black Bean Soup with Tomato-Avocado Salsa

Chicken with Ginger, Juniper Berries, Red Cabbage, and Potato Purée

Lemon Risotto with Spot Prawns

Curried Duck Breasts with Basmati-Saffron Rice

Curried Lobster Tails with Sticky Rice and Coriander Chutney

Oyster Risotto with Sevruga Caviar

Pineapple "Variation"

Coconut *Panna Cotta*

Valentine's Day Dinner
Dead of Winter Dinner

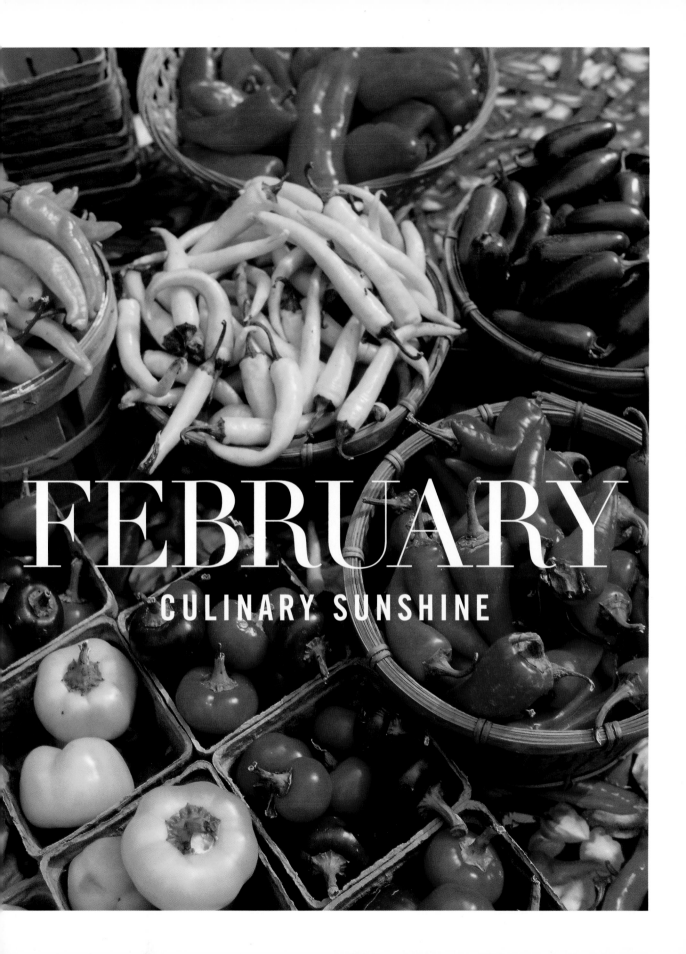

FEBRUARY
CULINARY SUNSHINE

The moment arrives at a different time for everyone, but at some point in February, those of us who live in cold-weather climates find that the novelty of winter has worn off. We lapse into an antagonistic relationship with the weather, cursing it under our breath and commiserating with strangers in elevators and taxicabs. By the time this short month rolls around, 30 days have elapsed since the holidays, with at least another 30 to endure before reaching spring's starting line.

At this time of year, it's as though a significant other is away on a long sojourn and we're left pale and lonely in the void created by the absence. Much of this has to do with how much we miss the sun and everything it brings—the way it turns up the lights on the great outdoors, heralds the end of cold and flu season, and invites us to dash outside without a moment's hesitation.

Miss anyone long and hard enough, and you might find yourself on a plane moving through the clouds toward what feels like a mandatory reunion. Similarly, February is the time when many people simply have to see the sun; they make like birds and fly south for the winter to the balmy shores of Florida, the Caribbean, or some other warm destination. It's amazing to arrive near the equator at this time of year, wearing one layer of clothes for the first time in months, and to find the sun waiting for you; like a lover, it embraces you at first sight, and life seems somehow transformed for the better.

Of course, the opportunity for this kind of escape is limited for all of us, due to the constraints of budget and time. So, I like to take a different tack with something I call culinary sunshine, engaging and igniting my taste buds with the sunny, the spicy, and the sensuous— unshy flavors that send the senses on a tropical getaway.

Fruits, particularly of the citrus variety, are especially reminiscent of the sun. Maybe that's why the first things I think of when I hear the word *oranges* are Florida and California—which is one reason I love eating them in winter. These fruits are used here in such dishes as Curly Endive, Blood Orange, and Tangerine Salad with Citrus Vinaigrette (page 329). On a similar note, Hawaii is conjured up by Pineapple "Variation" (page 350) and Coconut *Panna Cotta* (page 353).

To create a dish for February, logic suggests you visualize the snowy landscapes of, say, Alsace or Switzerland. But why not go instead to the dreamy, azure blue waters of Provence and imagine yourself eating Steamed Mussels with Fennel, Saffron, and White Wine (page 331), or take a mental journey to another part of the Mediterranean and enjoy a Lemon Risotto with Spot Prawns (page 339) on the Italian Riviera?

For days when it's bitter cold, go ahead and boost your temperature with spices. One of the few southwestern dishes I've offered at the Gotham—Black Bean Soup with Tomato-Avocado Salsa (page 333)—is included for this reason, as are Curried Lobster Tails with Sticky Rice and Coriander Chutney (page 346) and Curried Duck Breasts with Basmati-Saffron Rice (page 343), two Indian dishes that pack a real kick.

There's another aspect of almost all of these foods that's a happy coincidence for February—they are vibrantly colored, from the highlights of yellow in the lemon risotto to the tomato salsa in the black bean soup, to the blood oranges in the salad, to the saffron broth set against the black mussel shells, and the yellow pineapple-variation dessert with its bits of green lime zest.

If you're fortunate enough to be in love, there's one occasion when you're assured a different kind of warmth—Valentine's Day—strategically located right in the middle of February. There's a menu for two in this chapter that is one of the most sensuous in the book, the intention being to give you something extra to look forward to for the first half of the month, and to look back on fondly for the second.

PINEAPPLE "VARIATION" **(page 350)**

Oranges

As someone who grew up in the Northeast, I still find myself giddy whenever I see an actual orange tree. When we travel to visit family in Florida at Christmastime, I'm amazed that there are orange trees in every yard, and even more stunned that the oranges often go unpicked.

Columbus brought oranges to this country in 1493. Interestingly enough, Spanish missionaries continued what he began, planting orange trees in Florida and later in California. This fruit's season begins in December and runs through April or May. At whichever point you purchase them, all varieties of oranges should be stored in the refrigerator to maintain freshness.

Some of the principal varieties of oranges are Temple, Valencia, navel, tangerine, and blood orange. Tangerine is actually a general term for many smaller oranges including clementines and mandarins, many of which have similar characteristics, such as a loose skin that's easily peeled. Some of these smaller oranges are very sweet, with many seeds, and begin showing up each year in November. There are also several varieties of crossbreeds, such as the tangelo, which is a blend of mandarin, tangerine, and grapefruit. My favorite orange is the Minneola. Minneolas are identifiable by a characteristic bump and deep orange skin. My fondness for them clearly isn't based on appearance; I love their very sweet and concentrated flavor.

Valencias are a big commercial variety grown in Florida and California that are good for eating and juicing. The navel orange is a seedless variety with a characteristic bump of its own, this one a little orange growing within the skin. Navels are very convenient not only because they are seedless, but also because they are very easy to section, with well-defined portions, so are ideal for recipes that call for this treatment.

The blood orange is a distinctly flavored late-season variety. While they used to be imported from Italy and Spain, they are now increasingly available from California.

For all of the sweet oranges available domestically, bitter oranges are hard to come by in the United States; most, such as the Seville, still hail from Spain and other European countries.

Finally, orange zest is a wonderful ingredient with which to become proficient. It's one of the sources responsible for the forceful orange flavor in such classics as *Duck à l' Orange*. Orange liqueur can also be an effective way of deepening the orange presence in a recipe. As distinct and impactful as oranges are, they can be made even more complex with the addition of these readily available flavor enhancers.

2 tablespoons extra-virgin olive oil
1 cup diced onion
1 cup diced fennel
4 large cloves garlic, peeled and minced
2 strips orange peel, each approximately 2 inches by $^1/_2$ inch (cut with a vegetable peeler)
2 sprigs fresh thyme
$^1/_8$ teaspoon saffron threads
1 cup dry white wine
4 pounds cultivated mussels, scrubbed
4 $^1/_2$-inch-thick slices baguette, lightly toasted
Coarse salt and freshly ground white pepper to taste
1 tablespoon unsalted butter
4 teaspoons chopped fresh flat-leaf parsley

In a large soup pot, heat the olive oil over medium heat. Cook the onion and fennel, stirring, for 5 to 6 minutes, until softened but not browned. Stir in the garlic, orange peel, and thyme, and cook for 3 minutes longer, until the garlic begins to soften. Crumble the saffron between your fingers and add it to the pot. Stir to combine.

Add the wine, raise the heat to high, and bring to a boil. Cook for about 8 minutes to burn off the alcohol and extract the flavors. Add the mussels, cover the pot, and steam for 8 to 10 minutes, stirring every few minutes, until the mussels open.

Put a slice of toast in each of 4 large soup plates. Using a slotted spoon, lift the mussels from the steaming broth. Discard any mussels that have not opened and divide the rest among the plates, arranging them on the toast.

Taste the broth and reduce it over high heat, if necessary, to concentrate the flavors. Season with salt and pepper. Swirl in the butter to enrich the broth. Ladle the broth over the mussels and garnish each plate with chopped parsley. Serve immediately.

WHAT TO DRINK: Serve this with a Belgian white or wheat beer.

VARIATIONS: If you don't have saffron, leave it out but also eliminate the orange peel. I prefer to use Prince Edward Island mussels because of their reliable freshness and flavor. However, if you have a good source for local mussels, they'll be fine. New Zealand green-lip mussels are also trustworthy.

Steamed Mussels with Fennel, Saffron, and White Wine

MAKES 4 SERVINGS

All of the experimentation in American kitchens these days has generated an endless variety of recipes for steamed mussels, which take on the flavor of many accompaniments. Some of the most successful ones involve Asian ingredients such as coconut milk and cilantro—which, come to think of it, wouldn't be bad at all on a cold day.

But my taste for mussels leans toward the traditional. One of my favorite ways to enjoy them is with a *marinière,* a classic French composition of shallots, garlic, and white wine that is finished with parsley. This is the way they are generally consumed in France, with the simple accompaniment of French fries and a crusty white bread for soaking up the broth.

I've varied that recipe here, fashioning one in the spirit of a bouillabaisse, with fennel, saffron, and white wine. I recommend serving this atop a crouton spread with spicy rouille.

You'll notice that the influence of citrus makes itself known here as well—orange peel, added to the mussels, will infuse the broth with a sunny flavor.

Black Bean Soup with Tomato-Avocado Salsa

MAKES 6 SERVINGS

Though it's not the style I'm known for, I happen to love the bold flavors in southwestern cooking. This soup is visually stunning, with flecks of cilantro and chunky tomato salsa, not to mention the swirls of soothing crème fraîche. Black bean soups are often made with salt pork, but if you have a preference for chorizo or smoked bacon, their distinct flavors will work equally well here. (See Variations, page 334.) Be warned: This is a spicy dish, but the salsa, thanks in large part to the avocado, has a sublime, cooling effect.

THINKING AHEAD: The beans must be soaked overnight. You can make the soup a day in advance and store it covered in the refrigerator. Reheat gently over a low flame.

SOUP

1	bunch fresh cilantro
2	small jalapeño peppers, halved lengthwise
1	tablespoon olive oil
4	ounces salt pork, cut into small dice
1	medium red onion, finely chopped
8	cloves of garlic, peeled and thinly sliced
2	pounds black turtle beans, soaked overnight in cold water to cover and drained
5	cups White Chicken Stock (page 421)
	Coarse salt and freshly ground white pepper to taste

Pull the leaves from the cilantro stems and set aside the leaves to use as garnish. Put the stems and jalapeños in the center of a piece of cheesecloth that measures approximately 12 inches square. Gather the sides together and tie with kitchen twine to make a neat packet.

Heat the olive oil in a heavy-bottomed sauce pot set over medium heat. Add the salt pork and cook, stirring occasionally, until nicely browned and much of the fat has been rendered, approximately 8 minutes. Remove pork with a slotted spoon and discard.

Add the onions to the pot. Cook, stirring occasionally, until softened, about 4 minutes. Add the garlic to the pot. Cook until fragrant, about 2 minutes more. Add the beans, stock, and cheesecloth packet to the pot. Bring to a boil over medium-high heat. Skim any surface foam, reduce the heat to low, and simmer for about 2 hours and 20 minutes, until the beans are tender but still hold their shape. Using tongs or a slotted spoon, lift the packet from the soup, letting any liquid drip back into the pot. Set the packet aside in a small bowl to cool slightly so that you can squeeze it over the soup to extract all its flavors. When cool, squeeze it over the soup and then discard the packet.

SALSA AND SERVING

2	plum tomatoes, peeled, seeded, and cut into $1/4$-inch dice
2	tablespoons finely minced red onion
2	tablespoons chopped fresh cilantro

$^1/_2$	teaspoon chopped fresh garlic
2	tablespoons extra-virgin olive oil
1	tablespoon fresh lime juice
	Coarse salt and freshly ground white pepper to taste
1	large ripe avocado
$^1/_3$	cup creme fraîche

In a nonreactive bowl, combine the tomatoes, onion, cilantro, garlic, olive oil, and lime juice. Toss gently and season with salt and pepper.

Cut the avocado in half lengthwise. Using the heel of a small knife, remove the pit. Peel off the skin and cut the avocado into thin slices and then into $^1/_4$-inch dice. Fold it into the salsa.

Spoon about a third of the slightly cooled soup into the bowl of a blender or a food processor fitted with the metal blade and process until smooth (you may have to do this in batches). Stir the purée back into the soup to thicken it. Season with salt and pepper.

Spoon the salsa into the centers of 6 large soup bowls. Pour the soup around the salsa. Spoon the creme fraîche around the surface of the soup. Garnish with the reserved cilantro leaves and serve.

FLAVOR BUILDING: Place a seared scallop on top of the salsa in the center of each bowl, and ladle the soup over and around it. (See sidebar, page 305, and increase the number of scallops to 6.)

VARIATIONS: You can substitute 4 ounces of chopped chorizo or smoked bacon for the salt pork.

Chicken
with Ginger, Juniper Berries, Red Cabbage, and Potato Purée

MAKES 4 TO 6 SERVINGS

When I set out to create a new dish, seasonality plays a crucial role. I also look to the past, drawing on classic taste combinations, often building on a tried-and-true combination by personalizing, then modernizing, the idea.

Which is why I can't explain the thought process that led to this dish. I can only tell you that the flavors of crushed juniper, fresh sliced ginger, and garlic are intoxicating. I cooked roast pheasant this way at the Gotham Bar and Grill with spectacular results. Here I offer the recipe using chicken, my thinking being that high-quality, free-range or organic varieties of chicken will be more accessible.

This also seemed like a good time to share my favorite braised red cabbage recipe. Deliciously tart and smoky, its brilliant red color is captured by carefully timed cooking.

THINKING AHEAD: The birds will benefit from a long marinade of up to 48 hours. The potato purée can be made ahead and kept warm using the technique on page 37. The cabbage can be made a day ahead, stored tightly covered in the refrigerator, and reheated gently over a low flame, stirring to avoid scorching.

MARINADE

2	cups coarsely chopped onion
20	cloves garlic, peeled and thinly sliced
3	ounces fresh ginger, peeled and thinly sliced
5	tablespoons juniper berries, crushed
2	$3^{1}/_{2}$-pound chickens, backbones removed, split in half
	Freshly ground white pepper to taste

In a large bowl, combine the onion, garlic, ginger, and juniper berries, and mix well. Season the chickens with pepper and then toss them with the marinade, gently rubbing it into the chickens to cover each piece well on both sides. Cover the bowl with plastic wrap and refrigerate for 24 to 48 hours. Turn the chicken several times, making sure all surfaces are in contact with the marinade.

CABBAGE

1	tablespoon canola oil
4	ounces slab bacon, cut into 4 chunks
1	medium onion, thinly sliced
2	teaspoons caraway seeds
1	large head red cabbage, cored and cut into $^{1}/_{4}$-inch-thick slices
1	tablespoon coarse salt
	Freshly ground white pepper to taste
1	cup red wine
$^{1}/_{2}$	cup red wine vinegar
$^{1}/_{2}$	cup honey

In a large pot, heat the oil over medium-high heat. Add the bacon and cook for about 6 minutes, until nicely browned. Remove and discard the bacon but leave the rendered fat in the pot. Add the onion and cook for about 5 minutes, until lightly browned. Add the caraway seeds and cook about 2 minutes longer, until fragrant.

Add the cabbage to the pot and season it with the salt and pepper. Add the wine, vinegar, and honey, cover, and cook over medium-low heat for about 30 minutes, stirring occasionally, until the cabbage begins to soften. Remove the lid and continue to cook the cabbage for about 30 minutes, stirring, until the juices are reduced to a light glaze. Cover and set aside to keep warm.

PURÉED POTATOES

$2^3/4$ pounds Yellow Finn or russet potatoes, peeled and cut into uniform pieces
(about 2 inches thick)

$3/4$ cup unsalted butter, cut into pieces

$1/4$ to $1/3$ cup half-and-half

Coarse salt and freshly ground white pepper to taste

Put the potatoes in a large saucepan and add enough cold water to cover. Salt the water and bring to a boil over high heat. Reduce the heat and simmer for about 15 minutes, or until the potatoes are tender when pierced with a sharp knife. Drain and return the potatoes to the pan.

Set the pan over low heat and cook for about 3 minutes, stirring constantly, until the excess moisture evaporates. Rice the potatoes in a food mill or ricer into a bowl, or simply put them in a bowl and mash them with a potato masher. Add the butter, working it into the potatoes until blended.

In a small saucepan, bring the half-and-half to a boil over medium heat. Add it to the potatoes, stirring gently, until the desired consistency. Do not overmix the potatoes. Season with salt and pepper, cover, and set aside to keep warm.

SAUCE AND ASSEMBLY

$1/4$ cup canola oil

$1/2$ cup coarsely chopped onions

5   cloves garlic, peeled and finely chopped

1   ounce fresh ginger, peeled and finely chopped

2   teaspoons juniper berries, crushed

$3/4$ cup white wine

2   cups White Chicken Stock (page 421)

1   tablespoon unsalted butter

Coarse salt to taste

In a medium saucepan, heat 2 tablespoons of the oil over medium heat. Add the onions, garlic, ginger, and juniper berries and cook, stirring, for 8 to 10 minutes, or until softened but not colored. Add the wine, raise the heat to medium-high, and cook for about 10 minutes, until the wine evaporates.

Add the chicken stock and bring to a boil. Reduce the heat and simmer for 15 to 20 minutes, skimming any foam that rises to the surface, until reduced by about half. Strain the stock through a fine-mesh sieve into another saucepan. Still off the heat, swirl in the butter to enrich the sauce. Cover and set aside to keep warm.

(continued)

Preheat the oven to 400°F.

Remove the chicken from the refrigerator and wipe off the marinade. Let it come to room temperature and then season with coarse salt.

In a large skillet, heat the remaining 2 tablespoons of oil over high heat. Cook the chicken, skin side down and in batches if necessary, for about 6 minutes, until the skin is nicely browned. Turn and cook the other side about 6 minutes longer, until browned. Transfer the chicken to a roasting pan and roast for 18 to 20 minutes, turning it once, until no sign of pink remains near the bone and the juices run clear when pricked with a small, sharp knife.

Serve the chicken arranged on a serving platter. Spoon the potatoes and cabbage into serving bowls. Pour the sauce into a warmed sauceboat and pass it on the side.

VARIATIONS: You can substitute a pheasant or baby chickens (poussin) for the chicken.

Lemon Risotto with Spot Prawns

**MAKES 6 APPETIZER SERVINGS
OR 4 MAIN-COURSE SERVINGS**

THINKING AHEAD: To make risotto in advance, cook it until it has absorbed the second-to-last addition of stock. Then, spread it out on a sheet pan lined with parchment paper to allow it to cool quickly. Finally, transfer it to a container and wrap it tightly to ensure that the rice does not absorb any moisture. When you're ready to serve the risotto, transfer the rice to a hot pot, add the final addition of stock and the other ingredients and cook for 5 minutes, stirring continually.

Lemon risotto is a classic and versatile Italian recipe that I had long admired in cookbooks before making it myself. Although the recipe had been around a long time, I wanted to "build out" the dish and make it a little more interesting. Sweet, sautéed spot prawns, or just about any high-quality shrimp, make a perfect addition to the creamy, lemon-perfumed rice. And the abundance of fresh herbs keeps the palate interested and unifies all the ingredients.

Though this is relatively simple to prepare, be sure to use the full quantity of herbs indicated. Also, keep the unadorned lemon risotto in mind for a multicourse dinner.

2	quarts White Chicken Stock (page 421)
2	tablespoons unsalted butter
2	tablespoons extra-virgin olive oil
2	shallots, peeled and minced
1	pound arborio rice
2	teaspoons finely minced lemon zest
1	teaspoon chopped fresh thyme leaves
1/2	cup dry white wine

In a large saucepan over medium–high heat, bring the chicken stock to a boil. Reduce the heat and keep the stock warm over low heat.

In a large pot, combine the butter and olive oil, and heat over medium heat until the butter melts. Add the shallots and cook, stirring, for about 1 minute. Cook the rice, stirring with a wooden spoon, for 7 to 10 minutes, until it turns milky white and opaque, and begins to stick to the bottom of the pan. Add the lemon zest and thyme leaves and stir to combine.

Add the wine and stir for about 2 minutes, until nearly absorbed. Ladle about 1 cup of the simmering stock into the rice. Cook for about 2 minutes, stirring often, until the stock is almost completely absorbed. Add more stock, a cup at a time, stirring gently until the broth is absorbed by the rice before adding the next cup. After about 15 minutes, begin tasting the rice. At this point, add the stock judiciously. The rice should be firm, yet cooked through in 18 to 20 minutes total cooking time.

PRAWNS AND ASSEMBLY

12	large spot prawns or jumbo shrimp, in the shell
3	tablespoons unsalted butter, melted
	Coarse salt and freshly ground white pepper to taste
3	tablespoons fresh lemon juice
1/4	cup finely minced fresh chives

Preheat the broiler.

Using a sharp-bladed chef's knife, cut through the shells to split the prawns in half lengthwise. Arrange them, cut side up, in a shallow broiling pan. Brush them with melted butter and season with salt and pepper. Broil for 3 to 4 minutes, or until lightly browned and opaque in the center.

Stir the lemon juice and chives into the risotto. Taste and season with salt and pepper. Spoon the risotto onto warmed plates and garnish each serving with prawns.

FLAVOR BUILDING: Serve this dish with Lobster with Savoy Cabbage, Flageolets, and Roasted Garlic (page 239). Stir 4 ounces of sliced, smoked salmon, cut into wide strips, into the risotto just before serving. This recipe also accompanies Slow-Cooked Lamb Shoulder (page 375) very well.

Curried
Duck
Breasts with
Basmati-
Saffron Rice

MAKES 4 SERVINGS

MARINADE

4	8- to 10-ounce boneless Moulard duck breasts, with skin
1	tablespoon Madras curry powder
6 to 7	scallions, thinly sliced
6	cloves garlic, peeled and thinly sliced
4	large shallots, peeled and thinly sliced
1	ounce fresh ginger, peeled and thinly sliced

Using a sharp knife, trim any excess skin from the duck breasts. Score the skin lightly in a crosshatch pattern, but do not cut the flesh. Sprinkle the breasts evenly on both sides with curry powder.

In a small bowl, combine the scallions, garlic, shallots, and ginger. Sprinkle half the marinade in the bottom of a shallow non-reactive dish large enough to hold the breasts in 1 layer. Lay the duck breasts over the marinade and then sprinkle the remaining marinade over them. Cover with plastic wrap and refrigerate for 24 hours.

BASMATI RICE

2	cups basmati rice
3	cups cold water
6	tablespoons canola oil
2	tablespoons blanched sliced almonds
2	tablespoons blanched pistachios
1/2	cup finely chopped onions
1	cinnamon stick
1/4	cup seedless golden raisins
1	teaspoon saffron threads
1/2	teaspoon ground cardamom
1	cup milk
	Coarse salt and freshly ground white pepper to taste

Put the rice in a colander and rinse it well under cold running water for 2 to 3 minutes, or until the water runs clear. Transfer the rice to a bowl and add the water. Set the rice aside to soak for 30 minutes. Drain the rice, reserving the soaking water. Set the rice and water aside.

In a medium saucepan, heat the oil over medium heat. Add the

Indian cooking has long intrigued American chefs looking for new and exotic flavors and ingredients, and during the doldrums of February, the popular Indian curry is a perfect way to lift your own internal mercury and spirits. I would like to remind you that—as with any cuisine—the raw ingredients, in this case the curry itself, are of paramount importance. Make sure you select a high-quality curry powder, or—better yet—make your own using freshly ground spices. (See page 345.)

The method for cooking the duck merits some attention as well, because it avoids all the hassles of roasting. Essentially, it is cooked like a steak, which saves time as well, as the duck will be fully cooked in about 8 to 12 minutes.

As for the basmati rice, this recipe is a composite of all the variations I've enjoyed in Indian restaurants in New York City over the years. Texturally rich, with pistachios and raisins, it is perfumed with a powerful trio of cinnamon, cardamom, and saffron.

This is such a flavorful dish that it doesn't really need a curry sauce, but I thought to provide one anyway—for that especially bitter cold day when your senses really need a pick-me-up.

WHAT TO DRINK: Serve this with a Trappist ale.

almonds and pistachios, and toast for 2 to 3 minutes, until lightly browned. Slide the nuts from the pan and set them aside.

Add the onions to the same pan and cook for about 4 minutes, until softened. Add the cinnamon and cook about 2 minutes longer, until fragrant. Add the rice and cook, stirring, for 5 to 6 minutes, until it just begins to brown. Add the raisins, saffron, cardamom, milk, and reserved soaking water. Season with salt and pepper.

Bring to a boil over high heat, reduce the heat to medium, cover, and simmer for about 10 minutes. Reduce the heat to very low and, still covered, steam the rice about 10 minutes longer. Remove from the heat and let it rest for 5 minutes. Stir in the reserved nuts, taking care not to overmix. Cover and set aside to keep warm.

SAUCE AND ASSEMBLY

1	tablespoon canola oil
6 to 7	scallions, coarsely chopped
1/2	small onion, chopped
5	cloves garlic, peeled and sliced
1	ounce fresh ginger, peeled and chopped
1	teaspoon Madras curry powder
2	cups Brown Chicken Stock (page 422)
1/4	cup White Chicken Stock (page 421)
1	tablespoon unsalted butter
	Coarse salt and freshly ground white pepper to taste

In a saucepan, heat the oil over medium heat. Add the scallions, onion, garlic, and ginger, and cook for 3 to 4 minutes, until softened. Add the curry powder and cook for about 30 seconds, stirring constantly to prevent the curry from scorching.

Add the chicken stocks. Raise the heat to high and bring to a boil. Reduce the heat and simmer for 12 to 15 minutes, skimming any foam that rises to the surface. Remove from the heat and stir in the butter to enrich the sauce. Season with salt and pepper, cover, and set aside to keep warm.

Remove the duck breasts from the refrigerator and wipe off the marinade. Let them come to room temperature and then season with salt and pepper.

Place the duck breasts, skin side down, in a large, cold sauté pan. Then, place pan over medium heat and cook duck breasts for about 10 minutes, until nicely browned. Turn and cook for 2 to 3 minutes longer, until medium-rare. Transfer to a plate, cover with aluminum foil, and let rest for about 5 minutes. Slice into $^{1}/_{4}$-inch-thick slices.

Using a fork, fluff the rice. Serve the duck arranged on a serving platter. Spoon the rice into a serving bowl to present with the duck. Pour the sauce into a warmed sauceboat and pass it on the side.

VARIATIONS: You can substitute chicken breasts for the duck; they will cook in about the same time. You might also use squab, following the cooking times on page 245.

Madras-Style Curry Powder

Every cook makes his or her curry mixture a little different. Over time, you too should feel free to adjust the following recipe to suit your own taste, varying the amounts of certain ingredients. You might also add 1 or 2 cinnamon sticks broken into pieces, 4 to 6 whole cloves, a tablespoon of cardamom seeds, a tablespoon of black and/or white sesame seeds, and/or a few threads of saffron.

MAKES ABOUT 1 CUP

4	tablespoons coriander seeds
1	tablespoon fennel seeds
1 to 2	tablespoons dried, crushed red chile peppers
2	tablespoons cumin seeds
1	tablespoon black mustard seeds
2	teaspoons whole black peppercorns
2	teaspoons fenugreek
1	teaspoon ground turmeric
12	curry leaves (optional)

Combine all the ingredients except the turmeric and curry leaves. Place the mixture in a sauté pan and warm over low heat. Gently toast the spices, stirring frequently, until fragrant, about 5 minutes. Remove from the heat and allow the spices to cool completely, then add the turmeric and curry leaves, if using them, and grind everything together in a spice grinder. Store in a small bottle with a tight-fitting lid. Like all spices, store in a cool, dry place.

Curried Lobster Tails with Sticky Rice and Coriander Chutney

MAKES 4 SERVINGS

In introducing a curried compound butter to the lobster in this dish, I employ the same technique I use with grilled lobster (page 74) but do so in a pan, brushing the claws with butter as they cook and trapping the flavor inside the shells.

The coriander chutney can be purchased in an Indian or Middle Eastern food store. Its fragrant, intoxicating blend of cilantro and toasted black mustard seed is very interesting, but you can substitute another store-bought chutney.

The Japanese sticky rice is based on a recipe I use a lot at home. Replete with scallions, it has just enough bite to fit this context.

In the end, this is a relatively simple dish that doesn't use a lot of ingredients but tastes as though it does. In fact, your dinner companions will probably think you were shopping all day.

THINKING AHEAD: The curried butter can be made as many as 3 days in advance and kept wrapped in plastic in the refrigerator; it will taste better if made ahead of time. The lobster may be prepared the morning of the day you will be serving this dish.

CURRIED BUTTER

$1/2$ cup unsalted butter, at room temperature
2 tablespoons finely chopped shallot
2 cloves garlic, finely minced
1 tablespoon Madras curry powder
1 tablespoon finely chopped fresh cilantro
Coarse salt and freshly ground white pepper to taste

In a small sauté pan, heat about a teaspoon of the butter over medium-high heat. Cook the shallots and garlic for about 2 minutes, until they are translucent and the moisture has evaporated. Add the curry powder and cook, stirring constantly for about 10 seconds, until just fragrant. Remove the pan from the heat and continue to stir to prevent the curry powder from scorching. Set it aside to cool.

In a small bowl, cream the remaining butter with the curry mixture and the cilantro. Season with salt and pepper. Set the curried butter aside for at least 20 minutes to give the flavors time to develop, or wrap it well in plastic and store it in the refrigerator for up to 3 days. Bring it back to room temperature before using.

STICKY RICE

2 cups Japanese medium-grain rice
1 teaspoon coarse salt

Put the rice in a colander and rinse it well under cold running water for 2 to 3 minutes. Transfer it to a medium saucepan and add enough cold water to cover the rice by about $3/4$ inch. Set it aside to soak for about 15 minutes.

Add the salt and slowly bring the water to a boil over medium-high heat. Reduce the heat to low and simmer, covered, for about 25 minutes, or until the rice is tender and the water is absorbed. Remove from the heat and let the rice sit, still covered, until ready to serve.

LOBSTER AND ASSEMBLY

$^1/_4$ cup white wine vinegar

4   1$^1/_2$-pound live lobsters

    Coarse salt and freshly ground white pepper to taste

2   tablespoons canola oil

6 to 7   scallions, thinly sliced

10   fresh cilantro sprigs, for garnish

$^1/_2$ cup coriander chutney, optional, see page 346

Preheat the oven to 450°F.

Bring a large stockpot of salted water to a boil over high heat. Add the vinegar and then the lobsters and cover the pot. Return to the boil and cook for about 3 minutes. This will kill the lobsters and set the meat. The shells will turn red.

Drain the lobsters and, when cool enough to handle, remove the heads from the tails and claws with a heavy knife. Discard the heads or let them cool completely and then freeze them for another use, such as shellfish stock. Cut the tails in half lengthwise. Crack the claws. (If doing this ahead of time, transfer the lobster to a plate, cover it with plastic wrap, and refrigerate for several hours until ready to cook.)

Rub a shallow roasting pan with the oil. Arrange the lobster claws and tails, cut side up, in the pan. Season with salt and pepper. Generously spread the curried butter over the exposed lobster meat in the tails. Roast for 7 to 8 minutes, or until the lobster meat is cooked through.

Using a fork, fluff the rice. Stir in the scallions and transfer the rice to a serving bowl. Serve the lobsters garnished with a few sprigs of cilantro, and pass the rice, also garnished with cilantro sprigs, on the side. Pass the chutney, if desired.

VARIATION: As mentioned above, you can substitute a store-bought chutney of your choice.

Oyster Risotto with Sevruga Caviar

MAKES 6 APPETIZER SERVINGS

This is one of those recipes, loaded with luxury ingredients, that cries out "Only serve me for a special occasion!" Stirring something as potent as an oyster into a risotto is an experience to be treasured. The rice takes on its briny character, becoming something truly unique. Caviar, another of the sea's proudest contributions to gastronomy, tops the dish. I strongly recommend that, as you eat, you slowly stir the caviar into the risotto, where its salinity will provide wonderful peaks of flavor.

The crème fraîche adds a subtle acidity to this dish. I think of this as a perfect starter for a romantic Valentine's Day menu, but it's so rich (and expensive) that I recommend serving just a small amount as an *amuse-gueule* of sorts.

THINKING AHEAD: To prepare a risotto in advance, follow the instructions on page 339.

OYSTERS: It's best to purchase your own oysters, shuck them, and add them to this dish at the last minute. But you can use shucked oysters as well.

OYSTERS AND OYSTER STOCK

1½	dozen oysters, shucked, oyster liquor reserved (for shucking instructions, see page 266)
2	cups Clam Broth (page 349)
1½	quarts White Chicken Stock (page 421)

In a stockpot, combine the oyster liquor, clam broth, and chicken stock. Put the shucked oysters in a bowl, cover, and refrigerate them until ready to use. Bring the stock to a boil over high heat, reduce the heat, and keep it at a simmer over low heat.

LEEKS

2	tablespoons unsalted butter
1	tablespoon canola oil
4	leeks, white parts only, cut into 1½-inch lengths and julienned
	Coarse salt and freshly ground white pepper to taste

In a 12-inch sauté pan, heat the butter and oil over medium heat. When the butter melts, add the leeks, season with salt and pepper, and cook, stirring, for 12 to 15 minutes, or until the leeks are very soft. Transfer to a bowl, cover to keep warm, and set aside.

RISOTTO

2	tablespoons unsalted butter
2	tablespoons extra-virgin olive oil
2	shallots, peeled and minced
2	cloves garlic, peeled and minced
1	pound arborio rice
1	teaspoon chopped fresh thyme

In a large, heavy saucepan, heat the butter and olive oil over medium heat. Add the shallots and garlic, and cook, stirring with a wooden spoon for about 1 minute, or until softened. Add the rice and cook, stirring with a wooden spoon, for 7 to 10 minutes, until it turns milky white and opaque, and begins to stick to the bottom of the pan.

Ladle about 1 cup of the simmering stock into the rice. Cook for about 2 minutes, stirring often, until the stock is almost completely absorbed. Add more stock, a cup at a time, stirring gently until it is absorbed by the rice before adding the next cup. After about 15 minutes, add the thyme and begin tasting the rice. At this point, add the stock judiciously. The rice should be firm yet cooked through in 18 to 20 minutes total cooking time.

ASSEMBLY

1/2	cup crème fraîche
	Coarse salt and freshly ground white pepper to taste
1/2 to 1	ounce Sevruga caviar
2	tablespoons chopped fresh chives

With the risotto off the heat, stir in the shucked oysters, leeks, and crème fraîche. Season with salt and pepper. Spoon the risotto into warmed bowls and garnish each serving with a small spoonful of caviar and a sprinkling of chives.

Clam Broth

MAKES ABOUT 3 CUPS

1	dozen large clams, preferably chowder (quahog)
3	tablespoons vegetable oil
1	cup chopped onion
1/4	cup chopped celery
1/4	cup chopped leek, white part only
4	garlic cloves, unpeeled and crushed
1	cup dry white wine
1	teaspoon black peppercorns
4	sprigs fresh flat-leaf parsley
1	sprig fresh thyme
1 1/2	cups water

Scrub the clams under cold running water. Discard any that feel much heavier than the others (they may be filled with sand) or that remain open after washing.

In a large pot, heat the oil over medium-high heat. Add the onion, celery, leek, and garlic. Cover and cook for about 7 minutes, or until the vegetables are soft but not brown. Add the wine, peppercorns, parsley, and thyme, and boil for about 5 minutes, or until reduced by half. Add the clams and the water. Cover and cook, shaking the pot occasionally, for about 6 minutes, or until the clams open. Discard any unopened clams.

Strain the broth into a large bowl or container and cool completely. When cool, cover and refrigerate for up to 2 days, or freeze for up to 3 months.

Use the clams in another recipe.

Pineapple "Variation"

MAKES 8 SERVINGS

Musical composers and poets have been known to employ the phrase "variation on a theme" to indicate a fresh take on a classic piece. Here, the word *variation* denotes several recipes based on one primary ingredient and intended to be served together, which is a stimulating and creatively challenging way to design a dish. Sometimes I take this idea a few steps further and build a whole dinner around an ingredient, such as garlic, potatoes, or truffles, possibly even including it in the dessert (Black Truffle Ice Cream!).

Over the years, I have created variations of chocolate and caramel, as well as a pear variation that featured pear sorbet, poached pear, and a warm Pear Tart Tatin (page 213), which not only riffs on different cooking techniques, but also different temperatures.

As good as that dish was in October, this is February, and Pineapple "Variation" is just the thing to wake up those tired winter taste buds. The pineapple components—roasted with sugar, frozen in a sweet pineapple sorbet, and shredded in a beguiling pineapple

THINKING AHEAD: The sorbet, and therefore the pineapple preparation, must be completed at least 4 hours in advance. The poached pineapple must be made at least 2 hours in advance, and can be made the morning of the day you'll be serving it and kept, covered, in the refrigerator.

PINEAPPLE METHOD

2   large fresh pineapples

Using a heavy-bladed sharp knife, cut the tops and bottoms off of both pineapples. One at a time, stand the pineapples on a cutting board and, using the same knife and a very steady hand, cut straight down the sides to remove the tough peel, taking care to leave as much of the pineapple flesh intact as possible.

Turn one of the pineapples on its side and cut eight $1/4$-inch-thick slices from the top third of the pineapple. Stack the slices and, using an apple corer or small round pastry cutter, remove and discard the cores. Transfer the slices to a small plate, wrap tightly with plastic wrap, and refrigerate.

Cut the remainder of the first pineapple in half lengthwise. Cut out and discard the core from both halves. Cut one of the halves in half lengthwise again and slice the two resulting quarters into sixteen 1-inch-thick sections, cutting 8 sections from each quarter. Transfer the sections to a small bowl, cover tightly with plastic wrap, and refrigerate.

Cut the remainder of the first pineapple into medium dice.

Cut the second pineapple in half lengthwise and cut out and discard its core. Cut the entire pineapple into medium dice. Combined with the dice from the first pineapple, you should have 5 cups of diced fruit. Transfer the diced pineapple to a bowl, cover tightly with plastic wrap, and refrigerate.

PINEAPPLE SORBET

2   cups diced pineapple
2   cups canned or frozen pineapple juice
$1/2$ cup sugar

In a saucepan, combine the pineapple, juice, and sugar. Bring to a boil over high heat and cook for about 15 minutes. Remove from the heat and set aside to cool slightly for 15 to 20 minutes.

Transfer to a food processor fitted with a metal blade and process until puréed. You should have about 4 cups of purée.

Pour the purée into the container of an ice-cream machine and freeze according to the manufacturer's directions. Transfer to a covered container and freeze for at least 4 hours.

POACHED PINEAPPLE

3 cups diced pineapple
1/2 cup sugar
1/2 teaspoon grated lime zest

In a 12-inch sauté pan, poach the pineapple and sugar, stirring occasionally, over low heat for 14 to 16 minutes, until the pineapple releases its juices and softens. It will gently poach in its own liquid. Remove from the heat and set aside to cool. When cool, strain the pineapple. Transfer the pineapple to a container, add the zest, and stir to mix. Cover and refrigerate for at least 2 hours or until chilled.

CARAMELIZED PINEAPPLE AND ASSEMBLY

1 cup sugar
1 Tahitian vanilla bean, split
8 sprigs fresh mint

Remove the 16 1-inch-thick pineapple sections (not the rings) from the refrigerator.

In a large sauté pan, heat 2 tablespoons of the sugar over high heat until dissolved. When dissolved, add another tablespoon and cook until dissolved. Continue until all the sugar is used and it turns golden brown. Take care, as the sugar will be very hot.

Add the vanilla bean and cook until the sugar is dark brown but not burned (about 8 minutes). Carefully add the pineapple sections to the sugar and cook, stirring, for 5 to 8 minutes, until soft and caramelized. Remove from the pan and set aside. Remove and discard the vanilla bean and reserve the caramel sauce.

To serve, remove the 8 reserved pineapple rings from the refrigerator. Crisscross the caramelized pineapple on each of 8 dessert plates. Spoon the poached pineapple into 1-inch-round ring molds, pressing to mold it. Invert onto the plates next to the caramelized pineapple. Lay a pineapple ring on each plate and scoop the sorbet into the center of the rings. Spoon a little caramel sauce around the plates and serve.

salad in which the fruit is lightly poached, then punched up with lime juice and grated lime zest—complement one another very well.

If all of this seems too ambitious, make just one of these components at a time and enjoy them on their own.

Coconut
Panna Cotta

MAKES 6 SERVINGS

PANNA COTTA

¹/₂	cup crème fraîche
5	tablespoons mascarpone cheese
¹/₄	cup plus 2 tablespoons sugar
1¹/₂	teaspoons unflavored powdered gelatin
1	cup unsweetened coconut purée (available in specialty shops)
1	ripe passionfruit

In the top of a double boiler, combine the crème fraîche and mascarpone cheese. Heat over simmering water, stirring, until smooth and hot. Remove from the heat and set aside to keep warm.

In the top of a double boiler, sprinkle the gelatin over the coconut purée. Heat over barely simmering water, stirring, until the gelatin dissolves. Take care not to overheat the gelatin. Stir the gelatin mixture into the crème fraîche mixture until just smooth. Pour into 6 rectangular or round molds, such as espresso cups or small ramekins.

Halve the passionfruit and scoop about 1 teaspoon of fruit, including the shiny black seeds, onto the top of each mold. Cover with plastic wrap and freeze for at least 8 hours or overnight to set.

SAUCE AND ASSEMBLY

5	ripe passionfruits, halved, peeled, seeded, and flesh scooped out
4	kumquats, sliced
2	oranges, divided into segments
1	banana, sliced
1	cup diced fresh pineapple
	Sugar to taste
1	recipe Mango Sorbet (page 354)
	Sprigs of fresh mint

Remove the molds from the freezer. Dip the bottom of each one in a pan of warm water and then unmold it onto a platter, turning the molds upright. Refrigerate for no longer than 2 hours to thaw a little. As they thaw they will soften to a custardlike consistency but will retain their shape.

Combine the fruit in a nonreactive bowl. Sprinkle it with enough

Panna cotta, which means "cooked cream" in Italian, is traditionally made with milk or cream, flavored with vanilla bean, and bolstered with a modicum of gelatin, so that when it's unmolded, it just barely holds its shape. (The French cousin might be the *charlotte,* in which the mold is first ringed with ladyfingers.) A popular recipe pairs this custard with summer strawberries and a strawberry *coulis,* or sauce, which is delicious, but looking for some culinary sunshine in February requires greater resourcefulness; I thought of using coconut purée instead of regular milk, and the tropical fruits and flavors featured here naturally followed.

sugar to sweeten and to eliminate any tartness from the fruit. Cover and set aside at room temperature for about 1 hour to give the fruit time to release its natural juices and for the flavors to mingle.

Place the *panna cotta* in shallow dessert bowls, place a scoop of mango sorbet next to the *panna cotta*, arrange the fruit around them, and spoon some fruit juice around each one. Garnish with mint sprigs.

Mango Sorbet

MAKES 1 QUART

5	large ripe mangoes
2	cups water
1¼	cups sugar
1	teaspoon fresh lemon juice

Peel, halve, and pit the mangoes. Cut the flesh into small dice (you should have 5 cups of fruit). Combine the fruit, water, sugar, and lemon juice in a large nonreactive saucepot. Bring the mixture to a boil over a high heat and boil for 10 minutes, then reduce the heat to a simmer and simmer for 5 minutes more. Transfer the fruit to a blender or a food processor fitted with the metal blade and purée. Strain the purée through a fine-meshed strainer into a medium metal bowl. Place the bowl into a larger bowl of ice water and let it stand, stirring often, until completely chilled. Pour the mixture into the container of an electric ice-cream machine and freeze the sorbet according to the manufacturer's instructions. Scrape the sorbet into a container, cover it tightly with plastic wrap, and freeze until firm, approximately 2 hours.

Valentine's Day Dinner

This sensuous menu is perfect for a group Valentine's Day dinner.

SEARED FOIE GRAS WITH PEARS CARAMELIZED WITH
HONEY AND ROSEMARY **(page 230)**

OYSTER RISOTTO WITH SEVRUGA CAVIAR **(page 348)**

SQUAB ROASTED WITH POTATOES, PANCETTA, AND SAGE **(page 245)**

CHOCOLATE SOUFFLÉ WITH COFFEE SAUCE **(page 385)**

CHOCOLATE MACAROONS **(page 383)**

Dead of Winter Dinner

Make this dinner to lighten things up on one of the darkest, coldest days of the winter.

CURLY ENDIVE, BLOOD ORANGE, AND TANGERINE SALAD
WITH CITRUS VINAIGRETTE **(page 329)**

CURRIED DUCK BREASTS WITH BASMATI-SAFFRON RICE **(page 343)**

COCONUT *PANNA COTTA* **(page 353)**

Butternut Squash Ravioli, Parmigiano-Reggiano, Marjoram, and Oxtail Broth

Duck

Duck Confit with *Frisée*, Green Lentils, Beets, and Roquefort

Duck Terrine and Green Peppercorns

Pappardelle with Braised Duck, Root Vegetables, and Pecorino Romano

Chicken Cooked in Cabernet with Root Vegetables and Potato Purée

Slow Cooking

Slow-Cooked Lamb Shoulder

Veal Stew with Melted Leeks and Potato Purée

Roasted Rack of Venison with Winter Root Vegetables and Acorn Squash Purée

Chocolate Macaroons

Chocolate Soufflé with Coffee Sauce

French Dinners

MARCH
LAST CHANCE FOR WINTER

March is the home stretch of winter, the final lap that starts out on ground treacherous with ice and snow and winds up on the promising green grass of spring. When this month begins, I'm filled with anticipation because it'll only be a matter of days before April arrives. April, with its nurturing, shining sun, and . . .

But wait! As the spring thaw grows closer I feel an unexpected nostalgia. I'm not quite ready to move on to the next season. There's something about March I'll miss. Much of it, in fact. With the final frost, the lingering feelings of the holidays will be gone as well—those good feelings that seem to reverberate for as long as you can see your breath in the air. And, come to think of it, the chill doesn't seem quite so unpleasant when you know it's almost at an end.

What's more, it'll be months before we can again enjoy the complex, soul-nourishing foods of winter. Braised meats, softened by slow cooking until they fall off the bone with just the touch of a fork. Rich, dark stews with root vegetables providing hearty sustenance. Game and game birds that bring to mind a reassuring fire burning in the hearth of a rustic retreat.

As tiresome as the winter may become, even the most incidental culinary experiences take on extra significance—a cup of hot tea after a walk in the woods, or a bowl of oatmeal as a preemptive morning strike against the elements. When we eat in the winter, it's as if we're fueling our own internal furnaces. Food seems more important than ever during this time of year.

March is the last chance to participate in these rituals for a good six months. So these are the days when I enjoy saying a fond farewell to the restorative foods of winter. To my mind, this conjures a desire for classic French dishes, some because they represent early forms of preserving foods through the long winters before electricity, and others because their richness serves to reassure the body against the cold.

The gamey flavor of duck is especially appropriate to this sentiment. Here it's featured in three dishes including Duck Confit with *Frisée*, Green Lentils, Beets, and Roquefort (page 367) and Duck Terrine and Green Peppercorns (page 369). In the third, Pappardelle with Braised Duck, Root Vegetables, and Pecorino Romano (page 371), other mainstays of the

PREVIOUS PAGE: CHICKEN COOKED IN CABERNET WITH ROOT VEGETABLES AND POTATO PUREE **(page 373)**

season, including turnips and carrots, are featured as well. And the same vegetables are put to use in another game dish, Roasted Rack of Venison with Winter Root Vegetables and Acorn Squash Purée (page 379).

Nothing says winter more to me than slowly cooked dishes, and here is one of the classics—Chicken Cooked in Cabernet with Root Vegetables and Potato Purée (page 373), my version of *Coq au Vin*. Similarly, Butternut Squash Ravioli, Parmigiano-Reggiano, Marjoram, and Oxtail Broth (page 359) features an intensely flavorful broth that will provide enough memories to last you through the spring and summer. Other slow-cooked dishes include the Slow-Cooked Lamb Shoulder (page 375) and Veal Stew with Melted Leeks and Potato Purée (page 377).

To complement these dishes, the desserts in this chapter are in the classic French style as well, including Chocolate Macaroons (page 383) and Chocolate Soufflé with Coffee Sauce (page 385), as welcome in the winters of today as they were in those of days long gone.

You can prepare the ravioli a week ahead. To store them, lay them on a baking sheet covered with a layer of cornmeal and place in the freezer. Once the ravioli have hardened, separate them and store them in a Ziploc bag in the freezer. They can be cooked right from the freezer without defrosting, provided you extend the cooking time by 3 to 4 minutes.

The broth can be prepared as many as 3 days in advance and stored, covered, in the refrigerator.

Butternut Squash Ravioli, Parmigiano-Reggiano, Marjoram, and Oxtail Broth

MAKES ABOUT 50 RAVIOLI; 6 TO 8 APPETIZER SERVINGS

RAVIOLI

2	medium butternut squash
	Coarse salt and freshly ground white pepper to taste
1	tablespoon unsalted butter, softened
1	tablespoon canola oil
$^1/_2$	cup finely diced onion
1	teaspoon minced garlic
$^1/_4$	teaspoon red pepper flakes
$^1/_4$	teaspoon freshly grated nutmeg
2	tablespoons mascarpone cheese
$1^1/_2$	tablespoons finely grated fresh Parmesan cheese
1	large egg yolk
1	teaspoon chopped fresh marjoram
$^1/_2$	recipe Semolina Pasta Dough (page 364)
1	large egg beaten with 1 tablespoon water

Preheat the oven to 400°F. Line a baking sheet with aluminum foil. Cut the squash lengthwise and scoop out and discard the seeds. Season the cut sides of the squash with salt and pepper. Put a small amount of butter in the cavity of each squash half. Arrange the squash cut side up on the baking sheet (use 2 baking sheets if necessary) and bake for about 1 hour, or until very tender when pierced with the tip of a knife. Remove from the oven and set aside to cool.

Scoop the squash flesh from the skin and transfer it to a saucepan. Discard the skin. Cook the flesh over low heat, stirring often, for about 10 minutes, or until the moisture evaporates. Set aside to cool to room temperature. When cool, push the squash through a fine-mesh sieve into a mixing bowl, or purée it in a food processor fitted with a metal blade. You should have about 2 cups of purée.

In a medium saucepan, heat the oil over medium-high heat. Add

Its name may evoke images of an unapproachable Old World recipe, but cooking with oxtail is not nearly as challenging or complicated as you might think. Its name is actually a bit of a misnomer, because oxtail may come from any form of beef. Lest you think you need to trim it on your own, it can be purchased in crosscuts from your butcher, just like any other cut of meat. In short, it's another option to be added to your repertoire, no more or less user-friendly than the rest.

It's worth discovering oxtail because of its wonderfully intense, beefy flavor. Patient slow cooking yields a dense, fragrant, rich, and satisfying broth. (Because they lend themselves so well to long cooking, another conventional use is braised oxtails.)

(continued)

Here, an oxtail broth meets its match in two equally assertive components. The butternut squash ravioli is made with caramelized squash, mascarpone and Parmesan cheeses, as well as a dose of marjoram, which is also a classic oxtail seasoning. And the Reggiano-Parmigiano adds a final note of richness. Grate it at the last moment to preserve all of its crucial sharpness.

the onion, garlic, pepper flakes, and nutmeg, and sauté for 5 to 6 minutes, until the onion is lightly browned. Remove from the heat and cool to room temperature. Add to the squash purée.

Add the mascarpone cheese, Parmesan, egg yolk, and marjoram. Season with salt and pepper, and mix well. Transfer to a pastry bag fitted with a #5 plain tip.

Roll out a quarter of the dough at a time. Place the pasta dough sheet on a lightly floured work surface. Brush off any excess flour from the dough. Cut off any irregularly shaped ends, making a long rectangle, and then cut the sheet in half to make 2 equal-sized rectangles.

About 1 inch from the top of one rectangle, pipe out mounds of filling about $1^1/2$ inches apart. The mounds should be about $3/4$ inch wide. Pipe out another row of mounds parallel to the first, about 1 inch from the bottom of the dough. Brush the second rectangle with the egg wash. Place the second rectangle over the piped sheet, brushed side down. Using your fingers, gently press around each mound of filling to seal. Using a fluted pastry wheel, cut out ravioli about $1^1/2$ inches square, trimming away the excess dough as necessary. Put the ravioli on a semolina-dusted baking sheet. Repeat the procedure with the remaining dough and filling, using more baking sheets as needed. Refrigerate until ready to cook.

OXTAIL BROTH

4	pounds fresh oxtails, cut into 2-inch lengths
	Coarse salt and freshly ground white pepper to taste
6	tablespoons canola oil
1	medium onion, chopped
1	rib celery, chopped
1	medium carrot, peeled and chopped
$1^1/2$	quarts White Chicken Stock (page 421)
4	sprigs fresh flat-leaf parsley
3	sprigs fresh thyme
1	head garlic, split in half crosswise
1	tablespoon black peppercorns
1	bay leaf

Trim any excess fat from the oxtails and season them with salt and pepper. In a stockpot, heat 2 tablespoons of the oil over high heat. Add about $1/3$ of the oxtails and cook, turning, for about 10 minutes, until nicely browned. Take care not to burn them. Adjust the heat as necessary. Remove the oxtails from the pot and set them aside. Add more oil and another $^1/_3$ of the oxtails. Repeat the procedure until all the oxtails are nicely browned.

Pour most of the fat from the pot. Add the onion, celery, and carrot, and cook for 5 to 6 minutes, until lightly browned. Add 1 cup of the chicken stock and deglaze the pot, using a wooden spoon to scrape up any browned bits. Return the oxtails to the pot. Add the remaining chicken stock, the parsley, thyme, garlic, peppercorns, and bay leaf. Bring to a boil over high heat. Reduce the heat and simmer for $3^1/_2$ to 4 hours, or until the meat easily falls from the bone. Skim the surface of the stock as needed.

Lift the meat from the stock and set it aside until cool enough to handle. When cool, pull the meat from the bones. You should have about $^3/_4$ pound of meat.

Strain the stock through a fine-mesh sieve into a large bowl, pressing on the solids to extract as much flavor as possible. Discard the solids. Let the broth stand for about 5 minutes and then skim any fat that has risen to the surface. You should have about $^1/_2$ quart of broth. Set the bowl in a larger bowl filled with ice water to chill.

SAUCE AND ASSEMBLY
- 1 tablespoon canola oil
- 1 medium onion, very finely diced
- 1 medium carrot, peeled and very finely diced
- 1 rib celery, very finely diced
  Coarse salt and freshly ground black pepper to taste
- 3 tablespoons minced fresh chives
- 2 ounces Parmesan cheese, shaved

In a medium saucepan, heat the oil over medium heat. Add the onion, carrot, and celery, and cook for 3 to 4 minutes, stirring, until translucent. Add the oxtail broth and bring to a boil. Add the meat and season with salt and pepper. Cover and set aside to keep warm.

Meanwhile, bring a large pot of salted water to a boil over high heat. Add the prepared ravioli and cook for about 3 minutes, until tender. Carefully drain them in a colander.

Put the ravioli into 4 warmed soup plates. Ladle the warm sauce over them. Garnish with the chives and shaved Parmesan.

VARIATIONS: Short ribs can be substituted for the oxtails. Sugar pumpkin or buttercup squash can be substituted for the butternut squash.

Semolina Pasta Dough

MAKES ABOUT 1 1/2 POUNDS

1 1/4   cups unbleached all-purpose flour, plus additional for dusting the pasta dough
1 1/4   cups durum semolina (also called pasta flour)
4   large eggs, at room temperature
1/2   teaspoon extra-virgin olive oil
2   tablespoons water, or as needed

In a food processor fitted with a metal blade, pulse the flour and semolina for about 40 seconds to combine. In a small measuring cup, whisk together the eggs and olive oil. With the machine running, pour the egg mixture through the feed tube and then add just enough water for the dough to come together into a mass. This will take about 1 minute. Check the consistency of the dough. If it feels too soft and sticky, add a tablespoon or so of flour. If it is dry and crumbly, add a tablespoon or so of water. Process for about 30 seconds and check again.

Turn the dough out onto a lightly floured work surface and knead for 5 to 10 minutes, until smooth and resilient. Wrap the dough in plastic wrap and refrigerate it for 30 minutes to allow the dough to relax before proceeding.

Remove the dough from the refrigerator about 15 minutes before rolling it out to allow it to come to room temperature and soften a bit.

Duck

Duck is one of the great constants in classic French cuisine—contributing its flavor to such staples as foie gras, terrines, and duck confit. Since all of these are featured in this book, I thought a few notes on duck might be in order.

Although the most common duck in the United States is the Pekin (or Long Island), my favorites are Muscovy, which are produced largely in California and Canada. They simply have the most pronounced flavor and their breasts are ideal for sautéing or grilling. They're smaller than Moulards, with an average breast weight of about 16 ounces.

Mallards are wild ducks that, although generally very scarce, can be obtained at certain times during the year through specialty suppliers. At Griggstown Quail Farms, from which the Gotham gets its Muscovys, there's a designated area where they raise the wild Mallards in a simulated natural habitat. Truly wild Mallards can also be ordered from Scotland, with two caveats—you must be careful of actual pellets remaining from when they were shot, and they tend to taste like what they were eating just prior to being killed (possibly fish), which can produce a great taste variance. Mallards are very lean and are best enjoyed braised.

Moulard ducks are hybrids—a cross between a Pekin and a Muskovy—"engineered" in the United States to produce foie gras here. Most of them are raised in upstate New York, but there's also substantial production in California and Canada. Moulards are large ducks with a breast weight exceeding 20 ounces. They have a thick layer of fat that must be trimmed away. Their meat is a bit chewy, with an almost beeflike flavor. Because of this, Moulards can be cooked rare. Their legs are good for roasting, but are best enjoyed braised or in a confit-style preparation.

THINKING AHEAD: The duck must be marinated for at least 2 days before cooking. Or you can purchase preserved duck legs. (See page 426 for Mail-Order Sources.)

Duck Confit with *Frisée*, Green Lentils, Beets, and Roquefort

MAKES 4 SERVINGS

Confit, one of the oldest forms of preserving, originated in southwestern France, where it was an especially prized technique in the winter, because confit of duck, goose, or rabbit could be held for weeks (if not months or years) without spoiling. Like many recipes that date back several centuries, this one is a labor of love in which time and patience are among the most important ingredients.

In a classic confit recipe, duck legs are rubbed with a cut garlic clove, sprinkled with salt, and marinated for two or three days. In the method I was taught in France, the marination process becomes more important, with shallots, sliced garlic, thyme, cracked pepper, and rosemary added to the mix. Slow cooking is also essential—the ducks are removed from the marinade, their fat melted, and are cooked at just below a simmer for hours, until

BEETS AND LENTILS

4	small beets
3/4	cup French green lentils
1/2	cup White Chicken Stock (page 421)
1/2	small onion, halved
1	clove garlic, peeled and smashed
	Salt and freshly ground white pepper to taste

In a medium saucepan, cover the beets with cold salted water and bring to a boil over high heat. Reduce the heat and simmer for 40 to 45 minutes, until tender. Drain, and when cool enough to handle, slip off the skins and cut the beets in half. Set aside.

In a large saucepan, combine 1 1/2 cups of water, the lentils, stock, onion, and garlic. Season with salt and pepper. Bring to a boil over high heat. Reduce the heat and simmer for 20 to 25 minutes, until just tender. Remove from the heat and cool in the cooking liquid.

HAZELNUT VINAIGRETTE

1 1/2	tablespoons red wine vinegar
1	teaspoon Dijon mustard
	Coarse salt and freshly ground white pepper to taste
3/4	cup plus 1 tablespoon hazelnut oil (walnut oil may be substituted)

In a small, nonreactive bowl, whisk together the vinegar and mustard, and season with salt and pepper. Slowly whisk in the oil until emulsified. Set aside.

DUCK AND ASSEMBLY

4	confit duck legs (see page 233)
2	tablespoons minced shallot
1	tablespoon chopped fresh flat-leaf parsley
	Coarse salt and coarsely ground white pepper to taste
1	small head *frisée* (curly endive)
2	bunches watercress, large stems removed
2	ounces Roquefort cheese

the meat begins to loosen up and is barely holding to the bone. At this point, they are gently lifted out of the pan, and the fat is strained and poured over the legs.

In this dish, the creamy Roquefort offers an interesting counterpoint to the crispy duck, while the beets supply a sweetness that's as welcome here as their brilliant ruby color.

DUCK TIPS: To make confit, I prefer Moulard ducks to Muscovy or Pekin (Long Island), although Muscovy or Pekin legs, possibly remaining from another recipe in this book that uses the breasts, will be fine for braising, making sausage or pâtés, and other similar needs. Pekin ducks are less than ideal for recipes using duck breasts because they carry too much fat and have a small breast size.

In a 12-inch sauté pan, cook the duck legs, skin side up, over medium-low heat for about 15 minutes, or until the fat is rendered and the skin is crisp.

Drain the lentils and discard any pieces of onion and garlic. Put the drained lentils in a small, nonreactive bowl and toss them with the shallot and parsley. Dress them with about 1/4 cup of the vinaigrette, whisking the vinaigrette well before adding it to the lentils. Season with salt and pepper.

In another bowl, combine the *frisée* and watercress. Dress with the remaining vinaigrette. Crumble the cheese over the greens and season them with salt and pepper.

Divide the lentils among 4 salad plates. Put a duck leg on each mound of lentils. Garnish with the beets and a bouquet of dressed greens.

SPECIAL EQUIPMENT: Large (11$^{1}/_2$-by-3$^{1}/_2$-by-2$^{1}/_2$-inch) ceramic or enameled cast-iron terrine mold (do not use an uncoated metal mold); parchment paper; plastic wrap; large roasting pan to hold the terrine mold; an instant-read thermometer; 3 pieces of thick cardboard cut to fit the inside of the terrine, stacked and wrapped together with a double thickness of plastic wrap; 3-pound weight, or its equivalent.

TERRINE

12	ounces duck or chicken liver
1	pound plus 6 ounces skinless duck meat, from the breast or leg, cut into $^{1}/_2$-inch cubes
1	pound plus 2 ounces boneless pork shoulder, cut into $^{1}/_2$-inch cubes
9	ounces pork fatback, cut into $^{1}/_4$-inch cubes
2	tablespoons fine salt
4	teaspoons freshly ground white pepper
2	teaspoons sugar
1$^{1}/_2$	teaspoons saltpeter (optional), available from pharmacies
2	cloves garlic, peeled and thinly sliced
1	shallot, peeled and thinly sliced
2	teaspoons fresh thyme leaves
2	tablespoons Cognac or brandy
1	tablespoon port wine

Put the liver in a small, nonreactive bowl. In another bowl, combine the duck meat, pork shoulder, and fatback.

In a small bowl, mix together the salt, pepper, sugar, and saltpeter. In another small bowl, mix together the garlic, shallot, thyme, and Cognac. Sprinkle the salt-and-pepper mixture over the liver and the meat mixture, dividing it proportionally, about $^{1}/_4$ over the liver and $^{3}/_4$ over the meat. Divide the garlic-shallot mixture proportionally over the liver and meat, and then splash with port. Toss gently until all the ingredients are well mixed. Cover both bowls with plastic wrap and refrigerate for at least 1 day or for up to 3 days.

Duck Terrine and Green Peppercorns

MAKES 12 SERVINGS; 1-QUART TERRINE

Making a terrine from scratch is a rite of passage that will build your confidence and sense of accomplishment in the kitchen and place you a notch above most fellow home cooks. The terrine, or pâté, stands right alongside confit in the pantheon of classic French preparations.

Having a whole duck is a prerequisite for making a terrine, because one of the most vital ingredients is the duck liver, which imparts a distinct flavor throughout. The liver and meat are combined with pork, seasoned and marinated in Armagnac and port wine, then cooked in a terrine mold lined with pork fat, commonly referred to as fatback. With these ingredients, is it any wonder that the resulting dish is so incredibly rich and satisfying?

ASSEMBLY

1   tablespoon canola oil
2   large eggs, lightly beaten
2   tablespoons green peppercorns in brine, drained and rinsed

Preheat the oven to 400°F. Lightly butter the sides and bottom of a 1-quart terrine mold. Line the mold with parchment paper, leaving a 2-inch overhang on the 2 long sides. (The butter will allow the parchment paper to stick to the sides of the mold.)

In a 10-inch sauté pan, heat the oil over high heat. Remove the liver from the marinade and cook, stirring, for about 2 minutes, until seared on all sides. Add it to the bowl with the meat.

In a food processor fitted with a metal blade or a meat grinder fitted with a medium plate, chop the meat to a medium to fine consistency. Transfer the meat to a large bowl and stir in the eggs and peppercorns until well mixed.

Spoon the meat mixture into the terrine mold. It will mound approximately 3/4 inch over the top of the terrine. With dampened fingers, smooth the top so that it's rounded. Fold the overhanging parchment over the top of the mold to cover the meat. Tightly wrap the entire mold with a double thickness of plastic wrap. (The plastic will not melt in the oven.)

Put the terrine mold in a larger roasting pan and bake for about 10 minutes. Reduce the oven temperature to 275°F. Pour enough hot water into the roasting pan to come about 1 inch up the sides of the terrine. Bake for about 1 hour and 15 minutes, or until an instant-read thermometer reads 145°F when inserted in the center of the terrine. Put it through the plastic and parchment directly into the meat. As the terrine rests outside the oven, the internal heat will raise the temperature to 155° to 160°F.

Remove the mold from the roasting pan and discard the water. Return the terrine to the roasting pan and let it cool at room temperature for about 45 minutes. Unwrap the plastic wrap from the mold and set it on a baking sheet, which will catch any juices that overflow during weighting. Set the prepared cardboard pieces on top of the mold. Weight it evenly, using 3 cans of food or other weights. Refrigerate the terrine overnight.

Remove the terrine from the refrigerator and carefully run a sharp knife around the inside of the mold. Invert it onto a serving platter and gently tap the bottom of the mold. The terrine should slide right out. Remove the parchment paper and serve, cut into thick slices.

FLAVOR BUILDING: Serve this terrine with classic accompaniments such as *cornichons,* strong Dijon mustard, lightly toasted country bread, and a small salad of lightly dressed greens.

Pappardelle
with Braised Duck, Root Vegetables, and Pecorino Romano

This recipe departs from the more familiar tomato-based pasta sauces, opting instead for a slow-cooked, richly satisfying composition of winter ingredients. Duck legs are braised in red wine to create a thick, densely flavored sauce that is best suited to a heavy, broad noodle. A root-vegetable *mirepoix* of carrots, turnips, and celery—traditional duck accompaniments—cut the richness of the meat and offer a textural counterpoint as well. Shaved pecorino cheese melts into a blanket over the pasta, providing a final, unifying element.

This is a relatively practical dish since duck legs will be left over from most recipes that call for duck breasts. They can also be purchased from specialty butchers or by mail order. (See Mail-Order Sources, page 426.)

THINKING AHEAD: The duck sauce can be prepared as many as 3 days in advance and kept in the refrigerator.

MAKES 6 APPETIZER SERVINGS OR 4 MAIN-COURSE SERVINGS

DUCK SAUCE

4	Muscovy or Pekin duck legs, trimmed of excess fat
	Coarse salt and freshly ground white pepper to taste
2	tablespoons canola oil
1	large onion, roughly chopped
1	carrot, peeled and roughly chopped
1	rib celery, roughly chopped
8	cloves garlic, crushed
1	cup red wine, such as Cabernet Sauvignon
3	cups White Chicken Stock (page 421)
1	cup peeled, seeded, and chopped plum tomatoes or canned plum tomatoes, drained and chopped
1	tablespoon whole black peppercorns
1/2	teaspoon caraway seeds
3	sprigs fresh thyme

Preheat the oven to 300°F.

Season the duck legs with salt and pepper. In a large, heavy, ovenproof casserole, heat the oil over medium-high heat. Cook the legs, skin side down, for about 6 minutes, until nicely browned. Turn and cook for 3 to 4 minutes longer, until browned on the other side. Lift the duck legs from the casserole and set them aside.

Pour off all but 2 tablespoons of the fat in the pan. Cook the onion, carrot, and celery for about 8 minutes, stirring occasionally, until golden brown. Add the garlic and cook for about 4 minutes, until the cloves begin to soften. Add the wine and cook for about 6 minutes until syrupy.

Return the duck legs to the casserole and add the chicken stock, tomatoes, peppercorns, caraway seeds, and thyme. Bring to a boil. Reduce the heat, cover, and braise in the oven for about 1 hour and 20 minutes, or until the duck meat is so tender it falls off the bones. After about 15 minutes of braising, check the liquid. It should be barely simmering; if not, adjust the oven temperature up or down.

Using a slotted spoon, remove the duck legs from the casserole and set them aside until cool enough to handle. Pull the meat from the bones, discard the bones, and set aside the meat.

(continued)

Strain the sauce through a colander into a saucepan, pressing on the solids to extract as much flavor as possible. Discard the solids. Let the sauce stand for about 5 minutes, until the fat rises to the surface. Skim off and discard the fat. You should have about 2^1/$_4$ cups of sauce.

Bring the sauce to a boil over high heat and cook until it reduces by half and has a rich, thick consistency and concentrated flavors. Stir the meat into the sauce and season it with salt and pepper. Set aside, covered, to keep warm.

ROOT VEGETABLES

1 medium turnip, peeled and cut into large dice
1 large carrot, peeled and cut into large dice
2 ribs celery, cut into large dice

In a large saucepan of boiling salted water, cook the turnip for about 5 minutes, until tender. Remove with a slotted spoon and transfer to a bowl. When the water returns to the boil, cook the carrot for about 5 minutes, until tender. Remove with a slotted spoon and transfer to the bowl with the turnip. When the water returns to the boil, cook the celery for about 4 minutes, until tender. Remove with a slotted spoon and transfer to the bowl with the turnip and carrot. Set aside.

ASSEMBLY

1 pound fresh or dry pappardelle pasta
3 tablespoons finely chopped fresh flat-leaf parsley
^{1}/$_3$ cup freshly grated Pecorino Romano cheese, plus more for grating at the table

In a large pot of boiling salted water, cook the pappardelle over high heat until al dente. Fresh pasta will take 2 to 3 minutes; dry pasta 8 to 10 minutes. Drain well.

Add the root vegetables to the warm duck sauce and heat gently.

Divide the drained pasta among warmed pasta bowls. Spoon the sauce over the pasta and top each serving with parsley and cheese. Pass more cheese at the table.

VARIATIONS: If you prefer chicken to duck, prepare the sauce with chicken instead of duck. Adjust the recipe by using 2 sprigs of fresh rosemary instead of the caraway seeds and, if you like, white wine instead of red. You can vary the pasta, using fettuccine or rigatoni instead of pappardelle.

FLAVOR BUILDING: Ricotta cheese, seasoned with salt and pepper, makes a creamy foil to the rich duck sauce. Spoon a dollop over each serving.

Chicken Cooked in Cabernet with Root Vegetables and Potato Purée

MAKES 4 SERVINGS

As a young cook, I found the very concept of *Coq au Vin,* or Chicken in Red Wine, to be very enticing. Marinating a chicken in red wine for 2 or 3 days seemed like a can't-miss proposition, not unlike chicken cooked with 40 cloves of garlic or some other equally assertive technique.

In this dish, the chicken pieces are lightly browned, then slowly simmered until the meat is almost falling off the bone. It can and should be served with a simple accompaniment, such as buttered noodles, rice, or potato purée—anything that will soak up the flavorful juices. Since the chicken is prepared 2 or 3 days in advance, this is a perfect recipe for entertaining.

THINKING AHEAD: As you can see from the recipe, the entire dish should be made in advance.

CHICKEN AND MARINADE

1	5-pound chicken
3	cups Cabernet Sauvignon wine
1	cup roughly chopped onion
$^1/_2$	cup roughly chopped celery
$^1/_2$	cup roughly chopped carrot
1	head garlic, separated into cloves, peeled, crushed, and roughly chopped
3	bay leaves
6	sprigs fresh thyme
3	sprigs fresh flat-leaf parsley
2	6-inch sprigs fresh rosemary, roughly chopped
1	star anise, broken into pieces
1	heaping teaspoon whole black peppercorns

Using a heavy-bladed chef's knife or poultry shears, cut the chicken into pieces. Begin by removing the wing tips and setting them aside. Remove the leg and thigh sections and separate the legs from the thighs. Cut away the backbone and trim the chicken of excess fat and skin. Discard the excess fat and skin. Cut the backbone into 3 pieces. Split the breast lengthwise. Remove the wing pieces and cut the breast into quarters. You should have 10 chicken pieces plus wing tips, backbone, and neck.

In a large, nonreactive bowl, combine the wine, onion, celery, carrot, garlic, bay leaves, thyme, parsley, rosemary, star anise, and peppercorns. Add the chicken pieces and toss to combine. Cover with plastic wrap and refrigerate for at least 2 days and up to 3 days.

ASSEMBLY

$^1/_4$	cup canola oil, or more as needed
	Coarse salt and freshly ground white pepper to taste
2	quarts White Chicken Stock (page 421)
2	tablespoons unsalted butter
	Puréed Potatoes (page 337)

Lift the chicken from the marinade and pat the pieces dry with paper towels. Include the backbones, wing tips, and neck with the

WHAT TO DRINK: Serve this
with a big California cabernet.

rest of the chicken. Strain the marinade through a fine-mesh sieve into a bowl. Reserve the wine and vegetables separately.

In a 12-inch sauté pan, heat 2 tablespoons of the oil over high heat. Season the chicken pieces with salt and pepper, and cook, skin side down, turning it for 12 to 14 minutes, or until well browned. Take care not to crowd the pan. You may have to do this in batches, adding a little more oil as needed. Transfer the chicken pieces to a large pot.

Add the reserved wine from the marinade to the sauté pan and deglaze the pan over high heat, scraping up any browned bits from the bottom. Add the deglazing liquid to the pot with the chicken.

Wipe out the sauté pan and add 2 tablespoons of oil. Heat the oil over medium-high heat and sauté the reserved vegetables from the marinade, stirring for about 10 minutes, until lightly browned. Add the vegetables to the pot.

Bring to a boil over high heat and cook for about 8 minutes, or until the wine is reduced by half. Add the stock and bring to a boil. Reduce the heat and skim any fat that rises to the surface. Reduce the heat to low until the liquid is barely simmering. Cover and cook for 12 to 15 minutes, until the breast meat is cooked through. Remove the breast pieces from the pot and set them aside, loosely covered with aluminum foil to keep warm. Continue cooking the leg and thigh pieces about 25 minutes longer, until the meat easily separates from the bone. Remove the legs and thighs from the pot and set them aside, covered with foil to keep warm.

Strain the sauce into a clean saucepan. Discard the backbones, neck, wing pieces, and vegetables. You will have about 2 quarts of sauce. Cook over medium-high heat for about 25 minutes, until reduced, slightly thickened, and richly flavored. Return the chicken to the sauce and heat gently. Add the butter, a tablespoon at a time, swirling to enrich the sauce. To serve, arrange the chicken pieces and sauce on a platter. Serve with the potatoes on the side.

VARIATION: An excellent variation, and one of my favorite recipes, is Chicken *Vinaigre,* which is made by browning the chicken in a pan, then deglazing the pan with $1/3$ cup of high-quality, aged red-wine vinegar. Reduce the liquid over high heat until nearly evaporated, then, following the original recipe, add the red wine and follow the remaining steps. The reduced vinegar adds a note of acidity that lifts the heavy flavors of the dish.

Slow Cooking

Long, slow cooking results in a soft, melt-in-your-mouth quality. It's a style that is most closely associated with heavy, dark sauces and stews, and is therefore most appropriate to the colder months of the year.

There are several benefits to slow cooking, one of the most universal being that it breaks down the fat and connective tissues in tougher cuts of meat, which are, as a rule, more economical than leaner options.

There are two primary methods of slow cooking. The first, braising, generally involves browning the meat and vegetables, deglazing the cooking vessel with wine, and then adding aromatics and a *mirepoix* of vegetables and cooking slowly, covered, either on the stovetop or in the oven. Ultimately, the braising liquid becomes the sauce for the meat being cooked. The other umbrella category is long poaching or stewing, in which the meat is broken down after being simmered for a long time in a dark stock.

Slow-Cooked Lamb Shoulder

MAKES 6 SERVINGS

In this recipe, a paean to the merits of slow cooking, a piece of lamb shoulder is gradually cooked in the oven while being constantly basted with stock. To keep things simple, chicken stock is used here, but if you use a dark chicken, veal, or lamb stock, a wonderful rich glaze will develop.

1	4¹/₂-pound lamb shoulder roast, boned, rolled, and tied
	Coarse salt and freshly ground white pepper to taste
2	tablespoons canola oil
2	carrots, roughly chopped
2	ribs celery, roughly chopped
1	onion, roughly chopped
1	head garlic, broken into cloves and crushed with the side of a heavy knife
3	sprigs fresh thyme
1	teaspoon whole black peppercorns
2	cups drained whole, peeled canned tomatoes
1	cup full-bodied red wine
1¹/₂ to 2	quarts White Chicken Stock (page 421)
2	tablespoons coarsely chopped fresh flat-leaf parsley
2	teaspoons coarsely chopped fresh mint leaves

Preheat the oven to 300°F.

Generously season the lamb on all sides with salt and pepper.

In a large, ovenproof casserole or roasting pan with a lid, heat the oil over medium-high heat. Add the lamb and cook for 8 to 10 minutes, turning occasionally, until browned on all sides. Remove from the pan and set aside.

Add the carrots, celery, onion, garlic, thyme, and peppercorns to the pan and cook, stirring, for 6 to 8 minutes, until they begin to brown. Add the tomatoes and season with salt and pepper. Cook, stirring, for about 4 minutes. Add the wine, bring to a boil, and cook for about 6 minutes, or until the wine nearly evaporates.

Return the lamb to the pan and add enough chicken stock to come about a third of the way up the meat. Bring the liquid to a boil, remove the pan from the heat, cover, and place it in the oven. Braise for 3½ to 4 hours, until the lamb is fork-tender. After the meat has been braising for about 15 minutes, check to make sure the liquid is barely simmering. Adjust the oven temperature accordingly. Baste occasionally with the pan juices during braising.

Remove the lamb from the roasting pan and transfer it to a platter. Cut and remove the string tying the lamb, cover the meat loosely with foil, and set it aside to keep warm.

Strain the braising liquid through a fine sieve into a saucepan. Discard the solids. Let the liquid rest for about 5 minutes and then skim the fat that rises to the surface. Bring the liquid to a boil over medium-high heat and cook for about 15 minutes, until the sauce is reduced by half and is thickened and richly flavored. You should have about 2 cups of sauce. Season it with salt and pepper.

Slice the lamb into thick pieces. The meat will be so tender it will almost fall apart. Arrange it on a serving platter and spoon the sauce over it. Sprinkle with the parsley and mint, and serve. Pass the extra sauce on the side.

FLAVOR BUILDING: Root vegetables, buttered pappardelle, Swiss chard, or steamed spinach all work well with this recipe.

Veal Stew with Melted Leeks and Potato Purée

MAKES 6 SERVINGS

This is an updated version of the beloved French classic *Blanquette de Veau*—a veal stew cooked in a white sauce—modeled on the very traditional recipe I first encountered in one of Raymond Oliver's books. Rich, creamy, elegant, and delicious, *Blanquette de Veau* is a favorite among Francophiles, classically garnished with mushrooms, pearl onions, and baby carrots. Here, the soft, ivory color of the sauce is flecked with herbs and complemented by pale yellow-green leeks and the subtle perfume of lemon zest.

THINKING AHEAD: The stew can be prepared a day or two in advance, but do not add the crème fraîche until the stew has been gently reheated.

VEAL AND SAUCE

3	pounds veal breast, cut into 1-inch cubes
	Coarse salt and coarsely ground white pepper to taste
2	tablespoons all-purpose flour
$^1/_4$	cup canola oil
$^3/_4$	cup dry white wine
$1^1/_2$	cups coarsely chopped onions
$^1/_2$	cup coarsely chopped carrots
$^1/_2$	cup coarsely chopped celery
2	medium leeks, white parts only, cut into 1-inch pieces
2	cloves garlic, peeled and sliced
	Zest of $^1/_2$ lemon, removed in strips with a vegetable peeler
1	teaspoon whole black peppercorns
1	bay leaf
3	cups White Chicken Stock (page 421)

In a large mixing bowl, season the veal with salt and pepper. Sprinkle it with the flour and toss to coat.

In a large pot, heat the oil over high heat. Cook the veal, stirring for about 6 minutes, until all traces of pink are gone. You may have to do this in batches. Add the wine and deglaze the pan, scraping up any browned bits from the bottom. Cook until the wine reduces by about half.

Add the onions, carrots, celery, leeks, garlic, lemon zest, peppercorns, and bay leaf, and cook for about 8 minutes, until the vegetables begin to soften. Add the chicken stock and bring to a boil. Skim any fat that rises to the surface. Reduce the heat to low, cover, and simmer for about 1 hour and 20 minutes, until the meat is tender.

Strain the sauce through a colander set over a large bowl. Remove the veal and set it aside. Discard the vegetables. Return the sauce to the pot. You should have about 1 cup of slightly thickened, richly flavored sauce. If necessary, cook it over high heat to reduce it slightly and concentrate the flavors. Season it with salt and pepper.

(continued)

ASSEMBLY

    4   leeks, white parts only, cut on the bias into $1/4$-inch-thick pieces
    3   carrots, peeled and cut on the bias into $1/4$-inch-thick pieces
    2   cups peeled pearl onions
    3   tablespoons unsalted butter
        Coarse salt and freshly ground white pepper to taste
$3/4$ cup crème fraîche
    2   tablespoons finely minced fresh chives
    1   tablespoon finely chopped fresh tarragon leaves
        Puréed Potatoes (page 337)

In a large saucepan of boiling salted water, cook the leeks for about 4 minutes, until tender. Remove them with a slotted spoon and rinse them under cold, running water to stop the cooking. Transfer them to a bowl. When the water returns to the boil, cook the carrots for about 8 minutes, until tender. Remove them with a slotted spoon and transfer them to the bowl with the leeks. When the water returns to the boil, cook the onions for about 8 minutes, until tender. Remove them with a slotted spoon and transfer them to the bowl with the leeks and carrots. Reserve 2 cups of the cooking water.

Put the vegetables and reserved cooking water in the pan. Add the butter and season with salt and pepper. Cook over medium heat until the butter melts and the vegetables are warmed through.

To serve, heat the veal sauce over medium heat. Whisk in the crème fraîche. Add the reserved veal and cook until heated through. Add the chives and tarragon.

Spoon the potato purée into the centers of 6 dinner plates. Using a slotted spoon, spoon the veal over the potatoes. Garnish each plate with the warm vegetables.

VARIATIONS: Serve this stew on a bed of lightly buttered fettuccine or fluffy white rice, either of which will soak up the rich and flavorful juices.

Roasted Rack of Venison

with Winter Root Vegetables and Acorn Squash Purée

MAKES 4 SERVINGS

THINKING AHEAD: You can prepare the squash purée in advance and keep it warm according to the method described on page 37.

VENISON SAUCE

1	tablespoon canola oil, or more as needed
	Reserved trimmings from 1 rack of venison
2	shallots, peeled and sliced
2	cloves garlic, peeled and sliced
1	tablespoon juniper berries
2	teaspoons whole black peppercorns
1	sprig fresh thyme
1	cup dry red wine
1$^1/_2$	quarts White Chicken Stock (page 421)
	Coarse salt and freshly ground white pepper to taste
$^1/_4$	cup unsalted butter

In a large saucepan, heat the oil over medium-high heat. Brown the trimmings for about 10 minutes, until nicely colored. Transfer them to a bowl and set aside.

Add the shallots to the saucepan and cook, stirring for about 5 minutes, until browned. Add the garlic, juniper berries, peppercorns, and thyme, and cook for about 2 minutes, stirring, until fragrant. Add the wine and bring to a boil over high heat. Boil for 10 to 15 minutes, until the wine is reduced to $^1/_4$ cup. Add the chicken stock, reduce the heat to low, and simmer for about 1 hour, until the stock is reduced to about 1 quart.

Strain the sauce through a fine sieve into a bowl. Discard the solids. Return the sauce to the saucepan and simmer it over medium-high heat for about 20 minutes, until reduced to about 1$^1/_2$ cups. Season with salt and pepper. Swirl in the butter to enrich the sauce. Cover and set it aside to keep warm.

ACORN SQUASH PURÉE

2	acorn squash, each weighing about 1 pound
$^1/_4$	cup unsalted butter, at room temperature
	Coarse salt and freshly ground white pepper to taste

Preheat the oven to 400°F.

Cut the squash in half lengthwise and scoop out the seeds. Rub about 1 tablespoon of the butter over the cut surfaces of the squash and season them with salt and pepper.

Arrange the squash cut side down in a shallow roasting pan. Roast

Venison is uniquely tender, lean, and easy to cook. Like a steak, the full flavor of venison is quick to reveal itself after just a coating of salt and pepper and a quick grilling or sautéing. Because most venison today is farm-raised, with a delicate fine flavor, there is no need for a strong marinade or heavy seasoning.

Here, venison is paired with salsify, a root vegetable with long, thin roots which is also known as oyster plant or vegetable oyster because of its faint cream coloring. It has a bitter taste that is moderated by storing it in the refrigerator, where it will sweeten. Note that, like pears or apples, salsify will turn brown when exposed to the air, so brush it with lemon juice, or hold it in a lemon-water mixture, after slicing.

for about 45 minutes to 1 hour, until tender when pierced with a fork or the tip of a sharp knife. Holding the squash in a kitchen towel to protect your hands from the heat, scoop out the squash flesh and transfer it to a serving bowl. Stir in the remaining 3 tablespoons of butter and season with more salt and pepper. Cover and set aside to keep warm.

WINTER ROOT VEGETABLES
- 3 pieces salsify root, peeled and cut into $1^1/_2$-inch lengths
  Juice of $^1/_2$ lemon
  Coarse salt and freshly ground white pepper to taste
- 1 yellow turnip, peeled and cut into $1^1/_2$-inch dice
- 2 large carrots, peeled and cut into $1^1/_2$-inch dice
- 1 tablespoon unsalted butter

In a medium saucepan, combine the salsify and lemon juice. Add enough water to cover, and season with salt and pepper. Bring the water to a boil over high heat. Reduce the heat and simmer for about 8 minutes, until the salsify is tender. Drain and transfer it to a bowl, cover, and set aside to keep warm.

Bring a saucepan of salted water to a boil over high heat. Add the turnip and cook for about 10 minutes, until tender. Using a slotted spoon, remove the turnip from the pan and transfer it to the bowl with the salsify. When the water returns to the boil, add the carrots and cook for about 8 minutes, until tender. Drain, reserving about 1 cup of the cooking water.

Return the water to the pan. Add the salsify, turnips, and carrots. Add the butter and season with salt and pepper. Cover to keep warm.

ASSEMBLY
- 1 rack of venison, trimmed, bones frenched and tied (ask your butcher to do this for you)
  Coarse salt and freshly ground white pepper to taste
- 2 tablespoons canola or vegetable oil

Preheat the oven to 450°F.
About 15 minutes before you are ready to cook the venison, take it from the refrigerator to allow it to come to room temperature. Season it generously with salt and pepper.

In a 12-inch sauté pan, heat the oil over high heat. Brown the venison by searing it for 2 to 3 minutes on each side. Transfer it to a large roasting pan and roast for about 8 minutes. Turn it over and roast about 7 minutes longer for medium-rare meat. Transfer the venison to a platter and cover it loosely with foil to keep warm. Let the rack rest for about 10 minutes.

Place a spoonful of acorn squash purée on each of 4 warmed dinner plates. Reheat the vegetables briefly, if necessary, and, using a slotted spoon, place them on the plates, dividing them equally.

Cut and remove the string from the rack of venison. Carve the rack into 4 double chops and arrange them next to the vegetables on the plates. Spoon the sauce around the plate and serve with the remaining sauce passed on the side.

WHAT TO DRINK: Serve this with a California Zinfandel.

MACAROONS

4	cups plus 2 tablespoons confectioners' sugar
3¹/₂	cups almond flour
4	tablespoons unsweetened nonalkalized cocoa powder
8	large egg whites
¹/₄	teaspoon cream of tartar
¹/₂	cup granulated sugar

Preheat the oven to 350°F. Butter 2 baking sheets. In a large mixing bowl, sift together the confectioners' sugar, almond flour, and cocoa. Add 2 egg whites and fold until the mixture is crumbly.

In the bowl of an electric mixer set on high speed, beat the remaining 6 egg whites with the cream of tartar for 1 minute. Add the sugar and beat for another 1¹/₂ to 2 minutes, until stiff peaks form. Fold the egg whites into the flour mixture, mixing until the dough is smooth and light.

Spoon the dough into a pastry bag fitted with a large plain tip, and pipe cookies approximately 1¹/₂ inches in diameter onto the baking sheet. You should have 3 rows of 5 cookies on each baking sheet. Set the baking sheets aside at room temperature for 15 to 20 minutes, or until the surface of the cookies looks a little shiny and develops a thin skin. Bake for 15 to 20 minutes, until the cookies are firm and browned. Cool on wire racks.

GANACHE AND ASSEMBLY

¹/₂	cup chopped extra-bittersweet chocolate, such as Valrhona
¹/₄	cup heavy cream

In a small, heavy-bottomed saucepan or in the top of a double boiler set over very hot (not simmering) water, melt the chocolate, stirring until smooth. Whisk in the cream until thick and evenly colored. Spoon the ganache into a pastry bag fitted with a #3 plain tip.

Invert 15 of the cookies so that the flat bottoms are facing up. Pipe a little ganache on each. Sandwich with the remaining cookies, pressing the flat bottoms together.

VARIATIONS: You can substitute one of the following fillings for the chocolate one above. You may omit 4 tablespoons of cocoa powder and increase almond flour by 4 tablespoons when using the lemon or raspberry filling. For vanilla macaroons, delete the cocoa.

(continued)

Chocolate
Macaroons
MAKES 15 SANDWICH COOKIES

At the end of a long tasting menu, certain three-star restaurants in Paris, and more than a few top restaurants in New York, have taken to offering little plates of macaroons in place of petits fours. Filled with playful, fanciful-looking spreads like raspberry jam, lemon curd, and chocolate cream, they make a lovely conclusion to a meal, and are equally suitable to an afternoon tea.

Though commercial brands may have created a contrary impression, macaroons should be very light and fluffy. Use the best ingredients available (e.g., a high-quality cocoa powder for chocolate macaroons) and follow the same principle for the filling to create an impactful flavor throughout.

LEMON FILLING

- $1/2$ cup fresh lemon juice
- 5 tablespoons sugar
- 2 large eggs
- 1 large egg yolk
- $1/2$ cup heavy cream or crème fraîche

Grated zest of 3 lemons

Preheat the oven to 350°F.

In a bowl, combine the lemon juice and sugar, and stir until the sugar dissolves. Add the eggs, egg yolk, and cream, and whisk until smooth. Strain through a sieve into another bowl. Stir in the zest and then pour the mixture into a shallow, ungreased 8-by-4-inch or 8-by-5-inch pan.

Set the pan in a larger roasting or baking pan set on the oven rack. Pour enough hot water into the larger pan to come about halfway up the sides of the smaller pan. Bake for about 20 minutes, until thick. Set the pan on a wire rack and let the filling cool.

Use the filling to fill the cookies, as described on the preceding page.

RASPBERRY FILLING

- 4 pints fresh raspberries
- 1 cup sugar

In a saucepan, cook the berries and sugar over high heat, stirring, until the sugar dissolves and the mixture is thick. Strain through a fine-mesh sieve to remove the seeds. Return the strained raspberries to the saucepan and cook over very low heat for about 40 minutes, until thick. Set aside to cool to room temperature.

Use the filling to fill the cookies, as described above.

COFFEE SAUCE

2	cups heavy cream
$1/2$	cup sugar
$1/2$	cup espresso coffee beans, crushed with a mallet or the back of a skillet, or coarsely chopped
4	large eggs

In a saucepan, combine the cream, $1/4$ cup of the sugar, and the crushed coffee beans. Bring to a boil over high heat. Remove from the heat and set aside to steep for about 15 minutes.

Return the saucepan to the heat and bring back to a boil over high heat. Reduce the heat to low.

In a small bowl, whisk the eggs with the remaining sugar until sugar is dissolved and mixture is lemon colored, about $1^1/2$ minutes. Slowly drizzle about $1/2$ cup of the hot cream into the eggs, whisking constantly to prevent them from curdling. Slowly pour the egg-cream mixture into the remaining cream. Carefully cook mixture over medium heat, stirring constantly with a wooden spoon until mixture thickens enough to coat the back of your spoon, about 4 minutes. Strain through a fine-mesh sieve into a metal bowl. Put the bowl in a larger one filled with ice water and stir mixture to quickly chill. Before serving, let the sauce come up to cool room temperature.

SOUFFLÉS

$1^1/4$	cups chopped extra-bittersweet chocolate, such as Valrhona
5	tablespoons sour cream
$1/2$	cup unsalted butter
5	large egg yolks
3	tablespoons room-temperature water
11	tablespoons sugar, plus extra for coating molds
10	large egg whites

Preheat the oven to 375°F. Generously butter 8 ramekins or individual 5-ounce soufflé dishes. Sprinkle each with sugar, then invert to shake out the excess.

In the top of a double boiler set over simmering water, combine the chocolate, sour cream, and butter, and cook, stirring, until the mixture is smooth and evenly colored. Remove the pan from the heat and set it aside to cool.

In the bowl of an electric mixer set on medium-high speed, beat the egg yolks, water, and 4 tablespoons of the sugar for about 4 minutes, until smooth and fluffy. (If you need this mixing bowl to beat

Chocolate Soufflé with Coffee Sauce

MAKES 8 INDIVIDUAL SOUFFLÉS

Like so many recipes in this chapter, the soufflé is a classic French preparation that's often attended by a great deal of pomp. To this day, restaurants ask that you order a soufflé at the beginning of your meal, because they have to be baked to order. The image of a delicate soufflé baking in the oven, the chef guarding its surroundings to make sure no loud noises occur, has an almost cartoon familiarity. There are soufflé recipes out there that offer a bit more "sturdiness," but they lack the essential, almost cloudlike airiness that, to me, defines this dessert.

The success of this soufflé depends on gently folding the egg whites into the final mixture, at which point—as in a restaurant—the dessert becomes very time-sensitive and needs to make it from the oven to the table in rapid fashion to prevent it from falling.

the egg whites, scrape the mixture into another bowl with a rubber spatula. Wash and dry the mixing bowl and the beaters. Both must be clean and dry or the whites will not expand.)

In the clean, dry bowl with the electric mixer set on high speed, beat the whites to soft peaks. When the whites reach this point, begin adding the remaining 7 tablespoons of sugar. Beat the meringue until it reaches stiff peaks.

Fold the egg-yolk mixture into the chocolate mixture, scraping the bottom of the pan with a rubber spatula to lift the chocolate and folding to just mix, keeping the mixture light and airy. Do not overmix.

A third at a time, fold the chocolate mixture into the egg whites, just until there are no whites showing in the mixture. Spoon the soufflé mixture into the prepared ramekins, filling each one nearly but not quite full. Arrange them on a baking sheet and bake for 25 to 30 minutes, until puffed, risen, and set.

Serve the soufflés immediately. Tableside, insert a spoon in the center of each one, and spoon some sauce into the soufflé.

French Dinners

These menus practically turn your kitchen into a time machine. Enjoy a taste of the past with the classic recipes in both.

MENU 1

SALMON RILLETTE **(page 271)**

LEEK AND ROQUEFORT SALAD WITH MIMOSA VINAIGRETTE **(page 166)**

CHICKEN COOKED IN CABERNET WITH ROOT VEGETABLES AND POTATO PURÉE **(page 373)**

GOTHAM PROFITEROLES WITH CHOCOLATE SAUCE **(page 186)**

MENU 2

DUCK TERRINE AND GREEN PEPPERCORNS **(page 369)**

GARBURE **(page 276)**

VEAL STEW WITH MELTED LEEKS AND POTATO PURÉE **(page 377)**

RED WINE POACHED PEARS WITH MASCARPONE AND PISTACHIO NUTS **(page 250)**

Goat Cheese Salad with Beets, Braised
Fennel, and a Citrus Vinaigrette

Seared Squid, Shallot, and White Runner Bean Salad

Artichokes

Artichoke Risotto with Prosciutto and Lemon

Poached Atlantic Salmon *à la Nage*

Monkfish Braised in Red Wine with Potato Purée

Lamb

Roast Leg of Lamb with Haricots Verts
and Boulangère Potatoes

Veal Chops with Gnocchi and Broccoli Rabe

Charcoal-Grilled Porterhouse Steaks with
Potato and Wild Mushroom Gratin

Milk Chocolate *Petits Pots*

Banana Cake

Easter Dinners

APRIL

RETURN OF THE LIGHT

In our culture, there's a lot of negativity directed toward April. The first of the month is that malicious quasiholiday known as April Fool's Day, the poet T. S. Eliot named this "the cruelest month," and conventional wisdom dictates that "April showers bring May flowers," pessimistically implying a rainy couple of weeks ahead.

But I've always found April to be a very generous time, a few weeks when, one by one, the signs of an optimistic new season fall into place every day. Winter coats and sweaters disappear, plants and flowers begin to bloom, and the result is that you simply begin to feel more alive.

This change is palpable even in the asphalt jungle of New York City. When the sky turns blue and the air temperate, people take to the streets en masse. On the first day that it's warm enough to wear shorts, the city is mobbed with bikers, roller bladers, and strollers as everyone takes on an enthusiasm that's truly glorious to experience.

From a culinary standpoint, April is when we begin to move away from the heavier foods of the winter toward lighter cuisine. Among the recipes I've included here to suit this shift are Goat Cheese Salad with Beets, Braised Fennel, and a Citrus Vinaigrette (page 392), Seared Squid, Shallot, and White Runner Bean Salad (page 394), and Artichoke Risotto with Prosciutto and Lemon (page 397).

Of course, during April, cold nights are still apt to make a last stand. For those evenings when they do, I've included slightly more hearty dishes such as Veal Chops with Gnocchi and Broccoli Rabe (page 408) and Monkfish Braised in Red Wine with Potato Purée (page 402)—recipes that, like this month, straddle the fence between winter and spring.

April is also the first time each year that I venture out to the grill, and I'm so eager to do it that I've been spotted out there in a sweater or sweatshirt on more than a few occasions. One of my favorite ways to break in the grill for the season is with Charcoal-Grilled Porterhouse Steaks with Potato and Wild Mushroom Gratin (page 410).

Of course, the biggest event of this month is Easter. When I was a kid, Easter Sunday was a big colorful holiday. The soft tones on Easter hats stand out in my memories of church. And, of course, Easter egg hunts are a blast for all children.

Today, we always eat an early Easter dinner in the midafternoon. Usually it starts with a salmon dish like Poached Atlantic Salmon *à la Nage* (page 400). Then we move on to a lamb dish such as Roast Leg of Lamb with Haricots Verts and Boulangère Potatoes (page 405).

Easter baskets are also an important part of this holiday. When I attended the Culinary

Institute of America, classes were assigned in blocks. When it was my turn to take advanced pastry, it happened to be during the month of April, and Albert Kumin, who had formerly been the pastry chef at the White House, was my teacher. Just before Easter, he brought in antique chocolate molds, which, for me, were a revelation that started me collecting them, too—a hobby I continue to this day.

But, even though chocolates are still a very important part of Easter, I've stayed away from molded chocolate here, choosing instead Milk Chocolate *Petits Pots* (page 413). We do use the molds at our home, however, decorating our daughters' bedrooms with them during the days leading up to this first holiday of the spring.

Goat Cheese Salad with Beets, Braised Fennel, and a Citrus Vinaigrette

MAKES 4 SERVINGS

This simple *salade composée* pairs two classic duos—goat cheese and beets, and oranges and fennel—with a vinaigrette of orange juice, lemon juice, and extra-virgin olive oil. The accompaniments are so satisfying that you needn't marinate the goat cheese.

SPECIAL EQUIPMENT (OPTIONAL): A Japanese mandoline works well to cut the beet into thin slices.

BEETS AND FENNEL

1	large beet
	Coarse salt and freshly ground white pepper to taste
1	large or 2 small fennel bulbs, trimmed and feathery tops discarded
2	tablespoons extra-virgin olive oil
$^1/_2$	cup finely minced onion
2	cloves garlic, peeled and crushed
1	bay leaf
1	sprig fresh thyme
1	cup White Chicken Stock (page 421), optional

In a small saucepan, cover the beet with cold water. Season with salt and pepper, and bring the water to a boil over high heat. Reduce the heat and simmer for about 25 minutes, or until the beet is tender when pierced with a tip of a small, sharp knife. Drain and set it aside to cool. When cool, peel and slice the beet into $^1/_8$-inch-thick rounds.

Trim the root end of the fennel bulb, making sure not to cut too deeply. The fennel's layers should remain connected at the root so that the cut wedges hold together. Using a large chef's knife, cut the fennel in half lengthwise and then into 8 wedges.

In a saucepan, heat the oil over medium heat. Cook the onion, stirring, for about 6 minutes, until softened. Add the garlic, bay leaf, and thyme. Season with salt and pepper, and cook about 2 minutes longer. Add the fennel and enough chicken stock or water, or a combination of the two, to just cover it. Bring the liquid to a boil over high heat. Reduce the heat and simmer for 10 to 12 minutes, or until the fennel is tender when pierced with the tip of a small, sharp knife. Remove the pan from the heat and let the fennel cool in the cooking liquid. (The cooking liquid is so tasty, you should save it for another use. It freezes well.)

SALAD AND ASSEMBLY

3	oranges
$^1/_4$	cup fresh orange juice
2	tablespoons fresh lemon juice
$^1/_4$	cup extra-virgin olive oil

Coarse salt and freshly ground white pepper to taste
4   cups mixed greens
1   6-ounce log fresh goat cheese, cut into 4 equal rounds
$^1/_2$ cup toasted walnut halves

Peel the oranges and, holding them over a small, nonreactive bowl to catch the juices, cut between the membranes to section them. Set the sections aside. Squeeze the membrane to extract the juices, if necessary. Add enough fresh orange juice to the bowl to measure $^1/_4$ cup.

Arrange the beet slices in a circular pattern in the centers of 4 salad plates to cover the center of each plate with a thin, pretty layer of beets.

Add the lemon juice and olive oil to the orange juice and whisk to mix. Season with salt and pepper. Dress the greens with a few tablespoons of the vinaigrette and toss until the leaves are nicely coated.

Mound the greens in the center of the beets layered on the plates. Add a disk of goat cheese next to the greens and on top of the beets. Arrange the orange sections and walnut halves around the greens on top of the beets. The beets should be clearly visible on the plates. Spoon the remaining vinaigrette over the beets.

Seared Squid, Shallot, and White Runner Bean Salad

MAKES 4 SERVINGS

The simple, light, and satisfying flavors in this dish will be just as good in the upcoming warm months as they are in April. The delicate essence of squid is unlocked by searing it very quickly in a hot pan. It is then tossed with warm white runner beans, sliced shallots, lemon juice, and garlic, and is served atop a bed of peppery arugula. Note how blanching the shallots softens their character, allowing them to blend into this context.

THINKING AHEAD: The beans must soak overnight.

RUNNER BEANS

$^1/_2$ cup dry white runner or Great Northern beans, rinsed and soaked overnight
Coarse salt and freshly ground white pepper to taste

Drain the beans and put them in a large saucepan. Add enough cold water to cover, and bring to a boil over high heat. Reduce the heat and simmer for 20 minutes. Season with salt and pepper. Cover the pan and simmer about 20 minutes longer, until the beans are tender but firm enough to hold their shape. The cooking time will vary depending on the age and dryness of the beans. Drain and set the beans aside, covered, to keep warm. You should have about $1^1/_4$ cups.

GARLIC VINAIGRETTE

3 tablespoons extra-virgin olive oil
3 cloves garlic, peeled and halved lengthwise
4 teaspoons fresh lemon juice
Coarse salt and freshly ground white pepper to taste

In a small sauté pan, heat the oil over low heat. Add the garlic and cook for about 5 minutes, stirring, until browned on both sides. Take care to keep the heat low enough to prevent burning.

Remove the pan from the heat and allow to cool slightly, then lift the garlic with a slotted spoon. Discard the garlic. Transfer the oil to a small mixing bowl and set aside to cool. When cool, whisk in the lemon juice, and season with salt and pepper.

SQUID AND ASSEMBLY

4 large shallots, peeled and cut into $^1/_4$-inch-thick rings
2 tablespoons olive oil
12 ounces cleaned squid tentacles and bodies, cut in half horizontally
Coarse salt and freshly ground white pepper to taste
2 tablespoons chopped fresh flat-leaf parsley
3 cups loosely packed arugula leaves

In a small saucepan of boiling salted water, cook the shallots for about 4 minutes, until tender. Drain and set aside, covered, to keep warm.

Put the warm beans in a mixing bowl and set them near the stove.

In a sauté pan, heat the oil over high heat until very hot but not smoking. Add the squid and season with salt and pepper. Cook, tossing, for about 1 minute. Transfer the seared squid to the bowl with the warm beans, add shallots, and toss with the vinaigrette. Season with salt and pepper, and stir in the parsley.

Arrange the arugula on 4 salad plates or a serving platter. Spoon the warm squid and bean salad over the greens and serve.

VARIATION: This salad can also be served cold.

Artichokes

Artichokes, a member of the thistle family, appear primarily in two seasons, the first spanning August through October and the other March through May. Originally introduced to this country by French and Italian immigrants, they caught on especially in northern California where the cool, coastal climate is ideal for cultivation. In fact, Castroville remains the largest artichoke producing area in the United States, with more than 8,000 acres in the Monterey Peninsula. The predominant variety grown here is the globe artichoke, which represents almost the entire domestic production.

In color, artichokes range from purple to green and often show traces of both. When purchasing them, always check the stem where it's been cut to ensure that it hasn't turned black but, rather, is clean and verdant. The artichoke itself should be firm to the touch with no brown spots or blemishes, and the leaves should be tightly closed, not unlike the tips of asparagus.

Artichokes are delicious steamed whole and are also very good braised or sautéed. If not cooked with some kind of acid—usually lemon juice or a reduction of white wine—they take on a metallic gray color. Tender baby artichokes are often served raw and thinly sliced with just some extra-virgin olive oil, lemon juice, and Parmesan cheese shavings—a wonderful way to enjoy them, especially at the last minute when they're at the peak of their season.

Artichokes are famously difficult to pair with wine because cynarin, an organic acid in the artichoke, stimulates the taste receptors in some people, making the palate unusually sensitive to sweet sensations.

Artichoke Risotto with Prosciutto and Lemon

MAKES 6 APPETIZER SERVINGS
OR 4 MAIN-COURSE SERVINGS

This recipe showcases the first great artichokes of the year by layering them into the various cooking stages of a risotto. It also offers an opportunity to appreciate how the two key components of the risotto—the base (*soffritto*) and the stock—can be adjusted to really drive home the flavors.

Salty prosciutto cooked into the *soffritto* provides a sturdy base for this dish, and a lemon squeezed over the risotto just before serving wakes up all the flavors.

THINKING AHEAD: The artichokes and stock can be prepared a day in advance and kept covered, separately, in the refrigerator. The risotto can be prepared several hours in advance by following the method on page 339.

ARTICHOKES AND STOCK

	Juice of 1 lemon
4	large globe artichokes, each weighing about 2$^{1}/_{4}$ pounds
2	quarts White Chicken Stock (page 421)
	Coarse salt and freshly ground white pepper to taste
1	tablespoon extra-virgin olive oil
$^{1}/_{2}$	cup finely minced onion
$^{1}/_{4}$	cup dry white wine
$^{1}/_{2}$	teaspoon coriander seed

Stir the lemon juice into a large bowl filled with cold water. Using a sharp paring knife, pare off the thick green skin at the base of 1 artichoke. Remove the thick, dark, outer leaves to reveal the light yellow center. Reserve the outer leaves. Trim the leaf tips just above the "choke" (the fuzzy center of the heart). Cut the artichoke heart in half lengthwise and put it in the acidulated water to prevent discoloring. Repeat with the remaining artichokes.

In a stockpot, combine the reserved artichoke leaves and the chicken stock. Bring to a boil over high heat. Reduce the heat to medium and gently simmer the stock for about 30 minutes. Remove the pot from the heat and let the stock stand for about 10 minutes to give the flavors more time to develop.

Strain the stock through a fine-mesh sieve into a bowl, pressing on the artichoke leaves to extract as much flavor as possible. Discard the leaves. Season the stock with salt and pepper. Return it to the pot and keep it at a simmer over very low heat.

In a large saucepan, heat the olive oil over medium-high heat. Cook the onion, stirring, for about 6 minutes, until softened. Add the wine and coriander seed and cook, stirring, for about 1 minute. Add the artichoke hearts and enough of the artichoke stock to cover. Bring to a boil over high heat. Reduce the heat to low, cover, and simmer for 12 to 15 minutes, until the artichokes are tender. Set the pan aside and let the artichokes cool in the liquid.

(continued)

RISOTTO

2 tablespoons extra-virgin olive oil

2 ounces prosciutto, cut into strips

$^1/_2$ cup finely minced onion

2 sprigs fresh thyme

1 clove garlic, peeled and minced

1 pound arborio rice

$^1/_2$ cup dry white wine

Coarse salt and freshly ground white pepper to taste

2 tablespoons unsalted butter

2 tablespoons chopped fresh flat-leaf parsley

Juice of 1 lemon

In a large, heavy saucepan, heat the oil over medium heat. Add the prosciutto and cook, stirring, for about 4 minutes, or until lightly browned. Add the onion and cook, stirring, for about 6 minutes, until softened. Add the thyme and garlic, and cook for about 2 minutes, until fragrant.

Add the rice and cook, stirring with a wooden spoon, for 7 to 10 minutes, until it turns milky white and opaque, and begins to stick to the bottom of the pan. Add the wine, bring to a boil, and cook for about 3 minutes, until almost completely absorbed by the rice.

Ladle about 1 cup of the simmering stock into the rice. Cook for about 2 minutes, stirring often, until the stock is almost completely absorbed. Add more stock, a cup at a time, stirring gently until it is absorbed by the rice before adding the next cup. After about 15 minutes, begin tasting the rice. At this point, add the stock judiciously. The rice should be firm yet cooked through in 18 to 20 minutes total cooking time.

Bring the artichokes and their liquid to a simmer over low heat. Add to the risotto and season with salt and pepper. Gently stir the butter into the risotto to enrich it. Stir in the parsley and the lemon juice for a little citrusy edge. Spoon the risotto into warm bowls and serve immediately.

Poached Atlantic Salmon *à la Nage*

MAKES 4 SERVINGS

A *nage* is a finished court bouillon of sorts, because the poaching liquid becomes the broth in which the ingredients being cooked are served. While I love this technique, I've always found that the classic *nage* leaves vegetables tasting slightly pickled. So, here I've tinkered with the recipe to adjust the acidity. I've also balanced the aromatics, adding some green peppercorns for a unique accent. After preparing the *nage,* the vegetables—carrot rounds, thinly sliced celery, and sliced pearl onions—are spooned over the pink fish. The pale, delicate colors create a presentation that is perfect for early springtime.

THINKING AHEAD: This dish can be prepared as many as 6 hours in advance.

COURT BOUILLON

$1^{1}/_2$	cups dry white wine
1	cup water
8	baby carrots, peeled and thinly sliced into rounds (about $^{3}/_4$ cup)
8	pearl or small boiling onions, peeled and thinly sliced into rounds (about $^{3}/_4$ cup)
1	rib celery, thinly sliced on the bias (about $^{1}/_2$ cup)
3	strips lemon zest, each about $^{1}/_2$ inch wide and 3 inches long
1	tablespoon green peppercorns in brine, drained, optional
$^{1}/_2$	teaspoon coriander seed
1	bay leaf
1	sprig fresh thyme
	Coarse salt and freshly ground white pepper to taste

In a large soup pot, combine the wine, water, carrots, onions, celery, zest, peppercorns (if using), coriander seed, bay leaf, and thyme. Season with salt and pepper. Bring to a boil over high heat and cook for about 6 minutes, or until the vegetables begin to soften. Remove from heat and cover to keep warm.

SALMON AND ASSEMBLY

4	7-ounce salmon fillets, each about 1 inch thick
	Coarse salt and freshly ground white pepper to taste
6	tablespoons extra-virgin olive oil
2	tablespoons finely minced fresh chives

Season the salmon fillets with salt and pepper. Arrange them in a 10-inch sauté pan or a saucepan large enough to hold the fillets in a single layer without touching. Pour the hot court bouillon over the fillets and bring it to a simmer over medium heat. Cook for 3 to 4 minutes. The salmon will still be a little rare. Set the salmon aside in the broth to cool to room temperature for about 10 minutes; the salmon will continue to cook a little as it cools. Refrigerate it in the bouillon for at least 1 hour, until chilled.

Lift the salmon from the court bouillon and transfer the fillets to serving plates. Strain the bouillon through a fine-mesh sieve into a bowl. Remove the thyme and bay leaf. Scatter the vegetables over the salmon. Measure $^1/_2$ cup of the bouillon and pour it into a small bowl. Whisk in the olive oil and season with salt and pepper. Taste and adjust the sauce with a little more oil or broth as necessary to balance the acidity. Spoon a little sauce over each fillet and garnish with the chives.

VARIATIONS: Other fish with a high oil content, such as mackerel, will work in this context. The herbs can be made more interesting with the addition of tarragon, chervil, or—if making the dish with salmon—dill.

Monkfish
Braised in Red Wine with Potato Purée

MAKES 4 SERVINGS

Just as tuna is often treated like red meat in recipes (tartare, au poivre), monkfish lends itself to meatlike preparations not traditionally associated with fish. (Both of these fish are also often regarded the same way by fishmongers, who call boneless tuna and monkfish "loins" rather than fillets.) It's not at all uncommon to see monkfish accompanied by ingredients like braised red cabbage, smoked bacon, or lentils.

Here, monkfish fillets are marinated like a piece of red meat—in red wine, with garlic, shallots, thyme, rosemary, bay leaves, and peppercorns—though only for a few hours, as opposed to overnight. The monkfish is then braised like a cut of meat, but again for a shorter time, after which the marinade is reduced and strained to create a red wine sauce. Using monkfish in this hearty way seems to me the perfect way to reflect and accommodate the transitional temperatures of April.

MARINADE

1	cup dry full-bodied red wine
4	cloves garlic, peeled and finely sliced
2	shallots, peeled and finely sliced
4	sprigs fresh thyme
3	sprigs fresh rosemary
2	bay leaves, crumbled
1	teaspoon whole black peppercorns
4	monkfish fillets, each weighing about 7 ounces

In a nonreactive bowl, combine the wine, garlic, shallots, thyme, rosemary, bay leaves, and peppercorns. Lay the fish fillets in a shallow glass or ceramic dish and pour the marinade over them, turning the fillets a few times to coat both sides. Cover and refrigerate, turning occasionally, for at least 1 hour and up to 4 hours.

PURÉED POTATOES

$2^3/_4$	pounds Yellow Finn or russet potatoes, peeled and cut into uniform pieces (about 2 inches thick)
$^3/_4$	cup unsalted butter, cut into pieces
$^1/_4$ to $^1/_3$	cup half-and-half
	Coarse salt and freshly ground white pepper to taste

Put the potatoes in a large saucepan and add enough cold water to cover. Salt the water and bring to a boil over high heat. Reduce the heat and simmer for about 15 minutes, or until the potatoes are tender when pierced with a sharp knife. Drain and return them to the pan.

Set the pan over low heat and cook for about 3 minutes, stirring constantly, until the excess moisture evaporates. Rice the potatoes in a food mill or ricer into a bowl, or simply put them in a bowl and mash them with a potato masher. Add the butter, working it into the potatoes until blended.

In a small saucepan, bring the half-and-half to a boil over medium heat. Add it to the potatoes, stirring gently, until the desired consistency. Do not overmix the potatoes. Season with salt and pepper, cover, and set aside to keep warm.

ASSEMBLY

    2   tablespoons canola oil
         Coarse salt and freshly ground white pepper to taste
    1   cup White Chicken Stock (page 421) or Clam Broth
         (page 349)
  $^1/_2$ cup unsalted butter, cut into pieces

Remove the fish from the marinade, scraping off any that clings to the fish, and set the marinade aside.

In a 12-inch sauté pan, heat the oil over high heat. Season the fillets with salt and pepper, and sear them for about 4 minutes, turning them once to brown both sides. Remove the fillets to a platter, add the marinade to the pan, and deglaze, scraping up any browned bits sticking to the bottom. Add the stock and bring it to a boil. Return the fish to the pan, reduce the heat to medium, cover, and braise the fish for about 8 to 10 minutes, until it is cooked through and barely opaque in the center. Lift the fish from the pan and set it aside, loosely covered, to keep warm.

Raise the heat to high and bring the liquid to a boil. Cook to reduce for about 10 minutes until lightly thickened and richly flavored. Strain the liquid through a fine-mesh sieve into a small saucepan, pressing hard against the solids to extract as much liquid and flavor as possible. You should have about $^1/_4$ cup of liquid.

Set the saucepan over low heat and add the butter, a piece at a time, whisking after each addition. When all the butter is added, you should have about $^1/_2$ cup of ruby red, intensely flavored sauce. Pour the collected juices from the monkfish, which will release a fair amount of liquid, into the sauce and stir to mix. Season the sauce with salt and pepper.

Spoon the potato purée into the centers of 4 warmed dinner plates. Using a carving knife, slice each monkfish fillet into 3 or 4 thick slices and arrange them in a fan to the side of the potatoes. Spoon the sauce over the fish and serve.

Lamb

Spring lamb begins to appear at the market around February and remains available through March and April. During these months the price of lamb spikes, especially around Easter. Domestic lamb is the best and thus the most expensive. A lot of lamb is also available from New Zealand and, to a lesser extent, Australia.

Lamb is often used around the holidays because of its historical association with religious ceremonies, the most familiar example being the sacrificial lamb.

Most of the lamb in this country is produced in Texas, Wyoming, and California. As the sheep age, their flavor becomes stronger and the meat becomes firmer, which is why spring lamb—only three to five months old—has a very delicate flavor and a pale pink color. It's so tender, in fact, that it almost has to be cooked to medium to achieve a truly desirable texture. There's not much of a market here for mutton, which comes from older animals, although it does enjoy great popularity in Middle Eastern and Indian cuisine, where the high seasoning suits it very well.

Lamb is most often pan-roasted, roasted, grilled, or braised, with different cuts being suited to each of these cooking methods. The shoulder is good for roasting, and chopped meat from the shoulder works very well in lamb burgers. Rack of lamb comes from the rib, which is the most expensive and desirable cut and the one that, of course, is sliced for rib chops. Lamb chops also come from the loin of lamb, which is often boned and cut into medallions. The leg is generally roasted whole on the bone, although boning and marinating can also be a wonderful way of flavoring it. The breast of lamb can be braised, stewed, or cut into spare ribs.

The meat for shish kebob comes from the legs. Lamb shanks, which have attained great popularity in recent years, come from the foreshank.

The most common herbs used in the cooking of lamb are rosemary, thyme, oregano, savory, and garlic, although the meat also has a great affinity for exotic spices such as cumin, coriander, and cardamom, which should be explored and incorporated into every home cook's repertoire.

LEG OF LAMB

- 1   whole leg of lamb, about 7 pounds
- 12   cloves garlic, peeled
- 1   cup loosely packed, roughly chopped fresh rosemary leaves
- 2   tablespoons fresh thyme leaves
- 1   tablespoon coarse cracked white pepper
- 2   tablespoons extra-virgin olive oil
- 4   teaspoons coarse salt

Tie the lamb, or ask the butcher to do so. Cut 5 of the garlic cloves in half lengthwise, then thinly slice them. Make slits in the lamb and insert the garlic slices into the meat. Coarsely chop the remaining 7 cloves.

In a small dish, combine the chopped garlic, rosemary, thyme, pepper, and oil. Mix well and then rub over the lamb. Cover and refrigerate for about 1 hour.

Preheat the oven to 375°F. Lightly oil a large roasting pan.

About 20 minutes before roasting, remove the lamb from the refrigerator. Season it with salt. Put the lamb in the roasting pan and roast for about 1 1/2 hours, or until an instant-read thermometer inserted in the thickest part of the meat registers 134°F. Begin checking the temperature after 1 hour and 10 minutes, keeping in mind that the lamb will cook quickly once it reaches a temperature of 125°F. Transfer the lamb to a serving platter and let it rest, loosely covered with aluminum foil, for 30 minutes. Reserve the pan juices in the roasting pan to make the jus.

BOULANGÈRE POTATOES

- 2   pounds fingerling or small Red Bliss potatoes
- 2   tablespoons extra-virgin olive oil
- 2   onions, halved, quartered, and sliced (about 2 cups)
- 4   cloves garlic, peeled and thinly sliced
- 2   tablespoons finely chopped fresh flat-leaf parsley
- 2   teaspoons fresh thyme leaves
- 1   teaspoon finely chopped fresh rosemary
      Coarse salt and freshly ground white pepper to taste
      Approximately 1 3/4 cups White Chicken Stock (page 421)

Peel the potatoes and, as each one is peeled, drop it into a bowl filled with cold water. Slice the potatoes 1/2 inch thick and return them to the water to prevent discoloring.

In a 12-inch sauté pan, heat the oil over medium-high heat. Cook the onions, stirring, for about 6 minutes, until softened. Add

Roast Leg of Lamb
with Haricots Verts and Boulangère Potatoes

MAKES 6 TO 8 SERVINGS

This is a very literal and classic version of a *gigot d'agneau*. Ask your butcher to tie the lamb for you, if you like, which will improve upon the irregular shape of the leg, allowing it to cook more evenly. (Regardless of the effort you make, the meat will be more rare closer to the bone, which many cooks like because it creates different degrees of doneness, allowing for some well-done, some medium, and some rare slices.) Attention to a few crucial details will help you have great success with this recipe: Be sure to slice the garlic cloves very thin so that the individual slivers will be fully roasted when the lamb is cooked. It's also very important to let the lamb rest properly for the "carryover" cooking to be completed and to allow the juices to redistribute themselves. Keep the lamb loosely tented with foil while it's resting to ensure an even, pink doneness.

The boulangère potatoes are a comparably classic recipe in which the potatoes are cooked in stock, which both flavors them and reduces to a rich glaze. They pair extremely well with the lamb but should also be kept in mind to accompany other roast meats and fowl.

the garlic and cook, stirring, for about 2 minutes, until softened. Drain the potatoes and add them to the pan along with the parsley, thyme, and rosemary. Season with salt and pepper, and cook for 10 to 12 minutes, until the potatoes and onions begin to brown lightly.

Add 1 cup of the stock, stir well, and cook for 4 to 5 minutes, until the stock reduces a little. Add the remaining $^3/_4$ cup of stock and cook, tossing the potatoes and onions, for about 18 minutes, until the potatoes are tender when pierced with the tip of a sharp knife but still hold their shape and the stock has reduced to a thick, flavorful glaze. Set aside, covered, to keep warm.

HARICOTS VERTS

1$^1/_2$	pounds haricots verts or young green beans, trimmed
2	tablespoons unsalted butter, cut into pieces
	Salt and freshly ground white pepper to taste

In a large saucepan of boiling water, cook the beans for about 4 minutes, until tender but still firm. Drain and toss with the butter and season with salt and pepper. Set aside, covered, to keep warm.

LAMB JUS AND ASSEMBLY

1	shallot, peeled and finely minced
2	cups red wine
2	cups lamb stock or White Chicken Stock (page 421)
	Coarse salt and freshly ground white pepper to taste
2	tablespoons unsalted butter

WHAT TO DRINK: Serve this dish with a young French red Burgundy, an aged Bordeaux, or an Italian Barolo.

Pour off all but 1 tablespoon of fat from the lamb roasting pan. Set the pan on the stove, covering 2 burners. Add the shallot and cook, stirring, for about 2 minutes, taking care not to let it burn. Add the wine and bring to a boil. Deglaze the pan, using a wooden spoon to scrape up the browned bits sticking to the bottom. Transfer the contents of the pan to a saucepan.

Set the saucepan over high heat and boil for about 8 minutes, until the wine nearly evaporates. Add the stock and the collected juices from the resting lamb and return to the boil, skimming any foam that rises to the surface. Cook for about 12 minutes, until the sauce thickens. Season with salt and pepper. Strain the sauce, if desired, and swirl in the butter. You should have about 1 cup of sauce.

Carve the lamb and arrange the slices on a platter. Spoon the potatoes and beans into bowls and serve alongside the lamb. Pass the sauce in a sauceboat.

Veal Chops
with Gnocchi and Broccoli Rabe

MAKES 4 SERVINGS

One of my very first jobs in the restaurant business was at an Italian eatery by the name of Santora's, where I was trained to make a variety of fresh pastas, including huge batches of potato gnocchi in a gigantic, freestanding industrial Hobart mixer. Traditionally speaking, it was very good.

But, personally speaking, I find that mass-produced gnocchi is too heavy; even a small portion can leave you ready to call it quits, skip dessert, and take a nap. There's a good reason for this: it's much easier to make gnocchi with a lot of flour because the dough is easier to handle and they don't stick together.

I created the gnocchi in this recipe for the Gotham. They are relatively airy, made so by using a minimum amount of flour.

The veal chops are pan-roasted, essential to balancing the bitter broccoli rabe. They are sauced with a pan sauce made by deglazing the roasting pan with white wine and chicken stock.

GNOCCHI

1	pound russet potatoes (2 medium potatoes)
1	large egg, lightly beaten
	Coarse salt and freshly ground white pepper to taste
3/4 to 1	cup sifted all-purpose flour
2	tablespoons unsalted butter, at room temperature
	White truffle oil, optional

Preheat the oven to 400°F.

Wrap the potatoes in foil and bake them for about 1 hour and 15 minutes, until tender when pierced with the tip of a small, sharp knife. Do not turn off the oven. Unwrap and halve the potatoes. Using a large spoon, and a towel to protect your hands, scoop the potato flesh from the skins onto a baking sheet. Discard the skins.

Spread the cooked potato flesh on the baking sheet and bake it for about 10 minutes, stirring often to prevent scorching and to dry it out. Remove the potato from the oven and pass it through a potato ricer or food mill. Set the riced potato aside to cool completely.

In a mixing bowl, combine the cooled potato with the egg and mix gently. Season with salt and pepper. Using your hands, add the flour, working it into the potato only until the flour and potato form a soft dough that no longer sticks to your hands. Do not overwork the dough—you do not want to develop the gluten in the flour. Cover the bowl with plastic wrap and set it aside for 1 hour to rest.

Pinch off a small piece of dough. If it sticks to your hands or the work surface, dust both with a little flour or dust a little flour onto the dough. Roll the piece of dough into a 1/2-inch-thick cylinder and, using a sharp or serrated knife, cut the gnocchi into 1-inch lengths. Transfer the cut gnocchi to a baking sheet lined with parchment paper and lightly dusted with flour. Continue with the remaining dough.

In a saucepan of boiling salted water, cook the gnocchi for 3 to 4 minutes, or until they float to the surface of the water. Drain, toss them with the butter and, if desired, with truffle oil.

VEAL AND ASSEMBLY

1 bunch broccoli rabe (about $^1/_2$ pound cleaned), leaves removed and florets cut into 3-inch pieces
2 tablespoons extra-virgin olive oil
4 cloves garlic, peeled and thinly sliced
Coarse salt and freshly ground white pepper to taste
4 large veal chops, each weighing 14 to 16 ounces
$^1/_4$ cup dry white wine
$1^1/_2$ cups chicken stock
2 tablespoons unsalted butter

Preheat the oven to 400°F.

In a saucepan of boiling salted water, cook the broccoli rabe for about 3 minutes, until tender. Drain and immediately plunge it into a bowl of ice water.

In a sauté pan, heat 1 tablespoon of the oil over medium heat. Add the garlic and cook, stirring, for about 2 minutes. Add the broccoli rabe and sauté until heated through. Season with salt and pepper, and set aside, covered, to keep warm.

Season the chops with salt and pepper. In an ovenproof 12-inch sauté pan, heat the remaining tablespoon of oil over medium-high heat until it is very hot and just beginning to smoke. Sear the chops for about 3 minutes on each side. Put the pan holding the chops in the oven and roast for about 2 minutes. Turn the chops and roast about 4 minutes longer for medium-rare meat. Transfer the chops to a warm serving platter and set aside covered to keep warm. Pour off any oil in the pan and add the wine. Raise the heat to high and deglaze the pan by scraping up any brown bits with a wooden spoon. Add the stock and cook until the sauce is reduced by half or thickened and richly flavored. Remove from heat and swirl in the butter. Season with salt and pepper, pout into a warmed sauceboat and serve alongside the veal chops, gnocchi, and broccoli rabe.

WHAT TO DRINK: Serve this dish with a great Chianti or an aged Barbaresco.

Charcoal-Grilled Porterhouse Steaks with Potato and Wild Mushroom Gratin

MAKES 4 TO 6 SERVINGS

At the famous Peter Luger's restaurant in New York City, they serve only porterhouse steaks, which combine the attributes of strip loin and filet steaks. I'd probably do the same if I owned a steakhouse. I especially love a grilled porterhouse because the char flavor makes a wonderful contrast to the succulent meat, especially when it's kept on the rare side. Here, a grilled porterhouse is paired with a rich and creamy mushroom gratin. While this is a wonderful way to break in the grill for the year, this dish may also be prepared in the oven if you catch a particularly cool April evening.

POTATO AND WILD MUSHROOM GRATIN

1	tablespoon extra-virgin olive oil
1	pound wild mushrooms, such as chanterelles, morels, or cremini, trimmed and sliced
$1/2$	teaspoon fresh thyme leaves
	Coarse salt and freshly ground white pepper to taste
4	pounds Yukon Gold or russet potatoes
2	small cloves garlic, peeled and finely minced
$1/2$	teaspoon freshly grated nutmeg
2	cups heavy cream

Preheat the oven to 375°F. Butter a 9-by-11-inch casserole or gratin dish.

In a 12-inch sauté pan, heat the oil over medium-high heat. Add the mushrooms and cook, stirring, for about 6 minutes, until tender and lightly browned. Add the thyme and season with salt and pepper. Set aside to cool to room temperature.

Peel the potatoes and, as each one is peeled, drop it into a bowl filled with cold water. Slice the potatoes $1/8$ inch thick, keeping the slices together. (A Japanese mandoline works well for this.) Layer some of the potato slices in the bottom of the casserole, overlapping them to form an even layer. Spoon a layer of mushrooms over the potato slices and season with some of the garlic, nutmeg, salt, and pepper. Top with another layer of potatoes and mushrooms, and season with more garlic, nutmeg, salt, and pepper. When all the potatoes and mushrooms are used, the gratin will be about $1^1/2$ inches thick.

Pour $1/2$ cup of the cream over the potatoes and press down firmly to distribute the cream evenly. Add more cream, pressing on the potatoes, until there is enough cream to just cover the potatoes when they are pressed. This will determine the correct amount of cream.

Cover the dish with aluminum foil and poke a few holes in the foil. Bake for 1 hour. Remove the foil and bake about 20 minutes longer, until the cream is absorbed and the top of the gratin is browned. Keep warm until serving.

STEAK AND ASSEMBLY

2	double porterhouse steaks, each weighing about 44 ounces
2 to 3	tablespoons olive oil
	Coarse salt to taste
3 to 4	tablespoons coarsely cracked black pepper

Remove the steaks from the refrigerator 15 to 20 minutes before grilling to allow them to reach room temperature.

Build a charcoal fire in a grill and let the coals burn until covered with white ash. Spread them out in the grill, arranging them so that one section of the grate is over the coals and another section is not. Lightly oil the grill grate.

Put the steaks on a platter and coat both sides with olive oil. Generously season both sides of the steaks with salt. Season both sides with pepper, pressing the pepper into the meat. Grill over the hot coals for 8 to 10 minutes. Turn and grill about 10 minutes longer. Move the steaks to the section of the grill away from the coals and cook about 20 minutes longer, turning them once, until the sirloin side of the steaks is rare (the filet portion will be slightly more cooked). Slice the steaks and divide them among serving plates, spooning the gratin next to the meat.

NOTE: If using 12 to 14 ounce steaks, 1½ inches thick, cook them for 4 minutes on each side for rare; 5 minutes on each side for medium-rare. Because of the impressive size of these steaks, they can be "seared" on the grill (10 minutes each side) and then roasted in a 375°F oven for 15 to 20 minutes to coordinate their completion with the potato gratin.

THINKING AHEAD: The *petits pots* can be prepared up to 1 day in advance and stored, tightly covered, in the refrigerator.

Petits pots of chocolate are like an American pudding cooked on the stove, resulting in a pastry cream–like consistency. These are baked in the oven in a water bath for a French version of an American classic taken to new heights by the use of Valrhona chocolate. Serve them with high quality butter cookies.

1¼	cups sugar
¼	cup water
5	cups milk
9	ounces unsweetened chocolate, preferably Valrhona, coarsely chopped
15	large egg yolks
2	tablespoons coffee extract

Preheat the oven to 350°F.

In a saucepan, combine the sugar and water, and cook over medium heat until the mixture registers 220°F on a candy thermometer.

In another saucepan, heat the milk until it is very hot and small bubbles form around the edges of the pan. Do not let the milk boil. Put the chocolate in a heatproof bowl and pour the hot milk over it. Stir until the chocolate melts and the mixture is smooth.

Return the chocolate mixture to the saucepan and carefully add the hot sugar syrup, using thick oven mitts or pot holders. Heat the mixture gently over medium heat, stirring until smooth. Remove the pan from the heat.

In a large bowl, whisk the egg yolks. Slowly drizzle about a cup of the hot chocolate mixture into the eggs, whisking well to temper. Pour the tempered yolks into the chocolate mixture and whisk. Strain through a fine-mesh sieve into a bowl. Stir in the extract and set aside to cool slightly.

Pour the chocolate mixture into eight 5-ounce ramekins or custard cups. Set the cups in a large, shallow roasting pan and set the pan on the center rack of the oven. Pour enough hot water into the roasting pan to come about halfway up the sides of the ramekins. Bake for about 1 hour, until the custards are set. Remove and let cool in the water bath. Remove ramekins from water bath, cover with plastic wrap, and refrigerate until ready to serve.

Banana
Cake

The banana chips that garnish this dessert (which may also be prepared as individual tarts) are something special to add to your repertoire. Banana purée is combined with sugar, spread thin, and dried overnight in a low oven. The result is a chip with a very unique and concentrated banana flavor.

THINKING AHEAD: The banana chips can be prepared up to 3 days in advance and stored, covered, at room temperature for up to 3 days.

BANANA CHIPS

2	ripe bananas
2	teaspoons superfine granulated sugar

Preheat the oven to 200°F. Butter a baking sheet and line it with parchment paper.

In a blender, purée the bananas until smooth. Spread the purée on the prepared baking sheet, smoothing it with a spatula to a thin, even layer. Sprinkle the purée with the sugar. Place the baking sheet in the oven and dry for 8 hours or overnight.

Remove the pan from the oven and break or cut the dried banana into chips. They may be stored in a tightly lidded container at room temperature for up to 3 days.

CAKE

1	cup plus 5 tablespoons sugar
12^1/$_2$	tablespoons unsalted butter, softened
^{1}/$_2$	cup hazelnut flour
2	large eggs
1^1/$_4$	cups bleached all-purpose flour
^{1}/$_2$	teaspoon baking powder
^{1}/$_2$	teaspoon baking soda
^{1}/$_2$	teaspoon salt
^{1}/$_2$	cup plus 2 tablespoons sour cream
^{1}/$_2$	cup plus 2 tablespoons puréed bananas (about 1 large, ripe banana)
1	large banana, to decorate the cake Vanilla Bean Ice Cream (page 84)

Preheat the oven to 350°F. Butter and flour a 10-inch round cake pan, tapping out the excess flour; or have ready eight 4-inch nonstick molds.

In the bowl of an electric mixer set on medium-high speed, cream together the sugar, butter, and hazelnut flour until light and fluffy. Add the eggs, one at a time, beating well after each addition.

(continued)

Whisk together the all-purpose flour, baking powder, baking soda, and salt. With the mixer set on medium speed, slowly add the dry ingredients, mixing until just incorporated.

Using a rubber spatula, fold in the sour cream and then the puréed banana. Scrape the batter into the prepared cake pan or smaller molds, smoothing the surface with the spatula. Bake for 30 to 40 minutes for the cake and 15 to 20 minutes for the molds, or until the cake is lightly browned, springs back when gently pressed in the center, and a toothpick inserted near the center comes out clean.

Let the cake sit in the pan or molds set on a wire rack for about 10 minutes. Invert onto the rack and cool completely.

When the cake is cool, slice the banana into thin slices and arrange them on top of the large cake or smaller individual cakes. Set the small individual cakes on dessert plates, or cut the large cake into wedges and serve on dessert plates. Top with ice cream and decorate with the banana chips. Serve.

FLAVOR BUILDING: Dot the perimeter of each plate with Chocolate Sauce (page 187), as pictured on the preceding page.

Easter Dinners

POACHED ATLANTIC SALMON *À LA NAGE* (page 400)

ARTICHOKE RISOTTO WITH PROSCIUTTO AND LEMON (page 397)

ROAST LEG OF LAMB WITH HARICOTS VERTS AND
BOULANGÈRE POTATOES (page 405)

MILK CHOCOLATE *PETITS POTS* (page 413)

GOAT CHEESE SALAD WITH BEETS, BRAISED FENNEL,
AND A CITRUS VINAIGRETTE (page 392)

LEMON RISOTTO WITH SPOT PRAWNS (page 339)

SLOW-COOKED LAMB SHOULDER (page 375)

BANANA CAKE (page 414)

Mayonnaise

Basic Vinaigrette

White Chicken Stock

Brown Chicken Stock

Double Turkey Stock

Vegetable Stock

BASICS

Mayonnaise

MAKES ABOUT 1 CUP

1	large egg yolk, at room temperature
1	tablespoon fresh lemon juice
1/2	tablespoon Dijon mustard
	Coarse salt and freshly ground white pepper to taste
	Cayenne pepper to taste
1	cup canola oil

In a medium bowl, whisk the egg yolk, lemon juice, mustard, salt, pepper, and cayenne until smooth. Whisk in the oil, drop by drop, until the mayonnaise begins to thicken. Add the remaining oil a little faster. When all the oil is absorbed, taste the mayonnaise and adjust the salt, pepper, cayenne, and lemon juice, if necessary.

Basic Vinaigrette

MAKES ABOUT 3/4 CUP

1 1/2	tablespoons fresh lemon juice
1 1/2	tablespoons red wine vinegar
1/2	teaspoon Dijon mustard
1/2	cup extra-virgin olive oil
	Coarse salt and freshly ground white pepper to taste

In a small, nonreactive bowl, whisk together the lemon juice, vinegar, and mustard. Slowly whisk in the oil until emulsified. Season with salt and pepper.

White Chicken Stock

THINKING AHEAD: This stock can be prepared up to 4 days in advance, cooled, covered, and refrigerated. Or it can be frozen for up to 3 months.

6	pounds chicken bones, coarsely chopped (substitute wings if bones or carcasses are unavailable)
4	quarts cold water, or as needed
1	large onion, chopped
1	small carrot, coarsely chopped
1	small celery rib, coarsely chopped
1	head garlic, halved crosswise
2	sprigs fresh thyme
2	sprigs fresh flat-leaf parsley
1	teaspoon whole black peppercorns
1	bay leaf

Place the chicken in a large stockpot and add cold water to cover the solids by 2 inches. Bring to a boil over medium-high heat, skimming off any foam that rises to the surface. Add the remaining ingredients. Reduce the heat to low and simmer gently uncovered for at least 6 hours or overnight.

Strain the stock into a large bowl and cool completely. Skim off and discard the clear yellow fat that rises to the surface. Or refrigerate the stock until the fat chills, about 4 hours, then scrape it off with a large spoon.

Brown Chicken Stock

MAKES ABOUT 3 CUPS

THINKING AHEAD: This brown stock can be prepared up to 1 week in advance, cooled, covered, and refrigerated; or it can be frozen for up to 3 months.

SPECIAL EQUIPMENT: A very large stockpot, with at least a 12-quart capacity

10	pounds chicken bones, coarsely chopped (substitute wings if bones and carcasses are unavailable)
2	tablespoons canola oil
1	large onion, chopped
1	small carrot, coarsely chopped
1	small celery rib, coarsely chopped
8	quarts water, or as needed
1	head garlic, halved crosswise
2	sprigs fresh thyme
2	sprigs fresh flat-leaf parsley
1	teaspoon whole black peppercorns
1	bay leaf

Preheat oven to 450°F. Place the chicken in 2 large roasting pans. Roast, stirring occasionally, until the chicken is evenly browned, 40 minutes to 1 hour. Halfway through roasting, pour off and discard any accumulated fat.

Meanwhile, heat the oil in a very large stockpot over medium-high heat. Add the onion, carrot, and celery. Cook, stirring often, until golden brown, about 10 minutes. Reduce the heat to medium and continue cooking, stirring often, about 10 minutes longer, until very well browned.

Transfer the chicken bones to the stockpot. Place the roasting pans on 2 burners on top of the stove over high heat. Add $^1/_2$ cup of the water to each pan. Bring to a boil, scrape up the browned bits on the bottom, and pour the contents of the pans into the stockpot.

Add enough water to the stockpot to cover the ingredients by 2 inches. Bring to a boil over medium-high heat, skimming off any foam that rises to the surface. Add the garlic, thyme, parsley, peppercorns, and bay leaf. Reduce the heat to low and simmer gently, uncovered, for 8 to 10 hours, the longer the better. As the stock evaporates, add water to keep the ingredients barely covered. Strain the stock into a large bowl or container, pressing hard on the solids. Let stand for 5 minutes, until the fat rises to the surface. Then skim off and discard the fat.

Clean the pot. Return the strained stock to the pot and bring it to a boil over high heat. Boil until the stock reduces to a rich consistency, 1 to $1^1/2$ hours, depending on the size of the pot. You should have about 3 cups. Pour the brown stock into the container you plan to store it in (it will gel as it cools) and cool completely.

Double Turkey Stock

MAKES ABOUT 1 1/2 QUARTS

In risotto recipes that call for White Chicken Stock, replace it with this rich stock for a greater depth of flavor, as we do at the Gotham Bar and Grill.

THINKING AHEAD: This stock can be refrigerated for as many as 3 days or stored in the freezer for 3 months.

3	pounds turkey wings, chopped into 2-inch pieces
2	quarts White Chicken Stock (page 421)
3	cups water, or as needed
1/2	cup chopped onion
1/4	cup chopped celery
1/4	cup chopped carrot
3	garlic cloves, peeled and crushed
2	sprigs fresh thyme
2	sprigs fresh flat-leaf parsley
1	teaspoon whole black peppercorns

Place the turkey wings and stock in a large stockpot and add enough cold water to cover by 2 inches. Bring to a boil over medium-high heat, skimming off any foam that rises to the surface. Add the remaining ingredients. Reduce the heat to low and simmer the stock until well flavored, 3 to 4 hours.

Strain the stock into a large bowl and cool completely. Skim off and discard the clear yellow fat that rises to the surface. Or refrigerate the stock until the fat chills, about 4 hours, then scrape off the fat with a large spoon.

Vegetable Stock

2	tablespoons olive oil
1	large onion, cut into large dice
2	medium leeks, with 3 inches of dark green leaf, washed and sliced
1	stalk celery, cut into large dice
3	plum tomatoes, very ripe, chopped
1	small head of garlic, cut in half
2	large heads of fennel, cut into medium-large dice
1 1/2	teaspoons white peppercorns
1	teaspoon coriander seed
1	large bay leaf
2	quarts cold water
1	teaspoon salt or to taste
6	sprigs Italian parsley
2	sprigs fresh thyme
1/2	cup white wine

Heat the oil in an 8-quart stockpot. Stir in the onion, leeks, celery, tomatoes, garlic, fennel, peppercorns, coriander, and bay leaf. Cover the pot and sweat the vegetables, stirring occasionally, over medium-high heat until soft, about 20 minutes. Add the cold water to the pot, return the liquid to a boil, then reduce the heat to a simmer and cook 90 minutes. Remove the pot from the heat and stir in the salt, parsley, thyme, and white wine. Set the pot aside to cool and continue steeping. After the stock has cooled, strain out the liquid, pressing on the vegetables to extract all the flavor.

Mail-Order Sources

DEAN & DE LUCA

2526 E. 36th North Circle
Witchita, KS 67219
800–221–7714
212–226–6800
www.deandeluca.com
A Manhattan food emporium that mail-orders superior ingredients and equipment, such as aged balsamic vinegars, fine cheeses, pancetta, prosciutto, salted anchovies, caper berries, basmati rice, quick-cooking polenta, harissa, hoisin sauce, and almond flour.

URBANI TRUFFLES USA

2924 40th Avenue
Long Island City, NY 11101
800–281–2330
718–392–5050
www.urbani.com
A source for white and black truffles, caviar, foie gras, high-end extra-virgin olive oils, and 25-year-old balsamic vinegar.

D'ARTAGNAN

280 Wilson Avenue
Newark, NJ 07105
800–327–8246
973–344–0565
www.dartagnan.com
This company supplies the best restaurants in New York, and can also provide you with the same fresh game, foie gras, and free-range chickens.

J. B. PRINCE

36 E. 31st Street
New York, NY 10016
800–473–0577
212–683–3553
www.jbprince.com
A source for excellent professional equipment; where many New York chefs shop.

BALDUCCI'S

95 Sherwood Avenue
Farmingdale, NY 11735
800–225–3822
www.balducci.com
One-stop shopping for such excellent products as dry-aged beef and other prime meats and game, white truffle oil, fine cheeses, and other provisions.

BRIDGE KITCHEN WARE

214 E. 52nd Street
New York, NY 10022
212–688–4220
www.bridgekitchenware.com
Manhattan's famous kitchenware store, supplying both professional chefs and passionate amateurs. Look here for entremet rings, springform pans, mandoline-type slicers, and terrine molds.

KATAGIRI

224 E. 59th Street
New York, NY 10022
212–755–3566
www.katagiri.com
Purveyors of a wide range of Japanese cooking products and housewares, including such ingredients as yuzu and mirin.

WILLIAMS SONOMA

P.O. Box 9008
Farmingdale, NY 11735
800–541–2233
www.williams-sonoma.com
This company supplies both professional chefs and passionate amateurs. Look here for entremet rings, springform pans, mandoline-type slicers, and terrine molds.

KITCHEN ARTS & LETTERS

1435 Lexington Avenue
New York, NY 10128
212–876–5550
www.kitchenartsandletters.com
A bookstore and gallery devoted entirely to books on food and wine.

Index

Photographs are indicated by italicized page numbers.